A Watershed Moment

A WATERSHED MOMENT

The American West in the Age of Limits

EDITED BY

Robert Frodeman, Evelyn Brister, and Luther Propst

The University of Utah Press
Salt Lake City

The Defiance House Man colophon is a registered trademark of the University of Utah Press. It is based on a four-foot-tall Ancient Puebloan pictograph (late PIII) near Glen Canyon, Utah.

LIBRARY OF CONGRESS CATALOGING-IN-PUBLICATION DATA

Names: Frodeman, Robert, editor. | Brister, Evelyn, editor. | Propst, Luther, editor.

Title: A watershed moment : the American West in the age of limits / edited by Robert Frodeman, Evelyn Brister, and Luther Propst.

Description: Salt Lake City : The University of Utah Press, [2024] | Includes bibliographical references and index. | Identifiers: LCCN 2024016353 | ISBN 9781647692025 (hardcover) | ISBN 9781647692032 (paperback) | ISBN 9781647692049 (ebook)

Subjects: LCSH: Sustainability--West (U.S.) | Sustainability--Philosophy. | Land use--West (U.S.) | Conservation of natural resources--West (U.S.) | West (U.S.)--Economic aspects. | West (U.S.)--Social life and customs. | LCGFT: Essays.

Classification: LCC HC79.E5 W3778 2024 | DDC 333.70978--dc23/eng/20240716

LC record available at https://lccn.loc.gov/2024016353

Front cover design by Jessica Booth with resources from Freepik.com.
Errata and further information on this and other titles available at UofUpress.com
Printed and bound in the United States of America.

Contents

Foreword

Like so many who grew up elsewhere, the West—its rugged mountains, vast open spaces, and rich history—long beckoned before I ever set foot on its soil and eventually called it home. The journey began during the summer of 1967, when a college friend and I spent eight weeks driving throughout the region. After departing the Black Hills, we missed Gillette, Wyoming, not yet an epicenter for energy activity; we camped without cost in the Big Horns and Gallatin Range in nearly deserted national forest campgrounds; we encountered bears roadside while cruising through Yellowstone; and we had no problem finding unoccupied campsites, inviting swimming holes, wide-open rangelands, and stunning scenery everywhere. I do not recall seeing any condominiums, and there were few franchise businesses.

I returned in the mid-1970s and was soon ensconced in Laramie, where my wife and I enjoyed meaningful professional opportunities and a base to explore the region. Early on, we found uncrowded trails in the Wind Rivers, rooms readily available and affordable in Steamboat, Jackson, and Moab, and solitude in the Snowy Range and Canyonlands. We also witnessed sawmill towns withering, bitter legal struggles over energy leasing on undisturbed forestlands, and condominiums sprouting across ski country. Denver's LoDo was a jumble of drab old warehouses, punctuated only by the bright lights of Larimer Square.

Since then, in what seems a blink of the eye, the Interior West has filled up, putting ever-increasing strains on the region's communities, public lands, wildlife, and water sources. Along the way, local economies have reversed direction, the backcountry has attracted ever more adventurers, and prolonged drought has gripped the region. Once-quiet mountain towns have transformed into year-round resort settings with attendant housing, employment, and social cohesion problems. Nearby ranchlands are sold and subdivided, often to absentee owners, with little regard for wildlife impacts. Voices rarely heard a few decades ago are pressing for long-overdue recognition, and nearly every place faces immediate challenges and growing future uncertainties. An old West has given way to a new West. The overarching question is how to preserve the sense of place and community that has long distinguished the West from elsewhere while both accommodating and steering the inevitable changes afoot.

A Watershed Moment seeks answers to this question, which bedevils communities and residents across much of the Interior West. Without doubt, the region is filling up with more and more people demanding more from the landscapes and waterways that are essential to its existence and identity. The book's editors—veteran witnesses to this New West transition—have assembled a knowledgeable and talented cast of authors who have experienced firsthand the changes occurring and are engaged themselves on the front lines in ongoing efforts to meet the impending problems. In the chapters that follow, they not only address the legacies of yesterday—mining, logging, oil fields, overgrazing, and ill-placed dams—but also confront a tomorrow that has now arrived—land use conflicts, housing shortages, recreation pressures, wealth inequalities, water shortages, lingering racial animus, climatic changes, unprecedented wildfire events, and the list goes on. Today's amenity economy presents quite different issues than those that defined the past.

Overlaying these challenges is the pressing need to conserve the West's unique natural characteristics for both current and future generations. Whether framed in terms of sustainability, conservation, or resiliency, this formidable task focuses on the region's public lands, wildlife habitat, open spaces, migration corridors, free-flowing watercourses, and scenic beauty. Following the unchecked destruction of wildlife during the nineteenth century, we managed to protect and restore bison, grizzly bears, beaver, and later wolves, albeit not without conflict and some degree of compromise. Can we do the same for historical migration routes? Any chance of undamming rivers? Will conservation easements suffice to maintain open space, seasonal habitat, and the region's ranching heritage? Given past injustices, are we prepared to safeguard landscapes sacred to the region's Native inhabitants, such as Bears Ears National Monument or the Badger-Two Medicine country? How far are we prepared to go to preserve ecosystem integrity across the landscape?

Framed in this manner, the challenges of the New West call for an integrated approach, one that better knits the region's public and private lands together along with its precious water sources. As Wallace Stegner sagely perceived, the West is distinct, defined by its aridity and expansive public lands. He also lamented the region's history of exploitation, while memorably observing, "It is hard to be pessimistic about the West. This is the native home of hope. When it fully learns that cooperation, not rugged individualism, is the pattern that most characterizes and preserves it, then it will have . . . a chance to create a society to match its scenery." What science and experience have made obvious is that what occurs on the public lands impacts adjacent communities, private lands, and Indian reservations, while the converse is true too. And what occurs upstream affects nearly everything downstream. All of this essentially demands better federal-state-tribal-local cooperation to ensure the region's natural heritage and viable human communities.

The chapters in *A Watershed Moment* traverse across the West to make these points and more in examining the impending challenges facing the region and its diverse communities. The chapters range from the Southwest's Mexican borderlands to the Crown of the Continent, alighting along the way in Salmon, Telluride, Bozeman, the Absaroka Front, and other points on the Western compass. The authors—drawing upon personal experience and their own hard-won knowledge—put the problems facing individual communities and places in perspective, examine the ongoing efforts to address these vexing problems, and offer feasible suggestions for moving forward. Theirs is a clear-eyed look at what is transpiring with a keen sensitivity to the need to preserve community character as well as the region's natural attributes.

The book is timely, comprehensive, and thoughtful. Anyone who cares about Stegner's "Native Home of Hope" in this time of rampant change will find the chapters insightful about what is occurring across the region, the challenges presented, and potential solutions, tinged with a sense of optimism about the future amid today's struggles. The West has been through previous profound transitions and survived largely intact. *A Watershed Moment* alerts us that we are once again in the midst of a major transition and points the way toward navigating this New West moment.

Robert B. Keiter

Preface

In October of 2022, under blue skies, golden aspens, and the white-capped peaks of the Tetons, the editors and contributors to this volume met at Murie Ranch in Grand Teton National Park. We came together to think about the future of the American West.

Murie Ranch has been the site of similar conversations in the past. In 1945, Olaus Murie was named director of the Wilderness Society: he accepted the position on the condition that he could move its headquarters to the ranch. In the 1950s the ranch was the site for the first draft of what became the Wilderness Act of 1964. And in 1956, Olaus and his wife, Mardy, led an expedition to the Brooks Range that would eventually lead to the creation of the Arctic National Wildlife Refuge.

The Muries' conservation efforts were visible on our afternoon walks: grizzly bears had been munching on berries, and bald eagles were a common sight along the nearby Snake River. The West has prospered under the protections the Muries helped enact. But these successes have also led to new challenges. The population of the Intermountain West has increased from less than seven million in 1960 to over twenty-five million in 2020. With more residents and visitors, the region's natural resources and local communities are now stretched and stressed.

Inspired by the Muries, the goal of *A Watershed Moment* is to create better connections between communities across the West while highlighting our new age of limits. Each chapter focuses on a place and a problem and ends with suggestions relevant to communities facing similar challenges. A central belief unites the chapters—that we must change the paradigm that has driven land use decisions in the West since European conquest and settlement.

The American public overwhelmingly supports the protection of our national parks, forests, monuments, wildlife refuges, and other public lands. We cherish the clean water, wildlife and fisheries, agricultural landscapes, and opportunities for solitude and outdoor recreation that these lands provide. Greater public engagement will be necessary to strike a sustainable balance between our stewardship of wild areas, the protection of our Western character, and the social and economic needs of our communities. But to be successful, this engagement will need to challenge the old-time religion of endless growth. We hope that this edited volume encourages more people to join us in this conclusion.

Our thanks to the many individuals and institutions that have helped bring this project to fruition. Our editor at the University of Utah Press, Jedediah Rogers, has been steadfast in his support of this project since the beginning. Lane LaMure has offered financial support, and we have benefited from the wise counsel of Jonathan Thompson. Danya Rumore contributed insights during our conversations, particularly ideas about the title. Two anonymous reviewers have offered useful guidance for improving the volume. Amanda Propst was invaluable in her help with transcription. The financial support of the George B. Storer Foundation made the Murie Ranch workshop and follow-on activities possible. Finally, we thank the Teton Science School and the Northern Rockies Conservation Cooperative, both of whom have supported this project.

Robert Frodeman
Evelyn Brister
Luther Propst

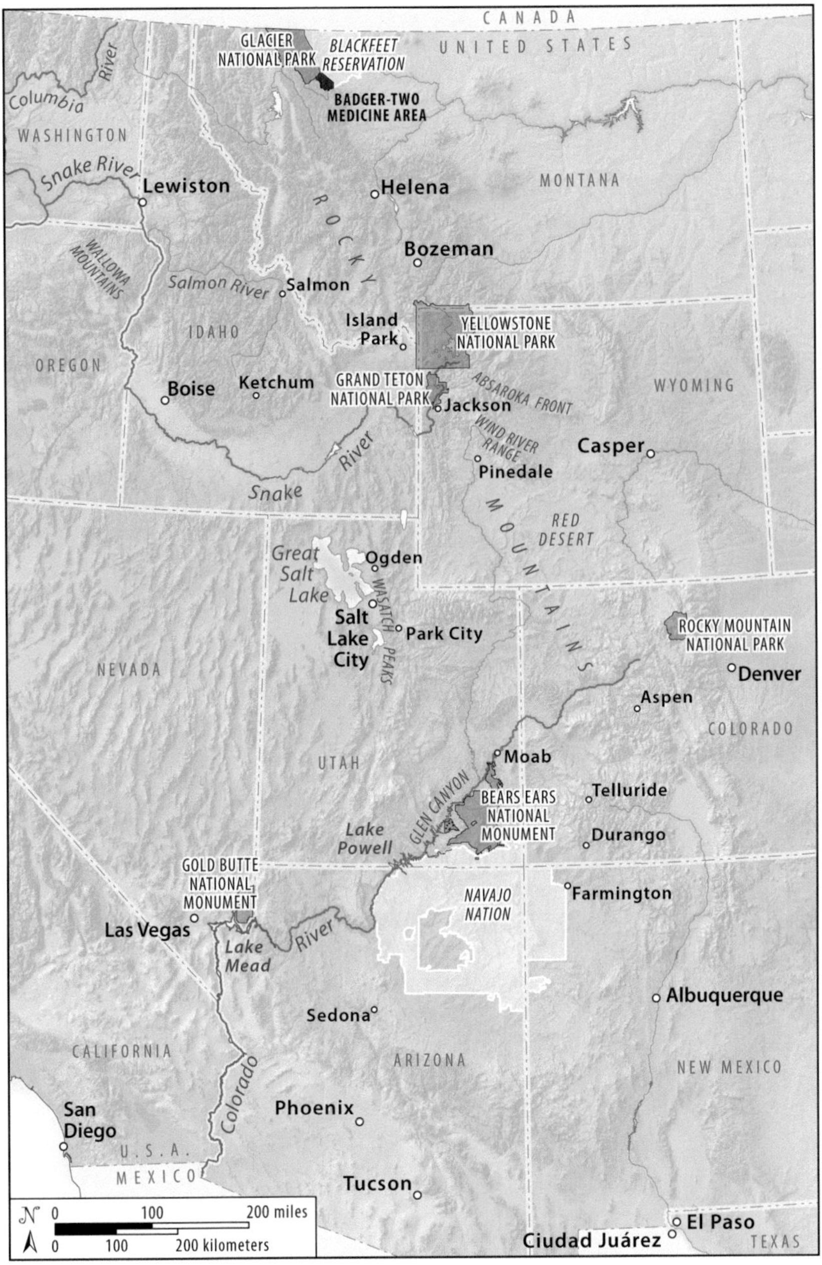

Figure P.1 Overview map of the Intermountain West, highlighting locations discussed in the volume. Map credit: Chelsea Feeney.

Introduction
Building Sustainable Communities in the Intermountain West

EVELYN BRISTER

With the Rocky Mountains on one side and the Cascades and Sierra on the other, together with the land that lies between, the Intermountain West encompasses about a quarter of the contiguous United States and a tenth of the U.S. population. This area includes the lowest elevation on the North American continent—Death Valley—and over fifty of its highest mountain peaks. Across portions of eleven states, the topography and ecosystems of the Intermountain West vary from desert to alpine forests and include vast rangelands, remote wilderness areas, and rich agricultural lands. Just two of its many river systems are the Colorado, source of water and power for much of the Southwest, and the Snake, a major tributary of the mighty Columbia.

Despite this geographical diversity, the Intermountain West is tied together ecologically via watersheds and wildlife migration routes and by its aridity. Dominant cultural influences have come from the westward movement of Euroamerican settlers seeking land, natural resources, religious freedom, and political independence. The region's character is grounded in the love that ranchers, conservationists, and recreationists express for the land itself. But the popular identification of Western identity with cowboy culture is built on older foundations of Native American and Spanish heritage and interacts with cultural influences brought from other areas of the United States and, in fact, the entire globe (Taylor 2004).

Though the land and people are diverse, the Intermountain West poses a distinctive set of land use problems that are the subject of this book. From the ski resorts of the Colorado Rockies to the red-rock buttes of the Navajo Nation and from the towering skyscrapers of downtown Denver to the dairy farms of the Palouse, the history and character of the West shape its land use problems and inform how solutions are proposed, judged, and enacted.

A Watershed Moment

The chapters of *A Watershed Moment* reveal tensions between a culture of economic growth and the ecological, economic, and social constraints set by community values and the land itself. The Intermountain West has undergone rapid urban growth at the same time that its water resources are reaching limits. A strong cultural thread in the West prizes private property and individual freedom, even as public oversight of resources is often required in order to prevent the collapse of human and natural communities. Both longtime residents and new arrivals appreciate the region's natural beauty, wildlife, open spaces, and opportunities for hunting, fishing, and other outdoor recreation, but in many communities, protected areas have become crowded with people and degraded by overuse. At the same time, the West continues its long-standing struggles to weather the boom-and-bust cycles of extractive economies, to sustain agricultural production in an arid region, and to overcome the legacy of Native displacement and loss of cultural identity. The West is facing a watershed moment where decisions could exacerbate partisan political conflict, greater economic disparities, cultural homogeneity that erodes the West's distinctive culture, declines in wildlife abundance, and greater risks from wildfire. These chapters provide workable ideas and resources for taking actions that will point us in the right direction.

It is not the aim of this volume to settle theory-driven debates about how culture, economics, and politics in the "New West" differ from the "Old West" or from other areas of the United States, nor is it our goal to settle debates about the degree to which underlying ideologies of land use and ownership vary as a result of class, duration of residency, cultural identity, or level of political participation (Robbins et al. 2009). Intersecting commonalities among socioecological regions in the Intermountain West provide a frame for how the chapters in this volume explain and address land use and land management challenges (Jones et al. 2019).

Aridity has shaped the West as a biophysical region, and today this limit affects decisions concerning agriculture, development, and wildlife conservation. Constraints on water resources will continue to drive policy changes as climate change alters precipitation patterns and exacerbates drought. Indeed, the effects of water availability and decisions concerning water resources are so important to communities in the West that the title of the volume invites readers to consider how water affects agriculture, fisheries, wildlife, recreation, development, and economic opportunities.

Another factor that shapes the West is the legacy of land use and land management decisions made by the U.S. government in the nineteenth century. These decisions still shape land use—most notably through the forced displacement of Native residents and the status of nearly 70 percent of the region as public lands. Public lands shape the West's economic and political landscape differently than in other regions of the United States: they limit where and how development occurs and, therefore, the tax base, and they are often managed for uses that are not fully compatible with one another, such as for range, oil and gas development, wildlife and cultural artifact conservation, and outdoor recreation.

Even recognizing these commonalities, Western counties also exhibit a high degree of variability. Although the population is growing overall, the rate of growth is uneven and localized (Jones et al. 2019). Economic activities are also distributed like a patchwork: there are areas of intensive agriculture and areas without agriculture; pockets of amenity and service economies and pockets where extractive industries drive the economy. Our authors have been influenced by previous analyses that call for the development of collaborative management approaches and integrated land use planning (Kemmis 2001; Travis 2007). But they also provide case studies that update these planning efforts to show the applicability of new tools and techniques. At the same time, some question whether collaborative planning provides sufficient resilience for communities that are harnessed to changes in the global economy, and other chapters question common assumptions about the negative consequences of residential development or highlight counterintuitive implications.

For those of us who live in and love the Intermountain West, it's important to devise strategies and explore solutions that preserve its cultural character while recognizing that change is inevitable—and often welcome. The chapters in this book describe what's worked and what hasn't. They take a pragmatic stance, sharing stories told from the perspective of lived experience and drawing on the knowledge of local experts. But there are also lessons for people living outside the Intermountain West: the themes that emerge—especially the importance of collaborative, data-driven problem-solving—are hard-won lessons that apply to other landscapes and ecosystems. For those readers, the Intermountain West offers an instructive account for anticipating and addressing issues in an ever-changing world. The West is already facing its watershed moment. Other regions have much to learn as they face their own.

Multidisciplinary Views on Western Places

The chapters in *A Watershed Moment* consider policy options for addressing a range of land use problems, whether these primarily take the form of economic, ecological, social, or political problems. Each chapter is grounded in a specific place and considers that place's historical context and future policy options. The authors have different professional perspectives—as lawyers, scientists, journalists, environmental consultants, historians, and anthropologists. They include fishery, wildfire, wildlife, and tourism managers, as well as community organizers and activists. Decisions about how to protect communities from wildfire, how to plan urban growth, and how to preserve traditional land uses—to take a few examples of the problems examined in the volume—require drawing on a diversity of viewpoints, including expert knowledge and diverse stakeholder perspectives. The authors explore a variety of approaches and identify particularities of local contexts against the background of large-scale economic, ecological, and social drivers. This volume is interdisciplinary not only in the sense that the authors come from different professional backgrounds but also in the stronger sense that the chapters integrate knowledge from different disciplines and recommend decision-making processes that encourage communities to share ideas, engage in dialogue, and reach for creative solutions.

The contributors to this volume's chapters break out of conventional silos to explore the ways in which social, economic, and natural systems are interconnected. The holism of natural and social systems is a fundamental assumption of this volume. This means that there will be more difficult trade-offs—and more unforeseen consequences—when we try to manage one part of an economic or ecological system without taking other parts into account. For instance, the chapters about community planning identify negative effects of increased traffic and sprawl for both wildlife and wealth inequality. Managing water resources, likewise, not only is a matter of rainfall and accumulated snowpack but also has to do with which crops are grown, patterns of urban development, the value of fisheries, and whether, for example, beaver are seen as pests or partners.

The sections are organized thematically, and the sections recognize the impossibility of segregating resource types or offering solutions from the perspective of a single professional orientation. In fact, many of the recommendations explicitly cut across areas of expertise and demonstrate the interconnectedness of systems. For instance, a holistic examination of wildfire management policy requires expanding well beyond fuel load, ignition source, and wind—the drivers of wildland fires—to also examine the landscaping aesthetic of homeowners who live at the wildland-urban interface and how to influence cultural values (chapter 19). Complex systems lead to complex problems and to complex solutions; this holistic approach is neither easy nor infallible.

Recognizing the importance of place, the editors asked each author to tell the story of a community, landform, or watershed, showing how the land policy challenges in that place are unique while also offering lessons for other places in the West and outside its borders. These stories focus on land policy and how communities are navigating competing demands on land use, complexity in environmental governance, and diversity of community values. Each chapter offers recommendations for preserving community character and resilience in the face of limits, both ecological and social. They recognize that the land and its governance systems are dynamic. While the focus is on the Intermountain West, these chapters are a resource for other regions that have faced—or will face—similar pressures. We are at a watershed moment: just as current issues are a result of decisions made a century ago, the decisions made today will affect future generations.

Collaborative, Creative, Evidence-Based Problem-Solving

A Watershed Moment seeks solutions that create balanced, livable communities in healthy landscapes. These are communities that fit into their landscapes and contain working lands alongside healthy natural ecosystems. The rules, norms, and practices that shape these lands and community relationships have been defined by the history of land use in the West, but they are also plastic and respond to new scientific knowledge, shifts in the legal landscape, changing social mores, and emerging economic opportunities. In the twenty-first century, public decision-making is increasingly determined by a blend of formal and informal governance that includes nonprofits, consultants, citizen groups, industry organizations, foundations, academic researchers, and private landowners, working in partnership with agents of municipal, county, state, federal, and tribal governments.

Most of the stories in this volume start with citizens—not government officials—who are concerned with how changes in land use make it harder for ordinary people to maintain security and quality of life. Jodi Brandt and her colleagues (chapter 21) write about a rancher working to restore streamflow on his land. The rancher has built a partnership with public land managers and university researchers to improve habitat for beavers, since beavers' dam-building activities create holding ponds that replenish and raise groundwater levels.

Other chapters center on the perspective of a natural resource or wildlife population, such as the Great Salt Lake or migrating mule deer, in order to examine how existing policies fail to offer adequate protection. The solutions that are available sometimes require inventing new legal tools or combining the knowledge and resources of different stakeholders. Emily Reed and Matthew Kauffman (chapter 17) share a story about how researchers identified a bottleneck in the mule deer migration path that threatened the existence of a specific herd. Preserving the migration pathway took the combined efforts and collaboration of university wildlife researchers, photographers and filmmakers, a private citizen who was dedicated to fundraising, financial contributions from many private supporters, and the cooperation of the Wyoming Game and Fish Department. Such cross-sector partnerships are effective at generating solutions that meet the needs and match the values of multiple stakeholders.

Even when governments are the initiators of policy shifts, public involvement and participation are essential for designing successful initiatives. There are many reasons to encourage widespread citizen participation in community decision-making about land use and economic development. Most importantly, citizens often have distinctive ideas, skills, and assets to contribute. Government-led public hearings and committees provide one venue for citizens to communicate with policymakers, but community organizations have an equally important role. People may be aware of a problem but lack a deliberative structure that helps them coordinate activities to address it. Regina Lopez-Whiteskunk's chapter (chapter 13) is one of several that describe this dynamic. She recounts the process by which representatives from five tribes organized a working committee and overcame political obstacles to persuade the Obama administration to designate Bears Ears for protection. And Robert Liberty (chapter 11) shows how a resident of Wallowa County, Oregon—with the support of 1000 Friends of Oregon, a nonprofit that advocates for sound land use planning—was able to save sensitive terrain from development that had been approved in violation of the county's democratically adopted zoning plan.

Several chapters offer cautionary tales about planning processes that stumbled by attempting to streamline decision-making at the cost of broad stakeholder involvement. In contrast, other chapters highlight steps that communities have taken to empower citizen action. An important first step is to bring all interests to the table early in the process, not just those with the most money at stake or those who agree with the leaders of an initiative. Even government offices and agencies with nearby jurisdictions and overlapping mandates can find it difficult to communicate with one another. Stewart W. Breck, for instance, highlights how important it is for public agents who handle human-wildlife conflicts to collaborate with organizations outside their usual circle (chapter 18). He observes that designing and distributing bear-proof garbage containers has many points of contact with homeowners, refuse collectors, and neighborhood organizations, and even coordinating different offices within a single municipality can be a feat in itself. Building collaborative networks should not be dreaded as a series of hoops to jump through or boxes to check but rather encouraged as a strategy for creating robust partnerships that can weather change. In many cases, partners on one initiative continue to build on their initial success and collaboration because, inevitably, land use policy must be updated.

Successful problem-solving often starts with collecting data about the distribution of costs and benefits. In economic terms, this may be viewed as evaluating whether all the costs of a decision are accounted for (i.e., internalized), or whether some costs are unaccounted for—hidden from view—and imposed on constituents or entities who are not receiving a benefit (i.e., externalized). Understanding the distribution of costs and benefits can help design fair policies. It can also help design an incentive or enforcement structure. Behaviors that are voluntarily encouraged through incentives rather than based on mandates can often garner wider support. A softer, more voluntary approach can be preferable so long as it is sufficiently effective; on the other hand, voluntary guidelines may disguise a lack of will to make real change. When public oversight is relegated to an advisory role, it can more easily be pushed aside.

An effective decision-making process collects, shares, and uses data as the basis for decisions. The ability to collect data cheaply, to analyze evidence rapidly, and to share it widely or to specifically targeted users, has enabled solutions to difficult problems. The project to identify and protect mule deer migration routes in Wyoming would not have been possible without wireless sensors that remotely tracked how the deer moved across the landscape and how long they spent in particular places (chapter 17).

Identifying the root causes of problems and finding leverage points can also lead to instituting new behavioral norms, either through incentives or through what behavioral economists call "nudges." Nudges preserve options but make a desired behavior the default or easiest path. Jennifer Wesselhoff's approach to tourism management in both Sedona, Arizona, and Park City, Utah, involves pursuing a number of techniques simultaneously, each of which might seem minor (chapter 10). Taken together, they create gentle pressure to shift visitors toward desired behaviors, such as taking shuttles to popular destinations, so that communities can comfortably coexist with the tourists who support the local economy. Her approach includes preferential marketing to target visitors whose expectations align with the community and distributing marketing content that sends subtle but consistent cues about sustainable choices.

Of course, creating new norms and changing behaviors is a difficult process that demands people be shown respect even when their priorities differ. In order to be effective, new norms must be culturally appropriate and align with local social values. Coeur D'Alene isn't Boulder, and Provo isn't Santa Fe. These chapters offer examples so that communities can learn from one another, but it's also important to recognize that solutions that have worked in one place may not have the exact same effect in another. Similar problems may actually be produced by different causes. The need to track the cause of similar-seeming problems and address them appropriately can be seen in the chapters by Joan May and Kristal Jones (chapters 7 and 9). Each examines a shortage of affordable housing, but Jones argues that the solutions that May recommends for Telluride, with its limited acreage of developable land, may not translate smoothly to Bozeman, where the community history, values, and ability to expand are different.

Developing policy solutions and enacting social change is an ongoing, stepwise process. Rather than expecting a definite end point, these authors show that it is often best to target measurable benchmarks while anticipating that each success will create new aspirations and opportunities. Gradual change and partial improvements are often preferable to all-or-nothing approaches. Drew E. Bennett's team provides an example: they have created conservation agreements that are temporally limited to protect grazing land as migration corridors for only those seasons of the year when these lands are essential wildlife habitat (chapter 14). Flexible legal agreements of this type can achieve conservation goals while preserving the value of working lands.

These stories of civic engagement also demonstrate another reason to solicit citizen involvement in land use planning: the process strengthens a sense of community. This is especially important because our social, economic, and environmental systems are undergoing constant change. A set of policies and practices that is an ideal fit for a community will inevitably need to be revisited as new economic opportunities or environmental challenges arise. Although inclusivity may seem inconvenient at times, insincere attempts to enroll the public or survey public desires are often inefficient in the long run because they risk generating pushback from people who feel left out. Aside from that prudential concern, designing inclusive decision processes is also the right thing to do.

Change Is the Only Constant

Strong, explicit support for diversity and inclusion is only one of many recent cultural changes that affect land policy. At the same time that culture changes, economic opportunities are shifting, technologies are improving (while creating unexpected side effects), and the climate is changing in ways that increase risks of drought, flood, wildfire, and insect infestations. *Resilience* has become a catchword that cautions us to make plans with change in mind. Fishery and wildlife managers incorporate adaptive management into their plans—a technique that integrates monitoring and learning from mistakes with the intent to update management plans accordingly. Even with the best planning, communities will face challenges, and the successful ones are those that bounce back. Consequently, many chapters point to the importance of building safety nets, knowing that one thing we can expect is the unexpected. The lesson is to hope for good times while hedging risks against the bad.

The most ubiquitous and pressing changes the region faces are related to climate change. Climate change does and will affect snowfall and rain, air and water temperatures, evaporation, the health of forests and fisheries, and wildfire activity—and it will have many direct and indirect effects on food webs, pests, agriculture, and human choices. Climatic shifts have increased drought, and already there is not enough water to support many important human uses, especially agriculture, as well as the sustainability of natural systems. Both drought and development reduce water availability, and shortages will force choices among agricultural, industrial, and residential uses (Hansen et al. 2002; Dettinger, Udall, and Georgakakos 2015). Natural systems, too, will come up short, and we ignore them at our peril. Bonnie K. Baxter shows how drought and overuse of water in the Great Salt Lake watershed diminish both ecosystem and human health (chapter 20). Grady Gammage Jr. and Wellington Reiter describe how water policy affects decisions involving agricultural production and urban growth surrounding Phoenix (chapter 2). And Josiah Heyman predicts a coming water shortage for Northern Mexico and El Paso, where water drawn from aquifers is essential for the people who work in manufacturing (chapter 3).

The chapters concerning water address the complexity of trade-offs. The value of water for ecosystem health in Great Salt Lake competes with its value for growing alfalfa in the surrounding watershed, the value of water for Arizona agriculture competes with urban development, and the aquifers in West Texas and Northern Mexico are stressed by the political and economic demand to site factories producing consumer goods on the border. In all these cases, tough choices will have to be made not just among current water uses but also between using water now and leaving it in the ground as reservoirs for future generations.

Technological advancement is another cause of problems that accelerate the need to examine existing land and economic policies. For instance, there are no longer any unknown places—no "back of beyond"—as people are able to geolocate every special spot. Social media have intensified people's desire to experience the Intermountain West's unique and magical landscapes. Increased visitation to public lands in the West, baby boomers becoming active retirees, and increasing numbers of people working remotely have led to both an increased need for service workers in many communities and a shortage of affordable places where they can live. The availability of reliable trip-planning information through platforms such as Airbnb and the influence of social media have produced explosive growth in the market for short-term rentals, and this, in turn, has raised prices in the real estate market, making it harder for ordinary folks, even longtime residents of the West, to buy or rent a home.

Tourism and the rise in remote work are two ways that information technologies have contributed to a shift from economies based on natural resources, such as ranching and mining, to economies based on natural amenities. Natural amenities like the desirable landscapes and climate characteristics of the Intermountain West draw visitors and new residents. In the 1990s, municipal and regional governments commonly viewed enhancing access to natural amenities as a way to attract economic development that would be less susceptible to market fluctuations for natural resources such as timber, fossil fuels, and precious metals. Thus, the virtue of capitalizing on natural amenities was that tourism and second-home ownership would buffer local economies against the boom-and-bust cycle of natural resource extraction. But the advance of amenity economies has been so successful in some places that economic gains have come at the expense of community values and the natural amenities that were the initial draw. Zion and Glacier National Parks have had to institute shuttles and timed entry passes, and the first trick to fly-fishing in Montana is finding a reasonably quiet stretch of river. In his chapter, Todd Wilkinson casts a critical eye on how the recreation—or, as he deems it, "wreckreation"—industry is out of step with the ethical impulse to admire and preserve wild places that was its genesis (chapter 16). While the authors of these chapters are critical of the wealth inequality and habitat degradation that tend to accompany growth spurred by amenity economies, their consistent aim is to find economic options that are compatible with conserving both community character and natural resources.

It's important to note that while value judgments guide land use choices, values are not static. Economic values rapidly change in response to market prices, and social and cultural values react to the availability of new opportunities, conditions, and experiences. We try out a set of policies or a way of life and sometimes find that we have not taken all the undesired implications into account. For instance, a pattern of residential development based on large lot sizes may be viewed as preserving rural community character until it creates sprawl that fails to provide the best qualities of either rural or urban communities (chapters 6 and 8).

In the late twentieth century, the long-term consequences of extractive industries to the environment became brutally apparent: uranium mining in New Mexico was responsible for high cancer rates in the Navajo Nation, and Butte, Montana, became the nation's largest superfund site as a result of copper mining. As a consequence, environmental regulations have raised expectations for how mining and other extractive industries operate. They still disturb wildlife, destroy plant communities, pollute water, require the creation of new roads, and concentrate heavy metals and other toxins in tailings while serving a culture of consumption that is responsible for climate change. But their negative impacts are much reduced compared to the last century, and as Shawn Hill explains in chapter 6, we are learning that the negative impacts of amenity economies, such as sprawling second-home developments, extend far beyond resort towns and have been underappreciated.

Development in the Intermountain West was desirable when it sustained population sizes and community character even as employment in productive and extractive industries dropped. But as more people have moved to cities such as Boise, Colorado Springs, and Missoula and the environs of Phoenix and Denver, the more negative consequences of suburban and exurban development have become apparent. The expansion of the wildland-urban interface has put more structures at risk from wildfire and more people and wildlife at risk for conflict. Moreover, some of the cultural expectations in the Intermountain West that prioritize individual liberties and private property rights create unfair consequences when populations are more dense.

Tailored Land Use Solutions

Several themes cut across the topical organization of the sections of this volume. These cross-cutting themes highlight the holistic nature of natural and social systems and, at the same time, demonstrate how the approach of these authors is unified around effective problem-solving. To take an example, wildlife management problems and solutions are closely related to how outdoor recreation and water resources are managed, and the options for managing certain wildlife issues are connected to the development of legal tools to promote conservation on private lands. Among the significant cross-cutting themes are sustainability, accountability, and collaboration across borders and jurisdictions.

Sustainability has a broad meaning that can apply to natural resources, ecosystem services, local economies, agricultural production, and relationships of all kinds, including with the nonhuman world. Sustainability is important but can set the bar too low. While our authors aim for sustainability, their case studies show that they are not merely aiming to preserve the status quo. Among other things, they aim to slow the rate of degeneration of natural amenities and community character and then to reverse negative trends. They support an ethic of making a place better—growing populations of animals that were endangered or threatened some decades ago, reintroducing animals that were widely exterminated in the early twentieth century, regenerating natural landscapes, and aiming for natural and economic recovery even while facing the pervasive challenge of climate change.

Pursuing sustainability is tied to considerations of environmental justice. Water rights enshrine nineteenth-century structures of political and economic power (chapters 2 and 20). Land policy in the Navajo Nation is also tied to outdated bureaucratic requirements that have inhibited economic development for Native tribes (chapter 12). Just land policy requires Native representation on committees such as the Management Advisory Committee to Bears Ears and other efforts to increase Indigenous involvement in the comanagement and preservation of cultural sites (chapter 15).

Accountability begins with acknowledging the reality of a situation and taking responsibility for decisions, but it also extends beyond acknowledgment to actions that repair relationships. Accountability is the difference between nodding in the right direction and actually making a difficult journey toward the desired goal. Policy tools, whether they set up penalties or offer incentives, are the guardrails that guide change in the right direction. In the context of zoning and land use policy, accountability requires that rules and guidelines be enforceable and not merely advisory. Accountability asks that we acknowledge the harm we do to ecosystems, that we not excuse economic arrangements that disproportionately burden the poor and vulnerable, and that we work to repair the harms that have been done to Native American communities.

The most innovative solutions are typically those that work across borders, boundaries, and jurisdictions. Water, wildlife, people, and goods move across property lines and political jurisdictions, but it is often the case that our ability to address a problem fails to extend beyond the lines drawn on a map. Public land management agencies such as the Bureau of Land Management, the U.S. Forest Service, and the National Park Service each have their own culture and set of rules and practices, and these agencies must often interface with others, such as the Department of Defense, Department of Agriculture, and the Environmental Protection Agency. Coordination can be difficult, and the problem is replicated at all levels, including among and within tribal, state, county, and municipal governments, which also interface with conservation and water districts. The U.S. Intermountain West shares two major international borders, not to mention obstacles that can impede communication among watersheds, ecosystems, legal frameworks, cultural identities, and political parties. Over and over again, these authors say there is one proven way to work across these many borders, and that is to build relationships.

Structure of the Volume

The chapters of the book are divided into five topical sections. The first section ("Resource Use and Overuse") contains chapters that examine the history and current status of problems related to water distribution, productive public lands, and resource extraction. The topic of the following section ("Equitable Communities") shifts to examine the implications that New West economies have for equity and community character. Chapters in the third section ("Preserving Private and Public Lands") look specifically at land use policy, including administrative obstacles to land ownership transfers in the Navajo Nation, comanagement of protected public land, and collaboration between agencies and private landowners to conserve wildlife habitat. How human societies can be designed to avoid wildlife and wildfire conflict is the subject of the fourth section ("Coexisting with Wildlife and Wildfire"). The final section ("Restoring Nature") contains a set of chapters that offer hope for restoring relationships between humans and nature.

Resource Use and Overuse. In the 1980s, scholars identified a constellation of cultural expectations and economic activities that they termed *the New West* to distinguish it from the Old West, which had been based on mining, fossil fuel development, ranching, farming, and logging. The New West has been described as "rural gentrification" as amenity-based economies attract new residents and shift the culture from working the land to recreating on the land (Pilgeram 2021). However, the appearance of amenity-based economies has not been uniform. Extractive and productive activities continue to be economically important for many in the West, and cities including Denver, Phoenix, Las Vegas, and Salt Lake City have followed the familiar growth pattern of suburban sprawl that is common throughout the country. The chapters in this section address tensions arising from shifts in traditional economies and, in particular, how the culture of economic production on public lands and presumptive water rights has shaped policies concerning resource use—especially the use of water. Historically, communities in the West have been subject to booms and busts tied to the availability of natural resources, commodities, and market prices, and this section examines the continuing precarity of Western communities as the nation undergoes an energy transition and the West adapts to climate change–induced water scarcity.

Equitable Communities. The chapters that address the growth of affluent communities such as Sedona, Park City, Telluride, Jackson, and Bozeman explore the growing socioeconomic divide between workers in these communities and visitors or residents whose income sources lie outside the community. The concern is that these places, like others in the West, are losing their traditional character and livability. In some places, traffic and travel times make the biggest difference, but in others, it is noise, development that obscures cherished views, a lack of affordable housing, or a shift in political outlook. The message of these chapters is to strive for balance in land use. In some places, there is a legitimate fear that the rural character of a community could rapidly diminish. While the outcomes are still unclear, a unifying thread is that development must create a balanced, livable community.

Preserving Private and Public Lands. Not only do zoning rules and planning objectives have significant impacts on residents' well-being, but they are also crucial for protecting land so future generations are able to enjoy it. These chapters focus on governance processes at the federal, state, and local levels. Some are unique and offer models to emulate; other chapters advocate for increasing flexibility to meet community development and conservation goals. Development in Oregon differs from other areas in the West because statewide rules set in the 1980s enshrined democratic decision-making, giving communities control over their own future. A common thread running through these recommendations is not to reject some tools in favor of others but to pick the right ones for the task at hand and adapt them to local contexts.

Coexisting with Wildlife and Wildfire. A special set of problems arises at the interface where undeveloped land abuts human communities. Processes such as fire that are typical or even essential for the health of some wildland ecosystems threaten human lives and the built environment. Increasingly, the boundary between wild and developed lands is indistinct, especially as climate change increases fire risk, as drought and habitat loss put pressure on wildlife populations, and as the extent of development and sheer number of people living in the West increase. When animals cannot make their living on wild lands but find rich sources of nutrition in nearby human-occupied environments, the stage is set for increased human-animal conflict. These chapters reveal the impact that human incursions into wildlife territory have on wildlife, and they examine the private-public-university partnerships that generate innovative solutions to preserve important wildlife habitat. There is no one silver bullet that will make it easier to coexist with wildlife and wildfire; instead, there is a tool kit of many initiatives that rely primarily on education and changing human behavior.

Restoring Nature. The challenge presented by climate change is already motivating many residents of the Intermountain West to rethink their relationships with the natural environment. A culture of controlling nature is yielding to a combination of scientific and traditional land management techniques, often derived from Indigenous knowledge, to find ways of life that harmonize with and support natural processes. Authors of the chapters in this section show that conservation needs and maintenance of quality of life for residents require updating antiquated water law and policies, and these values also demand cultural change to curb current levels of consumption. Initiatives in the West are using ecosystem restoration to mitigate some of the local effects of climate change, such as through beaver rewilding. These solutions work best when they can be customized to each community or landowner's needs and constraints. The volume closes with two chapters that demonstrate that we are living in a watershed moment when we have opportunities to recognize and repair the harm that past resource management decisions did to the natural beauty and abundant wildlife of the West. In the upper reaches of the Snake River and in the receding waters of Lake Powell, we see how resilient nature is as it reestablishes healthy fish and vegetation communities.

The Intermountain West is undergoing a watershed moment where its future will be different—perhaps very different—from its past. The chapters in this volume remind us that the choices we make as stakeholders, residents, land managers, researchers, and lovers of majestic spaces create channels that will carry us into the future we want to create. Because our choices pivot on our connections to natural and human communities, these chapters also remind us to build respectful relationships across our communities and to respect the limits of natural environments. This may require slowing down and living differently. But as these chapters show, watershed moments are a valuable opportunity to strengthen our communities and preserve the land we love.

The West as Myth and Reality

ROBERT FRODEMAN

Jagged peaks and serpentine canyons. Rivers rushing through narrow defiles; saguaros climbing desert slopes. Broad valleys filled with bison and elk. Native Americans gathered at river bottoms, mountain men and wagon trains, cowpokes driving herds of cattle. Endless vistas and limitless opportunities. Horace Greeley telling young men to go West.

These are the classic images of the American West. Reality matches these images if you catch things at the right time. But there are other views that don't make it into the coffee-table book, of $500-a-night hotel rooms and campsites that must be reserved six months in advance, underpaid and overworked staff, dead animals along highways, long commutes and housing prices that rival New York and San Francisco. Few rhapsodize about walking for a mile on asphalt before getting to the trail you want to hike.

Surveys of tourists in Yellowstone find that most people are delighted with their visit despite the congestion. But the juxtapositions are still jarring, cowboy images crashing into the realities of twenty-first-century life. Remote work has made it possible to have a job in Atlanta and live in Montana so you can hike when the crowds are gone. But check the prices of apartments and condos before moving. And know that the crowds are now here year-round.

A Watershed Moment asks, Is it possible to protect what we love about the West while remaining open to opportunity and promoting a sense of community? Each chapter focuses on a place and a problem, in towns large and small and across river drainages and animal migration routes. The authors explore Zoom towns and jammed roads, conservation easements and rewilding beaver, second homes and housing shortages, ranchland management and ungulate behavior, overtourism and environmental decline, wildfire, drought, and climate change.

What unites these accounts, the red thread that ties them together, is the recognition of the increasing divergence between our images of the West and the reality of life here. The frontier myth retains a powerful hold upon our psyche, but it is increasingly at odds with our social and environmental reality. Having long assumed endless space and resources, the American West must now contend with constraints both physical and cultural in nature. How do we navigate this new reality?

Water is the most obvious example. Drought is forcing changes in the Colorado River Compact, and the state of Arizona is flirting with limiting residential construction because of a lack of groundwater. But a similar point holds concerning wildfire: conflagrations have caused the largest casualty insurer in the state of California to stop writing new policies. And for tourism: Rocky Mountain and Arches National Parks now require timed entry permits much of the year, and at Zion, the Angels Landing hike involves entering a lottery. And for housing: driven by the lack of developable private land and the demand for homes by remote workers and retirees, the average price for a home in Jackson, Wyoming, is now more than $5 million.

Limits are a bad match with the myth of the frontier. The question is whether we can adjust our stories to harmonize with the social and environmental realities of a new era.

John Locke's America

John Locke died in 1704, yet you find his fingerprints all over the U.S. Constitution. They are visible in calls for "inalienable rights" and to protect "life, liberty, and property" (changed by Jefferson to "the pursuit of happiness"). His *Second Treatise of Government* (1689) remains one of the masterworks of political philosophy. In it, he imagines an original state of society consisting of Robinson Crusoes—self-interested individuals living in perfect freedom, who decide to give up part of that freedom to a government that will make their lives more secure, while still retaining ultimate control over their rights. Locke's legacy is the individualistic, libertarian political philosophy that defines American culture to this day.

Locke argued that claims to private property had an individual origin. Rather than being something given to you by the government, you acquire private property by mixing your labor with nature. Pluck an apple from a tree and the apple becomes yours. Likewise, plowing a field makes it yours. By this logic, Native Americans had no claim to the lands they inhabited, for they hadn't "improved" them. The argument was no less dehumanizing just because it was sincerely believed.

Three hundred years later, Locke's view of society still undergirds our attitudes and institutions. Yet this attitude depends on a specific set of environmental conditions. Locke justified the individual's possession of private property by the fact that the taking of the apple or the enclosure of a field doesn't leave anyone else with less: "Nor was this appropriation of any parcel of land, by improving it, any prejudice to any other man, since there was still enough, and as good left" (Locke [1689] 1980, § 33).

There could be "still enough, and as good left" because of the endless bounty of America. As Locke puts it in the *Second Treatise*, "In the beginning all the World was America"—endless expanses of virgin land waiting to be used. Given the population and the technology of the time, the claim made sense. America, after all, consisted of an entire *New World*. Europe had once been similarly abundant, but that continent had long since been filled. The discovery of America opened up a new way to organize society.

This truth still held at the beginning of the nineteenth century. Jefferson said as much in his 1801 inaugural address, when he claimed—and this was *before* the purchase of the Louisiana Territory—that there was "room enough for our descendants to the thousandth and thousandth generation." The population of the nation then totaled some five million, and life moved at a snail's pace. An ox cart traveled at two miles an hour; a sailing ship at six knots (or miles) an hour. Even decades later, and relying on a regular change of horses, a Pony Express rider in 1860 was limited to ten miles an hour. Travel from London to New York took six to eight weeks.

All this was about to change. The Pacific Telegraph Act of 1860 would put the Pony Express out of business: information now moved at the speed of light. The transcontinental railroad (completed in 1869) transported people and supplies at up to forty miles an hour, a twentyfold increase over an oxcart. The first gas-powered car was sold in the United States in 1896, and by 1900, the U.S. population had grown fifteenfold, to seventy-six million. The country was filling up, and technology made far-off places accessible. Rather than the thousand generations Jefferson predicted it would take to occupy the land, it took only four: the U.S. Census Bureau declared in 1890 that the Western frontier had closed.

But by then the frontier had become central to the nation's view of itself. The myth of the frontier served powerful needs. It underwrote the belief in American exceptionalism, that this was the "land of opportunity." And it implied that there was no need for an individual to moderate their beliefs, for no one was stuck in a place where they would be forced to compromise with others. One could just head West. The West was the nation's escape valve, the place where one could be free from stifling conformity. Thoreau expressed the point in 1851 in the essay "Walking": "Eastward I go only by force; but westward I go free."

David Hamilton Murdoch (2001) sees the rise of the frontier myth as a response to the trauma of the Civil War and the massive social changes that occurred in its aftermath. In the Civil War, America confronted its original sin of slavery; in the urbanization and industrialization that followed, it lost the conditions that made Jefferson's ideal of an agrarian democracy possible. Rather than a society of independent farmers, Americans were now increasingly huddled in cities under the thumb of captains of industry. The emergence of a new hero, the cowboy, embodied the qualities that Americans feared that they had lost. Fulfillment of the American Dream moved into the symbolic realm.

Locke did not name it, but he made the myth of the frontier possible. The frontier was that space of possibility that lay just beyond the horizon. Our Founding Fathers—his intellectual offspring—wove this attitude into our institutions. Then the evolution of post–Civil War American society made the myth essential to the nation's psychology. It became the touchpoint for economic activity (the entrepreneur) and politics (the outsider who would clean up Washington). The cowboy of myth embodied our suspicion of government even as we became more dependent on government and on one another.

The Frontier Myth

It's hard to speak of the frontier without reference to Frederick Jackson Turner. "The Significance of the Frontier in American History" (1893) divides Western history into two, before and after the Census Bureau's announcement of the closing of the frontier. Turner claimed that a continually receding line separating wilderness from civilization was the defining event in American history and in the formation of the American character.

In *The Legacy of Conquest* (1987), Patricia Nelson Limerick frames matters differently. Rather than an empty space awaiting the manifest destiny of Anglo-European culture, the West becomes the site of overlapping conflicts. Limerick avoids narratives of villain and victim, emphasizing that most Westerners inhabited both roles, often simultaneously. Skirmishes occurred not only between Anglo- and Native Americans (and Asian, Mexican, and Afro-Americans) but also across every stratum of society: mine owners and mine workers, homesteaders and ranchers, respectable and fallen women, senators and government bureaucrats, Lakota and Pawnee.

The point isn't to reduce Western history to relativism: some are more sinned against than sinning. But it is to replace certainty with complexity and to recognize the ambiguity of history. Similarly, the frontier thesis isn't dismissed; instead, its truth shifts as it becomes symbolic in nature. The rise of the frontier myth was part of an effort to create a usable past, to make it into a tool for shaping the ideology and ambitions of American culture. Turner didn't recognize that the frontier would never close—it would simply be transferred to new realms.

This is where Hollywood enters the picture and quickly becomes central to the story. In an era of multiple platforms for social media, it is difficult to imagine the influence the industry once held over American culture. Hollywood was the dominant art form of the early to late twentieth century. It was also radically democratic: particularly in the silent era, movies were accessible to audiences of every nationality and every degree of literacy.

From the 1900s, Hollywood provided the storylines of American life. In 1942, eighty-five million Americans—two-thirds of the country's population—went to the movies *each week*. The Motion Picture Production Code (created in 1934) ensured that the stories contained uplifting messages of Americanism, with good and evil marked by white and black hats, virtue rewarded and vice punished, and authorities held in high esteem. Hollywood created a common American (and to a significant degree, worldwide) cultural vocabulary. Or to put the point in darker tones, it represented an unprecedentedly successful vehicle for propaganda.

The technology of film arose at an opportune moment. Late nineteenth-century industrial and urban life—Twain's Gilded Age—had left many nostalgic for a more virtuous, agricultural, and Jeffersonian past. This explains the popularity of dime store novels (circa 1860–1900) and entertainments like Buffalo Bill's Wild West (1883–1913), both of which mined Western history for their accounts of heroes and villains. Hollywood rose as the next iteration of these stories, with the first Western, *The Great Train Robbery*, appearing in 1903.

With the move to California in the years after 1910, the movie industry had Western landscapes ready at hand. Stars like Bronco Billy (148 Westerns) and Tom Mix (291 Westerns) dominated the silent era. In the 1920s, perhaps half of all Hollywood movies were Westerns. Even with the rise of television in the 1950s, the Western kept its hold on the cultural imagination. As late as 1959, eight of the top ten television shows were Westerns. Other genres, such as the detective story (e.g., *The Maltese Falcon*, 1941), presented a similar character type—independent, suspicious of authority—transposed to the urban scene.

By the late 1960s, the Western seemed to have loosened its grip on the culture.

But the frontier had once again been relocated. Science embraced the metaphor: MIT Provost Vannevar Bush justified federal support for scientific research via a pamphlet titled *Science, the Endless Frontier* (1945), which led to the creation of the National Science Foundation in 1950. Politics utilized the metaphor as well: Jack Kennedy gave his New Frontier speech in accepting the 1960 Democratic nomination. The Western also moved into the space age. NASA's Mercury and Apollo space programs embraced the theme, with the actor William Shatner making the connection explicit in the opening monologue of the original *Star Trek* (1966–69) when he intoned, "Space . . . the final frontier."

Hollywood continues to place the trope in new settings. Viewed as a stronghold of liberal values, Hollywood storylines have in fact aided the rise of the libertarian right, placing antiauthoritarian "cowboys" in a variety of settings. The popularity of these films with famous (anti)heroes—*Dirty Harry* and *Billy Jack* (1971), *Rambo* (1982), *Die Hard* (1988), *The Bourne Identity* (2002), *Jack Reacher* (2012), the list goes on—has led each to become a movie franchise. The days when government was portrayed as the benevolent protector of civil liberties (e.g., *The Grapes of Wrath*, 1939) seem very long ago.

The Rise of a Western Aesthetic

But why focus on movies? Shouldn't we be addressing the issues actually confronting the West, such as the megadrought, wildfires and resulting smoke, loss of habitat, and lack of affordable housing? Shouldn't we give our attention to these problems rather than the clichés of Hollywood directors like John Ford?

The contrast between image and reality isn't so straightforward. There's not a list of physical phenomena in the world constituting so-called objective reality and another (false) set of things called myth or ideology. Decisions about how to address our problems are made by people whose beliefs are shaped by the stories they've heard.

What's more, ideologies rarely arise from the careful weighing of evidence or via an analysis of the cogency of an argument. We are moved by stories, not logic. Stories become the mental shortcuts or heuristics used to make decisions. These images or anecdotes may have been first heard in childhood. Or they formed part of the stock accounts in the community where we grew up. Or they are provided by the media environment we're exposed to.

For the better part of a century, Hollywood cinema was a dominant source of our culture's heuristics. People modeled their behavior on role models like John Wayne and Clint Eastwood, Audrey Hepburn and Meryl Streep. Genres like the Western told variations of the same story over and over again, providing models of how to react in different situations. The nineteenth-century poet Percy Shelley highlighted this power of art when he noted that "poets are the unacknowledged legislators of the world." It is the poet—in contemporary terms, the film director, the rap artist, and the writer of advertising copy—who creates the stories that help us make sense of experience. The same process occurs in politics: the successful politician is the one who campaigns in poetry, even if she must then govern in prose.

Aesthetics, then, presents us with a puzzle. Students majoring in art or English are criticized for being impractical, for science, technology, and economics are seen as the fields that pay the bills. But to contrast aesthetic concerns to more practical endeavors misses the ways in which aesthetics has infiltrated every aspect of our lives. And in an odd reversal, technology has made aesthetics more central. Watch people on the subway and at the gym, earbuds in place, listening to music or a podcast; note how one's smartphone is at the ready to fill in any empty moment with Instagram videos. The aestheticization of business, indeed of every moment of our life, is exemplified by Apple, which became the richest company in the world by making products that are cool as well as functional. Even their packaging is a work of art.

Aesthetics has been central to the experience of the American West. The nineteenth-century trade in beaver pelts was driven by the fashion trends of London and Paris, and died out not only because most of the beaver had been trapped but also through a change in fashion—the rise of the silk hat. On a greater scale, the landscapes of the American West confronted European culture with an alien aesthetic. Europe had the Alps, but there was no European analogue to the deserts and canyons of the West, much less to the sublime spectacles of Yellowstone and the Grand Canyon.

In the early days of European exploration, the Western landscape was viewed with a mixture of disdain and dread. In the well-watered East, brown means the plants are dead or the ground disrupted, and bare rock is a rarity; this made the West appear to be a forsaken landscape. In 1857 Joseph Ives led the U.S. Army Corps of Topographical Engineers to the Grand Canyon. He described the experience: "The region last explored is, of course, entirely valueless. It can be approached only by the south, and upon entering it there is nothing to do but to leave. Ours has been the first, and will doubtless be the last, party of whites to visit this profitless locality" (Ives 1861). Such attitudes about the West were once common. The Yellowstone region was first known as Colter's Hell, and nineteenth-century place names such as Dragon's Mouth Spring, Devil's Den, and Hellroaring Creek still abound.

Stephen Pyne's *How the Canyon Became Grand* (1998) describes the aesthetic revolution that taught people how to appreciate these unfamiliar landscapes. Painters Thomas Moran and Albert Bierstadt and photographer William Henry Jackson emphasized the sublime elements of Western landscapes, how they combined grandeur and fearsomeness, and the beautiful with the grotesque—exemplified by the geysers and bubbling mud pots of Yellowstone. Their art overturned attitudes toward the West: Moran's monumental painting *The Grand Canyon of the Yellowstone* was instrumental in persuading Congress to create the world's first national park in 1872. It still hangs in Statuary Hall at the U.S. Capitol.

While tourism in the American West dates to the early nineteenth century—Scottish nobleman Sir William Drummond Stewart left St. Louis in 1834 with a party of mountain men and stayed in the West for the next year, surviving encounters with grizzly bears—the economy of the region was long rooted in the extractive industries. A resource-based economy dependent upon mining, oil and gas, timber, and the grazing of cattle leaves a scarred landscape at odds with both ecology and tourism. The shift toward aesthetics was encouraged by the creation of the landmark environmental laws of the 1970s, which caused many extractive industries to move offshore to countries with more lax regulations (with the extractive industries that remained often hidden behind beauty strips). Since then, the economy of the West has increasingly been rooted in the attractions of its landscape.

The term tourism hardly captures the situation today. Rather than the traditional two-week drive-by of national parks with kids in tow, visitors and residents now find a multifaceted industry that generates nearly 2 percent of the American economy (ORSA 2022)—a figure that's much higher across the Intermountain West. Businesses now promote and communities depend on snowmobiling, downhill and cross-country skiing, hiking, biking, paddling, climbing, trail running, hang gliding, hot-air ballooning, fishing, hunting, and more—an entire industrial-amusement complex.

In their essays, Todd Wilkinson and Shawn Hill note that the shift from an extractive to a recreational economy hasn't worked out as hoped. It turns out that recreating in and subdividing the West can be as hard on the wildlife and the land as the extractive industries were—or even harder, given that subdivisions never go away. The environment today is stretched to the limit. Yet tourism and development continue to grow.

The Paradoxes of Growth

Tourists foreign and domestic, along with relocated remote workers, second-home buyers, and retirees are drawn to the West for reasons of aesthetics. People come for the weather, the views, the recreational opportunities, and the ideology. In doing so, they have created something new—the amenity economy.

The standard response to this influx is to expand the infrastructure: build more and wider roads; more hotels, apartments, and subdivisions; and hire more workers to service the needs of visitors and new (and often part-time) locals. Jackson, Wyoming, offers a case study of this approach. Jackson is a town of ten thousand, in a county (Teton) of twenty-five thousand. Visitors, attracted by Yellowstone and Grand Teton National Parks and its quaint downtown square, can on summer days bring the local cell phone count up to sixty thousand. The main thoroughfares are jammed. The response of the Wyoming Department of Transportation (WYDOT) is to widen the roads. There is also a massive development project proposed to address the affordable housing crisis called Northern South Park.

The land to be developed has a storied history. Homesteaded by Stephen Leek in 1888—whose photos of starving elk in Jackson Hole led to the creation of the National Elk Refuge in 1912—Leek sold the land to Bruce Porter in 1938 (Clayton 2020). Porter's descendants now want to develop parts of the still-working cattle ranch into a combination of market-based and affordable housing. The county's new neighborhood plan for this land would provide a significant increase in density (more than a 400 percent increase) while setting aside 70 percent of the units for affordable and workforce housing, with 30 percent of the housing units to be luxury homes sold at market rates.

Private, developable land is scarce in Jackson and Teton County. The county is 97 percent public land: Teton County includes the southern part of Yellowstone National Park, the entirety of Grand Teton National Park and the National Elk Refuge, and a large part of the Bridger-Teton National Forest. In addition, much of the private land that remains is held under conservation easements. Scarcity plus a beautiful location makes for very expensive property values.

The Northern South Park development would add as many as 1,800 units on the south side of two-lane High School Road, which borders the Jackson town limits. In a town with 5,300 dwellings, this would represent a 34 percent increase in housing in one fell swoop. Assuming an average of 2.5 people per unit, the development would also mean an additional 4,500 residents in a county of 25,000.

With housing comes cars and traffic. Figuring two cars for every three people would put another 3,000 cars on High School Road. This would increase pressure to widen the road and build other parallel roads. It would also add traffic to the town's main artery, Highway 89. Heading north, that road soon divides, running west toward the town of Wilson and on to Teton Pass and Idaho, and east toward the iconic town square and the national parks. WYDOT plans on expanding the road to the west, Highway 22, to five lanes, and to build other feeder roads through ranchland and meadows to accommodate growth.

The Northern South Park development would worsen traffic congestion. But on the other hand, it would provide a substantial number of deed-restricted housing units for teachers, nurses, and EMTs. It would get people off the couches where they've been sleeping in town, or out of the daily commute from Star Valley (forty miles to the south) or Teton Valley, Idaho (thirty miles to the west over Teton Pass). At least some of the local housing problems would be solved.

But would they be? The people who used to drive in from Star Valley and Teton Valley did much of their shopping and eating in those places. Now they would be going to Jackson restaurants and grocery stores. More business means hiring more employees for these establishments, as well as spurring the development of new businesses. Note too that the people who will buy the market-priced homes will create additional demand for personal service workers. Where will all these new employees sleep? On the recently vacated couches in Jackson and in the now-available housing in Star Valley and Teton County, Idaho.

This cycle has a name: induced demand. The classic case is transportation: traffic is bad, so you expand the roads, which makes the commute quicker, which encourages more people to commute from farther out, which makes the traffic bad again. But a version of this is also true for housing. There is an endless stream of people in St. Louis or Cincinnati wanting to come here who will fill the available homes and couches. In the end, traffic will worsen, and the housing situation will be no better than it was before. Nothing will have been fixed, and much will have been made worse.

What, then, is the solution to this problem? As the term is usually meant, there *is* no solution. Attempts to fix our housing and traffic problems by growing the infrastructure (roads, housing, parking, etc.) lead us to the same situation at a higher level. The only remedy, if this is the correct word, is to recognize that growth must end.

Similar points can be made about many of the other challenges facing the West. Yellowstone National Park received 4.8 million visits in 2021. Growing numbers will eventually lead to the establishment of timed entry passes. That is, to the instantiation of limits. Of course, such limits already exist in an indirect fashion—for instance, in the National Park Service's decision not to expand parking areas near popular trailheads. Similar rules have governed backcountry camping permits for decades—decisions justified in terms of the carrying capacity of the land. In truth, while restricting access is described in terms of ecology, these decisions are just as much a matter of aesthetics.

Carrying capacity is a familiar concept from ecology: go beyond it and an ecosystem suffers. The term means something different for human society. We have the ability to adjust our carrying capacity through technology as well as by adjusting our habits and expectations. This gives us flexibility to make the imposition of limits equitable, for instance by making campground reservations available to anyone with an internet connection. But other inequities will remain and in fact increase: for instance, the law of supply and demand means that people will be increasingly priced out of housing. We have long relied on technological work-arounds to push off our problems, but the future will require greater adjustments to our habits and expectations. Technology won't help us increase access to the Death Canyon hike in Grand Teton National Park.

Myths Old and New

Locke's political philosophy is another instance of mythmaking. Governments aren't created by Robinson Crusoe types coming together to balance freedom and security. Rather, each of us is born into and raised by a community. The individual only gradually comes into being, with their values being formed through a process of education and acculturation. Locke's origin myth biases our thinking toward radical individualism.

Locke's myth, however, did have two great advantages: it invited people to do exactly as they pleased—always a pleasant suggestion—and it was consistent with the environmental conditions of early America. Those environmental conditions are now disappearing. Long-standing social, economic, political, and ideological arrangements have been built upon Locke's assumption of infinite space and resources. What happens when these assumptions no longer match the world we live in?

This is the challenge facing the American West. And not just here: the United States as a whole and communities and nations worldwide are encountering similar situations.

There is a standard response to the presence of limits: technology will come to the rescue. Technological advance has been treated as a get-out-of-jail-free card: we can engineer ourselves out of our problems so that we do not have to change our expectations or behavior. Certainly, technology will play an important role in our adapting to new circumstances, whether through renewable energy, carbon sequestration, new crop strains, drip irrigation, new housing designs, or improved transportation. But technology can only do so much. We also need to change our values, reinterpreting our relationships to our communities and to the natural world.

Stories can help us imagine this new future.

We may turn to our artists, asking for new stories for our new times. Myths, however, are difficult to script. They rise organically—or not. And mythmaking today faces its own challenges. It is difficult to make self-restraint attractive; it calls upon a degree of maturity that society increasingly rejects. What's more, the modern media environment makes it hard for any story to achieve wide cultural sway. Our fragmented media landscape means that no single story is likely to gain too much prominence. Which only increases the tendency to fall back upon the old and now quite inadequate myths.

There's no simple solution to these dilemmas. The essays of this volume do not pretend to solve our problems. What they do offer are critical analyses and small steps toward a better future. In the midst of this, the overall goal remains what Wallace Stegner suggested decades ago: the creation of a society to match the scenery.

I
RESOURCE USE AND OVERUSE

1

The Myth of Homeland
Bunkerville, Nevada

BETSY GAINES QUAMMEN

The West, because of the many myths it carries, has become a sanctuary for contemporary mythologists—insurrectionists, Christian nationalists, and end-of-the-world preppers. When extremists bring separatist frenzy to old sawmill towns where extraction jobs have dried up, longtime residents might feel relieved thanks to the new revenue but heartbroken over the ugly politics, zealotry, and racism seeping into their Western communities. When towns, once booming, go bust, they can become terra nullius (territory without a master) to outsiders. Boom-and-bust cycles bleed jobs from communities, hollow out the middle class, and leave towns open to fevered dreams. Economic uncertainty and desperation can also lead to radicalization, lawlessness, and violence, as Western myths and religious fervor give way to dangerous acts of rebellion. And this doesn't just happen in towns but also on Western public lands.

Which brings us to a story of a collision of myths in a corner of southern Nevada. It's happening in Clark County, a place where old Western myths nestle together with the New West. Here the jet set enjoys opulent lifestyles next to working-class cocktail waitresses, construction workers, truck drivers, pit bosses, and one rather notorious rancher. They all share the same geography, though their homelands vary drastically. This place in the desert is a hot spot to indulge all types of hedonistic urges—be they gustatory, carnal, wagering, thrill-seeking, or armed rebellion. Here mountain bikers and hikers hit the trails of the Valley of Fire, Nevada's oldest state park, while off-roaders tackle rugged terrain amid Joshua trees, greasewood, and the Bundy family's trespassing cattle in Gold Butte National Monument.

Las Vegas calls to those seeking over-the-top live performances, expensive cocktails, and twenty-four hours of blaring jackpot slots, but head north toward the Utah border and the culture is far more sober. The towns of Overton and Glendale support populations devoted to a faith brought by early homesteaders to the region. As we will see, this story is one of cowboys, religion, and defense of homeland set within red-rock fins of sandstone, where the Virgin River winds beside towns defined by the needle-like spires of Latter-day Saint meetinghouses. There is no question: this is Mormon homeland and the site of the most central modern mythmaking event in the West, the 2014 Bundy standoff.

Roots of Rebellion

This event brought hundreds of armed rebels to an imagined homeland to play with cowboy and frontier vigilantism. But while the headlines date from 2014, the Bundy war actually began in 1989, when the desert tortoise was listed as endangered under the Endangered Species Act. (It was relisted as threatened in 1991.) The Bureau of Land Management (BLM) had begun implementing a tortoise recovery plan on public lands, including Gold Butte, a section of the Mojave Desert that stretches through Cliven Bundy's former allotment. That allotment became a designated national monument, drawing tourists with high clearance vehicles to navigate bone-jarring roads, rock hounds, and modern-day gold prospectors. Gold Butte abuts the Lake Mead National Recreation Area, where the Hoover Dam blocks the Colorado River, towering above a reservoir ever shrinking due to ongoing drought. This is a hard and dry place, hardly ideal for cows but pretty great for tortoises. All the same, it was a place viewed as homeland by and for the Bundy family.

A buyout program had been established in Clark County to serve as a compensatory system, whereby developers were given the go-ahead to build in tortoise habitat, so long as they contributed to a fund used to remunerate ranchers who agreed to retire their permits. The BLM informed Bundy that the new restrictions affected his grazing leases—most notably, limiting the cattle he could run in impacted areas. They also offered to buy him out. But Bundy didn't want the money. He wanted his grazing rights. And so he ignored them when his permit was canceled, continuing to graze his animals. He overlooked federal fines and fees left unpaid over the years. He also disregarded his neighbors' retired allotments, taking advantage of their absent cows and letting his own herd grow and expand onto public lands. He did not own this land, yet continued to use it as if he did.

Bundy has a number of hard-held beliefs tied to his church and to Western mythology. He thinks of this land as his own, à la manifest destiny. Gold Butte is part of Mormondom, land claimed by saints, who were told God promised them their Zion, a homeland. Bundy's idea of history starts and ends with white settlement.

In 2015, I sat with him in his living room and asked about his claim to the land, and he told me a story about the first Mormon pioneer down in the territory, his hypothetical ancestor. This guy traveled with a team of horses, a wagon, a wife, his family, and "maybe a milk cow tied behind" to what is now northern Nevada. When he and his family arrived at a place that looked promising for settlement, the first matter of business was for the imaginary horse to take a drink of the muddy Virgin River at the border of Bundy's actual property. "And when that horse takes the very first sip of that renewable resource," he said, "he is beginning to create a *beneficial use* of that resource." This is his claim to the creation of his water rights.

To Bundy, rights come through a white man's horse taking a drink from a body of water that the day before had been a Southern Paiute river. And this, in part, informs his notion of ownership today—the horse of an imagined Mormon family. Though Gold Butte is public land, Bundy insists it is his own: "It's what the range war, the Bundy war, is all about right now. It's really about protecting three things: our life, our liberty, and *our property*." He later expounded on these ideas to a crowd at a rally in Paradise, Montana, as he toured the West to find support. The event was held after a mistrial was declared over his role in the standoff. He spent seven hundred days locked up. He told the crowd of mainly supportive patriots that anyone who holds rights to public lands (he does not in fact have rights of any sort—he was at one time only a lessee) has acquired them "preemptively through beneficial use . . . created through our pioneer fathers." He claimed that these are "property rights, not privileges, not allotments." In fact, he said, "They [public lands] *are* your ranch!" Keith Nay, who'd lived near the Bundy place before his death in 1997, had advised Bundy never to call public land "an allotment"; those who leased federal lands, according to Bundy and Nay, should call the land something altogether different. Bundy told the ranchers in the crowd to go ahead and just "call it your ranch."

At the time of writing this, I've heard from friends that Bundy and his family were also trenching, illegally diverting water onto his property, and irrigating the Mojave desert at a time when drought holds the region in a vice. In his mind, it's his land—which a Mormon pioneer secured as his homeland with his thirsty horse.

The Battle of Bunkerville

In 1993, when Cliven Bundy stopped paying federal grazing fees for his cattle, he launched a religiously tinged, militia-backed, sagebrush-style insurgency. The Bundy cows continued to graze public lands across decades of legal disputes. After twenty years, the BLM finally got around to confiscating the family's cows. By then, the rancher had racked up over a million dollars in unpaid bills and fines. On April 12, 2014, hundreds of protesters, including members of various militia groups, gathered near Bunkerville, Nevada, taking their stand in solidarity with the Bundy family, whose grazing permit had been canceled decades earlier. They came to indulge in Western myths of righteous lawlessness, decisive standoff, and buckaroo justice. A number of folks in the crowd carried guns, and a few snipers aimed rifles at federal agents. Agents aimed back. Men in cowboy hats rode on horseback with a crowd pushing along to face Las Vegas police and BLM officers. Some of the protesters threatened the officers and yelled obscenities. Although sharpshooters had been in position throughout, the standoff ended without violence or bloodshed—but only barely.

Known as the Battle of Bunkerville, it ended when the feds and the police relented and retreated as Cliven's son Ryan declared to the crowd, "The West has now been won." This evokes a Western myth that goes back to Teddy Roosevelt's volume *The Winning of the West* (1889), which celebrates the violence of the Indian Wars. But the West was never "won." Indigenous peoples still are very much a part of the fabric of the West, although Ryan's hollered statement underlines just how important myth remains in the making of the West. In conceiving of a homeland, he used public sentiment spun from romanticized cowboy tropes and Hollywood Westerns to legitimize his homeland.

He also used religion. The Bundy family is absolutely convinced of their right to land. And in part, this is validated by Latter-day Saint belief. Although the family is not supported by the church, Ryan said of his ongoing rebellion, "My Mormonism plays a large part in what I do . . . the biggest part." One of the biggest tenets held in Mormon culture is the right to Zion—land God promised to the saints by way of the prophet Joseph Smith. So when considering the idea of homeland, the ties run into biblical notions of entitlement. This is the same motivation behind Zionism, the Jewish nationalist movement, and it inspired the revelations of Prophet Smith in conceiving Mormon Zion, an idea taken West with Brigham Young.

In their move to Southern Paiute lands in the 1800s, the Mormons, as well as miners not affiliated with the church, established settlements around precious water and atop game habitat, bringing scarcity to an Indigenous population that once had successfully made its living on the land. The Southern Paiute people were devastated by the damage to what they considered sacred homeland as well. These are a people who came as descendants of Tabuts, a wolf god. According to legend, "Tabuts blessed them and put them in the very best place," the same place that Brigham Young claimed. Of the Moapa Band of the Southern Paiute, who still reside along the banks of the Muddy River, some are Mormon converts while others stand in angry defiance against the church.

In the years since the standoff, members of the Bundy family have launched a campaign, meeting with thousands of people, supporters, and other ranchers and urging their followers to flout government regulations and join Cliven in his crusade to take back the West. His sons Ryan and Ammon took over the Malheur National Wildlife Refuge in Oregon a little over a year after the Battle of Bunkerville in the same spirit of defiance. The Bundy family's reach online is voluminous, if incalculable.

The Battle Spreads

When I first heard about the Bundys, their public land battles initially sounded like a fringe cause—an isolated family caught up in a quixotic battle with the government over a bunch of cows. But in fact, their crusade has inspired hundreds of thousands of supporters in the years following the Nevada standoff. Bundy's dismissal of environmental laws, his misinterpretation of the Constitution, and his take on entitlement are all very popular in some Western, libertarian circles. Writer Todd Wilkinson calls his influence the Bundyfication of the West. We might even consider it the Bundyfication of America after actors inspired by the family found their way to Washington, DC, on January 6, 2021. It's not hate that attracts most of Bundy's followers, who now proliferate throughout the intermountain states and beyond. It's the sense of power that these ideas—myths, misinformation, conspiracy theories—give those who feel helpless given the economic anxieties common in white rural American populations, amid booms and busts, corporate takeovers, environmental laws that feel overly restrictive, and new influences shaping Western communities.

The Battle of Bunkerville was one of the events from which Stewart Rhodes, the Oath Keeper from Nevada and Montana and lead instigator in the January 6 insurrection, drew his inspiration (Smith 2022). It was the springboard for Ammon and Ryan Bundy's political aspirations when they ran for governor of Idaho and Nevada, respectively. The Bundys, as Western "everymen," have become the heroic face of antigovernment agitators: they have made insurrection noble to other malcontents. They also made it into a religious ritual, a notion that others embrace in the creation of homeland among Christian nationalists in the American Redoubt—the movement in Washington, Oregon, Montana, Idaho, and Colorado that calls for the like-minded (arch-conservative Christians, Orthodox Jews, and Messianic Jews) to move West to await convulsions, from the outbreak of civil war to economic collapse to the coming of Latter-Days.

The Bundys have gotten away with illegal grazing, takeovers, standoffs, and expensive property damage. Their amalgamation of Mormon beliefs, libertarianism, and a right-wing reading of the Constitution continues to inform and embolden antigovernment activism as they wrap myth into their actions while they themselves engage in mythmaking—the winning of the West. And their idea of homeland has informed others. The Bundys feel entitled to the land, with their ties to early settlers and the promises of Joseph Smith. They control a piece of federal land that now is no longer regulated. It's lawless, and the BLM is no longer monitoring their illegal cattle.

The idea of a takeover is not unique to the Bundys. We've seen wave after wave of colonization and land rush in the West. It happened with homesteaders, prospectors, land speculators, and hide hunters who followed the lure of manifest destiny onto Indian land. It's happening with religious zealots building strongholds in communities and the über-wealthy forcing sanctuaries into wild places, blocking access to adjacent federal lands they don't own but do control, like Bundy and Gold Butte.

So continues the layering of the West, building on Indigenous sacred homelands, settlers' Edens, miners' mother lodes, trappers' paradises, the lush plains of the cattle baron, and Teddy Roosevelt's manly playgrounds over killing grounds. Add people who call public lands "their ranch." Trophy homes, strongholds for Christian nationalists, front lines for insurrectionists, safe havens for families in the foothills of the Rocky Mountains, and ongoing land use wars have become the places to entrench while watching America teeter ever closer to ruin.

How can we reconcile such destructive and unsustainable versions of homeland in a place that sits wedged between history, unrealistic expectations, and untenable, yet widely held, myths? Especially when the Bundys, motivated by all the same myths others embrace in their creation of homelands, are actually winning?

Homeland to Many

The West is stacked with "homelands." Refuges. Redoubts. Retreats, redos, wilderness, family steads, sacred ground, and battlegrounds. These are the various ways people interpret land and build culture, carving homelands into the flanks of the intermountain states. Newcomers and those already living here have created a precarious Jenga tower of dreams—some Edenic and others dystopic. Homelands pile atop homelands across the West, creating problematic political divides, income gaps, religious extremism, gun worship, and cultural isolation. Varying notions of how a place is perceived can rip communities and ecosystems apart.

There are reasons the West has become the ground upon which to build dreams and manifest ideals. People are lured by the myths that define this place, tall tales of profuse liberty, cowboy machismo, untrammeled and uninhabited lands, rugged individualism, "discovered" territory, blank slates, conquered spaces, and perhaps, and currently the most dangerous, the idea of a frontier front line. These are myths, hard-baked and stubborn, that tug at people trying to realize their imagined havens or bug-out shelters. The result is a mix of strange bedfellows pursuing the same myths.

One thing that makes the West so appealing is the feeling that it is a place where anything is possible. As Horace Greeley of the *New-York Daily Tribune* wrote in 1865, "Go West, young man, go West and grow up with the country." This idea has led to imaginings of a clean slate and new starts—a venue for people to reinvent themselves or launch new endeavors. People seek to "grow up" in this West, tantalized by myths this place should finally outgrow.

In many towns in Nevada, Washington, Idaho, and Montana, we can see tessellated homelands—varying manifestations all drawn on by mythos. A white nationalist separatist can live down the road from a retired financier building a $10 million wilderness retreat. The first sees homeland as a stronghold—a place with a high percentage of white people, some of whom may be open to his extremist ideas. He moved here to engage and gain power in ways he could not back home, and now he sits on a county commission and works to push state politics ever more to the right. The financier sees homeland as a retreat—a luxury getaway in wilderness, but a "wilderness" tailored to her needs now that she's rendered precious wildlife habitat unviable. She's here in her second home, not to build ties with the community, but to consume nature like a private delicacy and a retreat. Her property abuts public land, and she has gated an access road that runs through her place, much to the consternation of hunters and hikers shut out of land that belongs to them (Thuermer 2023).

A young family, newly wealthy from selling an app development company, moves nearby to build their idea of homeland—an escape with a panic room, a bunker, a greenhouse, goats, and a big backyard. While this family has moved to the Intermountain West to be self-sufficient and await economic collapse, across town, militants prepare for a holy war, awaiting broken seals, a pale horse, and end-times—perhaps they are planning to take over a wildlife refuge in an act of insurrection or engage in a standoff with the federal government. These could all be people living in towns scattered throughout this region, etching their imaginings and ideologies into Western landscapes. Playgrounds, sanctuaries, and front lines all fit together.

Of course, building homeland out West is nothing new. Nor is the supremacy that comes with it—the idea that some deserve this land more than others. The West has been a place of frontier fetishism since Europeans ventured to the Americas with their myths of dominion and lands to "discover." Western lands have been, and still are, considered sacred by hundreds of tribes, pueblos, and nations whose peoples walked here since time immemorial, far before colonization, white settlement, and ideas of ownership. To Native folks, lands and peoples are not separate. There is no notion that humans are superior and singular, created in the image of a Christian God. Land and wildlife are considered relatives, not possessions or lesser beings to be mastered—an idea laid out in Genesis, a myth of dominion.

As white people came West to settle, they began to commodify everything. Unlike in the beliefs of Indigenous populations, nature was seen as separate and had value not in its essence, but in its consumption. This ideology led to various rushes: gold, animal skins, ranches, copper, timber, land development, natural gas, and uranium. It later led to the popularity of parks as playlands (Yellowstone, Glacier, Zion), the building of opulent resorts, and the creation of safe havens in "wilderness," where people further consume nature.

The Myths That Built the West

To understand how this geography became so layered—and burdened—let's examine the myths carried by Europeans when they first came West. Building homeland atop homeland came with colonization, then settlement, fueled by the myths of "discovery," manifest destiny, and terra nullius. Though the West wasn't first encountered by white men, and people already lived here, the 1493 Doctrine of Discovery, codified in a papal bull issued by Pope Alexander VI, put forth that a land "discovered" by Christians was their land, making conquest over non-Christians legitimate, at least according to colonizers. Along with the myth of discovery came the idea of terra nullius, land free for the taking. This idea of "no-man's land" came from the Romans but was used by later Europeans to justify the colonization of lands and deprive Native inhabitants of sovereignty.

Settlers, as white Christians, felt that they were a more suitable culture to live in the West than the non-Christian, non-market-driven Native peoples. With the dispossession of Native lands came the myth of untrammeled wilderness, a falsehood embraced by the early preservationists and the modern conservation movement. In efforts to establish national parks and later wilderness areas, the history of Indigenous peoples' use of lands and their nomadic lifestyle across geography was erased (Spence 1999).

Discovery and terra nullius ushered in the idea of manifest destiny, a rallying cry to settle, procreate in, and make bountiful the West, despite its aridity. This presented pioneers with a God-given purpose to make gardens out of plains, deserts, and mountains. Indigenous homeland was overtaken during the frenzy of manifest destiny as people pushed to populate the mythic ever-expanding frontier. The West earned a reputation, courtesy of one of the biggest Western mythmakers, historian Frederick Jackson Turner, as a place that embodied real America and one that provided limitless opportunity and liberty. The cowboy became a perfect exemplar of these ideals. In spite of the fact that the lowly cowpuncher was a fellow often short on cash and thirsty for whiskey, his image got overhauled to represent authentic America and unbridled freedom. As Horace Greeley predicted, his image "grew up" with the West as it was settled.

After the Louisiana Purchase, various parties went out to map the West, bumping along routes traipsed by French Canadian mountain men trapping beaver. This practice, as well as bison hunting, later led to the near extinction of these species, challenging the myth of infinite abundance. Next, gold rushes beckoned folks westward, piqued by ideas of God's bounty, vast riches, and easy lucre, the myth of the mother lode. Wandering into the Colorado, Dakota, and Montana territories to claim their fortunes, they often lived in misery, eking out an existence in dingy, overcrowded mining towns. Cattle were brought up from Texas and left to graze lands now bereft of bison. This led to overstocking lands and terrible overgrazing while ranches struggled to be profitable with fickle markets and brutal winters.

Still, Teddy Roosevelt, after spending time on a ranch in North Dakota, wrote of the West as salubrious and a place to prove one's mettle. Ranching became emblematic of the hale-and-hearty American experience, again romanticizing both the West and the cowboy. Cowboys became icons America couldn't get enough of in both the twentieth and twenty-first centuries. From Calamity Jane and Tom Mix to Kevin Costner in *Yellowstone* and Emily Blunt in *The English*, the cowboy myth has summoned credulous infatuation.

Over the years, mining opportunities dried up. Timber towns shuttered mills, and family ranches were sold to hobby ranchers or corporations. As jobs in extractive industries disappeared, Westerners struggled to stay, while outsiders took opportunities to stream in, following in the footsteps of those seeking the promises of the West. They brought their own ideas of homeland, informed by notions of the last frontier where all things are possible.

Various myths do draw people to build homelands, but so too does the land itself. It beckons. This is a place where mountains, rivers, deserts, and plains stretch in seemingly boundless directions, and much of it is open to public access. Living here, or visiting, means the opportunity to freely wander across vast acreage. All told, Western states hold almost 50 percent of public lands, so Americans, especially Westerners, are free to move across and imagine their own meanings of this place. Because of this incredible privilege, folks might feel different degrees of ownership over these beautiful and wild places—Native lands divvied into national parks, wilderness areas, national forests, refuges, national monuments, and BLM areas. There are multitudinous ways these places are used and viewed. Homelands in the West are made on both private and public lands, and although the latter belong to all Americans, when a flag is planted and a homeland is claimed, even public lands become deeply contested and mythologized.

The Myths Evolve

Today, we see the consequences of the latest land rush. Wealthy recreationists have built ski resorts atop mother lode myths. Wildlands disregarded as too remote or without resources have been reimagined by even richer people as nature retreats, taking opportunities to limit or block access to federal lands that might border their private properties (Thuermer 2023). Western communities are changing as young affluent workers who operate remotely reshape agricultural landscapes, buying houses in subdivisions on former ranchlands rearranged by developers. In spite of the fact that the housing market is bullish and development seemingly unending, economic disparity in Western communities is causing the working class, and even the professional class, to struggle to buy homes.

As more and more people move West, they take to recreation in spaces that until the last few decades were mostly valued for mining, logging, and ranching—or left unpeopled. When old myths and new cultures jumble together, bitterness can bubble over. When tradition is confronted with the realities of modern economics and laws, it sometimes leads to the creation of darker notions of homeland—biblical promised lands, unending liberty, safe havens at the time of apocalypse, and battlegrounds. As I've mentioned, shared myths do not always manifest in the same ways. Some old mining towns have been reimagined as resorts, while some old logging and ranching communities have been rearranged into separatist states.

So how do we walk among these myths, address misunderstandings, and create resilient communities? How do we protect our resources from overdevelopment and public lands from blocked access? How do we ensure that our city commissions and school boards stay safe from takeovers by those who have undemocratic agendas? How can we secure counties from rampant extremism? I wish I had the answers to address these terrible pressures occurring in so many Western places. I don't. What I have are some ideas on steps that might help create buffers and connections to stave toxic elements.

First, our communities need strong relationships among people with differing politics. We have become increasingly angry over differing perspectives, losing sight of the fact that people are far more than Independents, Republicans, or Democrats. Getting versions of one another on social media or biased news outlets that lack any nuance makes us fall victim to reductivism and rage. We need to sit down and talk with one another. Though it sounds obvious, we should build relationships with neighbors, even those with campaign signs of politicians we oppose. Connections are imperative for healthy communities. Lack of trust can turn neighborhoods into angry, siloed households, and the only way we can push back on polarization and maintain community integrity is through concerted efforts to build ties and find common ground.

Further, towns need to work to protect newspapers. "News deserts" lead to low information, polarization, poor voter turnout, lack of trust in media, and corruption, according to a 2022 report from Northwestern's Medill School of Journalism. Invest in your community by volunteering, supporting community nonprofits and local businesses, and visiting libraries. Drive slow and cheer on teachers. Get to know your grocers, waiters, and mail carriers.

These ideas sound simple, but they are a place to start in building strong ties. Unless we are engaged in our communities and in dialogue with one another, the myths that lure dangerous elements to build homeland in Western geographies will persist. So too will their unlivable consequences.

2

From Reclamation to Reckoning
A Phoenix Story

GRADY GAMMAGE JR. AND WELLINGTON REITER

At 10:00 a.m. on the morning of March 11, 1911, former president Theodore Roosevelt stepped onto the balcony of Old Main, at what would one day become Arizona State University, and looked out at a crowd estimated at two thousand people—larger than the population of Tempe. He had come to the Arizona Territory to dedicate the dam that would ultimately be named after him, built sixty miles to the northeast in the Salt River Canyon. The dam was the first major project built under the National Reclamation Act of 1902. Roosevelt was expected to make only brief remarks, but feeling ebullient, he launched into an oration and a prophecy: "I firmly believe that as the east becomes better educated this will be one of the places to which visitors will come from all parts of the country. Moreover, I believe as your irrigation projects are established, we will see 75 to 100 thousand people here" (Roosevelt 1911).

Teddy was right, he just didn't look far enough ahead. Today the Salt River Valley—metropolitan Phoenix—holds just under five million. The story of the improbable ascent of this desert city is an emblematic saga of the West—the extraordinary success of national policy to encourage settlement and the resulting dilemma that we confront today. The question now is whether the legacy of that policy, created to encourage farming but which became the basis of an urban explosion, can continue to be sustained or whether it needs to be dramatically rethought.

The history of the American West is written in the physical relocation of water. Sunshine and land are not portable, but water can be moved and make dry land bloom. In central Arizona, the Hohokam figured this out first and as early as the first century CE built a civilization that represented a several-hundred-year-long adaptation to desert life based on diverting water from the Salt River.

At its height, the Hohokam population may have been as high as one hundred thousand. Their civilization included dense urban villages, sports venues, and even multistory "condos" like Casa Grande. By 1300 CE, they had dug nearly a thousand miles of dirt canals capable of irrigating up to one hundred thousand acres. Today we think the Hohokam declined over an extended period of drought lasting perhaps 150 years (Abbott 2003).

Phoenix was named after the mythical bird that immolates itself in search of rebirth because it sits atop the remnants of this native civilization. Given the stress on central Arizona's watering systems today, with a much larger population at risk, it is hard not to think about what happened to the Hohokam.

The Reclamation of Phoenix

The origins of Phoenix dispel one of the persistent myths of the American West: that settlement is the product of rugged individuals eking out their livelihoods from a hardscrabble personal struggle. The image of the cowboy, repeated through novels and movies, fuels this misperception. The reality is that it is not possible to survive in most of the arid West—in that area "beyond the hundredth meridian"—unless you get along well enough with your neighbor to share a plumbing system. The digging of an irrigation ditch is the equivalent of a New England barn raising: an occasion for the celebration of community (Gammage 1999).

Unlike other places in the West, the roots of Phoenix were not in mining or ranching. Phoenix was a farming town. The city's generally accepted modern history began in 1867 when Jack Swilling realized that the Salt River Valley offered rich farmland. Swilling was the picture of an iconic Westerner: a former Confederate soldier and deserter, a Union army freighter and scout, a prospector, a farmer, a land speculator, a drunk, and a scoundrel. By 1868, he had water flowing in an irrigation ditch. Swilling and his partners grew crops and sold land, seeking to profit from the enterprise of settlement. It was a pattern that would be repeated again and again.

The Swilling ditch set off two decades of active canal building. Many of the ditches followed the traces of the Hohokam canals, which were designed simply to divert water out of the Salt River and to follow contours out into a large, flat valley, falling primarily from east to west and only slightly north to south. This geography made it possible to gravity flow widespread irrigation. Canals were built by a variety of entrepreneurial companies seeking to grow crops or to increase the value of landholdings (Zarbin 1997).

The water in these canals was subject to an 1865 territorial law known as the Howell Code. Surface water usable for irrigation would be regarded as public property. Owners of arable land had the right to build public or private canals, and the use of water for farming was given a preference over other purposes. In times of scarcity, the law gave priority to the oldest water rights: "first in time, first in right."

Between 1867 and about 1902, the Salt River Valley changed from a wasteland to a garden of agriculture. Water was diverted to irrigate more than four hundred square miles, an area larger than that at the height of the Hohokam civilization. But the settlers did not know from one year to the next how much water would come down the river. Floods alternated with totally dry riverbeds. Inevitably, the settlers claimed more land than could consistently be watered. This resulted in manipulation, deception, and litigation over competing rights. The situation deteriorated when a serious drought occurred early in the twentieth century. It became clear to a group of settlers that they needed to develop a way to smooth out the erratic flow of the river: they needed a dam. The 1902 National Reclamation Act (also known as the Newlands Reclamation Act) would make federal funding for such a dam possible.

Reclamation was the concept that the federal government should construct great irrigation works—dams and canals—in the arid West to "reclaim" the land for agriculture. The projects would be financed initially by selling tracts of up to 160 acres to farmers with an allocation of water to irrigate. This mission was supported by Western boosters with a nearly religious zeal. Even the term *reclamation* expressed a kind of divine preference for farming. John Wesley Powell appears to have initially used the even more religiously loaded term *redemption* for what needed to happen to arid lands (Smith 1947, 39). Land left unfarmed was presumptively worthless. Water should be a tool to bring agriculture, and therefore civilized society, to an untamed region.

Powell's original notion included a sweeping reorganization of Western settlement. He proposed the federal government survey the West for appropriate sites for dams and canals, encourage settlement in rational proximity to those sites, scrap the rectangular Jeffersonian grid in favor of topographically designed and larger allotments, and create pasturage areas as a "commons," as had existed in Spanish settlements. Most of his vision was too late (and maybe too socialistic) for Western settlers. Dams and canals survived as federal projects, but settlement continued in existing patterns. The result has been the use of the federal government's extraordinary power to rationalize and justify Western growth for more than a century.

In Phoenix, as much as anywhere in the United States, the term *reclamation* was on target. Modern irrigation works built in the footprint of the Hohokam would indeed make the arid valley come to life once again. In 1903, the Salt River Valley Water Users Association (SRVWUA) was formed with articles of incorporation through which members would pledge their lands as collateral for a federal loan. In exchange, they would obtain rights to the water stored behind the proposed dam. Water, repayment obligations, and voting in the association would be allocated on a per-acre basis.

The SRVWUA ultimately became the Salt River Project (SRP), which controls six storage dams and reservoirs, hundreds of miles of canals and ditches, groundwater wells, and underground storage. It delivers about a million acre-feet of water annually to the Phoenix metropolitan area and also provides electricity to customers in a large portion of the area. Each acre-foot currently can support two to three families for a year.

The U.S. Bureau of Reclamation (USBR) became the largest water provider in the United States and the operator of thousands of dams and works in the seventeen states west of the Mississippi River. In the early part of the twentieth century, it replaced the entrepreneurial chaos of early irrigation efforts with a vast government command-and-control bureaucracy. USBR built the Hoover and Glen Canyon Dams and operated the Colorado River itself as a giant irrigation work.

That stable water supply allowed the farming community of Phoenix to begin to grow. But it lacked the traditional advantages of its Western rivals. It had neither the precious metals that made Denver thrive, nor the religious imperative of Salt Lake City, nor the location of El Paso on a major trade route. At the turn of the twentieth century, the comparative population reflected this difference in municipal population: Denver, 134,000; Salt Lake, 53,000; El Paso, 16,000; Phoenix, 5,500 (Gammage 2016).

The Growth Machine

The growth of Phoenix benefited greatly from the arrival of the automobile. Flat land and a grid of agricultural roads made every piece of land equally accessible. The desert was so hard, it did not even need to be paved to be drivable. Because Phoenix had never been a major rail location, trucking brought markets closer. As late as 1940, the growing metro area remained largely an agricultural economy. Phoenix reached a population of 65,000 in 1940, but by then, Denver's was 325,000.

From its earliest days, the settlers of Phoenix had eyed the sunshine and abundance of land as an opportunity to cash in. They viewed real estate profit itself as the motivating force for growth. The realization that development could be an industry all on its own came to Phoenix at about the same time that it was recognized in Los Angeles. This was a new idea: a future driven not by migration to employment locations but rather by developers motivated by profit who would seek out both employers and residents. Between 1900 and 1930, this formula grew LA by a factor of ten. But LA had attractions Phoenix lacked: temperate summers, the ocean, the Rose Parade. Phoenix needed more help.

World War II and its aftermath transformed Phoenix. First, two air force bases took advantage of great year-round weather conditions and brought thousands of GIs to the area. Many of them returned after the war with their housing and educational benefits. Even if you were not a veteran, the FHA programs made single-family mortgages attainable. Builders found the Salt River Valley a great place to develop: inexpensive land, no need for basements or frost protection, and a twelve-month construction calendar.

Most of all, Willis Carrier's invention of air conditioning in 1902 had begun to penetrate the consumer market with window units starting right after the war. Finally, there was a way to gain relief from the oppressive heat. Earlier generations had wrapped themselves in wet sheets and slept outside. Whole-home air conditioning was not prevalent until 1957, when the FHA allowed the cost to be added into mortgages. Air conditioning also contributed to Motorola's decision to begin manufacturing transistors, radios, and semiconductors in the valley. Air conditioning allowed the plants to be kept clean and the engineers comfortable. Those engineers happily agreed to relocate to Phoenix if their homes were also air-conditioned (Gammage 1999).

Starting in the 1930s, another federal program made groundwater available for Western irrigation. The Hohokam never made use of groundwater in their systems. In the mid-twentieth century, irrigators began adapting turbine pumps from the oil industry for use in water wells. To take advantage of this new well technology, farmers needed electricity. As part of the New Deal, the Rural Electrification Act of 1936 kickstarted the process in America. Suddenly, irrigated agriculture could move well beyond land reachable by distributed surface water.

By the early 1950s, Maricopa County was the fifth-most-significant agricultural county in the United States, measured by the value of crops (USDA 1950). But for any landowner, the most valuable crop of all is a production subdivision. As the postwar building boom kicked in, what boosters were calling the "Valley of the Sun" became a growth machine.

In one decade, the city of Phoenix's population increased by 311 percent, the highest growth rate among the nation's fifty largest cities. By 1960, Phoenix was the largest city in the Southwest, with a population of 439,000 (Gibson and Jung 2005). This growth was fueled by the easy conversion of farmland into development. Farming leveled the land, cleared it of creosote and other native vegetation, and built dirt roads to make every parcel accessible. The basic building block was a square-mile "section" of flat land bounded by farm roads that would eventually become four-to-six-lane arterials. Each section would include "shopping centers" on the edge and a school and park in the center. The rest of the acreage would be modest single-family ranch homes, with some apartments thrown in. This pattern of urbanization was repeated over and over as farmland was consumed by the postwar boom.

As these sections of land were converted from farming to subdivisions, water use went down by as much as 70 percent. The abundance of water supply developed for agriculture meant that subdivisions in the valley could be landscaped with grass and trees imported from milder climates. This was desirable in convincing Midwesterners to pick up their lifestyle and shift it to a warmer, sunnier locale.

As the city's growth consumed farmland, the areas being farmed began to shrink. In some cases, new land could be brought into crop production if it lay within the boundaries served by SRP. But the limits of Salt River water were within sight. Development also began to occur in the lusher deserts north and east of Phoenix, where luxury homes on larger lots were built because of scenic views. These developments, many of which were in Scottsdale and some of which included resort hotels and golf courses, put added pressure on groundwater supplies. The strong belief, however, was that everything would be OK in the long run, as people hoped that a new water supply from the Colorado River would soon materialize.

Colorado River Water Comes to Phoenix

The Central Arizona Project (CAP) started delivering Colorado River water to Phoenix in 1985 (Zuniga 2000). Arizona's relationship with the river referred to as the "lifeblood of the Southwest" has been complex, intricate, and often fraught with conflict. The Colorado gives the state its signature feature: the Grand Canyon. But it also has long represented a source of great frustration with neighboring states, especially the vast economic engine of California.

The Colorado, like the Salt, has been used for irrigated agriculture for hundreds of years. California began major diversions for large-scale commercial farming earlier than Arizona. In 1905, an aqueduct was built partially through Mexico to take water to the Imperial Valley (Gupta 2008, 208). Later, the All-American Canal, staying north of the border, was added (Imperial Irrigation District 2023). Farming in and around Yuma was extensive during these years but paled in comparison to what was developed next door.

In 1922, the U.S. Supreme Court ruled that the state of Colorado could not assert the right to all the water arising within its boundaries, which made possible the division of the waters between the seven basin states and Mexico. This would be accomplished by using the National Reclamation Act to build the largest dam the world had ever seen (Boulder, later Hoover Dam), impounding the largest artificial body of water in Lake Mead. The apportionment of the water was suggested by the Boulder Canyon Project Act: 4.4 million acre-feet to California, 2.8 million to Arizona, and 300,000 to Nevada. Arizona felt that it should receive at least as much as California, since the river flows through Arizona for more than three hundred miles before forming a common border with California, and California contributes virtually no water to the river's flow. However, California had long-term use (and a lot more congressmen) on its side (August 2007).

This dispute resulted in the last time one state brandished arms against another (known as the "misadventures of the Arizona Navy"), and in the longest-running case of original jurisdiction in the history of the U.S. Supreme Court. Ultimately the case was resolved in a decree that formalized the apportionment suggested in the Boulder Canyon Project Act, but that satisfied Arizona: it would settle for the 2.8 million, but the waters of the Gila (made up of the Salt and Verde Rivers) would not count against that total.

This resolution paved the way to realize the dream of bringing Colorado River water to central Arizona. In 1963, the legendary Commissioner of Reclamation Floyd Dominy, together with Secretary of the Interior (and Arizonan) Stewart Udall, announced the biggest reclamation project ever: the Central Arizona Project (CAP). The plan was to take water out of Lake Havasu and use immense pumps to lift it over a couple of mountain ranges to move between 1.5 to 2 million acre-feet to Phoenix. Arizona would repay to the United States the cost of building the canal, except to the extent it served federal purposes (Johnson 1977).

Congressional authorization for the CAP came at a price: the right to the water that would flow through the CAP had to be the "junior priority" on the river. In a time of shortage, California would be entitled to its entire 4.4 million before any water would be put in the CAP canal. Within Arizona, agricultural irrigation districts committed to buying all the water available from CAP until cities would need it. Federal policy continued to advantage farming in that Arizona's repayment obligation would bear no interest to the extent the canal was used to transport agricultural water. City water would carry interest.

In 1976, after President Carter had put the CAP on a "hit list" of projects to be killed (even though it was half built at that point), another concession was extracted from Arizona. The state at that point was annually pumping 2.2 million acre-feet of groundwater above the natural recharge rate (Connall 1982). Before the CAP funding would go forward, Arizona had to come up with a plan to curtail that pumping, generally to the point of "safe yield" or a sustainable level. The Groundwater Management Act (GMA) was the result. The act created "active management areas" (AMAs) of groundwater, administered by the State Department of Water Resources. In Phoenix and Tucson, AMA's new subdivisions would have to show the availability of a one-hundred-year-assured supply of water before they would be approved. Groundwater for farming was largely grandfathered.

Because of cost increases, CAP water was initially too expensive for agriculture. In a supreme irony, one problem was that farmers could continue to pump groundwater with electricity subsidized by the federal government, making it cheaper than CAP water. As a result, a deal was reached for cities to subsidize CAP water for farming in exchange for further limiting any long-term rights to agricultural water.

After cost overruns, construction delays, disputes over how much of the cost of the canal Arizona should bear, and litigation between the United States and the state of Arizona, the CAP canal was ultimately declared complete in 1993. Settlement of the lawsuits with the United States resulted in a major share of the water that the canal would deliver being dedicated to central Arizona Indian communities.

The Boom Begins to Fray

At the turn of the twenty-first century, the Sun Corridor seemed poised to boom without limit. Between 1991 and 2003, metro Phoenix added an additional four hundred thousand people. Pinal County, situated between Phoenix and Tucson, started seeing production home building replace farming. Growth was so evident as to threaten existing homeowners' lifestyles—meaning traffic was getting too bad. So in 2000, a proposition to draw growth boundaries around Arizonan cities was placed on the ballot by environmental groups. It went down to defeat in a wave of concern that population increase was the ultimate source of the area's economic future.

That apparently rosy future was interrupted, however, by the boom-and-bust reality of real estate. Real estate development is a volatile and cyclical industry in which the laws of supply and demand operate with relentless force. Homebuilding in the metro area exploded to fifty thousand starts in 2005, not because of some tectonic shift in the attractiveness of Arizona, but rather from creative financial wizardry.

From 2005 to 2010, the price of homes in Phoenix fell by nearly 50 percent (Streitfeld and Healy 2009). The state of Arizona went from creating 121,000 jobs between October of 2005 and October of 2006 to losing 183,000 jobs in 2009. In 2011, only six thousand new homes were built in Maricopa County. It was the biggest bust in a place with a long history of boom-and-bust (Gammage 2016).

All this led to relentless criticism by national commentators of the weakness of "Cities in the Sand." The outsider criticism of Western cities reinforced a longstanding skepticism about the wisdom of settling large numbers of people in a place without abundant rainfall. Of course, no major city can survive based on the natural resources within its immediate environs. A "resource shed" of imported materials like timber, concrete, copper, steel, electricity, and so on supports the concentration of people that build a community. Water is a commodity subject to transport. Western cities, thanks largely to the vast plumbing of federal reclamation, bring water from farther away. But to many Eastern observers, life in the desert never seemed rational.

As the economic downturn of the early 2000s gripped the nation and prompted questioning of the viability of Sunbelt cities, a much more threatening trend was masked. Significantly diminished annual rainfall meant that by 1999, Roosevelt Lake was only 40 percent full. By 2003, it was becoming clear that the worst drought in one hundred years had commenced.

Despite the slowly developing water shortages, the growth of Arizona's population continued in a pattern evident from the 1950s: as city growth replaced farming, water use declined. This relationship was largely the product of favorable geography. The conversion of farmland in the Salt River Valley to the cities of metro Phoenix allowed farmers to sell their land at good profits and cities to take over the water usage for homeowners. In this, Arizona differed from California, where people live on the coast but farming exists in the central valleys. That distinction has meant that in Arizona, farmers and cities have a cooperative history of shared benefit, and that benefit has kept water use remarkably stable. In the early 2020s, it became clear that the replacement of farming with urbanization was no longer going to sustain anticipated growth.

The Reckoning Is at Hand

As of this writing (2023), the confluence of three news stories appears to be signaling a crisis for central Arizona's water supply. First, Lakes Mead and Powell are at the lowest points since the dams were built. Each lake is only about 25 percent full. Second, the Arizona Department of Water Resources has essentially shut down further housing development dependent on groundwater in Pinal County and west of Phoenix. New hydrologic studies in these areas conclude there is not enough to last for one hundred years for all the planned uses. Third, a subdivision north of Scottsdale has found itself cut off from water delivery. Each of these represents a piece of failing policy.

The area with dry taps is an isolated but telling example of Arizona's antipathy to regulation. Rio Verde Foothills is a "wildcat" subdivision, a loophole in Arizona real estate law where houses are allowed to be built without any long-term water supply. These houses will likely be receiving water soon from one solution or another. The other two stories are much more serious—and much more emblematic of the collision of massive population growth, resource constraints, and legal systems built for a different time.

Twenty-first century Phoenix stands as a monument to the reclamation era. Despite the current negative press, Phoenix is probably better positioned than other cities of the arid Southwest to survive the next twenty to thirty years of likely aridification. In addition to the SRP and CAP systems that support the valley with hydrologically differentiated water supplies, over the last twenty years, more than twelve million acre-feet of Colorado River water have been "banked" underground on behalf of Sun Corridor cities. The state began an aggressive program of recharging aquifers in the Sun Corridor through direct and indirect recharge (Gammage [2011] 2021).

"Direct" recharge meant pumping the water hundreds of miles through ditches lined with concrete to avoid seepage and then spilling the water out into the desert specifically to encourage it to seep into the ground. "Indirect" recharge meant selling expensive Colorado River water to farmers below cost, in lieu of the use of groundwater they had a right to pump. The groundwater left in place is then treated as banked surface water. The state is not yet using this magic account but may soon start doing so. This water could sustain urban uses for a decade or more, but when it is used, it is gone forever and unlikely to be replenished.

There are other water sources. A less-than-full CAP canal could deliver other main stem river water transferred from agricultural use and will likely be used to transport groundwater from selective remote basins in western Arizona. Supplies can be further stretched by additional conservation, landscaping reductions, industrial efficiencies, and greater reuse of treated effluent. Cities need to consider policy choices about housing density and economic development opportunities that consider efficient water use. Operational efficiencies like redesigning reservoirs and limiting loss in municipal delivery systems can further stretch supply. Agricultural use may be preserved by more state-of-the-art irrigation techniques. Ultimately augmentation of existing supply is necessary, from ocean desalination or other long-range importation. Large-scale availability of such alternatives is probably decades, and certainly billions of dollars, away.

There are good reasons not to panic about the situation. But a day of reckoning is clearly at hand. Creative management of current water systems will only go so far. A horizon for existing growth that is twenty-five to thirty years out is not sufficient reassurance for long-term investment by either businesses or individuals still motivated to move to the West. Dramatically slowing the growth of the Sunbelt is a theoretical result advocated by some. But moving to Phoenix to live and work will likely remain attractive to thousands of future residents.

For the city to continue growing, however, a confrontation between agriculture and urbanization is becoming unavoidable. The federal policy decision to build great plumbing projects to encourage Western migration has been a stunning success. That policy prioritized farming as a near-religious imperative. More realistic than stopping growth is sustaining the West by revisiting the existing framework favoring agricultural use.

The Salt River Project system was built by farmers. The land they farmed was readily converted to urban growth, and a logical shift in use occurred without any serious conflict over competing uses. When CAP was built, it was designed to be paid for by urban customers, and farming was only a "holding" use until municipal growth took over. But much of Western water law was not set up to support a transition to urbanization. California and Arizona on-river farmers have a higher priority than urban Arizona. The CAP canal could theoretically go totally dry before any farming in California or western Arizona suffers any cuts.

The current moratorium of development on groundwater is the result of weaknesses in the Groundwater Management Act. Visionary for its time, the GMA today represents an all-or-nothing kind of regulation and includes distorted incentives to race for approval long before actual development. The GMA had a built-in preference for Pinal County farmers, allowing them to pump well beyond sustainable levels. Not so for housing in Pinal County, which had to demonstrate one hundred years of availability of groundwater. So housing is now at a standstill in that high-growth area, even though it would use less water than continued farming. And the federal government still supplies farmers with heavily subsidized electricity for pumping groundwater.

The reclamation era preferences for farming over municipal and industrial uses must change. Rigid and fixed priorities established when water was plentiful cannot answer today's allocation dilemma. Change can happen through regulatory reform, through legislation, or through market transactions, some of which are already occurring. A small allocation of main stem Colorado River water has been approved to move from an isolated location along the river to the rapidly growing Phoenix suburb of Queen Creek. A consortium of western Arizona farmers has offered to sell major annual water entitlements to central Arizona. Even California farmers have expressed willingness to transfer water.

These are complex and expensive propositions. Water markets are a relatively novel concept, and the price issue varies widely with the nature of the commodity. Are you buying a onetime block of water, an annual amount for a fixed term of years, or a permanent entitlement? Farmers who financed and relied on government-built water systems deserve compensation for their investments, and farming should not disappear from the West. But farming cannot automatically trump other uses. Urban uses deserve at least a more balanced position in the priority scheme. Readjusted priorities could mean cities compensating farmers for that shift and farmers learning to accommodate a less predictable water supply.

Western water, it is often said, "flows toward money." More accurately, it flows toward people, and that's where the money is. Too often, water transactions have been thwarted by an unwillingness to let market forces operate. There is a reason for this: water is a special commodity that has long been regarded as a right, not a privilege. But the efficient allocation of a diminishing resource requires creativity as limits are approached. Inevitably, economic bargains must be a critical part of such allocation.

Teddy's 1911 speech was not just about water. It was a valedictory about education, civic responsibility, the virtue of hard work, and a commitment to community. He saw the Salt River Valley as an embryonic piece of America—a place that could be made to blossom with the addition of a reliable, well-managed water supply. The occasion of that celebration was about one fundamental component of civilizing the West: the sharing of a precious community resource. Today reckoning with the legal mechanisms to sort out the sharing of that resource as it is diminishing is a critical challenge to the civilization built by "reclamation."

3

The Hidden Side of the West
The U.S.-Mexican Borderlands

JOSIAH HEYMAN

An enormous white blade waits in a line of trucks to cross the boundary from San Jerónimo, Chihuahua, to Santa Teresa, New Mexico. Hundreds of people have carefully assembled the molded and machined parts of the blade, toiling in a vast, low-slung building in Ciudad Juárez, Chihuahua. After threading its way through that sprawling border city, the blade is on its way to a wind farm in the U.S. High Plains.

The wind turbine blade is both a symbol of the transition to a more sustainable future and a tool for making that future happen. But the energy, water, and labor required to manufacture it is hidden by the wall at the U.S.-Mexico border. The physical wall has vertical steel slats that block migrant workers and asylum-seekers from entering the United States. The conceptual wall involves the estrangement between the two nation-states despite shared economies, peoples, histories, and environments.

The Mexican North and the U.S. Southwest resemble each other with respect to climate, aridity, water resources, wildlife, and vegetation. What's more, the entire continent is tied together by the production and consumption of commodities and the movement of people. This essay focuses on the environment shared by twin cities on the U.S.-Mexico border and on the impact of vast export industries on the Mexican side (a useful overview is Ganster and Collins 2021). In particular, it focuses on scarce and declining but essential water resources that pose a crucial environmental challenge for this arid region.

Viewing the political ecology of the U.S. Southwest through the lens of water resources shared with Northern Mexico shows that the relevant geographical space incorporates not just the borderlands but also large metropolitan areas in both countries that, while distant from the border, affect the supply and flow of goods, labor, and natural resources. Northern Mexico is tightly bound to the United States and Canada.

This analysis points to socially constructed borders as rarely acknowledged barriers to understanding shared environmental resources and, through that lack of understanding, the loss of a sympathetic sense of connection. Do natural resources recognize an arbitrarily drawn line on the map? Does such a distinction dull our recognition of similarities and connections? And how can we overcome these forms of alienation? After examining these challenges, I look to policy solutions that address the reality of shared water.

An International Border That Both Connects and Separates

Since 1965, U.S. and Canadian manufacturing and high-value agricultural production have gradually moved into Mexico, especially its northern states. The 1994 North American Free Trade Agreement (NAFTA, modestly updated to the U.S.-Mexico-Canada Agreement, USMCA, in 2020) facilitated export trade to Canada and the United States from all Mexico, especially from the near-border north (Cypher and Delgado Wise 2010). A notable result has been massive urbanization in arid areas (Kopinak 2004). For example, almost three million people work in *maquiladoras*, or export assembly plants (see Fernández-Kelly 1983 on this sector). The majority of *maquiladoras* cluster in Mexico's northern border cities. For example, in September 2023, Ciudad Juárez had over 306,000 export manufacturing employees, most of them assembly-line operatives, out of a total population of around 1.56 million (INEGI 2023). That is, in Juárez, one in every five human beings—counting babies and the elderly—makes auto parts, appliances, electronics, medical supplies, and so forth, for consumption in the United States and Canada.

This has amplified a long-term upward trend in internal migration and population concentration: many of the most populous Mexican cities, such as Juárez, lie in the northern part of the country, which was historically sparsely populated (see, e.g., Heyman 1991). Agricultural production of high-value export crops in parts of the countryside follows a similar pattern. Production of winter fruits and vegetables requires intensive irrigation and sometimes the use of greenhouses. The need for swift transport to U.S. markets demands that this production be situated closer to its destination in spite of the scarcity of water (Zlolniski 2019).

These economic opportunities attract impoverished internal migrants, including many Indigenous people from southern Mexico. Although products and sites vary, manufacturing and agriculture in Northern Mexico share an underlying connection to the political economy of North America. Mexico provides huge quantities of inexpensive labor to supply North American markets with goods.

There are different approaches to turning Mexican labor into high-priced goods. In Mexican cities on the border, the manufacturing is often very labor-intensive and not terribly sophisticated. In these *maquiladoras*, workers assemble components brought from elsewhere, soldering, screwing, and gluing together the final product for consumer electronics and appliances. In other cases, such as the near-border industrial behemoth of Monterrey, more demanding and high-skilled manufacturing takes place, though none paid to U.S. and Canadian standards.

Although some regional production is aimed at the Mexican market, this is less common than export production. Indeed, many consumer goods in Mexico are secondhand items imported back from the United States. Investment and operating capital are largely U.S. and Canadian, though European and East Asian corporations can also be found. Mexican businesses in the export sector tend to consist of smaller manufacturing subcontractors or real estate developers for extensive industrial parks.

This arrangement emerges from the unevenness of earnings and standards of living across the border: poor Mexican worker-consumers produce high-quality goods for prosperous U.S. and Canadian consumers and wealthy managers and investors, thereby linking the two countries. The value to be captured from unequal exchange between the prosperous north and the poorer south—for example, via low-wage manufacturing—encourages a marked concentration of people in cities in the Mexican north and especially along the border. Meanwhile, that poverty south of the border makes amelioration of environmental disorder difficult (e.g., via infrastructural investment; Heyman 2007).

In turn, the border tends to hide these economic connections. Of course, people with hands-on transnational roles from both countries—such as logistics managers—know about the linkages. Whatever the reality, workers in Mexican factories tend to view U.S. corporate counterparts as benevolent but distant executives, separated by physical distance and linguistic difference. They may even view their northern neighbors as "modern" people who live in an impressively wealthy and safe country compared to their own. Line workers tend to hold more resentment toward the Mexican managers, foremen, and other white-collar workers, of whom they have much greater knowledge and with whom they interact directly.

North Americans, in their turn, encounter consumer products, not people. In the United States, there is an acrimonious political focus on Mexican and Latin American migrants crossing the border into the United States, but the way that most Mexicans actually engage with the U.S. economy is not by crossing the border. It is through the transfer of labor via impersonal products. Connecting issues, experiences, and human value across the conceptual "wall" is difficult (Heyman 2012, 2017).

The border itself functions as a curtain. Each nation's perspective is reported inside that country, but analysis that combines and interprets information about interactions between the two nations, speaking to their interdependence and the many movements and flows between them, is harder to come by. National stereotypes remain pervasive and powerful. All poverty is viewed as Mexican, and all modernity as rooted in the United States (Vila 2000) even though both ideas are gross generalizations with only partial elements of truth. Worse than the economic and cultural stereotyping is the fact that these ideas perpetuate conceptual separation between two intimately interwoven countries, denying the reality of a shared arid natural environment and obstructing trust and relationships.

Aquifers Don't Have Political Borders

Cities, small and large, pair between Mexico and the United States: San Diego and Tijuana, El Paso and Ciudad Juárez, Laredo and Nuevo Laredo, Brownsville and Matamoros, and many others. On the Mexican side, growth has been based on various cross-boundary connections—manufacturing above all. As noted, the primary resource that Mexico provides the North American economy is people: hardworking but poorly paid, stimulating growth. The environmental crisis that plagues both sides of the border, but especially the Mexican side, is often a matter of simple human well-being. For example, given the scarcity of surface water, it is a challenge to provide sufficient clean drinking water and likewise difficult to extend wastewater removal and treatment. Wastewater service often lags behind the arrival of piped water, causing a contradiction of increased waste volume with no or substandard treatment and disposal.

The twinned border cities share surface and subsurface water, airsheds, microbes, and even dust and debris. My work as a public scientist has addressed the quality and quantity of water on each side of the border, as the local hydrological systems are bisected by the international boundary. In the case of Ciudad Juárez and El Paso, the Rio Grande / Río Bravo del Norte (the latter being the Mexican name for the shared river) serves as the border and shared channel for the two cities. The river is gauged, and shares are allocated by treaty to Mexico and

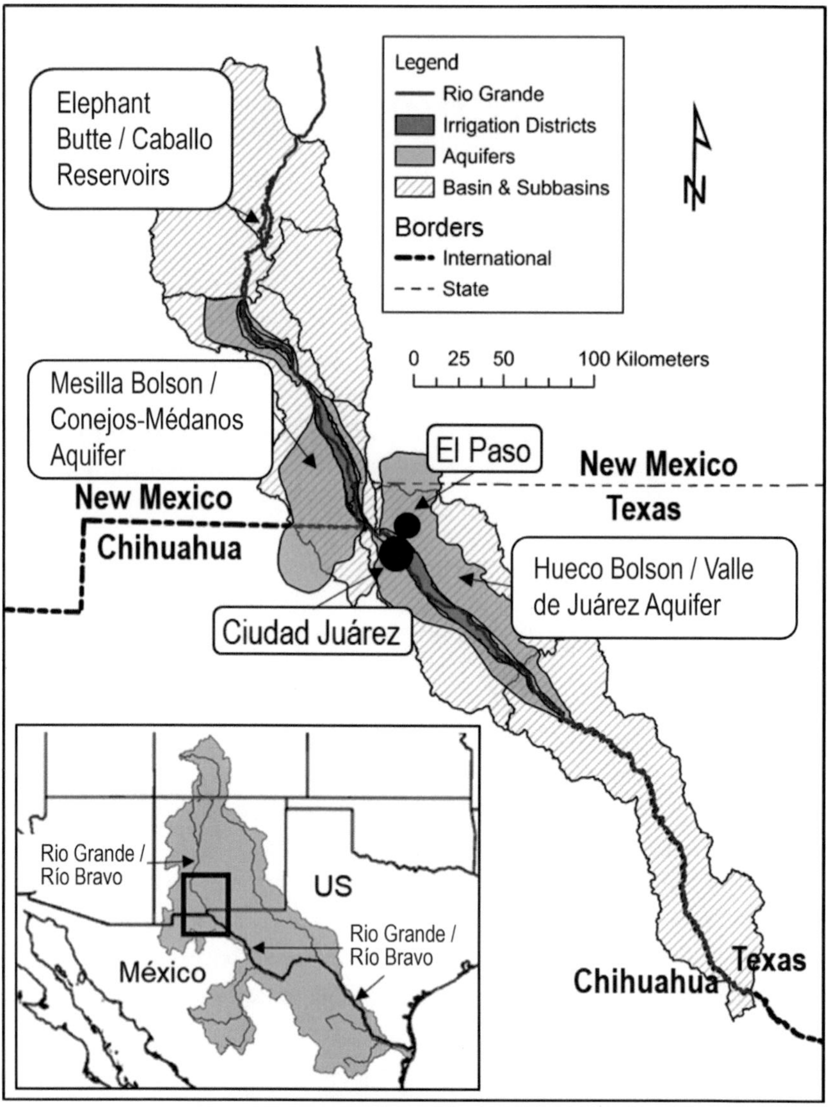

Figure 3.1 El Paso–Ciudad Juárez water sources and the international border. Source: Heyman, Mayer, and Alger 2022.

the United States, all dedicated to irrigated commercial agriculture. The city of El Paso has acquired some farm irrigation rights for municipal usage. (An up-to-date book on border water arrangements, or their absence, is Mumme 2023.)

In the case of the twin cities, two separate (in east-west terms) aquifers supply most (in the case of El Paso) or all (for Juárez) of the water used, while in the case of farms, well water provides a buffer against low-river years and a supplement to the river-sourced irrigation, allowing growers to plant thirstier crops such as pecans and alfalfa. The freshwater in the aquifers has declined slowly but surely for decades; in this desert setting, less enters than leaves when pumped. Pumps are gradually arriving at the saltier water below, which raises problems for drinking and farming without expensive desalination.

There is no border wall underground to stop the migration of water. In the past, when El Paso pumped more water, the aquifer contents moved toward the U.S. side, flowing through the underground rock and soil matrix to equalize elevation below the surface. Now, after decades of massive urbanization due to manufacturing in Ciudad Juárez, that city is drawing more water, and so groundwater has begun migrating toward Mexico. When I emphasize that the issue is shared, the sharing is concrete and physical—the hydrological system consists of a river above two underground aquifers that cross the international boundary.

The stress is exacerbated by extended periods of river drought and recent declining river flows due to climate change. The growing long-term drought means that less runoff from snowpack flows into the river systems from mountains in Colorado and New Mexico. As the river runs low, humans draw more from the declining aquifer (Hargrove et al. 2023).

The dilemma of sharing a limited supply of groundwater is worsened by the international boundary, even in a binational community that generally is aware of the people and concerns across the border, due to the absence of institutions to govern subsurface water (Mayer et al. 2021). Yet there is no shared administration of the water resources in a legal or political sense, since the responsible organizations are Mexican and U.S. urban utilities and irrigation districts that are not coordinated or comanaged. For example, the applicable fifty-year planning document of the Texas Water Development Board attends only to state-bounded supply and demand and ignores both Mexico and the U.S. state of New Mexico (TWDB 2021). The two aquifers even have different names in the two countries: the Hueco Bolson / Valle de Juárez Aquifer and the Mesilla Bolson / Conejos Médanos Aquifer (in each case the U.S. name is first).

The precise amount of fresh and saline water in each aquifer is not definitively known. Nonetheless, scientists in both countries have arrived at a consensus on useful approximations. Freshwater that lies near the top of aquifers has shown a long-term decline as brackish (somewhat salty) water intrudes. This brackish water is difficult to use and requires costly treatment. Thus, the region is not running out of water, but it is running out of cheap and easily accessible water.

Future water will be costly and difficult to obtain, requiring more elaborate processing. In the case of the Hueco Bolson / Valle de Juárez Aquifer, which is the one that serves the two cities the most, the best estimate is that its high-quality water has a remaining lifetime of thirty to forty years. This is not long at all. El Paso has some capacity to respond with more expensive treatment technologies and costly long-distance importation, though it is likely this will harshly impact poor people in a city that has a high percentage of people living in poverty (Heyman, Mayer, and Alger 2022). The situation is worse for Juárez. It has big factories, twice the population, and much less public wherewithal to craft alternative treatments and sources.

In 2020 and 2021, well-informed and engaged stakeholders from both sides met under the auspices of the University of Texas at El Paso and Universidad Autónoma de Ciudad Juárez to discuss options for the future of this crucial fount of life. But with all goodwill, they could not overcome the long-term logic of fresh groundwater exhaustion nor address the immediate dilemma that Mexico has far less public financing to recycle water and locate alternative supplies (Mayer et al. 2021).

Mexico's lower financial capacity to invest in future municipal water should not be a challenge for Juárez to face on its own. The city of Juárez is not just a Mexican city. It is a quintessentially North American city, home to Mexico's largest complex of export assembly factories serving the U.S. and Canadian markets. Factory workers drink that water, wash with that water, and flush their toilets with that water. Modest amounts are used inside the plants. (Typically, factories themselves use little water, albeit highly purified, but other Mexican exports, such as beer, fruit, and vegetables, use large quantities.) The generation of electricity for the factories, businesses, and homes requires considerable water. All this water is embodied indirectly in the turbine blade described earlier, as well as in every car part, hospital device, and television made there. Yet it proved difficult in our study, even among a group positioned to see across the border, to reach the conclusion that the United States ought to help finance major water-conserving and sourcing works in Mexico.

This is not merely a local challenge. Every twinned border metropolitan area has a version of these environmental problems, which are also human well-being problems, particularly for the poor. Take Nogales, Sonora, and Nogales, Arizona—known together as Ambos (Spanish for "both") Nogales. The U.S. side is still a small city, while the Mexican side has grown topsy-turvy, clinging to hillsides and ravines lining the tiny Santa Cruz River as people move there to serve the northbound fruit and vegetable trade and, of course, the profusion of *maquiladoras.*

The V-shaped form of Nogales, Sonora, collects stormwater and sewage that mix during particularly intense rainfalls due to the city consistently outgrowing its sewer and drainage systems, worsened by the Mexican municipality's inadequate funds for maintenance.

The northward channel brings this awful mix across the boundary, often interpreted as something bad that backward Mexico does to the clean United States, though the people who most suffer its consequences are poor Mexicans with homes in the ravines. The larger trash piles up against the recently installed border wall, creating a toxic backup into the heart of the city of Nogales, Sonora. There are storm tunnels under the wall, but they have dense grates (to prevent human migration) that easily clog, and the wall itself is a barrier cutting perpendicularly across the flow of water. Large water volumes persistently knock down the wall along the border, a phenomenon where nature overcomes human enterprise (Sadavisim 2018; Miroff 2020).

Nevertheless, Ambos Nogales is one of the sites in the region with the best record of binational cooperation. The Nogales International Outfall Interceptor is an 8.5-mile pipeline that travels from the U.S.-Mexico border, where it captures Nogales, Sonora, storm- and wastewater, bringing it to the Nogales International Wastewater Treatment Plant inside the United States. Long established (begun in 1972), this cooperative arrangement has struggled to keep up with the greater volume flows of *maquiladora*-driven urbanization, as well as physical wear and tear. Binational funding has helped, albeit incompletely. Ambos Nogales, El Paso and Juárez, and their other border cousins are arguably the places on the continent most prepared to cooperate because of long-standing mutual connections and respect. The challenge of cross-border cooperation is a difficult one, symbolized by the wall, but the connections are much more extensive than the borderlands themselves—for the boundary hides our knowledges, institutions, economies, and imaginations from one another, in the national interiors as well as the line itself.

Wider Implications

I've told this story so far as a local one about contiguous border cities that are hydrographically connected but also separated by an international border. But this is also a story of how we think about a shared continent. Why do we distinguish a "U.S. West"? Mostly it involves a contrast with the wetter part of the continent to the east and northwest. It would not be hard to imagine an extension of the

Interior West (the Great Plains, the Rockies) into Canada. But there is a racialized preference for imagining Canada and the United States together: neither country is purely white, but that *is* the image, by contrast with Mexico.

In fact, there are good environmental and historical reasons to conceive of Northern Mexico together with the dry Western United States and Canada as a single biocultural region. The great anthropologist Carlos Vélez-Ibáñez (2017) refers awkwardly but thought-provokingly to "Southwest North America." Environmentally, it is formed by massive mountain ranges dividing bleak desert basins with oases scattered across them. Even the distinctly Mediterranean climate and vegetation of the Pacific coastal strip of California extends into Mexico, as indicated by the proper geographical names Alta California and Baja California (upper and lower California). This part of the continent, comprising the Mexican North and the U.S.-Canadian dry West, was recently stolen from Native Americans, and the frontier experience—in both its dominant narrative and more recent critical counternarratives—applies to both sides of the U.S.-Mexico border. Beginning in the late nineteenth century and accelerating in the last half century, intensive capitalist development has induced massive urban nucleation throughout this landscape.

The example I used of Ciudad Juárez and El Paso is therefore representative. Not only do adjacent border cities share economies and environments, but the wider region also does. Take the vast metropolis of Monterrey, Nuevo León, the second largest metropolitan area in Mexico with just over five million people. Monterrey is known for its sophisticated manufacturing capabilities: it has the skilled workers, engineers, and managers needed for world-quality production, well paid by Mexican standards but significantly cheaper than comparable Canadian and U.S. labor. As a result, this center attracts investments aimed at the entire North American market. As I write, a new $5 billion Tesla plant has been announced, while many other advanced manufacturers of recent years could also be listed. Monterrey is not directly on the U.S. border, but it is just south of the land ports of Laredo and Nuevo Laredo—the former is now the single largest import-export port in the United States, recently surpassing Pacific coast ports. Monterrey also suffers water challenges that closely resemble those of the Western United States.

This metropolis, part of the Rio Grande / Río Bravo del Norte watershed, is not so much drawing water from the river as intercepting water before it reaches the river. Monterrey's climate resembles the arid basins and mountain fronts of the U.S. West. And unsurprisingly, it has encountered the same water crises that have recently plagued the U.S. West. In the summer of 2022, the metropolitan area ran low on water. As with every instance of water troubles, it has its place-based specificities: a random, but over time predictable, drought year; competition between agriculture and an ever-expanding city for water; undersized water supply infrastructure; and the delayed construction of a new aqueduct.

Predictably, poor and middle-class people suffer the most, lacking expensive water storage devices on their roofs. There was a momentary rescue by heavy rain in the fall of 2022—just the sort of magical rescue we have come to hope for in the U.S. West. But in the bigger picture and the longer run, the problem is systematic, not idiosyncratic. Monterrey has a regional water governance system that is embedded in state and national regulation and is institutionally stronger than in the United States. But even with such governance, the politicians and engineers in this pinnacle of Mexican sophistication are simply too local for what is a continental challenge. It is a continental challenge both demographically, stemming from Mexico's economic role supplying goods to the north, and geophysically, due to erratic water supply and the increasing heat of these arid sites affected by climate change. These are realities that should be familiar to all of us in arid North America.

Institutions for the Future

If we draw back the border curtain, then, we recognize the same scenario on both sides. It becomes possible to embrace our mutual interests and fate, working together to thrive in our dry portion of the half hemisphere. There are precedents for doing so. A small binational bank, the North American Development Bank (NADBank, https://www.nadb.org/), lends money for various environmental projects, above all for water purification for delivery to marginal communities and for wastewater treatment. It supports projects in both countries, although there is more need and thus a larger number of projects in Mexico. Through a previously independent agency, the Border Environmental Cooperation Commission (BECC), which is now included inside the bank, technical support is offered to communities seeking bank loans or loans coupled with grants from other government agencies in each country. The operating costs of these organizations are primarily funded by the United States, though the bank lends out and recovers its own capital. In this way, NADBank is emblematic of the combined but also markedly unequal development of the two countries.

NADBank, however, is quite limited and has grown little in its twenty-eight years of existence. It has a small amount of lendable capital, and its loans charge interest (albeit at a low rate) for projects that may realistically not generate profits (e.g., sewage treatment). Its border-region geographic scope is thus limited. What's more, the bank only addresses environmental issues. There are other domains that also deserve attention and support. In a bitter irony, for example, the U.S.-Mexico Border Health Commission had lapsed by the time of the COVID-19 pandemic. Nevertheless, NADBank shows how we can build policies and institutions to serve both sides of the border. Additional funding for the bank would allow it to widen programs for direct granting without charging interest, increase its geographic scope, and build and revive comparable organizations for issues other than environmental protection. But this will only happen if there is an essential change in vision and feeling behind the policies.

The U.S.-Mexico border is enormous in scope and organized around the main building blocks of current world society (territorial nation-states). In public discourse, it is a powerful symbol of separation and threat (Heyman 2017). But it is worth stepping away from this most dramatic of cases to ask about lessons that might apply more widely. There are two basic qualities of international borders that in altered form can be found elsewhere. First, border areas around Native American lands separate territory governed by sovereign tribes from the rest of the United States, and these areas, like the Mexico-U.S. border, are often characterized by inequities of wealth and opportunity. Second, borders between states or between different federal land management agencies (such as those managed by the Bureau of Land Management and the National Park Service) create zones of divided and complex governance even though they are environmentally continuous. In these cases, increasing pressures on water and other shared natural resources should be met with cooperative management approaches.

Borders, then, can point toward new and creative policies and governance institutions that acknowledge connectedness across difference (Heyman 1998). Our human and biophysical environment can be thought of as a web of mutually shared commons that provide for our well-being on this continent and, indeed, across the modern climate-changing world. Commons are goods that everyone can access, that everyone can use, and from which we all benefit. Yet since they are not singly owned, no single authority (whether a person, business, or government) has sole responsibility for caring for them.

An aquifer that several utilities and many farmers draw from, but over which no one has exclusive control, is a commons. Commons without cooperation are at risk of overuse and contamination due to the absence of mutual responsibility—the tragedy of the commons (Hardin 1968). Elinor Ostrom (2015) in reply proposed that commons are best handled through an ethos of mutual recognition where people are committed to the use and sustainability of the resources. The airsheds of cities (such as the closely twinned settlements of the U.S.-Mexico border) also are commons, as is the biological well-being of populations facing transmissible diseases.

From these characteristics—commons to be governed according to their geographic reach, spanning traditional boundaries—specific rules, institutions, and practices follow. The communities with significant interests in the commons must be involved in discussion and decision-making. A simple but telling example is that we need effective cross-border water and airshed councils. Decisions may include distant sites with significant involvement in the well-being of the local or regional geography, which given the economic integration of the continent, may involve U.S. and Canadian funding of projects in the borderlands and Northern Mexico. NADBank, with BECC, described above, offers a tested, successful model; it can be much better funded and expanded.

Projects could include water conservation (which can take investments and incentives), binational desalination, maintenance of waterlines and wastewater lines, and expansion of wastewater treatment facilities, especially in Mexican cities (also see Lara-Valencia et al. 2023). For air, investments in upgraded diesel—or better yet, electric conveyances carrying containers across the border—could greatly reduce the harmful particulates coming from idling trucks at the border ports of entry and sometimes at other sites. Toxic air releases can be greatly reduced in regional industrial processes by use of alternative production processes, often but not always more expensive but worthwhile in their preventative value. Investment in green spaces (using stormwater) and regionally suitable trees and shrubs can temper the increasingly worrisome summer heat in the region and reduce flash flooding. Campaigns to paint roofs and introduce white coloration to street paving and sidewalks can have dramatic impacts. Undoubtedly, other examples can be delineated.

All these policies are doable. The hesitation comes not from costs, benefits, or pragmatics; it is the politics of bounded national, or even local communities being willing to spend money on other people—poorer people, culturally and "racially" different people, people in other jurisdictions. To coexist on our shared continent, a crucial mix of knowledge and sentiment, however, must extend to places and people who are different from us, not just to ones we recognize as similar or related. There are many borders to surpass, then, such as citizenship and race. The quintessential one is the divisive but powerful image of the racialized nation-state, including the United States versus Mexico. That is the continental challenge that we face.

4

Farmington, New Mexico, and America's Energy Transition

JONATHAN P. THOMPSON

On an unusually warm February day, I drove south from Durango, Colorado, into the New Mexico portion of the San Juan Basin, a ten-thousand-square-mile, dinner plate–shaped geologic feature that straddles the state line. I was headed for Farmington, New Mexico. I passed farms and juniper and piñon forests, scrub-covered mesas and cottonwood-studded river bottoms. All of it functions as a facade hiding what lies beneath: vast stores of oil and natural gas, fossilized organisms that once plied the shallow inland sea that spread out across the region some seventy-five million years ago, and a thick bed of low-sulfur coal, the leftovers of fecund and sultry shoreline swamps.

For over a century, oil and gas companies and coal companies have been poking and gouging at the basin to get at the fossil fuel bounty, and it shows. From a high point, I could see the smokestacks of the two hulking coal power plants that churn out juice for hundreds of thousands of far-off homes. I passed dozens of pumpjacks doing their slow, relentless grind, looking like mechanical versions of the "Bisti Beast," a Tyrannosaurus that once roamed the Cretaceous seashores nearby. I got stuck behind a lumbering, mud-splattered gas-field water truck, tire chains dangling off its bumper like a medieval fashion accessory. And I made one of my customary stops at the St. Mary's Catholic Cemetery, where a Virgen de Guadalupe statuette stands atop one of the older graves, her hands clasped in prayer as she looks beatifically into the distance, less than one hundred yards from a complex of shiny, Byzantine spires rising into the contrail-streaked blue: the condenser towers of a huge methane-gas processing plant that rises up around the humble burial ground.

As I drove toward Farmington, the region's industrial, commercial, and population center, I felt as if I was looking out at the Anthropocene made physical, a place where the landscape is indistinguishable from the infrastructure, and where the very geology has been altered by so much development. The San Juan Basin is one of the only places on the planet where a twenty-six-kiloton nuclear device (double that of Little Boy, which obliterated Hiroshima) was detonated underground to free up natural gas from the rock—a nuke-frack job, if you will. "We've got so much pipeline in the ground, it's like rebar," a federal land management official once told me of the San Juan Basin. "If you had an earthquake, the ground wouldn't even shake."

The energy industry is similarly entwined with Farmington's and the region's economy and communities and even its culture and identity. You might say oil, natural gas, and coal extraction built this town, funding nearly every aspect of life, from teachers' salaries to the sleek, modern School of Energy at the local community college, from the public library to kids' scholarships to—indirectly—the Super Walmarts and proliferation of chain restaurants and other amenities. This puts the community at the mercy of regional, national, and even global oil, gas, and coal markets and prices, all governed by forces over which local officials have no control. It's a bit like being on an economic roller coaster ride, with whiplash-inducing climbs followed by violent downward plummets (Thompson 2015).

Since the 1980s at least, local leaders, environmentalists, and even oil and gas executives have been trying to diversify the economy by supplementing fossil fuels with tourism, agriculture, small industry, and the hard-to-define amenities economy—something to ease the economic and societal whiplash that is inherent to riding the volatile commodities waves. Mostly they've failed.

Now the efforts have taken on new urgency. The natural gas industry—once the region's cash cow—has been in a slump since 2009 and isn't expected to return. And in the summer of 2022, one of the two coal plants and its mine shut down, taking some four hundred high-wage jobs and millions of dollars in tax revenue with it. The second coal power plant and mine are expected to cease operating within the decade, depriving the community of hundreds more jobs. The topsy-turvy fossil fuel economic roller coaster is in free fall or, as a local oil and gas operator told me, it is now a "death train."

It raises a crucial question: Will the community finally come together and embrace a transition away from fossil fuels? Can they leverage federal cash for orphaned well cleanup and mine reclamation and use it to build a cleaner, more equitable community? Or are fossil fuels simply so entangled in the economy, culture, and identity of the community that phasing them out would be akin to ripping that energy infrastructure "rebar" from the earth, causing the foundation and everything on it to crumble into dust?

Geology Is Destiny

Humans have inhabited the San Juan Basin for millennia. The Chacoan society (850–1250 CE) of the Pueblo people was centered here, and Diné farmers have grown crops along the banks of the three rivers that come together in the basin (Brugge 1971). The first white settlers arrived in the late 1800s, drawn by those fertile, arable bottomlands. By the turn of the century, tens of thousands of fruit trees were producing peaches, apricots, cherries, and apples in and around the small town. The rail line that stretched up from Farmington, now the largest city in the San Juan Basin, to Durango, about fifty miles to the north, was called the Red Apple Flyer after its primary cargo, which was sent to Denver, Chicago, and even Europe.

But geology had different plans. Methane, especially, is so abundant that in some places, it oozes from the earth unbidden. Early white settlers drilling wells for water often ended up with natural gas wells. Tales abound of kids igniting methane bubbles in streams and of the gas building up in water wells and exploding. In 1921, a group of locals drilled the first commercial natural gas well in the San Juan Basin near the small town of Aztec, with the fuel piped into local homes for heating and cooking—and an explosion or two. And that same year, the first oil lease was issued by the newly formed Navajo Nation Tribal Council on land near Shiprock, not far from where the Four Corners Power Plant now stands. The region's first hydrocarbon boom was on.

The fledgling San Juan Basin natural gas industry was slow to truly take off because it was so far removed, geographically, from the big markets. Then, in 1950, El Paso Natural Gas built a large pipeline from near Farmington to California, igniting a boom of epic proportions. Construction workers spilled in from all over, followed by roughnecks from Oklahoma, Texas, and beyond.

Among the job-seeking migrants was Norman Norvelle's family, who rolled into the region in 1957, when he was just eleven, their belongings all loaded into a 1953 Chevrolet sedan and an aging half-ton pickup truck. At the time, the region still retained some of its agrarian roots, and Farmington still lived up to its name. "It was a beautiful place," he told me. "There was orchards and truck gardens everywhere." Norvelle remembers driving with his family north into Colorado and up to Kennebec Pass, high in the La Plata Mountains, and gazing out across the San Juan Basin. The air was so clear then, he could see the Sandia Mountains near Albuquerque, some two hundred miles to the south.

Farmington's population doubled, then tripled, and before long, the quiet little burg had ballooned to become the region's population and commercial center. Well pads, processing plants, gathering systems, and trailer parks sprouted where once stood orchards and melon-patches. The Red Apple Flyer carried pipes and other oil field equipment rather than fruit, and the community traded in its namesake livelihood for hydrocarbon extraction, which it soon discovered was more lucrative, and volatile, than ranching and farming.

"The Farmington economy was always oil and gas bust-and-boom," said Norvelle, whose father—a diesel mechanic—had to go to Alaska for work when the local industry slumped in the 1960s. "They used to have a bumper sticker that said, 'God, please give us one more boom, and I promise not to piss it away this time.'" Farmington certainly wasn't unique in this respect; oil and gas was booming all over. But what happened next sent the San Juan Basin into a whole new realm, fossil fuel–wise.

In the 1950s, to quench the burgeoning hunger for electricity, a consortium of utilities set out to construct six massive coal-fired power plants across the relatively sparsely populated Colorado Plateau, which would then ship power hundreds of miles along high-voltage lines to rapidly growing Southwestern cities. The San Juan Basin was to be home to not one, but two of the plants: the 2,000-megawatt (MW) Four Corners Power Plant, with its adjacent Navajo Mine, constructed about fifteen miles west of Farmington on the edge of the Navajo Nation, and about a dozen miles away and across the San Juan River, the 1,500-MW San Juan Generating Station and its feeder mine. The Navajo Generating Station on the Navajo Nation near Page, Arizona, was also part of this "Big Buildup," as scholar and author Charles Wilkinson termed it (Wilkinson 1992).

The smokestacks, still with scant pollution controls, spewed thousands of tons of harmful particulates, including the potent neurotoxin mercury, into nearby, predominantly Navajo communities. Shoddily contained coal-combustion waste piled up in the mines and next to the plants, its toxic contents leaching into groundwater or oozing into the Chaco River. In 1971, Peter Montague, a prominent environmental activist, in a Senate committee called the Four Corners Power Plant "the greatest single public health hazard in the Southwest and perhaps in the Nation—possibly even in the world." Norvelle's two-hundred-mile view was lost behind a sea of smog that would grow to blanket the entire region, one so persistent that most people under the age of fifty-five—myself included—have never seen the Four Corners Country's iconic landscapes unobscured except in brief moments following cleansing downpours.

"As children, we were used to seeing haze sitting around us, blotting out the view of the majestic mountains that mark our tribal cardinal directions," Wendy Atcitty, who grew up in the area, told me, "and never understanding that not everyone in our country hauled water and lit up a kerosene lamp to see at night." Atcitty's father worked at the plants, coming home each night covered in fly ash, but the family—like up to fifteen thousand other households on the Navajo Nation—didn't receive any of the power the plants generated.

It's a form of energy colonialism and environmental injustice best described in 1971 by Peterson Zah, who would later become the Navajo Nation's president: "The formula is very simple and politically sound. Indian land, Indian coal, and Indian water will generate Indian power. The power will be shipped across Indian lands to Albuquerque, Phoenix, and Los Angeles. The cities will get more and more power at no cost to their environment. The result will be Indian pollution."

It was all part of a trade-off between the community and industry—even if everyone wasn't in on it. In exchange for the smog and the poisoning of his favorite fishing holes, Norvelle got relatively well-paying work, first as a construction laborer on the Four Corners plant, then as a fuel and water analyst at the San Juan station, and later as a chemist for El Paso Natural Gas. A similar trade-off played out on a macro level—with higher stakes. The Navajo Nation got much-needed but meager royalties and lease payments from the owners of the mine and power plant, local governments received a steady influx of property and sales taxes, and the region got thousands of high-paying jobs.

Pollution was not the only price people paid for prosperity. Prosperity itself was a challenge. In the 1970s, when the coal plants were first firing up and global energy crises sparked an oil- and gas-drilling boom, the influx of workers and money overwhelmed services and infrastructure. Schools were so crowded that they had to have two shifts: half the students would go to class in the morning, the other half in the afternoons. Crime ballooned. Local high school students made sport out of beating up inebriated people, a ritual that culminated with the fatal 1974 beating of three Navajo men in Farmington.

Economic Roller Coaster

In hopes of offsetting some of these impacts, the state has, over time, created a taxing structure to capture some of the revenue. The fossil fuel companies and the myriad businesses that have sprouted to support them, from fracking chemical outlets to shoe stores to car dealers, pay gross receipts taxes to the state, city, and county on every sale. The businesses pay property taxes on their land, equipment, and oil and gas and coal production. Producers pay severance taxes on the gross value of oil or gas that they sell, and royalties to the federal government, the state, tribes, or private landowners. And the operator of the natural gas plant north of Bloomfield, where distillation columns tower like steeples over the Catholic cemetery, pays state natural gas processor's taxes.

These funds, in turn, pay for everything from firefighters' and teachers' salaries to roads to day-to-day governmental operations. Earnings from the state's $22 billion Land Grant Permanent Fund, which is fed almost entirely by oil and gas royalties on state lands, support New Mexico's public schools. The San Juan plant and mine paid $3.5 million annually in property taxes to the three-thousand-square-mile Central Consolidated School District that reaches deep into the Navajo Nation, according to a 2019 study by O'Donnell Economics and Strategy (O'Donnell 2019), and nearly $2 million to the community college. All this was supplemented by energy company donations to sports events, the public library, scholarships, and the symphony.

This huge infusion of cash into local and state governments effectively puts the government—and therefore the community as a whole—into the fossil fuel business. It also further embeds the industry into the economy and the identity of the community, where more than a degree or two of separation from the energy industry is quite rare. The upside is that those communities get to share in the profits. The downside is that everyone, from the tool pusher to the symphonygoer, is dependent on a volatile global market and polluting industries that can hurt other sectors of the economy, such as tourism and quality of life. And any efforts to rein in or regulate industry, or even try to add to the three-legged economic stool, are readily interpreted as attacks on schools, local governments, and really, the people who live here.

Jason Sandel, now executive vice president of Aztec Well, a conglomerate of drilling and oil field service companies run by his family, was just heading into middle school in the mid-1980s when the big oil and gas boom busted. His grandfather had passed away, and his father, Jerry, was at the company's helm. He only barely kept the company afloat. A "ghost town" feel settled into Farmington, Sandel recalled. And while the situation inspired some talk about diversifying the economy, folks mostly felt angry at their impotence in the face of geopolitical forces and volatile commodity prices, spawning what Sandel calls "a rise of conservative attitudes and nationalism as a result of feeling out of control."

Ironically, it would be the federal government's largesse that would extricate the community from its crisis—and allow it to delay economic diversification once again. Energy Department–funded research had led to the development of methods to economically extract methane adsorbed to coal beds—otherwise known as coal-bed methane drilling. At the same time, Congress offered tax credits on any unconventional wells drilled prior to 1992. This sparked a new boom in the San Juan Basin, where companies went on a drilling frenzy despite low prices for natural gas.

The federal government would step in again in the early 2000s to bolster fossil fuels. The George W. Bush–Cheney administration's Bureau of Land Management handed out drilling permits like candy at a parade. Construction of a third coal power plant in the region, Desert Rock, was proposed in 2003 to help meet burgeoning demand for electricity. Federal royalties from wells in the San Juan Basin topped $700 million in 2007, and state severance tax revenues were close to $1 billion. Schools got a per-pupil funding increase, allowing the Farmington district to hire more teachers and up their salaries. The local construction industry was going gangbusters to accommodate new businesses and residents. It seemed as if it would go on forever.

"I was caught up in it too," said Four Corners Economic Development CEO Arvin Trujillo, who was the executive director of the Navajo Nation Division of Natural Resources during that time, and a proponent of Desert Rock. "You would look at it all and say, 'The plants won't shut down . . . we're doing fine. If it's not broke, why try to fix it?'"

Now it is broke, or in the process of breaking. Natural gas prices crashed in late 2008 as abundant supplies from the Bakken and Marcellus shale formations glutted the market. Between October of 2008 and January of 2009, Aztec Well—the region's largest locally owned oil field services company—idled 75 percent of its equipment and almost as many workers. The company's annual revenues were cut in half. ConocoPhillips, WPX, and BP sold their assets to smaller companies and fled, taking high-level management jobs and their salaries with them.

The San Juan Basin alone lost an estimated five thousand jobs, and the Farmington metro area went from having one of the lowest jobless rates in the country to having one of its highest in just a few years. "It was ominous," said Farmington city manager Rob Mayes, who was faced with a sudden loss of nearly 20 percent of gross receipt tax revenues, the city's main source of funding. "It just fell off a cliff."

Low natural gas prices hit coal, too. The Desert Rock proposal—battered by tenacious local opposition—unraveled in 2009. Environmentalist lawsuits and divestment by California utilities forced both Four Corners and San Juan to shut down generating units and install costly pollution-control equipment in 2014 and 2016, respectively. The mines' owner BHP Billiton bailed, leaving the Navajo coal mine to the Navajo Transitional Energy Company—a tribe-owned entity—and the San Juan mine to Westmoreland, which entered bankruptcy in 2018.

And then, in 2017, the bombshell dropped: San Juan Generating Station would close in 2022 and Four Corners Power Plant was imperiled, too. "Now your foundational economic driver is going down," said Trujillo. "It's like a spiderweb, with the coal plants in the middle. When all these $70k to $80k jobs disappear, what do we do then?"

Diversify or Die

I had been asking the same question and figured the best place to start to find an answer was with Trujillo of Four Corners Economic Development, or 4CED. So I headed up to San Juan College, which is in the more affluent part of Farmington but studded with oil and gas wells nonetheless. I found his office in the School of Energy and sat down at his desk, scattered with papers and periodicals, the most recent copy of *Native Business* sitting on top. "Our economy has always been focused on energy," Trujillo, who grew up in the Nenahnezad chapter of the Navajo Nation, in the shadow of the Four Corners Power Plant, told me. "We need to look in other areas—to diversify our economy and market the quality of life."

It may seem like a no-brainer to an outsider, but it's still remarkable coming from Trujillo, who spent most of his career in the coal industry, working as an engineer in Powder River Basin coal mines before coming home and working with the San Juan Basin mines and at the Four Corners plant. He wrote a 2019 op-ed published in the *Albuquerque Journal* defending "much-maligned fossil fuels," which he said are "a critical lifeline for our state's success."

But this apparent inner conflict isn't uncommon in these parts. In fact, I've found that some of the most ardent champions of economic diversification are leaders of the oil and gas industry. Four Corners Economic Development got its start when T. Greg Merrion, then president of a local family-owned oil and gas company, collaborated with other community leaders to figure out how to mitigate the impacts of the 2009 gas price crash by turning to agriculture and tourism and courting light manufacturers and health-care providers. Sandel, the Aztec Well executive, is an ardent Democrat—an anomaly in these parts—and strong supporter of economic diversity as well as a contributor to Democratic governor Michelle Lujan Grisham, who champions the energy transition. He even blasted the local baseball team for naming itself the Frackers, since it would conflict with the "Jolt Your Journey" branding campaign aimed at emphasizing recreational opportunities and wiping away the "national sacrifice zone" stigma long attached to the region.

Nearly all these leaders believe in a qualified form of economic diversification: Looking for other means of revenue is fine, so long as it doesn't get in the way of fossil fuel development.

Sandel, for example, sat on the Farmington City Council, where he advocated for more bike paths, spiffing up the beleaguered downtown, and marketing the area's amenities. He also called for relaxing restrictions on in-town drilling (there are about three hundred oil and gas wells within city limits), despite the fact that gas wells next to homes and on golf courses and cozied up next to the Frackers' old training field doesn't exactly scream "quality of life." Now Sandel helms the citizens advisory committee for the Energy Transition Act, which New Mexico lawmakers passed in 2019 to support communities and workers affected by coal plant closures.

Farmington implemented an economic development sales tax, created an economic development department, added recreational amenities to the town reservoir, increased marketing of tourist attractions, and recently finished a "complete streets" overhaul of the downtown, making it more amenable to pedestrians and small businesses. Trujillo's organization has supported the Harvest Food Hub that links farmers up with local restaurants and retail outlets and backs an initiative to lure the outdoor recreation industry to town. He likes the idea of leveraging state-level incentives for the film industry to attract more moviemakers, and maybe even a production studio, to his corner of the state. And he supports plans to build three utility-scale solar projects in the area to help replace power generation lost from the closed coal plant. Farmington mayor Nate Duckett even dons Lycra and hops on a mountain bike to promote the recreational opportunities of the region.

Yet in spite of all these efforts, these people and organizations all cling almost desperately to fossil fuels in one way or another. Part of it is simple economic pragmatism: oil and gas drilling and coal mining create more jobs and usually pay higher wages than solar or wind facilities. But there's also something deeper. Over the years, industry, politicians, and ideologues imbued coal mining and oil and gas drilling with symbolism and mythology. Coal was not just coal, they argued. It was abundant, reliable, and deserving of a seat in the pantheon of American culture, alongside cowboys, guns—and, yes, freedom. Donald Trump attempts to invoke this symbolism when he says he'll save coal or restore America's "energy dominance" by slashing regulations. In Farmington, fossil fuels are an integral part of not just their national identity but also their local and regional culture. Giving it up is hard to do (Thompson 2017).

The Farmington municipal utility, for example, spent nearly four years and more than $2 million in support of an upstart energy company's bid to keep San Juan Generating Station running by installing technically and economically dubious equipment to capture the carbon and market it to oil fields to stimulate aging wells. Meanwhile, the utility discouraged residents' adoption of rooftop solar by tacking extra fees onto solar panels. Trujillo and Sandel—and for that matter, the state's governor—are big boosters of a proposal to use the region's natural gas, or methane, as feedstock and fuel for hydrogen production. Trujillo favors a similar idea of using methane for petrochemical factories.

"Energy is the key," Duckett said on his *Mayor's Table* video podcast in 2023. "When we're talking about retraining a workforce: What are you going to retrain them to do that allows them to make the kind of money they're making right now in the coal mine? It doesn't exist."

That's probably true, for now. "Wage differentials are a significant deterrent to change," notes a 2019 report on energy transitions from the Western Rural Communities Program, which includes a case study on the San Juan Basin. "In 2017, average earnings in San Juan County for jobs in oil and gas extraction were $105,662, mining $101,397, and all other jobs, a meager $39,917. Many workers are unwilling or unable to accept lower wages, even when they can find alternative work or access skills training. Instead, they choose to drop out of the labor force, commute long distances to other energy locations or simply leave" (Alexander 2019).

There are other drawbacks to shifting to an amenities economy. Tourism and retail jobs pay little, tend to be seasonal and without benefits, and the very same qualities that draw tourists tend to cause housing prices to rise, according to a 2020 Headwaters Economics report (Lawson 2020), thus widening the gap between wealthy amenity migrants and the working poor.

It's more than just economic practicalities, however. There's also an ideological and maybe even politically partisan element to it all. The same nationalistic turn Sandel remembers following the 1980s bust has returned, only now it's more fossil fuel–centric.

There is a tendency here to see the energy transition as a war, as an ideological battle in which the good working folk of Farmington defend themselves against outsider, Tesla-driving liberal environmentalists and to see true economic diversification as a weapon wielded by the left. In fact, the transition is driven by a combination of factors, environmental regulations being only one of them, and the push to diversify the economy is a response to the decline of the fossil fuel industries more than a cause. Republican politicians from the Farmington area who frame their fossil fuel fetish as an attempt to save jobs tried to kill the 2019 Energy Transition Act, which was passed in response to the imminent closure of San Juan Generating Station and has funneled tens of millions of dollars into the region for worker retraining and economic development. Duckett, the Farmington mayor, also falsely blamed the act for nixing the effort to keep the coal plant running, even though it provided a safety net for his community.

Aside from directly obstructing efforts to create a sustainable economy, the fetishizing of fossil fuels can also work at cross-purposes to economic diversification. Will "quality-of-life" retirees really want to settle downwind from a petrochemical factory? How many mountain bikers are eager to pedal single-track among hydrogen sulfide-oozing oil and gas wells? Fish-consumption advisories have long been in effect in lakes downwind from the power plants due to high mercury content, and the American Lung Association recently gave San Juan County a flunking grade due to high ozone levels. That said, Morgan Lake, the cooling reservoir for the Four Corners coal plant, is a windsurfing destination, despite literally falling in the shadow of the plant's smokestacks.

"I understand the instinct to stick with what you have," Camilla Feibelman, the Sierra Club Rio Grande Chapter director, told me, "but economic success is always paired with diversification, innovation, and creativity, not clinging to the past."

Optimism

After my interview with Trujillo, I took a little walk around the School of Energy. In some ways, it embodies the challenges here. The sign out front has a BP logo on it, even though BP sold out and left. The school offers degrees in petroleum production management, energy production foundations (focused on natural gas), natural gas compression, and tribal energy management. While the state gave the school $500,000 a few years back to develop a renewable energy center, the "Center for Excellence" curriculum—with hydrogen, electric vehicle, and lithium battery programs, but no wind or solar—is still under development.

If the region is transitioning away from fossil fuels, this is certainly not recognized by the college. Instead of focusing on retraining the workforce at the soon-to-close San Juan plant to help build the solar facilities—*solar* does not appear anywhere in the school's course offerings except as part of the astronomy class—the college partnered with Enchant Energy to equip the workers to run a plant with carbon capture. That effort fell apart, leaving the college with a curriculum about as practical as one aimed at typewriter repair.

The San Juan plant burned its last ton of coal in September 2022, and all the employees of the mine and plant were laid off soon thereafter. In March 2023, the operators got the go-ahead to demolish the plant and reclaim the mine, precluding the possibility of a revival. Local officials who supported the effort to keep the plant running were visibly upset and lashed out at environmentalists and policymakers. But there was also an underlying sense of relief: finally, they could let go of this quixotic cause they'd been chasing for the last four years, and the community could move into its next phase.

So far the plant's closure hasn't killed the local economy. In fact, the community as a whole appears to be moving on from coal—if not yet oil and gas—despite local officials' efforts. Construction recently began on a utility-scale solar array near the old coal plant that will plug into the regional electricity hub there. Two other solar installations are in the permitting phase. Together, they should replace the property taxes lost when the coal plant shut down, if not all the jobs. Energy Transition Act funds are being disbursed to displaced workers, retraining programs, and nonprofit initiatives ranging from growing the small-scale Navajo agricultural economy to building a pumped hydropower energy storage facility. At least one local oil and gas drilling company has largely switched over to plugging and reclaiming old wells, and a half-dozen methane emission mitigation firms have sprouted in the Farmington area—proof that the energy extraction infrastructure can also be used to give back to and heal the land while building a new industry.

The economic transition now underway in Farmington could be as disruptive as the midcentury shift from orchards to drill rigs. But it is also similarly inevitable, and local officials' attempts to obstruct the transition will only make the changes more painful. The least they can do is simply get out of the way. Better yet, they can embrace the change by putting the oil- and gas-related tax revenues that are still coming in toward economic diversification and quality-of-life improvements. They can go after an abundance of federal funds from the Infrastructure Investment and Job and Inflation Reduction Acts to build up a restoration economy and to incentivize clean energy manufacturing and development using existing infrastructure. The city's utility could embrace solar power rather than discourage it and make a concerted push to blanket every big-box store and sprawling parking lot with photovoltaic panels. They can use state incentives—along with the spectacular landscapes, relatively affordable housing, and the region's amenities—to lure the film industry not just to shoot movies but to set up shop in the area.

The way forward is simple, and yet it won't be easy to transform the culture and identity that was thrust upon it by geology. This became clear to me as I walked out the door into the vast, empty parking lot of the Energy School. I was dazzled by the bright sun and the tanks, pipes, and other apparatus of an oil and gas well complex. It's not a running well, but instead a training facility for the many courses offered here. There was not a wind turbine or solar panel in sight.

5

Booming and Busting in Salmon, Idaho
Cobalt and the New West

JARED L. TALLEY

In 1901, a prospector in central Idaho found a gray rock outcropping with a pink streak through it. The pink streak was a rare-earth mineral, cobalt, which at the time had few uses. In the century since, cobalt has become a critical mineral and is now center stage in global politics, five to ten times more valuable than copper.

Cobalt's importance has taken the rural community of Salmon in central Idaho by storm. Salmon was founded after gold was struck in the nearby mountains and has seen its fair share of mining boom-and-bust cycles. The recent activity surrounding cobalt mining is routine for this community, yet the social landscape for mining has changed. Mines now face a wide range of environmental and social considerations that add time and cost to operations, and demand has increased for critical minerals to advance our technological society. It is a dilemma that takes on an unaccustomed cast when the minerals are those that support a more environmentally sustainable future.

For a century, cobalt was useful as a component of magnets, munitions, and certain metal alloys. This has changed. Cobalt is now a critical mineral for the transition away from fossil fuels, used to stabilize the lithium-ion batteries that power our phones, computers, and a growing electric vehicle fleet. If we want to reduce our dependence on fossil fuels, we need cobalt along with other rare-earth minerals like lithium, manganese, and graphite. Moving toward an environmentally sustainable future requires the historically destructive practice of mining.

Intersecting with the changes in cobalt mining are social changes in the rural communities that support mines. Rural communities in the American West now receive a growing number of residents looking to escape the bustle of city life and be closer to nature. This demographic transition poses challenges to communities with a history and reliance on resource-based industries like mining, timber, agriculture, and ranching. Many towns are traversing these social transitions while simultaneously navigating the national and global transitions to a green economy with projects like cobalt mining.

These transitions present a series of juxtapositions. Cobalt mining can be environmentally destructive, yet this has to be weighed against the overall good it can do for the environment. Incoming residents looking to be closer to nature place new pressures on infrastructure and the community bonds of rural towns but then add to the economic and cultural diversity that can help a rural community adapt to a changing world. Such juxtaposition is a reality we must face as we navigate the environmental and social changes that occur as we move toward a more environmentally sustainable future. The story of Salmon is a story of challenges. But it is also a story of optimism that mining and social transitions can be done responsibly through the social, environmental, and economic boom-and-busts of the American West.

Background

The Idaho Cobalt Belt (ICB) is a sixty-four-kilometer stretch of forested mountains in east-central Idaho, just a few miles south of the largest wilderness area in the Lower 48 west of the continental divide—the Frank Church River of No Return (Bookstrom 2013). The ICB is the largest known reserve of cobalt in the United States, potentially providing as much as 10 percent of our current national demand. Developing these resources reduces our reliance on foreign-controlled mines and aligns with U.S. president Joe Biden's commitment to shoring up supply chains for domestically produced critical minerals (Exec. Order No. 14,017. 2021. 86 Fed. Reg. 11849 [Feb. 24, 2021]).

Globally, cobalt is rare and difficult to refine. An estimated 70 percent of global cobalt supplies come from the Democratic Republic of Congo (DRC), which holds more cobalt than all the other known cobalt reserves in the world. The cobalt mines in the DRC are notorious for human-rights violations, child labor, and what some have called modern-day slavery (Tsurukawa, Prakash, and Manhart 2011). If we want cobalt to fuel the green transition, we must look for stable access to socially responsible supplies.

Domestic production allows U.S. regulations to guide mining. Although mining can be quite environmentally damaging, modern regulations have made it considerably cleaner and safer. Historically, mining has been among the heaviest polluters of Western lands and waterways. More stringent regulations have reduced these impacts but have not removed them entirely.

Beyond environmental impacts, mining in the West has also impacted communities through economic phases known as the boom-and-bust cycle. Minerals are nonrenewable and difficult to extract, so the amount of minerals any particular location can provide is decided by the amount that exists in that location and the sophistication of the technology used to extract them. When local mines are running at full steam, local towns prosper from the money pouring in. When local mines run dry, these towns decline. What are now referred to as "ghost towns" in the West are often busted mining towns.

In Salmon's backyard, the demand for cobalt has driven prospecting in the ICB. The town has been preparing for the boom and the workers that come with it. The town has also been preparing for the bust when cobalt prices drop and mines get shuttered along with the local services they rely on. Fifty years ago, the boom-and-bust cycle that comes with the scale of these mines left many communities in shambles, like the neighboring town of Cobalt, which was bustling in the mid-twentieth century but is now a ghost town.

Salmon has diversified its economy so it is not hitched directly to the mines, and the mines themselves are championing responsible environmental, social, and governance (ESG) practices. If history is any indicator, a mining company's commitment to altruistic environmental and social causes runs about as far as its profit sheet. The landscape looks different than it did in the past, but some things haven't changed: promises of responsible mining and diversified economic portfolios are not enough to reduce the anxieties that have arisen from a history of boom-and-bust (Brueckner et al. 2013).

Something else is happening in the American West that intersects with the challenges of global mining in a rural community. People are moving. Idaho has consistently ranked in the top three fastest-growing states in the United States over the past decade, along with the other Western states ranking in the top ten. Economically, this is great for Idaho. Socially, however, it is causing growing pains.

Idaho is an agricultural state, and its many rural towns form part of what can be called the Old West—communities and economies based on commodity production in timber, mining, agriculture, and livestock. (Think tubers: nearly a third of the country's potatoes are grown in the Snake River Plain, an arc of land that extends across southern Idaho.) These are close-knit communities with quaint brick downtown strips, generational relationships to the land, and a fierce sense of place and identity.

In contrast, much of the recent growth consists of a shift from commodity production to service and amenity provision, focusing on providing human services, tourism, recreation, and environmental amenities rooted in idyllic landscapes. Vacation homes, recreational gear shops, and trendy restaurants are hallmarks of these New West communities. Talk about the Old and New West is shorthand for tracking how social attitudes, demographics, and economies are changing (Winkler et al. 2007).

Change is hard. Some of the difficulty of handling these Old West to New West transitions lies in the struggle to expand the infrastructure of a municipality—new homes and increased populations require water, sewers, roads, and electricity that must be built in anticipation of growth. Tensions over land use are also to blame: despite the relationship between environmentalism and outdoor recreation, recreation is not environmentally benign and is often in conflict with wildlife stewardship and commodity production. And it is difficult to maintain the identity of a community through economic change, especially if it is accompanied by an influx of nonlocal residents.

Thus, Salmon lies at the intersection of two critical transitions—the cobalt-driven green energy transition and the Old West to New West transition. On the one hand, the mines and new residents greatly benefit the Salmon community by boosting and diversifying the economy. On the other, mines can leave waters and land polluted as local businesses are shuttered while a wave of new residents can leave scenic landscapes spotted with suburban development and locals without affordable housing or the skills to prosper in a shifting economy. Although there are many ways to tell this story about Salmon, this one begins with cobalt.

Cobalt Mining in Salmon, Idaho

Although only forty-five miles due west of Salmon, the Jervois Cobalt Mine is nearly an hour-and-a-half drive through forested mountain roads. The mine, referred to as the Idaho Cobalt Operation (ICO), is the largest of many mining projects in the region and the only one currently permitted to mine cobalt. Historically, mining operations in the American West began almost immediately once the minerals were located. But now, after the flurry of environmental laws in the 1970s, new mining operations must comply with a lengthy permitting process that delays initial operations. Although this delay reduces the ability to quickly respond to global markets and demands, it has the benefit of allowing local communities to organize and strategize to reduce potential environmental and social impacts of the mines.

The Salmon community was prepared for a large-scale cobalt mine in the area. In 2004—prior to the recent cobalt activities—Salmon carried out a community review where twenty-seven professional community development experts toured the town, spoke with residents, and learned from local leadership. A community review is a holistic approach to understanding the existing resources and needs of a community, as well as anticipating future change. A few years later, in 2009, 325 residents (more than 10 percent of the total population of 3,100) met to develop a vision statement for their community.

> Salmon is a close-knit community that welcomes new residents and supports young people who want to make their home here. . . . Our community is a "place of hope" where people work hard to find a common purpose. Our small-town values mean we care deeply about each other and our community.
>
> We have a sustainable economy that builds from and diversifies our traditional natural resource and agricultural industries. . . . We have expanded our tourism sector into a vital part of the economy, renowned as a destination for rich outdoor and educational experiences that take advantage of our cultural heritage. (Salmon Community Review 2009)

The Salmon community's vision offers a way to navigate the transitions they are facing by *using* extraction—either in the form of natural resource extraction or as cultural extraction through tourism—to develop a "place of hope" where community bonds are cherished. In the wake of the 2004 and 2009 review processes, Salmon was poised to respond to the new mine. The community had agreed on a vision for their future, expressing what they collectively valued and what risks they were willing to take.

Out of this process came the recognition that the community needed a foundation to help collect and disperse community development funding, and thus the Lemhi Valley Community Foundation (LVCF) was born. With the LVCF and a shared vision, Salmon leadership entered negotiations with Jervois and their Idaho Cobalt Operation to develop programs that would help alleviate the boom-and-bust challenges of a mining economy. These conversations were made easier by Jervois's commitment to environmental, social, and governance (ESG) principles, meaning that they recognized the ecological and social risks of mining and would work to reduce those risks with local communities. ESG is often used to put a patina of environmental sensibility over hard business practices—sometimes called "greenwashing"—but for the community, it is better than nothing (Yu, Van Luu, and Chen 2020).

Jervois secured nearly $40 million of bonds for reclamation after the completion of the project, although the U.S. Forest Service has estimated that eventual reclamation could exceed $44 million. Reclamation bonds are secured at the beginning of a project to assure that there is money available to reclaim and restore the land, or otherwise mitigate long-term environmental impacts. Reclamation bonds are required, and securing them helps give the community peace of mind that there is a plan and funding to clean up the mine site after it is closed.

As a show of good faith and beyond the federally required reclamation bond, Jervois made an additional $150,000 annual commitment to fund restoration projects throughout the operational life of the mine. The Idaho Conservation League—an Idaho-based nonprofit dedicated to conserving Idaho environments—currently manages the annual fund in partnership with Jervois, requesting proposals for on-the-ground stream and habitat restoration in the area surrounding the mine. Of course, $150,000 pales in comparison to the estimated $44 million worth of reclamation that will need to be done. What might be seen as a show of good faith could also be interpreted as purchasing a social license to operate.

Even more surprising (although it should be standard practice) were the conversations Jervois had with the Salmon community for social renewal beyond ecological reclamation. With large mining development comes an increase in jobs, and with an increase in jobs comes an increase in workers. Mining towns in the West are no stranger to the impacts of mining booms or to the eventual busts when the mine runs dry and closes, followed by workers leaving, houses going vacant, and shops being shuttered. To help the community moderate the boom-and-bust cycle that typically comes with mining, Jervois and community leaders began conversations around a Community Benefits Agreement. During these conversations and during construction of the mine, Jervois awarded small grants (up to a thousand dollars each) to community organizations as a show of good faith—or perhaps, as with the restoration funds, as a social license to operate.

The Community Benefit Agreement, in conversation with Jervois, would consist of three efforts to mitigate social impacts. First, Jervois would contribute annually to a permanent fund for community development. Salmon had the foresight to develop such a fund, and the likely candidate for that funding was the LVCF, which had been created after the community review. This annual contribution would be held until the time the mine closed and then could be used by the community to help alleviate negative impacts from the closing. Second, Jervois would manage an annual community grant program (similar to the program with the Idaho Conservation League) that could be accessed during the operational life of the mine to mitigate negative impacts. Lastly, Jervois would develop and contribute to a scholarship fund through the Idaho Community Foundation to help Salmon students obtain an education. Many other organizations in the community offered small scholarships, so aggregating them in one fund bolstered by mining dollars would help award students with substantial scholarships that were previously unavailable.

The community understood their priorities and risks. But as is often the case with boom-and-bust cycles, things are never as secure as they seem. Although the restoration fund managed by the Idaho Conservation League was formalized, the Community Benefits Agreement was in essence an informal handshake agreement. Nothing had been signed.

Jervois had neared completion of construction on the mine at the end of 2022 and announced that operations would begin in 2023. Jervois and the Idaho Conservation League had already awarded $150,000 to three restoration projects: to remove troublesome culverts that blocked access for salmon (i.e., the fish, not the town), to continue stream restoration, and to acquire a key parcel of land along Panther Creek to preserve salmon habitat. For the Salmon community, everything looked great—the boom was approaching. In March of 2023, before the mine was even fully operational and before the full extent of the boom could be felt, the proverbial bust came. Global cobalt supplies caught up with demand, and the market price of cobalt quickly fell, resulting in Jervois shuttering operations.

Nearly 280 construction workers had been building the mine, but after the closure, only a few dozen were needed to maintain minimum operational standards. In a town of 3,100, the loss of over 200 jobs is significant. Over 200 well-paying jobs mean over 200 paychecks that are being spent in local businesses; those businesses can hire more workers, providing even more jobs in a small community. Though these had been merely temporary construction jobs, they had come with the promise of nearly 150 permanent operational, well-paying jobs; with the closure, those vanished before they had been created. The promise of the boom was gone before it had begun.

For the Salmon community, this was not a surprise. They have seen mines come and go, start and stop, boom and bust. The new cobalt conversations had begun nearly a decade earlier, and few in Salmon had high hopes. In the parlance of the Old West, not many hitched their horses to the cobalt wagon. But with cautious optimism, the community had hoped that the Jervois project would be different. The new community grants, scholarships, and endowments would have been a boon to a small rural community, helping them shore up risks, navigate the growth that comes with the New West transition, and tighten the community fabric.

The promise of the mine was the promise of help in making the community more resilient. The community is at the center of the Northwest's struggles with salmon recovery, wolf and livestock conflicts, increasingly destructive wildfire, aging and insufficient infrastructure, housing shortages, and skyrocketing prices on the homes available. Each of these is enough to stress a community, but taken together, they pose a web of risks that the mine could help address. But that's how boom-and-bust cycles work in these Western communities—when times are good, look forward. When they are not, look inward.

Looking Inward

The 2004 and 2009 community review and vision development processes helped Salmon articulate a sense of its own identity and the risks it faced. When Salmon began meeting with Jervois to detail the Community Benefits Agreement, community leadership hosted town hall meetings and, together with residents, reviewed the community planning and vision documents that had been developed before the recent cobalt mines arrived. The goal of these meetings was to determine which community needs might be impacted by the looming boom-and-bust cycle. Six community priorities were identified that would be tied to the Community Benefits Agreement: economic development, recreation and conservation, health and emergency services, housing, education, and public projects. Although this list was tailored to the impacts of the mines, it could just as easily have been developed to confront the impacts of any significant and sudden change in rural communities, New West development included.

Rural communities face challenges different from those of their suburban and urban counterparts. Rural economies are not nearly as diversified, making them more vulnerable to global market changes, environmental changes, and shifts in policy priorities. These economies are local in the sense that they employ local labor, they use local land, and their business infrastructure is often locally owned. Yet they are national and global in the sense that the commodities they produce are used in national industries (e.g., battery manufacturing) for national priorities (e.g., electric vehicle transitions), are highly controlled by national policy (e.g., federal mining laws), and are subject to global market swings. Having local and nondiversified production economies tied directly to national and global commodity markets is not a new phenomenon nor is it unique to Old West communities; global control of local prosperity is a scheme that has led to conquest, dominance, and imposed dependence for communities across history and across the globe

(Acemoglu and Robinson 2017). This juxtaposition of local communities and economies being whipsawed by global priorities and markets poses considerable risks to Old West communities—a boom-and-bust cycle they are all too familiar with.

In some ways, New West transitions are a benefit to these communities. Tourism and recreation—along with the service industries that support them—diversify and stabilize local economies through national market volatility. However, rural economies require a workforce that is difficult to attract and retain, especially as housing prices boom in the New West. Old West industries (mining, timber, agriculture, ranching) are losing local labor as young adults and families leave to find employment in more stable urban centers. When the next generation leaves, the intergenerational landowners do not have successors to take over the family business (for more on conflicts of succession planning in the West, see, for example, Wilmer and Fernández-Giménez 2015). When landowners are land rich and cash poor without a successor to take over the land, wealthy nonlocal land developers become an attractive option for late-life planning (i.e., retirement, medical bills). Working lands are subdivided and expensive houses are built to attract new residents, shifting local housing markets and pricing out longtime residents.

As more residents move in, the need for public infrastructure increases. Infrastructure needs abound, from aging buildings, roads, and utilities to outdated or absent digital internet access and insufficient health and emergency services. Funding public projects is more difficult, as Western rural communities have a low tax base, primarily due to the amount of federally owned public lands that are exempted from property taxes (Salmon is in Lemhi County, which is 93 percent federal land). Rural counties in the West receive federal PILT (payments in lieu of taxes) to offset the property taxes that they cannot collect on federally owned lands, but these are significantly lower than the taxes that could be collected on high-value property. Thus rural communities are incentivized to increase property values, often through the development of working lands. The cycle of new development requiring increased public services and development driving communities toward seeking a tax solution to pay for these services creates a feedback loop that leaves landscapes and communities in a precarious state.

These are some of the ways that New West transitions are challenging rural communities. At the core of these challenges lies the need for rural communities to provide economic and housing opportunities for their community members while simultaneously navigating significant transitions and national priorities in a quickly changing world. Among these opportunities—and critical to them all—is the need for education, both for a growing economy as well as to help local kids find meaningful ways to help their communities thrive. Yet it is more difficult to attract and retain qualified teachers for these communities, and the distance to higher education means students have limited access to resources that can prepare them for a quickly shifting technological world. If students leave to gain education but never return, then the local workforce is diminished, and working lands are more prone to development, creating ever more challenging feedback loops.

One answer to this web of challenges is for rural communities to use shifting national priorities, whether that be the green transition to electric vehicles or the New West transition predicated on environmental recreation and tourism, to reduce their risks. Cobalt mines promise jobs and an economic boom. New West transitions promise stabilized economies and increased taxes for public infrastructure. But they both promise something more to communities like Salmon. The juxtapositions of mining a natural area to transition to a green future and reducing housing opportunities for local residents while stabilizing the economy create new narratives around social and ecological responsibility that can help a community find balance through boom-and-busts. It may start with a community-visioning town hall meeting, or a Community Benefits Agreement with a new mine, but the challenge of the amenity-based New West has to be recognized before it is possible to work toward solutions.

Through it all, it must be remembered that rural communities are full of strengths and possibilities. Community bonds and intergenerational relationships help people organize quickly and efficiently to address a natural disaster, rally around a community member who has fallen ill, or raise the funds to purchase community resources like elementary reading materials. The land itself is also a source of this strength. It provides local opportunity, resources for a nation to pursue its priorities, potential for economic diversity, and a shared sense of place for its residents. The land and the community are the source of resilience and simultaneously the source of rural risk through either cobalt mining or New West development. For Salmon, finding balance in juxtaposition and stability through boom-and-busts requires coming together as a community, recognizing the strengths and needs of the community, and using the booms to manage the busts.

Looking Forward

Salmon will survive the latest case of boom-and-bust, just as they have survived other booms-and-busts in the past. To thrive, however, will require more. To thrive will require commitments from entities like the mining companies to help the community reduce the impacts of the bust that follows the boom. To thrive requires recognition from the mines, the Old West community, and the New West residents that they are intimately tied to global markets and national trends. Both the cobalt and the recreation opportunities in Salmon's backyard breed a cautious optimism that new social and ecological narratives can open up new opportunities to thrive.

Mining is significantly different now than in the past. Environmental consciousness is higher and has led to stricter regulations and monitoring. At the same time, green energy technologies require mined minerals. Social and cultural consciousness has grown and is forcing communities to look inward to focus on their own resiliency through mining's boom-and-bust cycles. But the challenges these communities face extend well beyond the mine's direct sphere of influence. The demographics of the West have changed: New West growth in Old West communities challenges degraded and insufficient infrastructure, traditional economies, and the close-knit ties that bind rural communities together. However, New West growth provides opportunities to adapt to a broader changing world.

Before Idaho became a state of scenic vistas, winding rivers, and striking granite peaks, a pink-hued mineral was formed in a slurry of volcanic activity. Now cobalt has fostered a dialogue between an internationally owned cobalt mine and a rural mining community to better understand the vision and needs of the community.

The mine may move forward when cobalt prices rise through the forces of global supply and demand. If so, the community will use the boom to prepare for the inevitable bust. Or the mine may never move forward, as battery technology advances and cobalt is no longer necessary. If so, the community will be left to navigate the national need for food, fiber, timber, and mineral production with the local challenges of New West transitions. In either case, the Salmon community will marshal its energy to negotiate scholarships, foundation donations, conservation grants, town hall visioning processes, and to provide a stable place for their youth to thrive.

The ground is constantly shifting in these communities, or to use a different belabored metaphor, they are building the ship as they sail. That is the nature of change, and navigating change is the underlying logic of their leaders. The juxtaposition of needing extraction and growth to foster community sustainability and resilience is a balancing act, and as they say, it takes a village.

II
EQUITABLE COMMUNITIES

6

The New West Economy
A Recipe for Social Unraveling?

SHAWN HILL

The New West describes the transition from an economy based on natural resource extraction (mining, logging, and agriculture) to one focused on consumer and professional services, tourism, and in particular, real estate development. The New West was widely believed to be the savior of the natural environment for the Rocky Mountain West. However, in some communities, it has had a deleterious impact on social equity and sense of community. Despite the hardships experienced by those who participated in the Old West economy, there perhaps was a sense that communities were in control of their destinies.

We are learning that the New West economy presents social equity challenges largely unforeseen before the advent of the "Zoom Boom" and the COVID-19 pandemic. Due to the uncoupling of income and lifestyle from specific geographic locations (usually large metropolitan areas), one can live virtually anywhere with a good internet connection. The Rocky Mountain West, once known for its harsh beauty, is now within the reach of an increasingly mobile elite—with the accompaniment of creature comforts heretofore afforded only by city living.

But doesn't a rising tide lift all boats? That is the key counterargument to consider: an influx of wealth from outside the region will boost the local economy and standard of living. In the experience of most mountain communities, the answer is that this rising tide will lift some boats while swamping others. Moreover, the embrace of the New West economy has revealed that economic gains often pale in comparison to the consequent wear and tear on the environmental and social fabric of Rocky Mountain communities. The price that must be paid for the prosperity promised by the New West is often the very soul of a community.

Although the particulars of any story about the transition from Old West to New West differ from one town to the next, the hopes and threats follow the same pattern: promises are made about future benefits that will come through attracting wealthy residents from elsewhere, but the full costs in terms of infrastructure and social change are rarely laid out for citizens to evaluate. One danger is that developers can write a playbook more quickly than communities can create strategies to achieve their own vision. Another risk is that the scale of community planning treats communities as though they are isolated even though planning's ill effects in one community can have dramatic effects on its neighbors. Finally, growth in the Intermountain West, especially the transition from rural to exurban and suburban community types, threatens the ecology that defines the region. These dangers can be illustrated by the history of planning and development in two communities that seem different on the surface: Morgan County, Utah, and Teton County, Idaho.

Morgan County is a remarkably bucolic community of thirteen thousand located within minutes of the Wasatch Front metropolitan area and its millions of inhabitants. Despite its proximity to Salt Lake City, Ogden, and Park City, it has largely kept its agricultural character intact, with most of the county's population located in the communities of Morgan City and Mountain Green. Many of Morgan County's inhabitants trace their ancestry to the Mormon pioneers who settled the area, and subdivision development has mostly hewed to traditional patterns, with homes and farms clustered along county roads, allowing much of the valley's open spaces to remain as productive agricultural lands or pristine nature.

Perhaps a harbinger of things to come, the nearby Snowbasin Ski Resort, which straddles the line between Weber and Morgan Counties, was purchased in the 1980s by the Holding family. The Holding family, who also owned the iconic Sun Valley Resort in Idaho, engaged in various planning efforts—including acts of the U.S. Congress—to position Snowbasin as a destination resort. The 2002 Winter Olympics catalyzed the effort, and Snowbasin was selected as the site for the men's and women's downhill and Super G events. Branded as a "Sun Valley Resort" replete with the benevolent, smiling sun logo of its namesake, Snowbasin's master plan was amended to include thousands of resort units across Weber and Morgan Counties.

Mountain Luxury Real Estate, an agency based in Eden, Utah, describes Snowbasin as "a sleeping development giant with over 4,800 units spanning Weber and Morgan counties, and the funding to execute. With final approvals delivered in both counties, land transfers complete, and water acquired, it is a matter of time before ground is broken, although no one knows exactly when" (Mountain Luxury Real Estate 2023). The fact that the resort has yet to be developed may have created a false sense of security in Morgan County, where the impact of resort development had yet to be felt.

Perhaps there is no greater contrast to the fleeting innocence of Morgan County than the experience of Teton County, Idaho. Located on the western slope of the Teton Range, Teton County, also known as Teton Valley, was known as the sleepy sister to nearby Jackson Hole, Wyoming. However, in the mid-aughts, land speculators descended upon Teton Valley, resulting in a spectacular development boom—and an equally spectacular bust—that has stripped the region of any notion that community character will be preserved if the New West development machine isn't kept in check. In contrast to Morgan County, Teton Valley has experienced the awakening of development giants and taken decisive action to bring them to heel.

A New West Savior Comes to Morgan County

In 2017, one of the last vestiges of pristine mountain land in Utah's Wasatch Range was sold. Known as the Gailey Ranch, the Morgan County property was an extreme rarity in that it was one of the few large, privately owned lands along the eastern slope of the Wasatch Range that had not been given over to resort development. It couldn't be any more different than the sprawling resort conurbation of the Park City area to the south. The twelve-thousand-acre property features over four thousand feet of vertical drop, eleven mountain creeks that feed the blue-ribbon trout fishery of the Weber River, and countless topographic undulations sprouting forests of conifers, aspens, and deciduous brush. The purchaser of the property was Wasatch Peaks Ranch, a newly formed LLC composed of owners unknown. Their pitch? The creation of a high-end, 750-unit residential development featuring a private ski resort, golf course, a lodge containing restaurants and spas, and all other amenities necessary to sustain a mountain retreat for the well-heeled and bring jobs, wealth, and prestige.

The problem facing the Wasatch Peaks Ranch proposal was the fact that the property was under a type of zoning district common in undeveloped Utah mountain areas: one unit was allowed per every 160 acres, with steep slopes factored out. Because the lion's share of the property was located on a steep mountainside, the development potential was limited to twenty-seven units. Moreover, the Morgan County General Plan, which was adopted following an unprecedented community effort, designated the property as "Natural Resource and Recreation," essentially locking in the land use designation for a generation or so. The community had spoken: the vast mountainside that rose above Morgan Valley would remain in its current form.

Then Wasatch Peaks Ranch came to town. Assisted by representatives from Denver-based landscape architecture firm Design Workshop, the developer initiated a propaganda campaign that contained three essential elements:

1. The development would be hidden from view from the valley below
2. It would add $9 million to Morgan County coffers annually
3. It was less intense than development concepts that were envisioned by other developers

Despite the public story, the technical information submitted by the developer indicated otherwise. The spine road was to be built along an existing dirt two-track that followed contours around 6,000 feet in elevation. Since the valley floor—where most of the population lives—lies at an approximate 4,800-foot elevation, it would be quite visible not only due to its location above the valley but also because of the many road cuts that would be necessary to navigate the steep mountainside. The Wasatch Range is one of the youngest mountain ranges in the Rockies, second only to the Tetons, and is known for its steep vertical drop resulting from a relative lack of erosion afforded by its geological youth. Pods of development were proposed across the entire twelve thousand acres of steep mountainside terrain, and the homes proposed had no size limit. One only needs to travel south to Summit County, Utah, to see the massive residential developments built on mining-claims-cum-mountainside subdivisions and the visual impacts that have become lessons learned from planning mistakes made a generation ago.

The economic analysis submitted by the developer claimed that if everything went according to plan, the development would yield $9 million annually to county coffers after a thirty-year build-out. However, a third-party review found that only a third of this revenue project was likely to be realized—and it was also premised on the condition that build-out of the development would occur without any significant hiccups. This was questionable given the experience of many large mountainside developments, most notably the Yellowstone Club in Big Sky, Montana, a similar private ski resort community plagued by bankruptcy and scandal.

With regard to the development potential of the property, the developer claimed that proposals with up to 10,000 units had been envisioned. Therefore, the current proposal for 750 units should be much more palatable. The problem with this claim is that proposals are just that—a pitch that a community must be convinced to accept and which, in this case, would require jettisoning the vision enshrined in its General Plan and implemented through its low-density zoning.

That there were worse plans possible was no reason to think this one's proposal to overturn the planning vision was legitimate.

The comparison also left out of consideration many other possible futures for these lands, from conservation easements to public acquisition or, as the county's General Plan envisioned, very-low-density development. The developer's claim that what others have envisioned should be the only comparisons by which a community considers acceptable development potential is in line with the advertising that has plagued the Rockies since the Homestead Act. Cooperative and coordinated planning to benefit all has often been suffocated by the mythology that landowners ought to be able to do what they please—never mind that this region is all land the federal government stole from Native Americans.

Development Enabled by Confusion and Lack of Oversight

In the months leading up to the approval of Wasatch Peaks Ranch (WPR) in November 2017, the developer's campaign successfully suppressed what was a simple consideration by Morgan County: Should the General Plan and Zoning Map be changed to allow this development? Should the community allow twenty-seven homes, as per the plan they had previously adopted, or 750 homes? Planning decisions are rarely this straightforward. However, Wasatch Peaks Ranch and Design Workshop worked to ensure that a straightforward account of reality—planning that followed the long and fair prior process of democratic decision-making—would not be the one to guide the decision.

Because of the massive site area, the developer was allowed to submit a Google Earth file in lieu of a site plan of adequate scale. This map, produced by Design Workshop, should have made plain the visual impact of the development. However, at the first public hearing, Design Workshop president Becky Zimmerman claimed that the planning staff had created the map and labeled it "garbage." Instead, she urged the Morgan County Planning & Zoning Commission to only consider a balloon five feet in diameter floated over the site in order for the community to assess true visual impact. Wasatch Peaks Ranch (WPR) CEO Ed Shultz emphasized that Morgan County schools would be flush with cash as a result of property taxes paid by future homeowners on this site, potentially $9 million annually. Zimmerman and Shultz made note of the dozens of "coffee-table conversations" they had had with stakeholders and decision-makers, something that most planners regard as ex parte communication.

A word about ex parte communication: it is problematic because when local governments consider development applications, it is widely understood that communication between a decision-maker and an interested person occurs in a public forum—not in private conversations. Ethics in government dictate that all who participate in a public hearing process have access to the same information; representations made in private conversations are widely regarded as incongruent with transparent governance. This is particularly true with development applications, as they are often considered "quasi-judicial" and subject to similar standards of evidence that pertain to court proceedings.

Though such planning procedures seem arcane to some, they exist to ensure that weighty matters receive their due consideration. Real estate development spurred by the New West economy cannot be reclaimed or restored like the mines and timber cuts of yesteryear, especially given the massive fragmentation of ownership that results from subdividing property. Once planning and development decisions are made, they are all but irreversible.

On a more practical note, haste indeed makes waste—especially for developers. Suppressing thorough, transparent public discourse for expediency created problems down the road. The Morgan County community was not ready to throw out their earlier plan despite a 6–1 county council vote to approve the development. On November 6, 2019, several Morgan County residents filed a petition with over a thousand signatures of other residents seeking to overturn the county council's decision. This referendum and associated legal actions wended their way through the justice system, ending with a hard-fought settlement

When the public and democratic community decision-making process failed to achieve the desired result, the developer was willing to consider tactics to manipulate public opinion, threaten residents, and skirt legal processes. The *Standard-Examiner*, a newspaper based in Ogden, Utah, reported that WPR and its surrogates reached out to petitioners, telling them that WPR would sue each personally, even telling one petitioner that she would be sued and lose her house. The *Standard-Examiner* also obtained an email from WPR outlining a "Plan B" if the petition was upheld, which included "plans to incorporate the development area or try to get it annexed into [abutting] Davis County; and 'back door efforts' to seek politicians' support. Those to be approached included former state Rep. Logan Wilde, said to be close to a judge, and [Utah] Gov. Spencer Cox, who as lieutenant governor took action to shut down an initiative petition" (Shenefelt 2022).

At the core of the Wasatch Peaks Ranch saga, the Morgan County community was given the standard New West pitch. In exchange for generous zoning allowances, the developer offered a vision of perpetual economic prosperity for the community. To many, this promise rang hollow, as evidenced by the developer's need for a biased public review process, silencing of citizens seeking recourse, and Plan B work-arounds. The New West pitch seemed too good to be true. Some saw it as something much worse—a Faustian bargain to sell a community's soul.

A Community Goes against the New West Grain

Should such bargains tempt communities across the New West, then it is perhaps worth looking at a community that has proverbially gone to hell and back. Teton County, Idaho, lies some two hundred miles up the intermountain spine from Morgan County. Teton County, colloquially known as Teton Valley, was once defined by its fragile pastoralism and laissez-faire planning and zoning. In the lead-up to the adoption of Teton County's first-ever Comprehensive Plan in 1983, some in the valley believed that planning and zoning would "stifle" the free market, which was believed to be "holding [development] in balance" (Meyer 1983). In the 1990s, Driggs and Victor, two of the county's communities, were surrounded by agricultural fields and green space. Less than thirty years later, both towns have expanded such that development extends in a broad exurban fringe, as shown in figures 6.1 and 6.2.

Nowadays, the Teton Valley community is much less sanguine about development outcomes. The county's first zoning ordinance was lax and found to be incapable of regulating development. Teton Valley became infamous for its creation of over eight thousand vacant lots in a county of barely ten thousand residents. These vacant lots were the result of a massive amount of subdivision approvals, and chopping up the land resulted in thousands of vacant building sites teed up for building permits. Teton County is now actively working to reduce the impacts of past decisions where policy solutions are possible—and bracing for those that are not.

A 2007 Doris Duke Charitable Foundation–funded study found that the biggest threat to the ecological integrity of the Greater Yellowstone Ecosystem (GYE) was development in Teton Valley. The U.S. National Park Service describes the GYE as "one of the largest nearly intact temperate-zone ecosystems on Earth." Checkered across a landscape once dominated by the organic geometry of riparian corridors, rolling foothills, and asymmetrical, fault-break mountain peaks, new subdivisions strained the Teton Valley ecology through its ramrod straight lines imposed by the Homestead Act's section and range system.

Aerial Photo of Driggs, 1994 | Aerial Photo of Driggs, 2021

Figure 6.1 Development in Driggs, Idaho, 1994–2021.

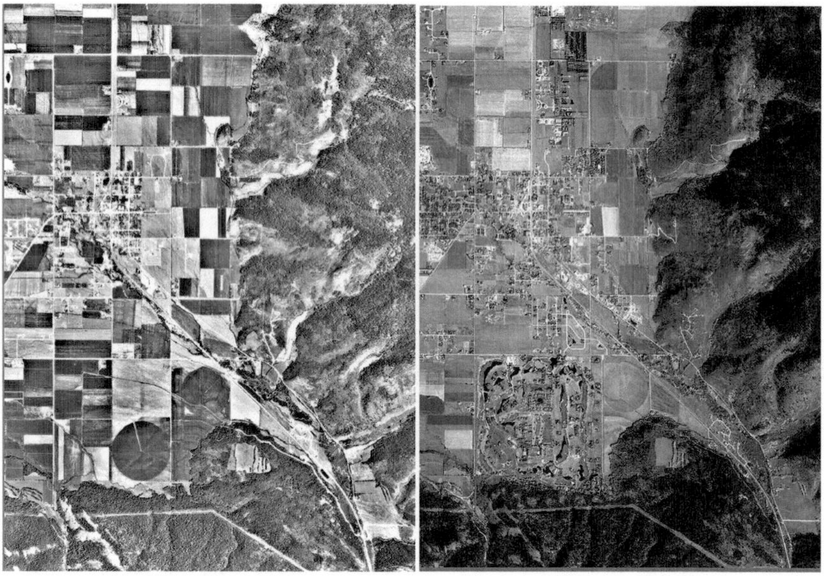

Aerial Photo of Victor, 1994 | Aerial Photo of Victor, 2021

Figure 6.2 Development in Victor, Idaho, 1994–2021.

Of higher importance, Teton Valley's social system began to buckle under unchecked and unplanned development pressures in the early aughts, particularly in the months leading up to the Great Recession of 2007–9. Like many of its peers, Teton County, Idaho, economically speaking, hits it out of the park. Its phenomenal economic growth has made it Idaho's most affluent county, and unemployment has all but been eliminated for most of Teton Valley's residents. This is especially true for those employed in the hospitality industry: a chronic labor shortage has turned tourism enterprises into an employment crapshoot. The question is not only whether a tourism business will be successful but if it can retain employees during peak season.

There is a harsh disconnect in the labor situation in Teton Valley: jobs are plentiful but affordable housing is not. Jonathan Schechter, an economist based in nearby Jackson Hole, has summed up the current mountain town labor conundrum: "Escalating property prices will make it increasingly difficult for the local tourism industry, whose success depends on large amounts of low-cost housing" (personal communication with author, November 23, 2022). As described in other chapters in this volume, low-cost housing is difficult to sustain in local economies that become driven by real estate and the provision of luxury amenities.

Despite the prosperity of mountain towns, there is a sense among many that life is harder than ever before, and the sense of community once afforded by remoteness has given way to itinerant residents enabled by incomes untethered to a specific location. Master-planned communities offer an accessible pied-à-terre for those who seek mountain life but with the comforts of the city. It is not uncommon for such communities to provide comprehensive concierge services such as rides from the airport, the stocking of groceries, snow shoveled from sidewalks and patios, and private lounges housed at nearby ski resorts. These high-demand households then generate employment demand for all manner of workers, not just in the hospitality industry but also in retail, health care, education, and other industries where pay is inadequate to secure housing in the hot real estate market.

Teton Valley, a community that has recently crested the twelve-thousand-resident mark, has not only seen more than its fair share of vacant lots but also master-planned golf course communities—four large developments with a combined total of over two thousand lots are either under construction or have been approved. Full build-out would be achieved but for labor and construction shortages, the only saving grace for a community that has lots of jobs—but no affordable housing.

In 2022, Teton County, Idaho, overhauled its zoning ordinance after eleven years of Sturm und Drang that stemmed from localized culture wars pitting old-timers against new residents. Front and center in this new zoning ordinance was the elimination of the planned unit development tool that had been used to approve the golf course developments. New development now is to be in the form of rural lots spaced out at one-unit-per-thirty-five-acre densities, and the community is poised to address the staggering affordable housing deficit resulting from a decades-long experiment with high-end resort development. The New West economy that was once seen as inevitable or even desirable is now something to be avoided lest the community fabric fray even more.

What is the cause of this fraying? We don't quite know yet. The comparison of household incomes between in-migrants and out-migrants, the number of sign-ups for little league sports teams, the percentage of housing stock owned by out-of-state residents, and other eclectic phenomena have been suggested as measures of community character. The decoupling of employment and geography, accelerated by the COVID-19 pandemic, certainly plays a role. So does the rise of social media, which allows us to interact with friends and relatives the world over, which may seem to create less of a need to do so with our neighbors. It can also dehumanize those with whom we share a community due to a lack of face-to-face interaction. Due to the ubiquity of in-home entertainment, it may not be at all uncommon for part-time residents to limit their entertainment to what's offered at their Rocky Mountain pied-à-terre.

The latest chapter in the Teton Valley story features decisive action, but few are under the illusion that the broken promises of the New West will be remedied immediately. In neighboring Teton County, Wyoming, also known as Jackson Hole, decisive action was taken when that community essentially banned new resorts eleven years ago with the adoption of its 2012 Comprehensive Plan. The New West gambit that has played out in that community will likely take generations to fix, as evidenced by an affordable housing shortage that experts estimate will require $2.5 billion in public subsidies over the next five years if meaningful progress is to be made (Boyd-Fliegel 2022). That's a staggering figure even for America's wealthiest county.

There are many challenges that face Jackson Hole and Teton Valley. However, the prospect of unlimited growth is not one of them. Both communities have adopted planning and zoning regulations that take a decisive stand for limits on development, rejecting the uncertainty of leaving real estate markets to their own devices. Unlike Morgan County, these communities have lived through the hellish experience of development run amok and will be reminded of such as they continue to address its impacts.

Turning the Corner on Environmental Awareness?

In communities like Jackson Hole and Teton Valley, can we at least notch one New West victory for the environment, even if the social equity has nose-dived? After all, the lessons learned from the New West development boom include a renewed sense of urgency to protect the Rockies and the Greater Yellowstone Ecosystem. Ignoring the issues of social inequity, have recent development plans at least managed to secure benefits for the natural environment? Or is it too little, too late? Is it always necessary for a community to go to hell and back before it saves its soul?

Communities defined by exurban and suburban development, such as Teton Valley and Jackson Hole, experience high levels of public concern for the environment. Those defined by rural landscapes, such as Morgan County, less so. Unfortunately, this may result in a vicious cycle where we must degrade wildlife habitat before becoming aware of it, let alone committed to protecting it. As such, it remains to be seen if exurban and suburban communities can play catch-up quickly enough. Mitigation of development impacts is common in the planning profession, but the restoration of degraded habitat is a far harder task. By the time we get around to fixing our mistakes, they have become more costly, more complex, and more politically fraught than if the environment had been left alone in the first place.

The transition of rural lands to suburban and exurban communities also appears to be an economic loser. Lands within cities almost always offer a weightier property tax return, as development is inherently more dense and, thus, more valuable. Unincorporated Teton County, Wyoming, for example, contains some of the most expensive single-family residential units in the world. Homes located on modest five-acre lots garner up to $40 million, yielding about $50,000 in annual property tax collections. However, in the town of Jackson, a condo building located on a half acre can yield ten times this amount.

Low-density suburban sprawl has fallen out of favor in many North American communities for many reasons. The adverse economic impacts are less known even though developing within existing cities and towns can reap extraordinary tax benefits. The cores of incorporated cities almost always generate more taxable income than the suburban and exurban lands—even when such lands contain extraordinarily valuable single-family homes. The public's return on investment is clearly better when growth is directed to the existing built environment. Suburban and exurban lands don't pay their fair share and require a subsidy from those who live in town. This is because sprawling single-family development requires more services (e.g., mail delivery, road maintenance, water and sewer infrastructure) than its more compact multifamily and mixed-use counterparts in cities. This denser development, in turn, generates more taxable revenue because homes, businesses, and other taxpaying activities are more concentrated.

If exurban and suburban development is a bad deal in terms of environment and economy, are there at least social benefits to be had? Mounting evidence suggests there are not. In 2018, Teton County, Wyoming, became the wealthiest county in America. Not soon after, it also became the most unequal. This phenomenon is chronicled by Justin Farrell in his groundbreaking book, *Billionaire Wilderness* (2021). As I wrote earlier in this chapter, there is a palpable sense that the tight-knit social fabric that once defined mountain town life is fraying like never before. We still don't know exactly why, but *Billionaire Wilderness* and other social science research is casting some light on the subject.

At the Mountain and Resort Town Planners Summit, an annual gathering of city planners, designers, conservationists, and elected officials, the fraying of social fabric is a recurring topic. At the 2022 event in Aspen/Snowmass, Jonathan Schechter gave a talk entitled "The Great Unraveling: Yes, Things Really Are Changing That Fast." The central theme of the talk was that, in terms of New West economic metrics, mountain towns were hitting it out of the park. However, the loss of community character and the fraying of community fabric creates a sense that despite the economic spoils of the New West economy, something of greater value is being lost. Schechter summarizes this phenomenon: "Our communities are rapidly changing from ones hallmarked by location-dependent economies and a sense of shared sacrifice to ones hallmarked by location-neutral economies and a sense of 'having it all'" (Schechter 2022).

Whether it be through true hardship or fleeting inconvenience, mountain life has been defined by a sense of scarcity. Eschewing the abundance of the lowlands is central to mountain town life. Arguably, this creates a unifying effect, as all are subject to the shared sacrifice that, prior to the dawn of the New West, was the hallmark of mountain town life. Now life in Jackson Hole, Aspen, Sun Valley, Bozeman, and virtually every other Western community with fast internet and proximity to an airport requires little sacrifice (for the well-heeled, anyway) in exchange for the natural and recreational amenities of the West.

Where We Go from Here

Unfortunately, there is no silver bullet to counter the fallout from the New West economy. The issue is so new that there is little consensus on how to define the problem, let alone how to solve it. Planners, administrators, engineers, and other technocrats will seek answers through tweaks in public policy. The conflict-averse will steer us toward education, dialogue, and process for process' sake. Those at the losing end of the New West economy may demand a new economic order. The experiences of the marginalized are often severe enough that any solution is simply the end of suffering.

Perhaps our silver bullet is the dismissal of silver bullets. Ironically, the planning profession has embraced elements of the New West economy known as "smart growth," which is a silver bullet response to the silver bullet previously known as the automobile. The New West is arguably the silver bullet to the Old West economy of resource extraction, with the promise of economic prosperity alongside social equity and environmental stewardship. A high-end resort may not be the silver bullet to Morgan County's historically paltry coffers, as cautionary tales from the Tetons would suggest. Ultimately, economic, social, and environmental success in the Rockies may very much look like our past—achieved by recognizing that we've got it good already. We need to realize that our communities are positioned for maximum leverage when we simply understand that it's OK to say "No, we're good."

In order to gauge the value that a development may or may not have, I've found the following policy questions useful in cutting through the noise:

1. Will this development or planning decision lessen the affordable housing deficit in the community? By how much? Who will it house? How will we ensure perpetual affordability (i.e., will the housing units be deed-restricted?) Having a recent Housing Needs Assessment (less than ten years old) on hand that clearly quantifies housing units needed by income category, tenure (own vs. rent), household type (singles/couples, families, etc.) is necessary to answer these questions.
2. Will this development or planning decision generate jobs? If so, what type of jobs and how many? Will the jobs that will be generated pay enough for those who hold them to live locally? Having a recent (less than ten years old) Employment Generation Study is necessary to answer these questions.
3. Will the environment be better off as a result of this development or planning

decision? In most cases, denser infill development will result in better environmental outcomes than low-density suburban sprawl. Conversely, those who seek to develop agricultural or virgin lands will almost always increase environmental degradation.

4. Is the sole benefit of this development or planning decision the prospect of increased tax revenue? If so, then we don't need it. The most resilient economic returns are achieved by hewing to democratically decided development patterns that reflect community values.

In sum, these policy questions lead to clarity about a situation that is easily understood by all. Lack of clarity creates confusion, chaos, and uncertainty about the future, which, for special places and those who love them, is a description of hell. There are no New West saviors. A community will only be successful if it is true to its values and respects the people and nature within and around it.

7

Shelter for the People
In Telluride, Community Suffers without Adequate Housing

JOAN MAY

Long ago, the abundant natural resources of the San Miguel River Valley offered seasonal hunting grounds for the Ute tribes. In the late 1800s, with the rush West to extract hard metals, miners forced out those who were already here, obliterating the treaties that had reserved the land for Native inhabitants. After that, hard-rock mining booms came and went, leaving neglected remains of the quest for riches. The year 1972 ushered in the current ski era with its own brand of resource consumption in the form of hotels, a golf course, luxury home construction, and high-end real estate sales (Telluride 2023).

The area was settled as San Miguel County. It spans over a thousand square miles of rugged, high-altitude terrain in southwestern Colorado. Most residents live in the eastern corner of the county, nestled in the mountains, in what is now Telluride. It's as close to Albuquerque or Salt Lake City as it is to Denver—which is to say, not very close at all—roughly 350 miles from any urban area. San Miguel County is the very definition of rural, with a mere 6.3 people per square mile. Residents proudly boast that the county has no traffic lights.

With about 2,600 residents, the town of Telluride is the county seat and economic engine of the region. Known for its ski resort and selfie-inspiring Main Street, the town joined the list of America's notable places in 1961, when it received the rare designation of National Historic Landmark for its vestiges of mining history and Victorian-era architecture. Mountain Village, incorporated in 1995, is the adjacent resort-amenities town, home to about 1,265 full-time residents (and many more part-timers) and connected to Telluride by a beloved, free—at least for now—gondola transit system.

Telluride itself takes up only about two square miles of land. Instead of suburbs, twelve-thousand-plus foot peaks encircle the town. Developing the surrounding area is virtually impossible because of the steep terrain, most of which is protected by the U.S. Forest Service or by covenants the community put in place to preserve the area's bucolic character and fragile landscapes.

Beauty combined with a scarcity of buildable land has resulted in predictable supply-and-demand price-hiked housing. In 2023, the average home sale price in the towns of Telluride and Mountain Village was over $3 million, according to analysis from the local title company. With a median income of $69,000 (*Telluride Affordable Housing Guidelines* 2023) those who want to live and work in the Telluride area are excluded from free-market homeownership unless they have substantial outside means of support. It follows that rental housing is also scarce. Yet the need for a reliable workforce is high, as the area's population more than doubles when tourism and second-home owner influx reach seasonal peaks.

That helps explain why about 75 percent of the Telluride area's workforce commutes, sometimes from hours away, on narrow and often icy mountain roads. When much of the workforce lives far from the jobs, the community that remains is compromised. Safe, stable, and affordable housing is a known social determinant of health—especially mental health—with housing insecurity correlated nationally with higher anxiety and depression levels and poorer health outcomes. For the well-being of the community, as well as for environmental, safety, and equity reasons, the goal of local leaders is for about 70 percent of the workforce to live close to their workplaces, flipping the current ratio (recognizing that some people prefer to make their home in other communities).

The only thing more prevalent in the local newspaper than real estate ads are "help wanted" ads, offering upwards of $25 an hour plus generous benefits for entry-level positions that go unfilled. Meanwhile, housing rental ads are extremely rare. In a recent issue, there were four pages of job offers and just three lonely long-term rental ads, ranging from $12,000/month to $15,000/month for three-to-four-bedroom homes.

In Telluride, affordable housing is the primary concern of virtually every young person, every employer, and every community leader. Housing supply is low. Housing anxiety is high. Governments can—and do—build lots of housing for locals. Over 1,200 units of government-provided housing have been built over the last thirty years in a county with only eight thousand year-round residents. That's a lot compared to most other resort towns, but it's not enough, and the shortage intensifies year after year. The ever-increasing demand has not been driven by large new commercial development in the area; there have been no new hotels built in over fifteen years. It's driven instead by a booming real estate economy that drives up prices and removes free-market options from the workforce housing pool.

The demographics of Telluride's population—like that of so many other quaint, attractive towns—were transformed at an accelerated pace by a COVID-19-driven mass exodus from cities by remote workers who can afford to live wherever they want, as well as Gen Zers seeking a more outdoorsy, small-town lifestyle. This migration has exacerbated the housing shortage, as wealthy newcomers buy up what were previously "ski-bum" rentals. Houses are remodeled or built new, resulting in bigger, fancier homes that require lots of workers to build, renovate, and maintain. (Good luck finding a carpenter, plumber, or electrician for a small emergency. The tradespeople who can afford to live and do business in the region are all booked on large projects for months in advance.)

For every home that was once a ski-bum house or an immigrant's first local residence and has since been remodeled, people are displaced. When we think about someone for whom Telluride is their only home, who has a full-time job supporting the regional economy, and who volunteers as a coach or for a nonprofit, that's a person we don't want to force out of this community. They make the community. They are the reason we need to solve the housing problem.

Competing in the Real Estate Frenzy

Mason Osgood moved to Telluride in 2019 to take a position as an AmeriCorps VISTA service member for the environmental advocacy nonprofit Sheep Mountain Alliance. He first lived in the Boarding House, a town of Telluride–owned launchpad with shared bathrooms, bunk beds, and a communal kitchen. Next stop was a rental house, from which he was evicted on short notice when a remodel was planned by the owner. Mason subsequently moved to various places with a lot of roommates and not a lot of privacy. He is now the full-time executive director of Sheep Mountain Alliance and an active volunteer in the community with a two-year lease on a shared house about fifteen miles from Telluride. He feels lucky to have a place to live for now, but his long-term situation is by no means secure.

Mason articulates the sentiment of many in the community: "There's a strong sense of vulnerability in looking for housing. It's a constant topic of conversation. It's really stressful when housing is always in the back of your mind. You know that when you lose your housing, even if you do by some luck find something else, you will likely be paying $2,000 per month per person or more, plus first and last month's rent, and maybe a security deposit. That means you pretty much always have to have $6,000 on hand. And that's for the lucky ones who find the rare place available to rent."

There are affordable-housing shortages in all desirable cities in the United States. And there's been a housing shortage in Telluride since at least the 1970s. Ask someone who's lived in this area for decades what it was like when they got here. The answer is the same: it was easy to find a job, but there was virtually no housing for workers.

So is this really a crisis? DeLanie Young thinks so. In her time in Telluride, she and her family have always rented from private owners, so she understands housing insecurity. Her experience as the Telluride Regional Housing Authority's programs manager from 2006–15 led her to run, successfully, for Telluride town council in 2017 and then for mayor. She is now the director of community services for the town of Telluride. In her tenure, she's seen what she calls the "real estate feeding frenzy" explode. San Miguel County's full-time, year-round population was already growing—and then it jumped almost 20 percent during the COVID-19 pandemic.

What was already shaping up to be a perfect storm was intensified by aggressive, effective marketing and a social media bonanza, which helped make once-sleepy little Telluride a household name. Tourism visitor numbers have exploded too. Domestic travel increased when international travel was restricted by the pandemic; remote work and school made it possible for people to travel at any time. The nonprofit and government sectors, as well as private businesses, have had to grow to keep pace with visitor and resident demands. But employers can't hire enough workers because workers can't find housing. How do you support a service economy without workers?

Other free-market dynamics have further diminished housing supply. In the past, some homeowners built accessory dwellings for on-site caretakers or local renters. But this is increasingly uncommon, as technology allows owners to monitor their properties from afar, and the superrich don't need rental income or the hassle of being a landlord. Similarly, in the past, it was common for those who bought free-market homes in the 1970s, '80s, and '90s to live in those homes themselves or to rent all or part of the space to locals. Now, as that population ages, many of these homeowners are moving away and are enticed to sell to someone (or more commonly an LLC) who will use the property as a vacation home or as a short-term rental. This increases the ratio of part-time residents and decreases the sense of community.

Community begins to erode when those who work in a place can't live there. Diversity also erodes, as people who aren't fluent in English or have less formal education have more trouble navigating the complex challenges of securing housing. Ultimately, will only the white and wealthy remain? Maybe they'll just bring their own workforce on their private jets.

Government officials are limited in their ability to solve the housing crisis: after all, wealth inequality is a global problem that can't be solved by any one little community. Yet governments are tasked with protecting the health, safety, and welfare of residents, of which housing security is a cornerstone.

I successfully ran for San Miguel county commissioner in 2006. I served for three four-year terms on a platform of balancing community, economy, and environmental preservation. Candidates these days run on similar platforms, with the strongest emphasis on workforce housing. In my twelve years as a commissioner, we grappled with similar problems, worked hard on solutions, and just like leaders today, got further behind on the goal of housing locals.

The Challenge of Short-Term Rentals

Adding to the local housing crunch is the effect of short-term rentals (STRs) such as Airbnbs and Vrbos. "The boom in STRs has definitely affected long-term housing," says DeLanie Young. "The lodging businesses and real estate community say it's anecdotal. But everyone I talk to in ski towns in the West concurs that STRs have wildly exacerbated the housing crisis."

She's not the only one who thinks so. Almost every person I interviewed who has lost their rental housing brought up, without prompting, that they and their peers have been kicked out in order for the house to sell to someone who intends to use it as a vacation home or to rent it short term, or both.

No one is saying that no STRs should be allowed. For some longtime locals, renting their primary residence during peak tourism seasons a few times a year is the only way they can afford to stay. And there is no doubt a great demand for this type of lodging. But according to many, things are out of balance. They argue that these units should be regulated the way hotel rooms are.

Melanie Montoya-Wasserman served as the director of housing for the Telluride Housing Department from 2017 to 2023, managing town-owned long-term rental properties, for which there are extensive waiting lists. She told me that several times a week someone calls or comes into the housing office lamenting that they lost their rental to someone who is going to rent it as an STR. It doesn't take a shrewd businessperson to extrapolate that homes are being sold at astronomical prices with the promise that if the new owners short-term rent, they can recoup some of the cost. Young notes that Telluride has the highest percentage of STRs of any municipality in the Colorado Association of Ski Towns network. Some Colorado communities, like Crested Butte, Breckenridge, and Steamboat, along with other resort towns across the American West, are starting to rein in STRs by limiting the number of licenses or increasing taxes and fees.

With consistent voter support, local governments—including those of Telluride, Mountain Village, and San Miguel County—have been building subsidized housing since the early 1990s. From one perspective, it looks like we have done an admirable job of providing a diverse array and large quantity of workforce housing, creating a variety of tiered occupant requirements, and securing funding to create this supply. Nearly half of the year-round residents of the Telluride area live in government-created community housing of various price levels and styles, including owner-occupied, rentals, single family, apartments, condos, dorms, the Boarding House, tiny homes, and parking spaces allocated for hardy folks willing to weather a Rocky Mountain winter in their vans or small RVs. There are homes for low- and medium-wage earners. Some of the owner-occupied units have appreciation caps (i.e., the resale price is limited).

Despite these efforts, needs assessments show that the area perpetually faces a seven-hundred-unit deficit in local housing. Getting supply ahead of demand is an ever-elusive goal because the free market, once a viable contributor to workforce housing, has gotten too expensive for those who rely on local work to pay their housing bills.

When the workforce housing programs began, the idea was that subsidized housing would provide entry-level homes for locals, who would eventually move up to the free market, opening up government housing for new first-time homeowners or entry-level renters. That didn't pan out. Both free-market and government-subsidized prices have risen continuously since the Great Recession and, in fact, increased almost 50 percent in 2022 alone. A handful of local senior management positions do pay six-figure salaries, but even these top earners can't afford multimillion-dollar free-market homes. Those who bought early have stayed in their subsidized homes rather than "moving up" to the free market. This has limited the turnover that governments envisioned at the beginning of the program and is creating a segregated housing market where, increasingly, all but the ultrawealthy must live in government-subsidized homes.

What more can governments do to address this ongoing crisis? To many local leaders, building as much housing as possible and prioritizing who qualifies for that housing is the best approach. But how should the town prioritize? Everyone agrees that teachers and first responders are especially important community members. But how about grocery checkers? And if grocery checkers are a priority, then are liquor store employees in that category? Ski patrollers are essential in a community that revolves around risky snow sports. Are lift operators also essential? The ski resort generates income that supports the community's economy, but is it the government's job to provide subsidized housing for corporations like Telluride Ski and Golf, or should that be the responsibility of those profiting directly from private enterprise?

What about retirees? If someone has been contributing to the community for decades through work, volunteering, and being a good neighbor, does that make them essential enough to keep their subsidized housing, when that home could be opened up to someone younger who is more active in the workforce?

And what is the purpose of all this housing that communities are racing to build? Is it intended primarily to support the local economy? Or is the purpose more about preserving the elusive notion of community? Defining the constitution of a community isn't a hard science, leaving us with tricky questions about social engineering.

In an attempt at fairness, Telluride relies on weighted lotteries to fill its subsidized housing. This low-tech process involves spitting balls out of a hand-cranked lottery machine. People deemed to have higher priority get more balls than those who meet fewer criteria. Everyone who enters the lottery must qualify by income, net assets, and local employment. Those with federally defined essential jobs get extra balls. A Telluride twist on prioritization gives extra points to those who graduated high school in the region—this is to encourage generational continuity. Telluride is working on tweaking this system. Currently, there is no priority for those who have invested the most time into the community. Extra points are being considered for longtime residents who have lost their housing or never had a secure place to live.

Natasha Hennessy is mystified that the longtime resident provision is not yet in place. She and her family lived in the same rental house in Telluride for eleven years until the house suddenly sold for $3.5 million cash. Scrambling to find housing, they drew the sixty-second spot in a lottery for one of twenty-four apartments in the town-county rental development called Sunnyside, despite having the most qualification balls possible. Devastated by the loss, the family has since qualified for and purchased a government-subsidized apartment for $600,000. "It's me and three large guys in seven hundred square feet," says Natasha. But she is relieved. They have a home.

Another Sunnyside lottery participant, Mark Rineer, has worked in the tourism service industry for more than a decade, mainly managing restaurants in Telluride. He and others I interviewed recounted tales of living in every type of housing imaginable—including a van and a tent in the woods. Multiple families sharing a studio apartment is not uncommon. One person I know of has a bed in a closet under a stairwell. Temporary couch surfing while looking for more permanent housing used to be the domain of young, single ski bums but is now common among families.

Rineer, along with all the other applicants, waited eagerly on the Sunnyside lottery day. With only twenty-four apartments available, his number came up thirty-fourth. Disappointed but still holding out hope, he and his family bided their time along with the others on the waitlist in case someone ahead of them wasn't able to claim their spot. On the cusp of losing his housing, and just nine days before Sunnyside's move-in date, Rineer got a call from the housing department offering him a Sunnyside apartment. When he heard the news, he collapsed on the floor, sobbing. "Eleven years of stress, of not knowing if our housing was secure—that stress was suddenly gone. I can't describe the relief."

Courtney McEleney is the manager of the San Miguel Regional Housing Authority. The housing that she manages includes "deed-restricted" homes, meaning a slew of requirements are attached to the properties' legal deeds. In the town of Telluride, for example, to qualify to purchase a home managed by the housing authority, potential occupants must prove they work at least 1,400 hours locally each year and cannot exceed area median-income parameters. Due to federal laws, applicants must provide proof of citizenship if the project is even partially funded by grants from the federal government. They may not own any other real estate in the defined geographic area, and they can only qualify for a place with no more bedrooms than human heartbeats. No guest rooms, no planning for a bigger family, and no staying put after the nest empties.

McEleney explained that residents of deed-restricted properties must continue to meet qualifying criteria for as long as they live in the unit, confirmed through biennial compliance checks conducted by her office. This irks some people. It's their home, they have the responsibility of a mortgage or rent, and yet the housing program requires that they reveal personal information about assets and income and who lives with them. They may be evicted if their situation changes. "People don't always feel like sharing their private information, and I get that," says McEleney. "But the purpose of these programs is to try our best to keep our community intact. Local leaders have decided that providing housing for those who live and work here is our best hope of preserving our community, and people who live in this sort of housing have to comply with the restrictions. I know it can be tedious, but there are so many people in need, and in fairness, we need to house those who meet qualifications first."

Whose Backyard Gets Housing?

Governments are doing their best to backfill the shortfall caused by the combined dynamic of inventory loss and increased demand. The Telluride region is a leader in this pursuit, as is evidenced by the high volume and high quality of workforce housing along with the high number of residents who happily live in these units. It's fair to say that all the deed-restricted neighborhoods are well loved and hospitable. Neighbor dinners, ride-sharing, impromptu playdates, barter-system childcare, keeping an eye out for each other, and lifelong friendships are the norm.

But now that the most easily developed land has been gobbled up, tensions are growing around how—and even if—to develop the remaining parcels. All three of the local governments are trying to speed up the process to address the crush and are facing "Not in My Backyard" (NIMBY) backlash. Whether or not it's justified, NIMBYism inevitably extends timelines, increases costs, and threatens to stymie creative solutions.

The Meadows, where I live, is a dense pocket of workforce housing in Mountain Village. When I bought my three-bedroom, 1,300-square-foot townhouse in 1992, it was the first for-purchase deed-restricted housing in the county. Since that time, the Meadows has been filled with condo and single-family home developments, resulting in an impressive 325 housing units—home to 60 percent of the town's population on 3 percent of its land.

Mountain Village recently fast-tracked a new deed-restricted condo project in the Meadows intended for "essential workers" (health-care, emergency response, education, and government personnel), priced at over $350,000 per bedroom. Workers can't afford this, so taxpayer-supported special districts such as schools, fire departments, and the medical center are stepping forward to buy the condos to rent to their employees, ensuring a sort of indentured-servant system. (If you change jobs, you lose your housing.) This also means that the taxpayers who fund the construction of these units are additionally funding the purchase of the units. Voters have approved tax increases over the past year to support affordable housing in virtually every special district in the region. As one longtime first responder said, "I'm paying so much in taxes for employee housing that I can't afford my own housing." San Miguel County has some of the lowest property tax rates in the country (Wisevoter 2023), which is part of the allure for second-home owners. But because values have skyrocketed, actual taxes have also jumped very quickly, and locals are having a hard time keeping up.

Neighbors are asking why subsidized housing can't be spread more evenly throughout Mountain Village. The answer is, at least in part, that attempts by the village to build housing in other neighborhoods have failed after protracted lawsuits by people who prefer not to see the "riffraff" out the window of their luxury homes. Neighbors are also asking if deed-restricted workforce housing to be sold for over a million dollars per unit is really the niche governments should be prioritizing.

Over in Telluride, the town has made an exception to allow buildings that are taller than historic guidelines dictate if it is for community housing. This has some residents and the Historical and Architectural Review Commission up in arms. Additionally, when and if the town attempts to develop the vacant lots that it owns that are sprinkled throughout the historic district, it will undoubtedly contend with opposition from neighbors.

The third local government entity, San Miguel County, has created a new Community Housing Zone District that truncates the traditional, lengthy five-step Planned Unit Development review process. The first application of this was the 2022 purchase of thirty-nine acres a few miles outside of town for a development that could provide between 240 to 780 densely situated units on what had been a thirty-five-acre ranch-character parcel (Cheavens 2022). Neighbors were not happy, particularly because the purchase was sprung on them without community input. They filed a lawsuit, arguing that the county did not properly follow its own master plan. The judge ruled in favor of the neighbors in the lawsuit and again on appeal.

Continued Development Compounds the Problem

Efforts to quickly increase the supply of community housing will never be enough, even without new enterprises needing additional employees. Yet today there are at least three enormous commercial development projects in the works. These projects will require even more new workers to service them.

In Mountain Village, a Four Seasons hotel has been approved that will include 53 dedicated hotel rooms, 38 "branded residences" that constitute an additional 77 rooms, 29 condominiums, and a mere 10 employee apartments. A second new

Mountain Village hotel was approved in 2023 that includes 50 hotel rooms, 20 condos, and 21 lodge units. It will have a mere 18 dorm rooms and 2 employee apartments. Where are the rest of those workers (estimated to be 300 per new hotel) going to live?

During the planning process, very few residents of Mountain Village (save the ski company owners) said they wanted new hotels. Locals, in general, are not asking for tourism-based economic development. Why would they? The sentiment among residents these days is that more tourists further increase the crowds and traffic, diminishing both the visitor experience and the quality of life for those who live here.

Also in 2023, the county approved a public-private development that will contribute land for a desperately needed regional medical center and a vitally important wastewater treatment plant expansion, along with new commercial development that was a necessary bargaining chip in the negotiations. County planner Kaye Simonson told me that the employee housing mitigation for this project is only the standard 15 percent that was "grandfathered in" when the developer bought the land.

The dots are easy to connect. Even without (and even more so with) new hotels and other commercial development driving the need for new employees, a growing population of transplants increases pressure on housing. As the last parcels of available land get developed, the persistent housing shortage worsens.

Past Decisions, Present Dilemmas

Decades ago, could the region have changed the trajectory of its housing crisis? Could past leaders have imposed deed restrictions on entire towns? What if Telluride had some neighborhoods with a "need to reside" provision? What if we had instituted house-size limits—would that have helped keep homes affordable? What would Telluride be like now if past leaders had been willing to compromise the historic character by loosening design guidelines to allow for less expensive construction? Did governments miss an opportunity during the recession to gobble up property for future public needs, when the economy ground to a halt? Should we have protected less open space, sacrificed habitat protection and carbon sinks, and in doing so, changed the region's quiet, natural character?

We can speculate about how we could have done it differently—either better or worse—but the crucial point is that the Telluride region, like countless attractive communities in the West and around the nation, currently faces a desperate workforce-housing shortage. And despite adding new community-subsidized homes every year, we are not moving the needle toward the agreed-upon goal of housing 70 percent of our workforce locally. Clearly, we can't build our way out of this problem, as there is an effective infinity of people attracted to the mountain lifestyle. No matter how much housing governments build, there will always be more demand than supply.

So what can be done, in addition to governments continuing to construct as much housing as they can while balancing other community priorities? An extensive study published by the Northwest Council of Governments in 2023 concluded that the only way to effectively overcome the crisis in ski towns is with a combination of government-subsidized housing, down-payment assistance, and market regulation.

Here are some strategies that communities facing such challenges are effectively employing:

- *Treat shelter like a basic human right.* As with water, sewer, and electric utilities, everyone should pay to ensure access to housing as a basic human need. Additionally, we can learn from Canada and European countries, where workers earn respectable salaries plus benefits for tourism careers. Their far bigger safety nets treat all residents like valuable community members.
- *Recognize limits to growth.* There are a limited number of beautiful resort areas, and each is going to see increasing growth pressure. It's incumbent upon governments to make the hard decisions to recognize social and environmental limits on growth. Despite the best efforts of well-intentioned pioneer planners, regional density models decades ago were based on best guesses that assumed free-market forces would balance resident and nonresident housing. That didn't work. No one predicted the construction of twenty-five-thousand-square-foot homes requiring armies of workers or a global pandemic that would reshape the profile of rural populations. The new hot-button phrase is *carrying capacity*. It is heard alternatively as "I'm here, so shut the door," and "What is the number of humans that our infrastructure and natural resources can safely support?" Regardless of one's lens, growth models must continually be revised, taking into account current realities including resource limitations and social and environmental values. It may be that we cannot accommodate previously platted densities and must say no to some proposals—even if it means digging deep to purchase development rights from current owners.

- *Tax the rich!* The disparity of wealth has caused land and building prices to become out of reach for "regular" people, and housing mitigation fees are one way to counter this. The deck is stacked so heavily in favor of those with family money, enormous salaries, and large investments that it will take unprecedented, substantial subsidies to even begin to help those who don't have the financial privilege to make this place home.
- *Prioritize existing housing stock for locals.* We must figure out ways to better utilize the resources that are already in place and create huge incentives for homeowners to rent out a room, a lock-off, or an accessory dwelling unit. These incentives could be monetary and also less tangible, like support for a culture where renting to a local worker is the norm. Governments might also spend tax revenue on purchasing existing homes and retrofitting them for multifamily employee dwellings.
- *Cultivate public-private and public-private-philanthropic partnerships.* The Telluride Foundation's nonprofit Rural Homes Initiative secures grant funding and works with private developers to build for-sale homes in rural towns. Some private businesses are buying homes to house their workers, and governments can encourage more of this through tax incentives.
- *Undertake unbiased studies on short-term rentals.* Plans for managing STRs should be based on those studies. We can also learn from other resort communities that are ahead of us in regulating these for-profit rentals.
- *Negotiate with developers.* Developers often have vested rights to build, but hard conversations between the local government and landowners will help reach the highest possible public-private benefit. This has worked in the past when administrators and elected officials negotiated with developers to ensure sizable contributions to the community.
- *Increase mitigation requirements.* New commercial development should mitigate close to 100 percent of the housing needs they create. Not everyone wants to live close to where they work, but shifting the burden of housing provision to developers and employers could alleviate much of the housing pressure.
- *Prioritize process.* Fast-tracking some community housing makes sense—as county planner Simonson pointed out, requiring developers to go through a five-step review just to build a few small homes for workers drives up costs and slows down building. At the same time, the best large developments in the past made sincere efforts to include neighbors and other interested parties in discussions right from the beginning. Though such efforts take

time, they ensure that neighbors and the community at large feel invested and respected—and won't file years-long lawsuits that delay the project anyway.

Envisioning the Future

The Telluride Valley rivals our best national parks in its beauty: a once-discussed federal parkland designation would have resulted in a very different Telluride with little or no development. Since that didn't happen, it's up to current residents to determine the right level of growth versus protection.

Speaking for myself, I hope that generations to come can benefit from the community resources and natural surroundings that are ever more valuable in our digitized, socially distant world. But how do we do that in a way that doesn't kill the very things we're trying to protect—the community and the natural environment?

I moved to Telluride after graduate school "for one ski season" and was instantly drawn into the eddy of the community, the lifestyle, and the mountains. I couldn't pull myself away. By my great fortune, not only did I find housing where I would eventually raise my son, but I found a lifetime of meaningful work. Not everyone is so lucky.

That first year, I worked as a bread baker and lift operator. I posted a note in the laundromat seeking a rental and was lucky to be offered a spot in a shared, woodstove-heated miner's cabin in a neighborhood east of Telluride known as Liberty Bell. Survival skills included endless snow shoveling, wood splitting, dressing in many layers (the cabin had negligible insulation), and contributing to frequent potluck dinners.

Many who come to live here now do so for the same reasons I did in the '80s. Being here nourishes the body, mind, and soul. Today's twentysomethings hone their own survival skills. Making themselves indispensable to the community remains the common denominator of Telluride's workers and residents. Their vision is what will shape the Telluride to come. They need the structure of clear land-management planning and fair taxation to bring that vision to fruition.

I am envisioning a new generation of Telluride inhabitants who emulate the qualities of those who came before: who honor the Ute people's sense of place, who have the resolve of the miners, who are inspired to dream like the shapers of the ski era, and who possess the collective will to build a community that future generations will be committed to protecting.

8

Exporting the Costs of Growth
Jackson Hole, Wyoming

LUTHER PROPST

Motorists driving over northwestern Wyoming's Teton Pass climb some two thousand feet in elevation from the valley floor of Jackson Hole, encountering steep grades, hairpin turns, and plummeting drop-offs along the way. It can be a white-knuckle trip in the summer; in the winter, driving Wyoming Highway 22—one of the snowiest stretches of highway in the Lower 48—is downright harrowing, plagued by avalanches, high winds, and snow-tire-defying black ice.

And yet, on any given morning, even during a February blizzard, a relentless stream of headlights heading east snakes up the pass from Idaho. The cars and trucks that then descend into the valley below belong to teachers, carpenters, firefighters, electricians, baristas, and nurses. Every day, they make this forty-five-minute-plus commute from Victor or Driggs, Idaho—or even farther afield. Some of these workers will earn $60, $80, even $100 per hour for their labors. But it's still not enough to afford to buy or rent even the humblest housing in Jackson, where in 2022, the average price for a single-family home topped $5 million.

It's been four decades since a median-income Jackson Hole household could afford a median-priced house. The COVID-19-exacerbated "Zoom Boom"—an out-migration of highly paid remote workers from cities into mountain towns, resort areas, and national park gateway communities—widened the long-growing gap between wages and housing. It quickly transformed Teton County's long-standing housing crunch into a full-blown crisis. The Zoom Boom was more than matched by the continued growth in the number of wealthy retirees, second-home (and multiple-home) owners, and the überrich taking advantage of Wyoming's low state taxes, which are highly favorable for protecting wealth.

In addition to a housing crisis, Teton County's popularity as a place to visit has further inflamed commuter traffic congestion over Teton Pass—and along the thirty-five-to-seventy-mile commute up the Snake River Canyon from Alpine and Star Valley, Wyoming. In a futile attempt to alleviate congestion, the Wyoming

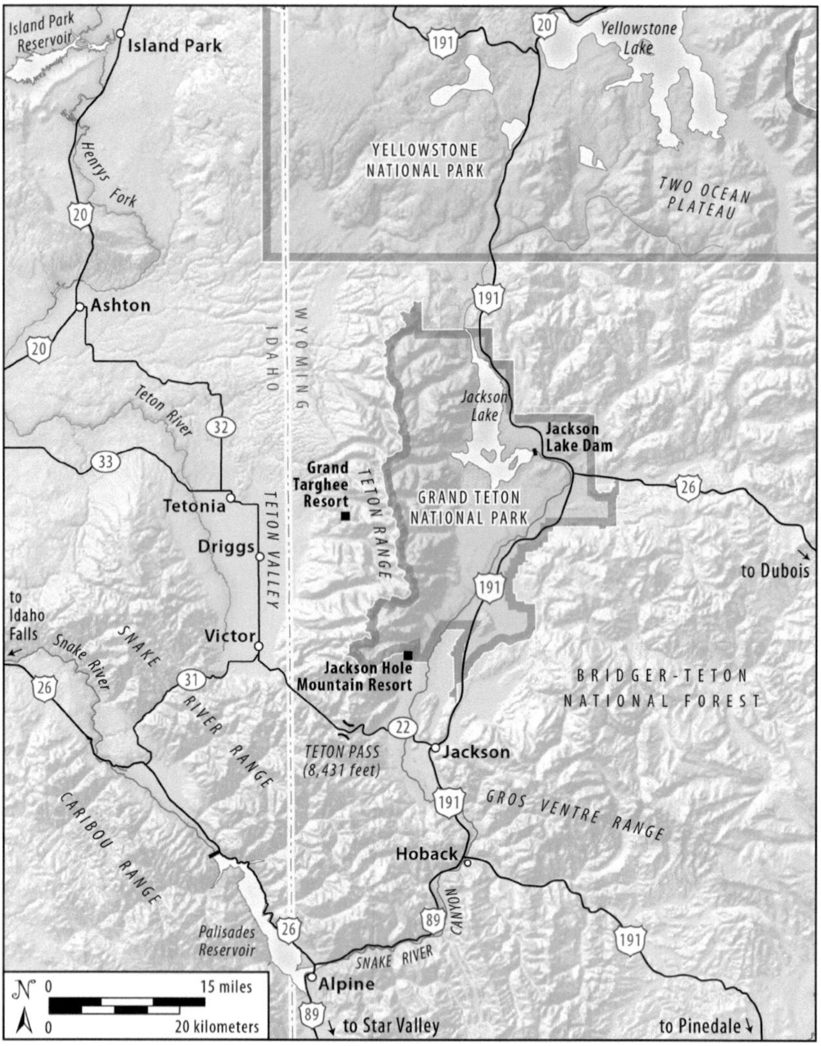

Figure 8.1 Map showing Grand Teton National Park and the Jackson Hole "commutershed." Map credit: Chelsea Feeney.

Department of Transportation recently expanded the highway south of Jackson to the Snake River Canyon from two to five lanes. This has sped up traffic and made the highway even more deadly for wildlife and people who live in neighborhoods south of town.

In March 2023, during one of the snowiest winters on record, the agony of the Teton Pass commute was compounded by a steady stream of big rigs and overloaded pickup trucks that ran off the road or jackknifed, snarling traffic for hours and preventing commuters from getting to work at all—or from getting home for dinner or to pick up kids. The rigs shouldn't even have been there: Semitrucks and vehicles hauling trailers are prohibited in the winter, since losing traction could result in a five hundred-foot plummet down a precipitous slope.

So why did so many drivers defy the winter ban? In an irony that crystallizes the laissez-faire attitude toward growth that defines many Western communities, the trucks were making the treacherous trip to move a couple hundred shipping containers from the Pacific Coast to Teton Village, the slope-side community at the base of Jackson Hole Mountain Resort. They were to become part of a new self-storage rental facility, providing half a shipping container for about $350 per month, to give homeowners a place to store a snow machine or drift boat in the offseason, or just excess stuff. The Wyoming State Board of Land Commissioners approved the self-storage facility on state trust land, bypassing local regulations for fire safety, wastewater treatment, and traffic congestion, while spawning two lawsuits.

That its residents have so much excess stuff to store is another sign of Teton County's spectacular wealth. That the trucks carrying those storage bins blocked the commute of those who serve and teach and heal the wealthy Jackson residents on the other side of the pass is a symbol of the ever-widening inequalities that exist in many mountain towns or "amenity economies" of the West.

A Distinctive Place

These phenomena aren't unique to Teton County. Aspen's gardeners and restaurant workers and even lawyers and doctors face a daily commute as much as two hours from down-valley communities such as Glenwood Springs and Rifle, Colorado. The folks who build and tend to the palatial homes in Telluride and Mountain Village—often occupied for only a few weeks each year—traverse a mountain pass and a narrow, windy road from Montrose and Delta. Sedona's hotel-room cleaners make their way up the red rock from Cottonwood and Verde Valley. And now even former bedroom communities are becoming too costly for the average worker, forcing them to drive ever farther to find housing.

But Jackson Hole—the spectacular valley east of the Tetons—is in a league of its own. Teton County residents have the highest per-capita income in the country, and the gap between total income and average wages is wider than anywhere else—even wider than in Manhattan (Farrell 2020). Except for a relatively small number of deed-restricted and subsidized affordable houses, even well-paid workers can't afford the cheapest homes—with luck, $650,000 might purchase a hotel-room-sized condominium. At the same time, Teton County needs ever more workers to staff high-end restaurants, build new mansions, clean and maintain luxury short-term rental units, and provide a wide range of goods and personal services to tourists, retirees, highly paid remote workers, and second-home owners.

Ninety-seven percent of Teton County is public land—including Grand Teton National Park, nearly half of Yellowstone National Park, the massive Bridger-Teton National Forest, and the National Elk Refuge. The result is a striking imbalance between the number of jobs in the community—tourism, personal services, construction, health care, and increasingly wealth management and finance—and the land available to build housing for those workers.

Teton County has a classic distorted housing market in which demand far exceeds the ability of the market to provide housing. As a result, Teton County exports a growing number of workers into its sprawling, fingerlike "commutershed," the area or landscape traveled by workers who do not live in the community where they work. To the west, workers routinely commute from not only Victor (24 miles) and Driggs (32 miles) but also Rexburg (80 miles). To the south, they drive from Alpine (37 miles) and Afton (69 miles). And to the southeast, they come from Bondurant (30 miles) and Pinedale (77 miles).

This dynamic produces several unfortunate consequences: the expense and wasted time of a long commute, wildlife-vehicle collisions, traffic congestion, greenhouse gas emissions, air pollution, unattractive wildlife fencing lining our highways, social segregation, and the creation of communities (especially in neighboring Teton County, Idaho) that can't generate the tax revenue required to meet basic public services (ECONorthwest 2022).

Local leaders often contend that the situation is beyond their control, which is partly accurate. They can't ban wealthy people from moving to the community or spending $5 million or $25 million on a vacation home. The crisis is indeed exacerbated by several federal, state, and local-level decisions and policies. For example, due largely to the tax revenue and royalties from rich low-sulfur coal deposits, Wyoming has the most favorable state tax code in the United States for preserving wealth, creating one of the world's most scenic tax havens and luring billionaires with its "cowboy cocktail" of finance and tax laws (Cenziper and Fitzgibbon 2021).

Teton County has an extraordinary history of conservation leadership, especially when it comes to protecting public lands. In the 1920s, John D. Rockefeller Jr.

acquired some 220,000 acres across the foothills and valley east of the Tetons. After many battles with local opponents, in 1943, he transferred the land to the federal government to later be added to Grand Teton National Park. Since this gift to the public, private landowners have protected much of the balance of the county's private land under conservation or agricultural easements. The Rockefeller family also maintained the JY Ranch until 2007 as a family retreat within the national park. This high-profile summer retreat may have contributed to the growing popularity of the area as a summer retreat (and later winter ski playground) for the wealthy. On the other side of the coin, after strong initial opposition, local landowners and leaders realized that tourism could provide the foundation for a prosperous economy. Over the last seventy years, they have successfully promoted large-scale, year-round tourism, second-home ownership, and retirement living for outdoor folks. At the same time, they have by and large failed to address, until recently, housing for the workers that such growth demands. Today this creates a Dr. Jekyll and Mr. Hyde approach to local land use and conservation: land conservation limits the supply of land for affordable housing, and strong national and even global demand raises the price of housing while the growth economy generates robust numbers of new jobs. It also dampens the political will to implement meaningful policies to address the problem.

An Isolated Community

Jackson Hole is often held up as an archetypal Old West community. Yet while much of the American West became a natural resource colony after Indigenous peoples were displaced, Teton County's geology and isolation largely spared it from extractive industries. Isolation discouraged logging. Mining prospectors and fossil fuel explorers came up empty here. The climate was too cold for most farming. Thus homesteading didn't begin in earnest until the 1880s. Technology—or more exactly, the lack of it—for many years also protected Teton County. No railroad was ever built into the county. Unsuitable soil conditions made building roads a special challenge. Roads into town remained rough (and in many cases, dirt) until well after World War II.

While the traditional natural resource industries were held at bay, the region was not protected from growth due to tourism. The natural wonders of the area drew sightseers, and the wildlife lured well-heeled hunters and anglers. In the early 1900s, Yellowstone was already pulling in tens of thousands of visitors per year—remarkable given the remoteness of the park at the time. By the time Grand Teton National Park was established in 1929, the shores of Jenny Lake had already been built up to accommodate flocks of tourists.

After World War II, the tourism industry exploded as Americans looked to experience one of the few places unsullied by industrialization. Yellowstone and Grand Teton National Parks attracted more than a million visitors annually throughout the 1950s, and any semblance of the old Mormon agricultural settlements that sprouted in the late 1800s just north of Jackson had been wiped away. Jackson still banks on the cowboy myth that infected Hollywood for decades, even today portraying itself as the "Last of the Old West" (a prominent wooden sign at the top of Teton Pass proclaims, apparently without irony, "Yonder Lies Jackson Hole—Last of the Old West"). Most of the working cattle operations were transformed into dude ranches, subdivisions, or private estates, allowing urban folks to play at being wranglers for a weekend, a precursor to today's billionaire hobby ranchers. The Jackson Hole Mountain Resort opened in the 1960s, turning Teton County tourism into a year-round affair.

Many other Western communities, from Aspen to Tahoe, from Bozeman to Tucson, from Santa Fe to Moab, were also embracing tourism and outdoor recreation. But most were doing so to replace the recently busted mining economy, whereas Teton County had been immersed in tourism from nearly the beginning of European settlement. That gave Teton County a head-start on fostering industrial-scale tourism—by the late 1960s, it even had daily commercial flights and had the busiest airport in Wyoming. Jackson and its amenities attracted millions of visitors each year, but for the most part, they were just that: visitors. They came on vacation, visited the parks, rode dude horses, went hunting or skiing, and then returned home. The same was true, to one degree or another, in other Western tourist towns.

By the late 1970s and 1980s, as the old extractive industries continued to consolidate and fade and as Americans became more affluent and mobile, tourism begat the recreational real estate industry. It was no longer enough to just visit these beautiful places; folks wanted to own a piece of them, even if only as a part-time residence. Subdivisions and condominiums sprouted at the base of ski areas. Out-of-towners bought and fixed up old miners' shacks. Subdivisions and "ranchettes" sprawled across former cattle pastures and prime wildlife habitat. Spurred by the times and the lyrics of John Denver, many disaffected young adults moved to Western mountain towns—seeking a "Rocky Mountain High" and staying to sell real estate (Teton County, population 25,000, has 700 realtors). Short-term profit outbid long-term vision.

With no community vision and lax local land use regulations, new development ignored traditional architecture, building in the mold of what they thought newcomers would want. And the newcomers started businesses—not only selling real estate but also opening restaurants, building new houses, starting white water rafting companies, teaching visitors to ski, guiding for trout—thereby drawing more folks like themselves. This marked the birth of fully integrated amenities economies across the West.

Teton County's population more than tripled between 1970 and 2000 (from 5,000 to 17,000), with development following apace. Initially, most of the growth was within Jackson, the county's population center and only incorporated municipality, and along nearby highways. But second-home owners would pay a premium for the "wilder" areas, especially near Jackson Hole Mountain Resort or adjoining the national forest, where they knew that the next wave of newcomers' homes would not sully their views.

From Wendy's to Albertsons, from McDonald's to big-box retail stores, corporate chains displaced the old mom-and-pop shops. More recently, international banks have displaced chain restaurants and convenience stores. High-end art galleries, clothing stores, coffee shops, restaurants, and interior decorators—along with real estate offices, of course—have replaced the greasy spoons, hardware stores, and bars downtown. This in turn has attracted more tourists and part-time residents, who have found comfort in the familiar. Most of the relatively scant acreage of private land not under conservation easement has been gobbled up by development, causing land and housing prices to skyrocket. At the same time, the burgeoning commercial sector requires more and more often-seasonal, low-wage workers to prepare dinners, whip up espressos, clean hotel rooms, and service the mansions.

Over the years, local leaders generally permitted and promoted this growth. Today, despite extensive local planning and regulatory initiatives, community character and social balance continue to erode. The ethic to protect public lands and the efforts among private ranchers to protect agricultural and conservation easements often do not extend to local land use decisions. As a result, efforts are inadequate to protect Jackson's Western heritage and ensure that public services and housing affordable to local workers remain in balance with development. State leaders, meanwhile, do all they can to promote growth in Teton County. This includes fashioning friendly tax and finance laws to lure the ultrarich.

By the late 1970s, local conservation advocates were beginning to see that the relative absence of the extractive industries of the Old West had paradoxically opened Teton County up to New West problems. Rural sprawl, affordable housing shortages due to the vast imbalance between wages and cost of living, wealth inequality, traffic congestion, and unprecedented levels of tourism were proving to be every bit as threatening to the wildlife, water quality, ecosystem health, and community character as what the late Western scholar Charles Wilkinson labeled the "Lords of Yesterday"—mining, oil and gas, logging (Wilkinson 1992; Larmer 2011).

In 1980, the Jackson Hole Alliance for Responsible Planning (now the Jackson Hole Conservation Alliance) formed to stop the development of a shopping center adjoining Grand Teton National Park in Kelly, Wyoming. They were successful, as were their later efforts to block other egregious proposals, such as a waterslide park across the highway from the National Elk Refuge in the late 1980s and a grizzly bear theme park in the early 1990s. But conservationists weren't nearly as successful in preventing the incremental but ubiquitous development of high-end residential properties for second homes, retirees, and remote workers. Nor have they managed to stop the continued development of high-end hotels and luxury short-term rentals or slowed the widening gap between the average price of a home and the average local income. Likewise, with the tremendous financial return from luxury development, they have been unable to convert proposals for high-end housing or lodging into workforce housing. Instead, recent additions include new amusements, such as zip lines and alpine coasters. Local government, by and large, has shown little effective interest in policies and regulations that would restrict all-out development.

Today Jackson and the Greater Yellowstone region are more popular than ever. Sales and use tax revenues have soared alongside skier days and visitor numbers at Yellowstone and Grand Teton National Parks. Demand for high-end real estate has skyrocketed, and the population of multimillionaires and billionaires has shot up as well. But it's not just Jackson Hole. The cost of living in Jackson's former bedroom communities—Driggs, Victor, Alpine, Hoback, even Pinedale—is getting ever more pricey.

This causes Jackson's commutershed to expand farther out into the region, leading to more traffic, wildlife-vehicle collisions, and emissions. Commuting directly lowers the quality of life for the people who commute and contributes to the deterioration of the very amenities that draw new residents.

The large number of commuters across state and county lines also creates an unhealthy public finance situation in neighboring counties. This is especially stark in Teton County, Idaho. Due to rapid growth and a state law that caps county revenue increases despite rapid population growth, the county simply cannot raise the revenue needed to provide basic public services. As a result, one of the most desirable, spectacular wildlife-rich regions on the planet is in full-on crisis mode.

Taming the Lords of Yesterday

The eighteen to twenty counties of the Greater Yellowstone region have had little regional or systemic success addressing the myriad threats posed by our now global economy. Mitigating the impacts of amenity-driven growth on Teton County—and increasingly on counties all around Greater Yellowstone—requires a robust and multifaceted regional approach. Otherwise, the region will continue to lose both the wildlife and natural values for which it is known globally and the distinctive unconventional outdoor vibe that has long distinguished mountain towns from cities and suburbs.

The political will to make meaningful regional—or even local—changes in growth policy is lacking. The 2020 joint Teton County–Jackson Comprehensive Plan starts with an inspiring vision statement: "To preserve and protect the area's ecosystem to ensure a healthy environment, community and economy for current and future generations." This lofty vision is often repeated but only sporadically followed.

Just as mining towns were once beholden to absentee mine owners from the East Coast or abroad, so too has the Greater Yellowstone Region allowed less centralized but powerful interests to push industrial tourism and wealth-based growth. Industrial-scale high-value tourism, a state tax code that is the most favorable in the nation for preserving wealth, and state trust laws that attract hidden capital finance a disproportionate share of Wyoming's budget and create prosperity and wealth in Jackson; however, these things are also degrading the foundation upon which this prosperity was built—wildlife, open space, and sense of community—and replacing it with wealthy part-time residents and the commuters who serve them.

Several factors undermine the political will for decisive change, including a shared memory of the area's history of poverty, isolation, and a highly volatile seasonal economy; well-funded, cynical, and sophisticated developers and their consultants; and a population that is too tired, overworked, distracted, or disenchanted to press for solutions. Political will to protect community values is sparse in both Teton County and other counties in Greater Yellowstone.

For example, Gallatin County, Montana, home to Bozeman, is about half private land. It has a relatively modest amount of acreage under conservation easement and has seen rapid, sustained population and economic growth for years. Growth is both sprawling outward across the countryside and rebuilding downtown Bozeman with increased density. Even if the county or local municipalities were to attempt to effectively manage growth, they would run into Montana's anticonservation and anticommunity state politics. State legislators have recently passed legislation that preempts local control and local authority to protect natural resources (Shain 2023).

Across the West, the federal government has provided leadership in managing growth in a few special areas, but not in Greater Yellowstone. Notable examples include the bistate Tahoe Regional Planning Compact in Nevada and California and the Columbia River Gorge Commission in Washington and Oregon. Farther afield are the federal Coastal Zone Management Act and the Coastal Barrier Resources Act, which help manage unwise development in coastal areas. Public land managers in the Greater Yellowstone region, through the Greater Yellowstone Coordinating Committee, have done a credible job promoting regional cooperation for protecting the region's national parks, national forests, wildlife refuges, and public lands. But no such leadership for addressing community development and sprawling growth is foreseeable in Greater Yellowstone. It's up to nonprofit advocacy organizations to catalyze such leadership on community development matters.

The Way Forward

For Jackson Hole and surrounding communities, the key to combating overdevelopment does not lie in better environmental or biophysical science, more sophisticated land use planning tools or scenarios, or more thorough social and economic analysis. Rather, the limiting factor is a deeply ingrained societal commitment to perpetual growth and the dearth of political will and community engagement at the local and state levels to question this commitment.

After toiling in this arena for over thirty-five years, I offer the following recommendations for aligning land use policy—points I see as relevant not only to Jackson Hole and Teton County but also to many cities and counties throughout the West.

In 1997, I coauthored a book entitled *Balancing Nature and Commerce in Gateway Communities* (Howe, McMahon, and Propst 1997). I am struck by the degree to which my perspective has changed over the past three decades. *Balancing Nature and Commerce* barely mentioned the importance of engaging effectively in local politics. Instead, the focus was oriented toward planning and public engagement tools and techniques (e.g., develop a shared vision, build on local assets, etc.). Times have changed and so has my impression of what is required to protect Western communities from homogenization and the loss of community character and the region's wildlife and natural values.

Today, I counsel people who ask how to protect their community from poorly planned development to fully engage in local politics, governance, and advocacy and to question the assumptions that growth is always desirable and inevitable. Public engagement is the foundation for positive local action. Engagement includes two complementary but distinct methods: work through nonprofit advocacy organizations and elect allies to local and state offices.

Here are my top six suggestions:

1. *Support your local growth management advocacy organization.* If you don't have one, create one. Local progress requires a local nonprofit organization whose mission is to protect against the loss of local values due to rapid, unmanaged development. Many local and regional conservation advocacy organizations remain reluctant to address development and private land issues; however, in rapidly changing Western communities, the impacts of poorly planned development are often the most pressing threats to wildlife, water quality, and community character.

   In Teton County, the Jackson Hole Conservation Alliance (JHCA) has played this role since 1979. The foundation of JHCA's long-term success is that it fully embraces a two-part mission: protecting both wildness and community character. More recently, Jackson residents have created Protect Our Waters Jackson Hole to complement the JHCA, focusing on protecting and restoring water quality. Jackson residents have also recently created Shelter JH to advocate for workforce and affordable housing. In neighboring Teton County, Idaho, Valley Advocates for Responsible Development (VARD) plays a similar role advocating for smart growth and conservation in the Jackson Hole bedroom communities of Victor, Driggs, and Tetonia.
2. *Build regional coalitions to advocate for better growth management.* Growth pressures are regional in scale, so the response to regional growth must be regional advocacy. In Jackson Hole, the number of jobs far exceeds the number of houses available to those who hold those jobs. Land use policies in Teton County and the town of Jackson—intentionally or not—export housing their workers to neighboring counties. In turn, this situation makes

it nearly impossible financially for these counties to provide basic public services.

Early in my conservation career, the Greater Yellowstone Coalition (GYC) assisted communities throughout the eighteen-county region through a program led by longtime conservation leader Dennis Glick called the Private Land Stewardship Program. The program's goal was to mitigate the negative wildlife and community impacts of sprawl and unplanned community development. Over the years, this focus on community development policies disappeared, leaving a significant void in the region's advocacy for managing growth.

The premier Western example of regional advocacy for improved land use (statewide in this case) is 1000 Friends of Oregon, whose work is described in this volume's essay by Robert Liberty. Since 1974, they have worked to protect and strengthen Oregon's unique land use planning system. To paraphrase Patrick Geedes (who is credited with coining the phrase *think globally, act locally*), the key to protecting communities and landscapes is "think regionally, act regionally."

3. *Elections matter, so engage fully in politics.* In Teton County and throughout the United States, advocates for conservation and community values almost always emphasize (or overemphasize) support for "charitable" activities through nonprofit organizations that qualify as tax-exempt under section 501c3 of the Internal Revenue Code (IRC). These advocates too often overlook the importance of recruiting, electing, and supporting allies to local and state offices. A detailed description of organizing to recruit and elect candidates is beyond the scope of this essay; however, the Bolder Advocacy website provides an excellent introduction. The key point is that the IRC and state law permit nonprofit organizations, unincorporated associations, and individuals tremendous opportunity to engage in local elections. Using modern voter data, clear and simple messages, and year-round political organizing, the most important way to create better communities is through elections.
4. *Articulate a compelling vision for the future of your community, repeat it often, and act to realize the vision.* Repeat a simple vision and tell stories based on local values to convey the vision, rather than rely entirely on science, economics, and analysis. Martin Luther King Jr. did not lead the civil rights movement of the 1960s through position papers and policy analysis but through a personal and compelling vision, including his 1963 "I Have a

Dream" speech: "I have a dream that my four little children will one day live in a nation where they will not be judged by the color of their skin but by the content of their character." Jane Goodall, one of the most effective science communicators of our time, brings a plush chimpanzee with her to her speeches, not only demonstrating mastery of primatology but also humanizing her and her message. A compelling vision and empathetic stories are necessary, but not sufficient. Without persistent public action, they lead nowhere.

5. *Promote a balance of regulatory and market-based tools.* The crux is balance. Many communities rely too heavily on zoning and other land use regulatory tools. Many other communities rely too heavily on private incentives, such as conservation easements. The most effective programs balance public land use tools and private intervention in the real estate market. For example, in Jackson Hole, perhaps the most effective effort to protect community character in the past several years is a community-driven partnership to protect the Café Genevieve block in downtown Jackson. The Save the Block campaign in 2019 protected a few acres of valuable downtown green space, historic structures, and three beloved eateries popular with visitors and locals while providing a site for a historical museum. The campaign raised several million dollars in public and private funds to eliminate a proposed ninety-thousand-square-foot luxury hotel that would have employed some one hundred people while providing only a very small fraction (perhaps 10 percent) of the housing required for those employees (Woods 2021).
6. *Embrace intergovernmental cooperation rather than externalizing the costs of growth.* A community does not provide leadership in conservation or sustainable development when it externalizes much of the costs to neighboring communities and wildland managers. Economists call these costs negative externalities. Jackson's economy excels in creating negative externalities due to the disproportionate reliance on low-wage, often-seasonal jobs serving wealthy visitors and part-time residents. This imbalanced economy creates the premier negative externality: a lack of affordable housing for the people who work in the community. In addition, those who enjoy the benefits of wildfire mitigation, water quality, and other local values should bear the costs of those goods rather than exporting them to neighboring jurisdictions or public land managers. This principle applies not only to Teton County, Wyoming, and surrounding counties but to regions throughout the West—Sedona and Cottonwood Valley; Aspen and Roaring

> Fork Valley and the Interstate 70 corridor; Santa Fe and Rio Arriba County; Tahoe and Reno; among others. For example, in the Tetons and elsewhere regional governmental structures rather than a single municipality or county should oversee regional services such as transit, wastewater management, and affordable housing. Also, an effective community development program should not only catalyze development of affordable housing but also ensure a reasonable balance between the number and type of jobs in a community and the number of dwelling units that those workers can afford.

To quote Wallace Stegner, "The West is still the native home of hope; it has a chance to create a society to match its scenery" (Stegner 1997). In the county with the widest disparity in wealth in the country and some of the most acute regional impacts from development policies, there is nevertheless reason for hope. But hope starts with a clear acknowledgment of the problems and implications of land use decisions. One of the core problems that must be acknowledged is that externalizing costs to poorer neighboring communities is not an answer.

This is a call for Teton County, the town of Jackson, and state and federal agencies, as well as communities throughout the West, to adopt a new approach to community development based on the premise that growth should not be viewed as inevitable. Pressure to grow alone does not justify growth when there is little to no consideration for the consequences for wildlife, ecosystems, water quality, the community, and neighboring communities. There are indeed limits if we want to protect and sustain what matters in the Tetons and Greater Yellowstone—and the American West.

9

Room to Grow but Growth for Whom?
Balancing Change and Priorities in Bozeman

KRISTAL JONES

Things are happening in Southwest Montana. This has created a new happy hour conversation for locals in Bozeman: Has the region reached a tipping point that requires different management and planning to keep things from changing too much? Which features are changing for the worse (common answers: traffic, encroachment on wildlife corridors, a second high school and subsequent impacts on high school sports), and which for the better (Whole Foods, music venues, direct flights to more destinations)? Ultimately, the question being discussed is, How many visions of Bozeman, the Gallatin Valley, and Southwest Montana can coexist in policy, planning, and community engagement?

The West is defined by a distinct set of social and ecological conditions that have driven waves of in-migration and economic booms over the past two centuries, and the culture and identity of communities have evolved apace (Jones et al. 2019). Many small towns in Southwest Montana were mining hot spots and booming regional hubs in the early 1900s but saw a major decline in economic and social activity with changing global economic patterns. Bozeman started as a fort and as an outpost for European settlers seeking resources and power over lands that had supported Native people for hundreds of years. Over time, the trading posts became less relevant than the railroad tracks, and the key resource of the Gallatin Valley—prime agricultural soils and relatively abundant water—created an economic base that was steadier than other forms of natural resource extraction.

The community identity of Bozeman coevolved alongside economic growth, a distinct mix of influences from land-grant university faculty, and the surrounding ranchers and potato farmers. The growth of the recreation economy across the West since the 1970s added another influence and layer to the social fabric of the region. A 1993 headline from the *New York Times* summed it up well: Bozeman, "Montana's Cow Town with Charm" (O'Brian 1993).

For Bozeman and places like it, the evolution from Old West (with a focus on natural resource extraction economies and relatively modest incomes) to New

West (with an emphasis on recreation, amenities, and a services economy) has until recently moved slowly enough for local identities and policies to keep pace. The changes in the Gallatin Valley over the past three years, however, have felt to many residents like they have happened overnight and with an intensity unable to be managed or directed in ways that meet community needs. Underlying the casual and consistent happy hour conversations about what is happening to our town, from high rents to staffing challenges and more, is the feeling that Bozeman is no longer the same small community it once was. The implications and impacts—for old-timers, recent transplants, and the waters and animals of the region—of what feel like unpredictable outside forces are a constant topic of conversation, and not just because people like to grouse. The community is seeking to understand itself as a first step toward identifying solutions. Is Bozeman experiencing a boom, like many other places in the West have experienced many times before? If so, how can we avoid a bust or at least soften the blow when it comes? Looked at a different way, responding to the questions of what creates community character and how many visions for a place can coexist requires something other than vigilance against worst-case outcomes. It requires a creative reimagining of how to maintain the character of place and community that have drawn waves of people here.

Once a Mountain Town, Always a Mountain Town?

Bozeman, as the central node in the social and economic landscape of Southwest Montana, has a complicated identity. It has been a paradise for dirtbaggers, with a ball named in their honor. Bozeman is also a regional hub, with the only hospital in a several-county radius, Montana's land-grant university that draws young people from around the state, and the largest commercial airport in the region. Agriculture, an important economic anchor for Southwest Montana, continues to be a significant economic driver in Gallatin County.

Jobs in education, health care, and, more recently, information technologies are prevalent here. And of course, there is the service sector. There has always been a tourist season, with the need for service providers to work in retail, as guides, waiting tables, cooking meals, and changing hotel linens. In Bozeman, there have always been people more than willing to jump gigs from season to season in order to support their ski/bike/kayak/climbing habit and to make it work despite financial challenges so they can live and recreate in Southwest Montana.

The towns of Livingston and Ennis are similar. Hemingway jump-started the Livingston literary scene almost a hundred years ago, and Ted Turner has been a large landowner in the Madison Valley around Ennis since the late 1980s. However, these celebrity sightings were noteworthy because they were the exception to the rule. Outside of the tourist economy, much of the region's income came from agriculture until Hollywood money began to flow to Montana as '90s stars bought ranches and came to play cowboy. The draw of Montana reflects the myth of the Old West—it is remote, different, wild, and untouched. Twenty years ago, those with money who came here to buy land seemed almost embarrassed about it: I returned Michael Keaton his skis after a tune-up at the local ski shop where I worked in the early 2000s, and it wasn't until he handed me his credit card that I realized it was Batman under the ball cap and sunglasses.

All this is to say that Southwest Montana has for a long time had local cachet, some privilege, and more economic resources than many parts of the Northern Rockies. However, until recently, Bozeman and similar places felt like well-kept secrets, small towns that provided big rewards in terms of access to beautiful and wild places if you could make it work financially to live here. The Gallatin and Paradise Valleys had a cosmopolitanism that was quiet and crunchy, not flashy and dominant, and the negative trickle-down impacts on locals weren't experienced in most of the fundamental parts of daily life.

After all, who among those who migrated here in the 1970s and 1980s, from either ranches in the surrounding areas or middle-class places around the country, was looking for opulence and private river access? As people came to the Bozeman area over the past several decades, the town's self-identity evolved into being a respectable mountain town with a strong environmental ethos as well as a proud agricultural history and a commitment to small-town ideals that owe more to Midwest communalism than Western independence. A professional job's salary was enough to buy a house in town, and additional success or willingness to plow your own driveway meant that you could buy a few acres within twenty minutes of town on one side of the Gallatin Valley or another. Rent was affordable with a job or two that still left time for plenty of fun, and competition for housing didn't inspire frantic and heartfelt letter-writing explaining why you should get that garage apartment that doesn't allow pets for $2,000/month.

Since the start of the pandemic, more people have moved from cities to small towns to take advantage of remote work opportunities, and as a result of several coinciding trends, Bozeman has been experiencing a new wave of growth. In the past, Ted Turner was an anomaly as a large landowner in the region who bought with no prior history. Now there is plenty of money in the hands of a few nonlocals to buy vast areas of ranchland in Paradise Valley. It's also worth noting that a significant portion of that land has been put in conservation easements, where it is protected from development in perpetuity, which highlights the ambiguous impacts of economic resources in the region. Similarly, owning a condo at Big Sky used to be the height of privilege. Now the Yellowstone Club and other luxury resorts in the Gallatin Canyon have re-created a complex ecosystem in which people wait with bated breath to see if Justin Timberlake will make an appearance at a party composed of C-list celebrities.

What does this mean for formerly workaday towns like Bozeman? What does the influx of extreme wealth mean for the rest of us and for the region? There are some trickle-down impacts that are quite material: prices of day-to-day goods and services have gone up, and it's hard to find service workers if a business can't pay top dollar. The impact on prices for all types of housing and thus on sprawl and the broader ecosystem are more complicated.

Bozeman as a Boomtown

Bozeman has always been an affluent community, and in the past decade, it has pulled away from the state and national medians in terms of income. But something new has happened since 2018—Bozeman has become a boomtown in the classic sense of the word (Little 1976). The resources are space, natural beauty, and (during the COVID-19 pandemic) libertarian values that played faster and looser with public health mandates than many parts of the country. The influx of people and financial resources made Bozeman a more affluent community.

This has had an outsized impact on housing prices. The median value of owner-occupied units in Gallatin County increased by 30 percent from 2018 to 2021, while the median household income increased by just under 10 percent (all data adjusted to 2021 dollars; "Table H-8: Median Household Income by State" and "Table B25097: Mortgage Status by Median Value" in U.S. Census Bureau 2010–21).

The boom has destabilized the region in ways that both amplify past trends and are qualitatively different. Until the past five years, Bozeman was affluent but not exclusive. There are lots of middle-class people here—two-income households that can make it work because they bought real estate before 2019. Of course, there are always lots of renters in places like Bozeman, and similarly, they could make it work, even if rent was higher than national averages and landlords held a lot of power. However, the increases in home values, purchase prices, and rent over the past three years have shifted the housing balance, and if you stay at happy hour for a second drink, you'll get discourses on theories as to why.

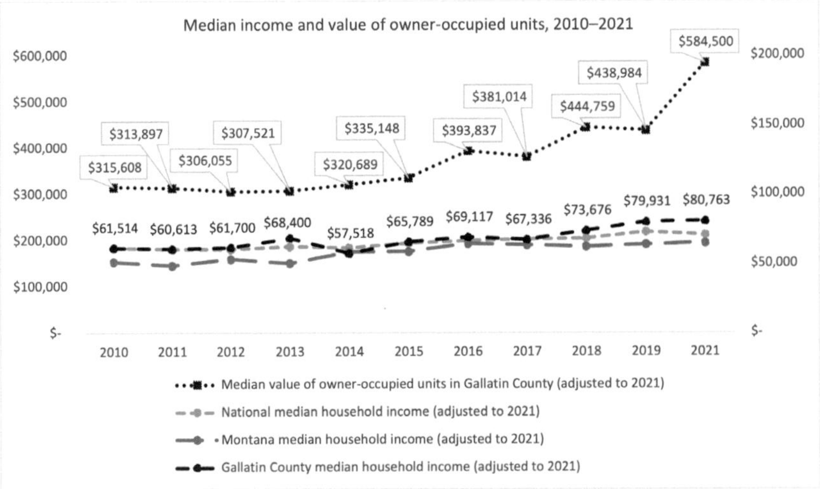

Figure 9.1 Trends in median household income and value of owner-occupied units in Gallatin County, 2010–21. Data source: "Table H-8: Median Household Income by State" and "Table B25097: Mortgage Status by Median Value" in U.S. Census Bureau 2010–21.

First, there are too many short-term rentals catering to visitors and remote workers, which means that there are fewer rental units for long-term local renters and fewer units on the market for owner-occupied purchases. Second, there are just too many people moving to the Gallatin Valley, and building and infill haven't kept pace. Worse, some of these people are second-home owners, who take housing stock off the market for locals and leave it empty much of the year. Third, and somewhat intertwined with the first two explanations, is the possibility that investment in real estate that drives up prices and supercharges further exurban development is coming not from newbies to the region who want to live here full- or part-time but from financial firms that see real estate in Bozeman as a source of wealth and a solid economic investment.

Underlying these three theories is the idea that the confluence of growth in the short-term rental market and remote work (both supercharged, though not initiated, by COVID-19) has created a new situation that looks unfamiliar to people who have been here for a while. Interestingly, the data does not support short-term rentals as a primary driver of housing costs. In April 2019, there were an estimated 320 Airbnb listings in the Bozeman area (about 0.5 percent of the total housing stock in the county). As of April 2023, there are 451 listings, down from a high of 568 in January of the same year (All the Rooms 2023). While a 40 percent increase from April 2019 to April 2023 sounds significant, the overall number of short-term rentals remains a very small proportion of overall housing stock.

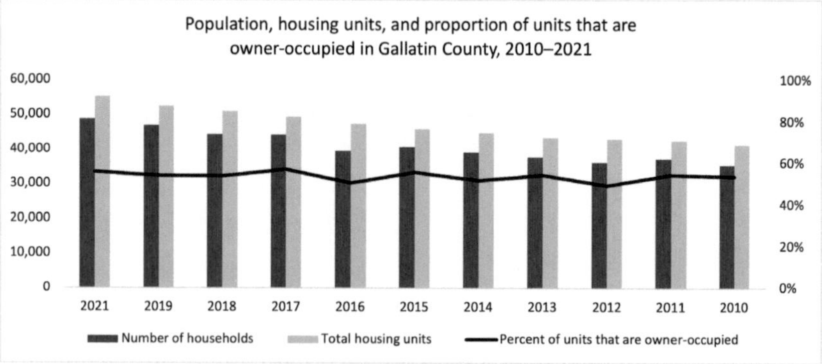

Figure 9.2 Trends in total households, total housing units, and proportion of units that are owner-occupied in Gallatin County, 2010–21. Data source: "Table CP04: Comparative Housing Characteristics" and "Table DP05: Demographic and Housing Characteristics" in U.S. Census Bureau 2010–21.

A second and possibly more impactful explanation could be the presence of largely vacant seasonal, recreational, or occasional-use housing units, which over the past several years have been estimated at about three thousand units or around 5–6 percent of the county's total housing stock. However, overall housing stock has largely stayed steady with population growth in Gallatin County over the past decade, and the proportion of units that are owner-occupied has hovered right around 50 percent during that time period (the national average is about 65 percent; "Table CP04: Comparative Housing Characteristics" and "Table DP05: Demographic and Housing Characteristics" in U.S. Census Bureau 2010–21).

The numbers suggest that the impact of money that originates from and flows back to individuals with no stake in the local community does not seem to be an adequate explanation for high housing prices and associated goods and services (see figure 9.2). The overall housing stock seems to be consistent with population growth, and it does not appear that the purchase of housing units for short-term rentals has greatly displaced homeowners, though it undoubtedly has an outsized and nontrivial impact on renters in the region. At the same time, the wealth that is driving up real estate prices does seem to be coming largely from outside the county, since median household incomes have not increased at anywhere near the rate of home valuations (see figure 9.1). The day-to-day experience for many people in the region, as well as some excellent journalists' writing, seems to support the idea that Bozeman and Southwest Montana are experiencing the impacts of speculation, just as the West was impacted by waves of natural resource speculation in the past (Bullington 2023).

Real estate speculation in high-amenity communities can be considered what political economists call extractive capitalism, in which the economic value of natural resources flows away from their local source to concentrate in the bank accounts of investors or firms based far afield. Boomtowns used to be based on lodes of gold and silver, with resources from outside the region providing capital to drive local economic growth but also to extract even more value, creating profits that did not stay in the community. Bozeman and places like it could be experiencing real estate speculation based on the natural amenities of the place—beauty, recreational access, open space—the mythos of the West.

At first glance, amenity appreciation is not extractive because it does not remove the resource and export its value elsewhere. It might even lead to preserving open space and wildlife habitat, if large landowners value those resources. However, if the attraction of communities like Bozeman is their proximity to wildlands and their quaint small-town character, then the boom increases the population and development pressures to the degree that the resource is diminished. And as with other extractive economies, if a real estate bubble bursts, then developed land cannot be quickly returned to a natural state. Once they are built, homesites remain on the landscape. Unlike modern mining regulations, there is no requirement that developers mitigate long-term damage once the built structures are no longer profitable.

While it is tempting to point fingers toward pressures that originate outside the region, Westerners should also reflect on their own role laying some of the groundwork for the challenges now being experienced in terms of housing availability and accessibility. In Bozeman over the last twenty years, there has been a general trend—not uncommon in other college towns and desirable micropolitan areas across the country—toward managed growth that prioritizes single-family homes, discourages density and diversity in housing types, and tries to balance the generally liberal values of maintaining affordability while limiting sprawl. The latter is especially salient in Bozeman and Livingston, as awareness of the ecological role that the Gallatin and Paradise Valleys play in the Greater Yellowstone Ecosystem has increased and, with it, the tension between clustering development near the urban cores and the private property rights of county residents to subdivide as they wish.

At the same time, Bozeman and much of Southwest Montana have experienced pressures that have come from a time of general economic growth and wealth consolidation in the United States. More people have larger amounts of disposable income, and much of that income has been generated through intergenerational transfer or professional incomes from firms based on the coasts. Increased national wealth has expanded air travel, and suddenly the Bozeman airport looks like a viable option for getting to an unexpected meeting in Seattle or San Francisco (or even, at certain times of year, New York City) on a direct flight. Some of this increased disposable income, mobility, and interest in outdoor recreation has driven economic growth for Montana, which as of 2021, ranks second only to Hawaii in the proportion of state GDP attributable to the outdoor recreation economy (Headwaters Economics 2023).

It seems most likely that all these explanations are a part of the story of why Bozeman has been experiencing an inequitable and increasingly exclusive boom over the past five years. There has not been enough data collected nor time passed to really understand what is driving the increase in housing prices, platted subdivisions, and rental rates. Overall national economic growth and consolidation of wealth, alongside a desire among those who hold that wealth to decamp from cities to small amenity economies, is certainly a part of the story. Zoning regulations, development policy, and a general orientation toward maintaining a certain version of small-town growth patterns have not helped the situation.

The question facing Bozeman now is how to proactively address the equity implications of a boom, which could look like an economic or housing market bust due to degradation of the natural resource base that makes this place desirable. Busts are hard on people, of course, and in the case of Bozeman and the surrounding areas, a bust could mean that those natural amenities that are no doubt driving these economic changes have been "loved to death." This is not only bad for people and the economy but would likely mean the destruction of a remarkable and irreplaceable ecosystem (Smith 2023). An equally important aspect of the current boom in the Gallatin Valley and places like it, whatever the drivers, is the increasing exclusivity that is pushing out renters, young people, farmers, county employees, and many others whose livelihoods and priorities are still based in the local community.

Room to the West (and in Your Backyard)

Bozeman is not Jackson or Aspen—not hemmed in by public land or multimillion-dollar private landowners. Bozeman is not Telluride, hemmed in by geography. Bozeman is not Boulder or Logan, proximate to major metropolitan areas. Bozeman is by all measures still a relatively small town in a fairly remote location, situated in an exceptional ecosystem. The combination of a history of natural resource and agricultural economies with a university and a recreation economy means that there has been economic growth and inequality but not extreme exclusivity like some other places. And the topography and land ownership patterns mean that there is room to grow.

But Bozeman and some other places across the country—Whitefish and Boise but also Asheville—have over the past few years experienced an increasing disconnect related to housing. Prices far exceed what local wages and median household incomes can sustain. The current housing crisis spirals out into development questions that don't have win-win answers—how to balance growth, conservation, entitlement, diversification, and equity.

The narrative in many amenity destinations in the New West is about the replacement of old-timers and worry over exclusion and inequality. But in many places that have not yet butted up against natural barriers or long-standing property ownership regimes that limit further growth, there is also a narrative about community, culture, and who and what belongs in this backyard. In the Gallatin and Paradise Valleys, where there is still room to grow (for Bozeman, growth can and will happen primarily to the west of the urban core), there is an opportunity to do something about the hand-wringing concerns related to how to manage the real estate and tourism booms and how to ensure that there is not a burst bubble in the near future. These concerns are for both the human and nonhuman communities that call Southwest Montana home, and the dynamics of balancing the needs and priorities of each are currently heightened but not necessarily new.

Bozeman is uniquely positioned at one end of the Greater Yellowstone Ecosystem and in the middle of the Rocky Mountain chain. With that location comes opportunities for growth, economic opportunity, desirability, and questions about community character, responsibility, inclusion, local control, public lands, and wildlife. The Gallatin Crest wilderness debate is one example where the bureaucratic process that is updating a national forest management plan became a source of great vitriol on all sides over the past five years. The Gallatin Forest Partnership submitted pragmatic proposals to protect large chunks of the Gallatin Wilderness Study Area, but the conservation professionals who expressed support for a compromise position were met with threats of personal violence (Belote 2019). Their opponents called for more science to better understand potential impacts to wildlife and the ecosystem, dismissing the evidence that supported a compromise position because it did not go far enough. In effect, opponents of compromise applied a purity test, where expressing pragmatism and a willingness to negotiate disqualified a proposal. To them, insisting on Wilderness with a capital *W* was the only way to stay true to the conservation mission.

The same calls for science and evidence are less present in local conversations about urban development and land use planning. Infill, upzoning, and density are all development approaches and techniques that studies by researchers and professionals in planning, architecture, and sociology have shown can reliably improve the environmental impact of urban development. These innovative approaches to development policy are evidence based and have been shown to encourage land-sparing (concentrating development in smaller areas to maintain more open space) and lack of conversion of land from open space or agriculture to subdivided development. Done well, innovative planning and zoning can also support a diverse and accessible community core.

However, many of the same types of voices that seek purity in management of the regional ecosystem have pushed back on changing development patterns within Bozeman. The concern is that there is a mismatch between infill and the less dense character of existing neighborhoods. The neighborhoods on both sides of Bozeman's Main Street, for example, are largely single-family homes and a few small, two-story apartment buildings. In the few transition blocks between Main Street and the neighborhoods, light industrial lots are being turned into ten-story apartment buildings, and these developments have generated considerable pushback related to infill, with some local community leaders calling for a full moratorium on any new development in the city limits until stricter zoning requirements can be enacted.

Smaller infill opportunities have seemingly been met with less pushback, but the calls for development moratoriums and changes in zoning sometimes include dislike of accessory dwelling units and similar approaches to creative use of small spaces in the urban core. The critiques levied by opponents to all these kinds of projects include the way that they change the community character, while others quibble with the expensive price tags of shiny new apartment units. At the same time, a lack of incentives and some state-level regulatory changes limit the ability of local government to ensure that some number of units in new developments are priced affordably. Thus a confluence of influences from across the political spectrum converges to keep innovative and equitable development from taking hold.

The BridgerView development in Bozeman is trying a different approach to addressing the affordability question. It is using the sale of full-price homes to subsidize those sold at an affordable price. The goal is to support professionals who live and work in Bozeman, and there are strict requirements about the proportion of income that comes from a local job, as well as income limits. However, what counts as affordable for BridgerView is not in line with what most people assume. When a single woman with a graduate degree earning 10 percent more than the median household income applied for a mortgage for a one-bedroom home, she found that she needed more than a 20 percent down payment—amounting to $60,000 in cash—to make the math work. When she brought her case to the housing land trust, they suggested she ask her family for resources, which is not an option for her or most people. The idea of affordable housing is that access to housing should not depend on the inheritance of generational wealth. The suggestion to ask for family money underscores some of the assumptions about who lives in Bozeman and highlights the multifaceted challenges of affordability and equity.

How Western Myths Can Support Contemporary Adaptation

The Old West economy was heavily reliant on natural resource extraction. To a certain extent, this reliance created limits to the population growth that was possible on the landscape. The New West is also limited by the natural resource base, since recreation destinations are valued to the extent that they are not used by too many people. Undiscovered destinations have extra cachet. When a trail or river gets too crowded, its appeal goes down, and so does some of the tourism revenue and demand for real estate.

One explanation for the recent and confusing changes happening around Bozeman and across Southwest Montana, and in similar communities across the West, is that economic growth and influx of resources are not tightly connected to the natural resource base of the region. When the carrying capacity of the land, in terms of the natural resources that can drive local economic activity, is decoupled from economic growth and overall development patterns, the trends can go haywire. Remote work, real estate speculation, a moment of intergenerational wealth transfer—there are many explanations for how so many people can afford to own housing in Bozeman even as prices skyrocket.

Whatever the combination of forces, there seems to be an implicit understanding across the political spectrum that something predatory is going on. When viewed from the left, greedy landlords and laws that protect the default assumption that single-family-home ownership is the preferred development pattern get blamed. When viewed from the right, the environmentalist identity of New West residents and the apparent elitism of the "Cosmopolitan West," exemplified by the creation of tenants' rights organizations in Bozeman and Missoula, are seen as supplanting the individualism and respect for private property rights that have long defined the region. Consistent across many diverse perspectives, however, is a desire to maintain a certain community character that has defined the West since European settlement. That character involves a balance of independence, embeddedness in the natural environment, and the ability to simply move on (usually, farther west) if the place gets too crowded. But these traits are increasingly at odds with our understanding of how the human and nonhuman ecosystems are interconnected and how they are affected by broader social and economic structures.

One source of the desire to maintain balance is a conception of the natural world as independent of human impacts and, ideally, devoid of humans. People across the political and social spectrum see that the Greater Yellowstone Ecosystem is a unique resource and landscape to be conserved. Wildlife of all sizes rely on the overall lack of development in the region to feed, breed, and migrate. The headwaters of the Missouri and the longest undammed river in the Lower 48 (the Yellowstone) define much of the Southwest Montana landscape. Maintaining these and other natural resources requires compromise and creativity, as well as both policy sticks and carrots at all levels of governance.

There are countless examples of collaborative conservation in the region, from the Big Hole Watershed Council, which forges agreements between irrigators and recreationalists about minimum water flows and river closures, to the Gallatin Valley Land Trust's work with legacy landowners and wealthy newcomers to protect open space, even when it has already been subdivided on paper. In many of these approaches to collaborative conservation, there is an alignment of old, new, and cosmopolitan values that provide a starting point for envisioning a future for the region.

The Old West offered residents space, freedom, and the ability to be away from the constraints of densely populated cities in a place where they could live off the land. The New West prefers keeping natural resources in the ground and on the landscape, but we continue to value the space and freedom integral to the nickname "Big Sky Country." Some of the tensions surrounding the management of natural resources are inherent in the conversation about what is causing the current exclusivity of Southwest Montana. However, limiting sprawl and ranchette subdivisions will only increase exclusivity if there are not creative approaches to creating other types and locations of housing.

Interestingly, many of the newcomers from the coasts who have income and the ability to afford a diversity of housing options might actually prefer those that prioritize density and walkability. Infill, midrise apartment buildings, and the establishment of small commercial cores throughout the Bozeman city limits could make Bozeman more inclusive and economically diverse. But these planning priorities will change the character of the place yet again, toward a more Cosmopolitan West that embraces some lessons learned from other parts of the country.

One of the limitations of the popular understanding of the boom-bust cycle is the idea that growth and impact happen sequentially and in linear fashion. In fact, while real estate and tourism boom in Southwest Montana, many people are right now experiencing the downsides. Rather than waiting to deal with the consequences once interest moves on or we love the place to death, the resources and momentum that are driving this boom can be channeled to mitigate and redirect some of the potential negative impacts. Policy mechanisms like local option sales tax (not currently allowed by Montana state law) and resort taxes (allowable only for small communities that meet specific resort-related requirements) could redirect some of the wealth that is enabling the boom into investments in community services and infrastructure. Local limitations on short-term rentals have the potential to positively impact the challenges faced by renters—especially young people and older people on fixed incomes—by decreasing competition with tourists for rental units. Conservation easements can ensure minimal human pressure on the open space that undergirds ecosystem function and a strong regional economy.

These formal tools will need to be coupled, however, with hard and honest community conversations about the limits to growth and visions for the culture and character of the region. Here the myths of the West—old, new, or cosmopolitan—might max out their ability to describe the future. The myth of independence has always been mostly a myth, and Southwest Montana, along with many other places in the West, must grapple with both the opportunities and challenges inherent in recognizing how interdependent the social and natural ecosystems in this place are with resources, pressures, and structures that operate around and beyond the region.

Further, community development planning is an ongoing, adaptive process and is equal parts zoning regulation and taxes, and honest conversations about the human and environmental impacts of those decisions. Community character, including who feels able and welcome to live here, will be shaped by decisions to adapt or retrench, and the independence that is a through-line for all permutations of the Western mythology can create opportunities for innovative change and tough decisions.

10

Tourism and Turmoil Challenge Sedona's Future

JENNIFER WESSELHOFF

Red Rock Country will always be beautiful. But the emotions surrounding the politics of tourism in Sedona turned red-hot years ago. The community is inching toward integrating a tourism-based economy with its beloved small-town quality of life, but City Council meetings can still turn tense when tourism comes up. Community conversations then turn to finger-pointing over heavy traffic, trash, trail congestion, ATV noise and dust, and in the case of those living near trailheads, people pooping on their property.

The impact of three and a half million annual visitors on a town of fewer than ten thousand residents permeates everyday life. Driving to the supermarket at peak times means fighting traffic and long checkout lines. Scoring a reservation at a favorite restaurant feels like winning the lottery. More concerning is the fact that Sedona's population is shrinking as the lure of tourism-generated revenue causes more people to move out and convert their property to short-term rentals (STRs). In addition, skyrocketing home prices mean that aside from the often retired well-to-do, potential newcomers can't afford the limited available housing.

Sedona Dissonance: Needing and Hating Tourism

Anti-tourism sentiment is an issue with a human heart. It is wistfulness for the past, a desire to "hairspray" the town—that is, to keep it set as it was the day you moved in. Sedona is experiencing this phenomenon on steroids. Most residents moved from elsewhere and are invested, financially and psychologically, in the town as it was: semi-rural and isolated yet with world-class amenities, surrounded by the majesty of the red rocks that make you feel small and mighty at the same time. Why would anyone want to change that? The attendant rise in property values is good if you are a homeowner, but many ask, Is the cost too high?

The emergence of short-term rentals booked via the internet crystallizes the issue. In 2022, the Sedona area had over 3,500 available STR rooms, a number that exceeded hotel room inventory for the first time. Neighborhoods sometimes feel besieged by a revolving door of weekend vacationers who park on the street, party loudly, create more trash than the average homeowner, and make people feel like strangers on their own block. The STR tornado has also sucked in long-term rentals formerly available to working residents, exacerbating the housing crisis and the population decline—not the kind of vortex for which Sedona wants to be known.

The city has responded with a twenty-four-hour complaint hotline, a licensing requirement, and incentives for STR owners to rent to long-term residents (City of Sedona 2023). These are helpful steps but insufficient to stem the powerful profit potential stirring landlords, homeowners, and out-of-town investors.

Discomfited Sedonans are rebels with a cause. Their target: tourism. In Sedona's 2018 "home rule" election, anti-tourism residents focused on the Sedona Chamber of Commerce & Tourism Bureau (the Chamber), blaming it for all tourism-related woes. They personalized their attacks—accusing the Chamber of lying, creating Facebook memes comparing Chamber leaders to Hitler, and showing the CEO (me) running over residents with a motorcoach. Their efforts to eliminate the Chamber's destination management contract with the city failed but garnered almost 34 percent of the vote. The election brought long-simmering anti-tourism sentiment into full view.

The subsequent Sustainable Tourism Plan process included public meetings and surveys that showed that a majority of Sedonans wanted balanced tourism management (Arizona State University 2023). They wanted a plan that acknowledges tourism's importance to families and livelihoods while protecting the city's small-town lifestyle and environmental heritage. There was also a well-organized "no tourism, no compromise" contingent, marshaled mainly by retirees and others with no direct connection to tourism. These opposing forces have kept anti-tourism on the front burner as Sedona's most politically volatile issue.

The conflict underlines residents' existential angst. Many Sedonans believe their "discovery" of Red Rock Country, which they naturally personalize, is slipping away, triggering a feeling between anger and panic. They protest new development, create angry social media campaigns, and strive to elect anti-development, anti-tourism candidates. For example, an environmentally sensitive and landscaped parking garage that would take hundreds of vehicles off Sedona's insufficient main-drag parking lots has been in limbo for years due to opposition from anxious neighbors. Resistance to such planning—where NIMBYism meets sentiment—is overtaking many Southwestern destinations grappling with similar issues.

In the postpandemic rush to outdoor spaces, Sedona has seen government policymakers look two ways at once. Since 2021, the City Council has refused to approve budgets marketing Sedona as a sustainable destination that expects visitors to adopt responsible behaviors while at the same time approving tourism programs advancing the state's first Sustainable Tourism Plan, which includes marketing Sedona as just such a place. Changes in political and Chamber leadership have added to the lack of direction, as one step forward and two steps back has become a common Sedona dance.

In April 2023, a dramatic new chapter in Sedona's tourism history dawned when it became clear the City Council planned to extend its "pause" on marketing budgets indefinitely, despite the impact on Sedona businesses and families. In response, the Chamber's board of directors voted unanimously to end its twenty-year tourism contract with the city, opting to explore private regional partnerships, a nonpolitical management structure, and new funding sources for marketing and other costs (Graham 2023). Since then, the Chamber has solicited funds from members for tourism promotion and begun exploring the idea of a tourism improvement district. Meanwhile the City of Sedona has formed a tourism advisory board and taken tourism marketing and management "in house" (Perry 2023).

The Search for Stability

As the twenty-first century dawned, Sedona was whipsawed by seasonal tourism. Spring and autumn, the most climatically congenial times of the year, were busy if not fast growing. However, businesses starved through the cooler winter months and again in the heat of summer. Sedona needed a year-round tourism economy providing a steady stream of customers and reliable full-time jobs.

Arizona is the forty-eighth state, admitted in 1912, and Sedona, like many rural Arizona locales, is a fairly new municipality, incorporated in 1988. The first City Council levied 3 percent sales and bed taxes to support city services. That same year, a new state law required that city-levied bed taxes (considered a discriminatory tax) be used to support tourism marketing and promotion. However, Sedona's bed tax was grandfathered; the city was not required to use it for tourism. Instead, bed taxes go into Sedona's general operating fund.

Back then, the business community viewed tourism as the future for this rural ranching town and lobbied to use the bed tax as seed money for tourism development via a city partnership with the Chamber. At the time, the Chamber already had a thirty-year history of tourism promotion and was (and still is) the region's only certified destination management organization (DMO). But it took until the early 2000s for the City of Sedona to match Chamber members' tourism promotion contributions and give birth to a formal City-Chamber tourism partnership.

This partnership led to a decades-long boom in tourism. The Chamber's work widened to include attracting corporate groups, small meetings, conferences, weddings, and international tour business while expanding its once-modest visitor center to handle as many as three thousand daily guests. Today, volunteers welcome throngs of first-time visitors dazzled by their first glimpse of Red Rock Country. They explain Leave No Trace principles, hand out trail guides, offer directions, suggest dining and lodging venues, run water bottle refill stations, and more. By 2019, tourism had become a billion-dollar-annual industry tied to ten thousand local jobs—the area's dominant economic linchpin.

As tax revenues and visitation increased, so did the demand for infrastructure and city services. Not being legally obligated to use bed tax revenues for tourism promotion, the city began easing off tourism contributions and spending bed tax dollars elsewhere. The lodging industry responded in 2017, proposing an increase in their bed tax burden with the proviso that at least 55 percent of the total tax collected promotes tourism, administered by the Chamber. The Council agreed. For a few years, as tax revenues set records and the Chamber led a community drive that resulted in the Sustainable Tourism Plan (Eland 2023), the Council's and the Chamber's visions aligned.

But as tourism increased, so did traffic congestion. Anti-tourism sentiment rose, and in 2020, the City Council eliminated the 55 percent agreement and adopted an essentially zero-based budgeting process. This change put the City Council firmly in charge of tourism management funding—adjusting the budget up or down by consensus rather than statute. This placed the Chamber in the position of seeking Council support for each product development, marketing, and tourism management strategy. Changing the rules had decisive effects. The Council's decision to withhold funds for destination marketing, for example, shut Sedona out of the major markets of Chicago, New York, and Southern California. By taking direct control, local elected officials became Sedona's tourism managers, changing the balance of a twenty-year tourism partnership that produces 75 percent of the city's operating budget and obviates the need for a city property tax.

The immediate post-COVID-19 era unleashed a tsunami of domestic travel to outdoorsy destinations such as Sedona, where fresh air and wide-open spaces are the raison d'être for travel. The explosive growth of metro Phoenix, whose northern fringes are just ninety minutes from Sedona, fed a steady stream of day-trippers into Red Rock Country as Sedona joined other smaller destinations overwhelmed by jammed roads and trails, trash, off-highway vehicle use, and packed restaurants. Ending strategic marketing to out-of-state visitors who stay longer and spend more did not diminish overtourism problems. Instead, the flood of day-trippers seemed like a biblical plague to many locals. Since most visitors drove home to Phoenix in the evening, hotels struggled to achieve pre-COVID-19 occupancy rates (though the average price for a hotel room rose significantly).

By 2023, high gas prices, inflation, and an economically uncertain future had diminished visitation. Tax revenues were in decline, and local businesses were vocal that a return to sustainability-focused out-of-state marketing was critical to their survival. But successive Councils remained determined to withhold advertising, settling for reaching out to arriving visitors about sustainable behavior. In an atmosphere where Chamber tourism managers and the Council spoke past one another, the Chamber board opted to detach from the city's financial control and direction.

As I left Sedona for Park City, Utah, in 2020, I felt frustrated that attainable consensus was eluding us. Sedona can meet tourism's challenges with creativity and common sense, as evidenced by the 2019 Sustainable Tourism Plan. But patience and trust were eroded in an emotionally laden atmosphere of crisis. The City Council sided with the anti-tourism voting bloc over tourism management. As a consequence, "unmanaged tourism" has resulted in more unsolicited day-trip traffic from Phoenix, while Sedona's absence from out-of-state markets has cut off opportunities to attract overnight visitors who value sustainability.

Sedona's Challenge May Sound Familiar

The Airbnb and Vrbo revolution has transformed travel for millions, complicating tourism management in Sedona and most semi-rural, outdoorsy destinations around the Mountain West. Despite its unique aspects, Sedona's experience carries lessons for all.

The explosion of short-term rentals (STRs) in Sedona is fueled in part by the Arizona legislature's refusal to allow municipalities to ban or limit the number of

STRs in their jurisdiction. For Phoenix-area residents who live so close to Sedona, the expanding number of Sedona STRs makes a quick Red Rock visit more accessible. Meanwhile, the vast Phoenix market and enormous profit potential have moved STRs to the center of the Sedona housing and lodging picture.

Close to 15 percent of Sedona's residential housing is short-term rentals, distorting the local lodging industry and severely curtailing long-term rental availability for residents. In addition, the early STR model of mom and pop renting out a room or a second home is giving way to corporations buying homes as full-time STRs, often at above-market prices, which tears at the fabric of neighborhoods.

The STR regulatory restraints placed on local governments preclude Sedona from determining where and how much of this new type of commercial lodging it will allow. Cities traditionally consider land management law, infrastructure availability, and community benefit when zoning for the appropriate number of lodging units. They establish parking, lighting, security, and other requirements. But in Arizona, short-term rental houses are immune from such regulation.

The impact of short-term rentals cannot be overstated. It has changed tourism and communities—and not for the better. Ironically, many residents who once benefited from renting out space to visitors now feel besieged by noise, trash, and traffic as house after house becomes full-time, whole-property short-term rentals. It is painful to lose connection to the place you call home, one of the underappreciated consequences of the STR phenomenon.

Around the West, no community has found a one-size-fits-all solution. How much regulatory control municipalities can exercise varies by state, and each community has different ideas about the applicability of zoning ordinances and municipal inspection powers. A survey of fifteen Western cities with a strong tourism base—from Salem, Oregon, to Bozeman, Montana, to Scottsdale, Arizona—shows only four require inspection of a permitted STR property, and just five of these fifteen cities have a geographic limit on where STRs can operate (National League of Cities 2023, vi). A rule setting the maximum stay at thirty days is common but not ubiquitous. Some cities permit only the property owner to serve as host, while others permit tenants in rental units to, in effect, sublease temporarily to a visitor. In California, where government powers are more far-reaching, San Diego (Nikolewski 2022) limits STRs to just 1 percent of total housing stock—a solution more complex than it sounds.

STR effects are broad and varied. In Sedona, for example, many residents leave when they convert or sell their homes as STRs, but the phenomenon is different in Park City. There, 70 percent of all homes are occupied less than two months a year, and so a great deal of housing stock sits empty much of the time. If the wave of STRs continues, Park City could see its population (and visitation) explode quickly, much as it did during the COVID-19 years. For Parkites, the questions are, How do we address the possibility that most of our housing could eventually become STRs, and how do we maintain a sense of community responsibility with the many homeowners who are mostly absent? And how do we balance these issues with an owner's property rights?

Issues beyond Short-Term Rentals

Each Western destination faces unique challenges. When it comes to public use versus preservation, for example, Sedona must reckon with the fact that Red Rock Country is almost entirely within the Coconino National Forest. Thus it is beyond municipal control and is made available to all by the mandate of the U.S. Forest Service. In March 2022, for example, the USFS declined the City Council's request to limit off-highway vehicles (OHVs) on Forest Service roads, stating it "would not be the correct management action" and that OHVs are a legitimate use of Forest Service land.

Sedona's response could be applicable anywhere. In 2021, the Chamber formed the voluntary Red Rock OHV Conservation Crew (RROCC), including more than a dozen OHV rental and guide companies that agreed to dedicate 1 percent of sales to the USFS for rider education, a commitment that could total $500,000 annually. Originating from the City of Sedona's OHV Work Group, RROCC members include the USFS, Arizona State Parks, local law enforcement, Arizona Game and Fish, and Tread Lightly, the OHV industry nonprofit promoting responsible outdoor recreation. RROCC posts volunteer ambassadors along trails to educate riders about speed, noise, and dust and to seal off trailside "donuts," where riders perform high-speed circular maneuvers that damage the land and churn up dust.

The Forest Service's foundational perspective is that national forests are open to all, including OHV users, mountain bikers and e-bikers, bird-watchers, equestrians, long-term campers, runners—literally anyone. Rangers in the West have the unenviable task of getting discordant users to live together. They have dealt with horses versus hikers, hikers versus mountain bikers, bikers versus e-bikers, and now, a conflict that pits everyone against OHVs. Famously ponderous and thorough, the Forest Service will eventually find ways to mix OHV enthusiasts with other users, whether with a permitting system, time-of-day restrictions, limited access, or another solution.

The burden of addressing "soft" quality-of-life issues such as STRs falls first on local governments, the authorities to whom small-town residents have the most direct access. However, local government, which commonly works closely with developers and business interests, often creates distrust by being insufficiently diligent in the hard work of constantly communicating with residents. An often unrecognized governmental communications flaw is failing to help residents understand private property law—that many projects, while they can be modified or ameliorated, cannot be stopped. In the absence of effective communication, residents take aim at every project that comes forth.

In 2021, the Sedona City Council decision to direct the Chamber of Commerce to cease all marketing without explicit Council approval presumed that marketing Sedona exacerbates tourism-related problems. The failure to educate visitors and set expectations is viewed by Chamber tourism managers as a missed opportunity. Although a Respect Red Rock Country theme and a partnership with Leave No Trace greet tourists as they arrive, branding Sedona as a preservation-conscious destination *before* travelers leave home could better impress upon travelers that sustainable behavior is part of the Sedona experience. It could also preferentially attract visitors who instinctively respond to the message—that is, sophisticated, responsible people eager to participate in overtourism solutions.

Tourism Challenges Local Elected Governance and Federal Management

Tourism is the new sheriff in town. The millions of people determined to visit the West (and spend billions to do it) affect every aspect of life in destination communities and national forests: traffic, culture, jobs and wages, tax revenues, emergency services, infrastructure, roads and transportation, water management, land management, air quality, and more. The increasing demand for recreation will eventually require a revision of the underlying philosophy of federal public land use, with recreation taking top priority, displacing grazing, mining, and timber. This is inevitable.

The U.S. Forest Service land use policy is likely to face irresistible demand for a comprehensive review. Reorienting land management to accommodate tourism's growth will be the greatest institutional challenge the agency has encountered, generating an internal cultural earthquake resulting in recreational management and customer service becoming job one. In addition, funding for recreational management and fire suppression, which are expensive but necessary services, will have to increase in the face of heavier public use. The process will take considerable time and may even require a generational shift in Forest Service management, which is why it should begin immediately.

There are no obvious statutory actions that could curtail record-setting visitation to smaller, remote destinations in the West. Americans will go wherever we please in exploring our continent-sized country, which begs for a holistic approach to destination marketing and management. Reactive solutions like closing an area to parking, adding garages, providing transit to trailheads, and instituting reservation systems are not long-term management solutions. Like patching a leak in an old garden hose, sealing off one hole often causes a breach elsewhere.

Marketing's Role in Achieving Sustainability

Some believe halting tourism marketing will solve overtourism. However, the Sedona City Council's marketing ban leaves the media landscape to other agendas. For example, Scottsdale continues to market Sedona as an up-and-back hours-long excursion to enhance your Scottsdale experience. In the greater Phoenix area post-COVID-19, Sedona is increasingly seen as a quick day trip for a hike, lunch, and selfie, a drive-by experience that increases traffic and environmental damage. With Sedona not telling its story of responsible recreation, arts, spirituality, and high-end resorts, the void is filled by social media selfies taken by day-trippers with little sense of Sedona's culture and environmental sensitivity. Voiceless, Sedona is vulnerable to negative portrayal by competitors as overvisited and congested.

The marketing ban is a symptom of polarization produced by Sedona's crisis atmosphere. In terms of the marketing aspect of managing overtourism, the Chamber, now independently, is seeking to change Sedona's tourist culture so that responsible users supplant careless overuse. Well-considered marketing campaigns are an essential component of managing tourism sustainably in increasingly overvisited Western mountain communities. Destination branding creates the distinctions that allow us to distinguish Arizona from Utah, for example, though they share a border, beautiful landscapes, and a recreation-based tourism economy. Persuasively communicating a place's authentic characteristics and values—in Sedona's case a commitment to the environment and small-town lifestyle while celebrating world-class amenities—helps visitors decide which places match their travel goals and personal values.

Social media's dynamism is the perfect venue for helping Sedona and destinations threatened by overtourism disperse and educate visitors. Sedona's trailhead shuttle (more below) and Sedona's Secret 7, a campaign to divert visitors to less congested but still spectacular sites, are two projects tailor-made for social media. Voluntourism, such as trash cleanups in spectacular Oak Creek Canyon, can turn someone into an Instagram or TikTok hero. These platforms can be harnessed in strategic, integrated social media campaigns rather than left solely to individual businesses, Instagrammers, and influencers. The Chamber's strategic goal—which includes promoting Sedona's stylish arts, spirituality, and wellness scenes—is not to attract more visitors. Sedona seeks fewer but "high value" travelers who stay longer and spend more.

Steeped in every tourism-related challenge that could harass a small Western destination, Sedona entered a marketing void in 2021. Reestablishing Sedona's qualities in the minds of sophisticated travelers may be challenging, time-consuming, and expensive. In a larger sense, marketing has a role in transitioning the image of the Mountain West. In recent years, our destinations have emerged as glittering playgrounds for the well-to-do—a combination of wide-open spaces and outdoor activities with first-class resorts, cuisine, arts, and culture. The next step is to show the Mountain West as a place of caring, stewardship, and sustainability and set the expectation that visitors must be ready to do their part.

For example, Park City is "Winter's Favorite Town," a brand that captures the glitter and fun of the Wasatch Back. Under that rubric, the Chamber delivers sustainability messages, furthering our image as a town aware of the balances we must achieve together (Wesselhoff 2023). Other communities, such as Mammoth Lakes, California, are doing the same (Mammoth Lakes Tourism 2023).

Creative Partnerships with the Private Sector

Businesses can function as sustainable tourism's shock troops and the face of sustainability-focused marketing. Tourism has many touchpoints: hotels, restaurants, tour companies, galleries, shops, spas, and rental companies. Visitors naturally, even subconsciously, look for cues on how to behave and what to do; businesses have tremendous influence over their choices. Businesses can translate sustainable messages into action. In Sedona, a concierge network promotes the Leave No Trace Seven Principles of responsible outdoor recreation to guests as they arrive, a message also promoted on streetlight banners and at the visitor center. The Chamber's recently created "Meet Sedona Again" campaign aims to bring the message to feeder markets like Los Angeles and Chicago, prepping visitors to receive on-the-ground advice when they arrive.

Traffic congestion, air quality, noise, and safety are typical concerns in Western destinations. When businesses and government work together, sustainable programs can be actualized. In Park City, the City Council and the Deer Valley Resort, a critical venue in defining Park City as a ski destination, showed how this can be done. Deer Valley proposed an ambitious expansion of its base area, Snow Park, which includes the construction of new underground parking, expanded transit, a hotel, new residential and commercial units, and enhanced access to Deer Valley ski lifts. Deer Valley has development rights on the location, which is primarily surface parking lots today, but requires municipal accession to vacate some public right of way, approve adjusted traffic patterns, and take possession of a Deer Valley–owned road.

The proposal was debated openly in numerous public forums for eighteen months. It met considerable opposition due to concerns about traffic, safety, and the impact on nearby residents. However, an understanding of Deer Valley's value to the community combined with a determination to find amicable solutions. This, along with consideration of the public mood, respect for one another's perspectives, and a shared vision of the community good produced agreement instead of disarray.

In December 2023, the two parties agreed to a modified expansion and to work together to maximize Snow Park's public benefits. Deer Valley agreed to reduce underground parking slots by 15–20 percent and to contribute $15 million for expanded regional transportation infrastructure and workforce housing, two essential civic needs, while the city vacated the roadway as requested (Manson 2023). Though opposition has not entirely abated, the agreement addresses public concerns, adheres to the precepts of the Park City Sustainable Tourism Plan, and permits Deer Valley to move forward—in ongoing consultation with and the approval of the Park City Planning Commission, it should be noted—with a project that will grow the local economy significantly while enhancing local quality of life with new amenities and leisure venues.

Already in Park City, transit infrastructure is sufficiently robust to support the concept of car-free ski vacations. Many resorts and hotels promote "car-free PC" as manageable and preferable. Free government-operated shuttles run from park-and-ride lots and go directly to the slopes. The shuttles are nonpolluting electric vehicles, further impressing sustainability values on visitors.

Whether subsidized or cost-recovery, hotel shuttle service can slash vehicle traffic and parking demands on small-town streets. Jackson, Wyoming, hotels offer shuttles almost as a matter of course to restaurants and shopping, dovetailing neatly with Jackson's free local bus service, provided since 1987.

The Sedona trailhead shuttle launched in 2022, ferrying hikers from two park-and-ride lots to four of the most popular Red Rock trailheads at no cost. In a model of cross-agency partnership, the city owns and operates the service (purchasing the shuttles in part with federal transit dollars), and the Forest Service encourages use by closing parking lots at two of the trailheads when the shuttle is operating. The Chamber promoted the service through its communications platforms. It was an immediate success, approaching one hundred thousand boardings in its first year. One lesson is that visitors will embrace sustainable processes when they are available and add to their convenience.

Building on the experience of cities like Sedona, Park City municipal and county governments recently recognized the Chamber-led Park City / Summit County Sustainable Tourism Plan to address overcrowding and economic inequality, preserve community character, protect the environment, and more. The plan is a North Star toward which we can constantly steer in the years ahead.

DMOs: Positioned to Lead Western Transition

Destination management organizations are well positioned to lead disparate stakeholders, including residents and visitors, in creating a shared vision for tourism's future and a concrete plan to achieve it, complete with metrics, timelines, and responsible parties. Park City and Sedona have proven the model. Such plans necessarily include a marketing framework that empowers a partner (logically, the DMO) to pursue a marketing course with the advice of the community. However, to achieve the necessary community trust, DMOs must shift their priorities from destination marketing to destination management in a way the community—including businesses—feels is appropriate.

The traditional DMO funding mechanism of a bed or transient-room tax paid by lodging industry guests has biased DMOs toward increasing visitation, tax revenues, job growth, and "heads in beds." Establishing key performance indicators (KPIs) that include quality-of-life issues such as small-town character, historic preservation, residential connectedness, and environmental impacts means taking a fresh look at who drives the process and how it is funded.

The influence of DMOs can change community perceptions of tourism and its management, enlist businesses and government, and affect visitor behavior. From the intersection of the business sector, visitors, the government, and the community, the DMO perspective can promote change through planning and diplomatic skill.

The transition to tourism management requires community support—and seeking it does not come naturally to many DMOs, since they are accustomed to increasing visitation utilizing reliable tax-based funding. Communicating, building relationships, and finding allies are among the many challenges. In Park City, for example, we reinforce our place in the community with regular communication through local media and ads that spotlight the people behind our small businesses. Programs like Community Give Back Day and initiatives like the Seasonal Workers Resource website demonstrate our responsiveness to community needs. Other destinations are looking toward sustainable tourism strategies such as off-the-beaten-path experiences that disperse visitors, promotion of longer stays to encourage engagement, efficient transportation to lessen carbon footprints, support for locally owned businesses, water and energy conservation, and ways to respect local lifestyles.

Venice and Tahiti manage tourism's impact by reducing visitation in ways the government can control, like limiting the number of cruise ships. This strategy is easier for islands or destinations only accessible by toll road. But in surveying the Mountain West, complex legal, political, and social questions arise. Determining who defines the meaning of "carrying capacity" and sustainability criteria are the most basic, assuming a community finds such a direction palatable. The full range of stakeholders—full-time residents, regular visitors, property owners who are part-time residents, day-trippers, STR owners, the lodging industry, tourism-dependent small business owners, people passionate about one form or another of recreation (and the list goes on)—must be consulted and accommodated to maintain comity. Of course, it is possible that policies that signal "only so many visitors are welcome under the following conditions" could become counterproductive. My experience tells me most destinations want tourism management that welcomes everyone while protecting, promoting, and preserving what is good and valuable about their home communities. A complex task to be sure, but smaller, semi-rural Western communities are cohesive and committed enough to undertake it.

As Western destinations define their course in the face of overtourism, destination managers will be central to community discussions about achieving more sustainable habits. DMOs should embrace this opportunity to lend their expertise in product development, tourism-related data analysis, visitor relations, and marketing for the good of all. In fact, it is hard to imagine effective action without DMOs at the fore. It goes without saying that DMOs themselves have an existential stake in the long-term viability of their communities.

Western DMOs can help blaze the trail to achieve economic balance, environmental health, and happiness in communities—places where visitors feel welcome and are ready to recreate sustainably. But this will take imagination, a unified organizational vision, a considered strategy, a willingness to lead, and the perseverance to commit to a strenuous task. Creating such a healthy, aware, and balanced outcome is a shared responsibility, from which no one—government, DMO, resident, or visitor—is exempt from doing their part.

III
PRESERVING PRIVATE AND PUBLIC LANDS

11

Wallowa County and Oregon's Half-Century Battle against Urban and Rural Sprawl

ROBERT LIBERTY

The snowy granite summits of Oregon's Wallowa Mountains rise to just under ten thousand feet. Elk, mountain goats, wolves, and even a small herd of moose live in and around the Wallowa Mountains. Wallowa Lake, cut by Pleistocene glaciers, is cradled by a rampart of moraines rising hundreds of feet from the valley floor. Brilliant green in spring, golden in summer and fall, and white with snow in the winter, the moraines are so perfect they have been used to illustrate the mechanics of glaciers in textbooks. A visitor, arriving blindfolded and then shown the grand scenery before her, might exclaim, "I love Montana!"

The mountains and lake are part of Wallowa County, which sits in Oregon's northeastern corner, bordered by Washington to the north and separated from Idaho to the east by Hells Canyon, the deepest canyon in North America.

Just 7,600 people call Wallowa County home. At the foot of Wallowa Lake is the little community of Joseph, population 1,200. It is named after "Chief Joseph" (also known as Young Joseph), whose actual name was Heinmot Tooyalakekt, which in the Nimiipuu (Nez Perce) language means "Thunder Rising to Lofty Mountain Heights." This area is the ancestral home of the southern band of the Nimiipuu. Despite living peacefully with the white invaders for many years, the southern Nimiipuu lands were signed away by leaders from bands in other regions, leading to their tragic pursuit and defeat by the U.S. cavalry in 1877 (Sharfstein 2017).

Not many years after Heinmot Tooyalakekt's surrender, Wallowa Lake began attracting tourists. But its remoteness—more than three hundred miles from Portland by car—insulated it from development pressures for much of the twentieth century. That began to change in the last half of the century. Oregon was growing rapidly, and it was growing in exactly the same ways as the rest of the country.

Across the West, in the background may be "the purple mountains' majesty," but in the foreground there is the parking lot with a convenience store, a coffee

Figure 11.1 Wallowa Lake and the East Moraine in Wallowa County. Photograph by Leon Werdinger.

shop, and a big-box store surrounded by a dead-worm splatter of cul-de-sacs bordered by big homes for small families, all from the same social and economic class, spreading out from the decaying historic downtowns. Farther out, across the valley and crawling up the foothills of the mountains are the low-density, high-end ranchettes converting the majestic into the mundane.

Sprawl in all its ugly and destructive forms has become the uniform pattern of development in the United States. Across much of America, the only way we might be able to tell whether we are in Orlando, Anchorage, or Denver is by identifying the plants in the landscape strip between the sidewalk and the drive-through fast-food chain restaurant or by comparing the temperature with the calendar.

A Legislative Beginning

That is what Oregonians did not want to happen to their state. They did not want to become New Jersey with ponderosa pines. They wanted to remain special.

But wanting, hoping, and wishing mean nothing without action. In the 1970s, Oregonians were exceptionally lucky to have elected as governor a gifted politician who rallied his allies inside and outside of government to translate their anxiety into action. Republican governor Tom McCall opened the 1973 legislative session with a clarion call for statewide planning legislation.

> Oregon is an inspiration. Whether you come to it or are born to it, you become entranced by our state's beauty, the opportunity she affords, and the independent spirit of her citizens. . . . Our thoughts today and deliberations to come, must spring from our determination to keep Oregon lovable and even more livable.
>
> But there is a shameless threat in our environment and to the whole quality of our life, and that is the unfettered despoiling of the land. . . . Sagebrush subdivisions, coastal condomania, and the ravenous rampage of suburbia here in the Willamette Valley, all threaten to mock Oregon's status as the environmental model of this nation.
>
> We are dismayed that we have not stopped misuse of the land, which is our most valuable finite resource.
>
> Umbrage at blatant disrespect for sound planning is not taken just here in Salem, because just less than a month ago Jefferson County's commissioners [in Central Oregon] appealed to me for a moratorium of subdivisions in that county, because the speculators, the speculators, have outrun local capacity for rational control. We are in dire need of state land use policy, dire need of new subdivision law and new standards for planning and zoning by the counties and cities of our state. . . . The interests of Oregon for today and in the future must be protected from grasping wastrels of the land. . . . We must respect another truism—that unlimited and unregulated growth leads inexorably to a lowered quality of life. (McCall 1973)

Two legislators took up the challenge of translating McCall's rhetoric into the reality of effective legislation. Republican state senator Hector Macpherson was a dairy farmer who represented a rural district in the Willamette Valley. Macpherson was reserved, gentlemanly, and very much committed to the cause. He found an unlikely partner in Democratic state senator Ted Hallock of Portland. Hallock, who ran his own public relations firm, was liberal, high energy, and occasionally caustic, and his private speech was richly seasoned with profanity.

Drawing on the expertise of people from outside the legislature, they put together an ambitious and comprehensive legislative package, Oregon Senate Bills 100 and 101 (S.B. 100/1). Toward the end of the session S.B. 100 passed, just barely, and not without some dexterous maneuvering around the many critics, skeptics, and opponents from both parties.

Oregon was not alone in passing planning legislation in this period. During the 1970s and 1980s, many states—including California, Florida, Maryland, and New Jersey—passed planning legislation that was much heralded. But those laws were heavy on process, based on the belief that planning, in itself, would yield something better through coordination and consultation, a belief that is reflected in Montana's 2023 Land Use Planning Act. This is why many parts of the West *without* land use planning and without strong land use regulations look exactly the same as those *with* plans and regulations (Montana 2023).

Planning and coordination are content-neutral—you can plan and coordinate for any kind of place. In fact, much of the nation's worst sprawl is the result of planning. Oregon's approach put the emphasis on the outcomes to be achieved rather than the process of planning. Put another way, what planning in Oregon is meant to produce is a place, not a document.

Keeping Cities Compact

You may like a salad, a steak (or tofu), and an ice cream sundae for dinner, but you would not put them into a blender and eat the resulting slurry. And that is what urban and rural sprawl does with the city and the country, resulting in a landscape that degrades the habitat for people and wildlife and creates places that are too big to mow and too small to plow.

One simple idea lies at the core of Oregon's planning and land regulation: keep the city and the countryside, the urban and the rural, separate and distinct, not combined in a blurry slurry of low-density sprawl.

The core idea of keeping the city and country separate is implemented in many ways, the best known being urban growth boundaries (UGBs). Every city in Oregon, regardless of size, from Joseph to the Portland metropolitan region, was required to establish a UGB. Inside that line growth and development would occur (subdivisions and apartments, stores, factories, parks, schools—everything urban), and none of those things would be built outside UGBs. Once in place, those UGBs must be regularly reevaluated to ensure that they contain enough land for housing, jobs, and public facilities, including parks and open space.

But S.B. 100 was also concerned about what happened inside UGBs, not just stopping leapfrogging sprawl. It recognized the benefits to taxpayers of building traditional neighborhoods with smaller homes on small lots, which require fewer miles of roads, water, and sewer lines.

The biggest obstacle to more compact urban development has been residential zoning regulations. Beginning early in the twentieth century, zoning in American cities was used to separate people by class, to protect the most expensive, single-family home areas from contamination by higher-density homes and especially apartment buildings. Economic segregation was a constitutionally acceptable way of achieving racial segregation. This history, known to scholars for decades, has finally risen to national prominence and is spurring reforms of residential zoning across the country. But Oregon got there first by several decades.

As a result of S.B. 100, all Oregon's cities were required to reform their zoning to allow for more multifamily housing and smaller residential lots. By 1982, within the urban growth boundary for the Portland metropolitan region of twenty-four cities and parts of three counties, the amount of land zoned for apartment buildings had tripled and the average minimum lot size for undeveloped residentially zoned land had fallen from 12,800 square feet to a bit more than 5,000 square feet. Changes to residential zones were carried out across all cities and county-administered lands inside UGBs, including wealthy suburbs. Cities that resisted were faced with enforcement proceedings, including losing their authority to administer residential zoning. In addition, the cities in the Portland metro regional UGB were required to zone lands to achieve minimum density targets.

In 2017, in response to the housing affordability crisis, the legislature required all cities with populations of 2,500 or more to allow accessory dwelling units (additional small housing units, detached, attached, or internal conversions, often referred to as ADUs) on all lots zoned for single-family homes. In addition, the law barred local governments from adopting regulations that would inhibit the construction of ADUs, such as requiring additional parking on site, subjecting them to design review based on subjective aesthetic standards, or requiring the applicants to face their neighbors in a public hearing (which would never be required to build a home on a vacant lot). This was followed in 2019 by legislation that required local governments to authorize up to four units of housing on all residential lots in cities with populations of 25,000 or more and duplexes on residential lots in cities of 10,000 to 25,000.

More housing choices, close to one another, means shorter trips to get to work, school, shopping, or recreation. It also creates the density that works well with transit. Together these things mean less greenhouse gases. That is why making urban development more compact is an important part of California's ambitious greenhouse gas reduction strategy. More housing and transportation choices in our cities, big or small, reduce economic and social segregation and offer more efficient use of taxpayer investments and less contributions to the climate crisis.

Keeping the Countryside Rural

Under S.B. 100 and 101, almost all the land outside the UGBs is zoned for farming, ranching, and forestry—not just the "prime" soils. About 96 percent of the private land in Oregon (about twenty-five million acres) was, and is, zoned for farming, ranching, forestry, or some combination. Key elements of farm, range, and forest zoning are the regulations governing land divisions and the construction of new houses. These are also the most politically controversial.

The concept of a "minimum lot size" is derived from urban and suburban residential development zoning regulations. It has no relationship to farming, ranching, or forestry, which are commercial activities for the production of food, fiber, and other products—not houses. The proper minimum size of parcels used for farming and forestry has to do with the economics of those industries—the smallest piece of land that can be managed efficiently to generate a net income. No farmer is going to move a herd of cattle ten miles to graze a twenty-acre parcel. Nor can you use a pivot irrigation system on a piece of land smaller than 160 or 320 acres.

Land division regulations are needed to maintain a supply of parcels of a size that can be efficiently put to farm use, even if not contiguous to other parcels, and taking into account the existing supply of parcels of different sizes. Dividing big parcels into smaller parcels increases price per acre because potential buyers value the lot as a rural homesite. Forest lands are different because trees require only periodic management. But again, those management activities only make business sense when applied to larger parcels, assuming the forests are to be sustained and not logged once prior to development.

Restrictions on rural housing may be the most politically difficult thing to accomplish in planning. But it is also the most important because low-density rural sprawl is a plague rapidly advancing across the American landscape. Professor Dave Theobald at Colorado State University analyzed land development patterns in the United States as of 2000 and found seven times as much land in exurban residential development densities (roughly two to forty acres per house) as in urban and suburban development. He forecast that by 2020, 14.3 percent of the land in the United States would fall into the category of low-density exurban sprawl density (Theobald 2005).

Oregon's farm and ranching zones allow homes for specific purposes, situations, and locations—homes for farmers and ranchers, homes for seasonal farmworkers, temporary homes for relatives, and "nonfarm dwellings" on lands generally unsuitable for farming or ranching. Of these, the most controversy has been associated with farm and nonfarm dwellings.

Oregon's land use laws are meant to protect land for commercial farming, not for their landscape value. Consequently, those laws have struggled to distinguish between hobby farming and ranching and farming as a business. Oregon has allowed new "farm dwellings" based on the demonstration they are needed for commercial operations. Past experience with issuing permits for homes based on farm management plans—promises to farm—had shown it to be an avenue for rural residences for people whose farming was, at most, a form of recreation.

Today, on the most productive lands, a farm dwelling can be approved only if the resident shows they have operated a farm grossing around $100,000 a year for three of the past five years. A gross income of $100,000 translates into a net income of $15,000—not enough to live on but enough to show the applicant for a home is seriously engaged in agriculture.

As for nonfarm dwellings, the idea is that there would be no loss of farmland if a home were built on unproductive land, such as a rocky outcrop. In addition, a nonfarm dwelling is only allowed if found not to result in conflicts with farming and ranching (open gates, litigation over dust and sprays, pet dog harassing and killing livestock, etc.). And the nonfarm dwelling may not destabilize the land use pattern in the area—that is, it cannot increase pressure for additional residential development.

In 1993, following years of litigation and political controversy, a regrettable compromise was reached to allow forest lands to be cut into 160- and 80-acre parcels that could have houses without any relation to forest management built on them. Additional houses would be allowed in areas where the ownership had been fragmented so much as to compromise the value of the land for producing timber. Oregon's laws also required the protection of wildlife but with less rigor than was given to farming, ranching, and forestry and more reliance on other state and federal protections.

Implementing Senate Bill 100

In the 1980s and 1990s, many other states considered adopting planning legislation intended to curb sprawl. But in most cases, legislators were influenced by opposition from many local officials who rallied under the banner of "local control." As a result, local governments were allowed great discretion in how they implemented these new laws. Oversight by the state was often weak or minimal, which seriously compromised the effectiveness of the legislation. Another flaw was reliance on vague goals and standards or simply the trust that content-neutral "planning" would somehow change the pattern of development.

By contrast, the Oregon legislature recognized that "local control" had been tested and had utterly failed to stop sprawl. In fact, facilitating or mandating sprawl was often a source of campaign contributions for local elected officials. Ultimately, Oregonians made it clear that local control was an abstraction that was less important than creating the kind of places, urban and rural, that Oregonians wanted.

Senate Bill 100 and the amendments and regulations that followed created a rigorous system of state oversight and enforcement for the system of planning and land regulations that replaced the old system of local control. Cities and counties were required to carry out a public process of adopting binding (i.e., mandatory) comprehensive plans and regulations to implement those plans. Once adopted, these were transmitted to the Department of Land Conservation and Development (DLCD) for public comment and staff review. The department staff reviewed the plans and regulations for consistency with state goals and laws, drawing on their own expertise and formally responding to public comments.

The next level of review occurred through a public hearing by the Land Conservation and Development Commission (LCDC). Plans and regulations could be—and were—rejected by the commission and sent back for revision. The commission's approvals were often appealed to the court of appeals by 1000 Friends of Oregon and other organizations. The Oregon appellate courts, unlike courts elsewhere, did not defer to LCDC's or local governments' interpretations of the law and thereby forced the agency and local governments to honor the actual wording of the laws and regulations. In addition, the DLCD and LCDC were given special powers to enforce the duty of local governments to adopt and correctly implement plans and regulations. These enforcement powers were used infrequently but effectively.

In Oregon, as in all other states, local governments are vested with the power and responsibility to make individual land use decisions based on formal findings of fact and application of the law. This is known as "quasi-judicial" decision-making because local governments are charged with acting in the same manner as a court.

The Oregon legislature took local governments' quasi-judicial fact-finding role seriously. The legislature eliminated the system of allowing trial courts to review local governments' findings of fact and legal conclusions. Instead, a new tribunal was created, the Oregon Land Use Board of Appeals (LUBA). LUBA heard all appeals from local government decisions in the same fashion as an appellate court. LUBA considered the adequacy of findings and legal reasoning but did not revisit the facts of a case. This meant that the legislature could impose relatively short deadlines for appeal decisions to be issued.

Another feature of this system was that the legislature abolished nineteenth-century doctrines about "standing" to appeal, finding that everyone had a stake in the implementation of the land use laws. Thus, anyone who participated in the local proceeding had standing to appeal. The LUBA appeal process was cheaper, faster, and helped both applicants and opponents. Now average citizens were able to represent themselves on appeal—and many did. Despite the abolition of archaic standing requirements, the volume of appeals remained very modest, a few hundred each year, compared to the tens of thousands of legal proceedings filed in the trial courts.

The complex and contentious decade-long effort to implement Senate Bill 100 was turbulent. There were plenty of raucous local meetings on proposed plans and regulations, with armed sheriffs standing at the ready in the back of the meeting room. Local officials were recalled over their support for Senate Bill 100. There were dog shootings, tire slashings, and death threats.

Between 1973 and 2007, Oregonians voted on seven ballot measures to abolish, weaken, or reaffirm Senate Bill 100, directly or indirectly. This history contradicts the common assertion that Oregon's system is "top-down." The first measures to repeal or weaken the laws failed. To the shock of many, Oregon voters approved "property rights" measures in 2000 and 2004 that would have crippled most zoning, not just the land use laws. Focus group research and polling showed that many Oregonians voted for the measure because they thought it was a restatement of existing property rights protection. Then when the law's actual impact became evident, the voters reversed course in 2007 and reinstated the land use laws but with a minor modification of allowing for the construction of a few thousand rural homes across the state in limited circumstances when the family had owned land before farm and forest zoning went into effect. That vote, with 62 percent in favor—including counties east of the Cascades—demonstrated again the depth of support for Oregon's effort to stop sprawl.

Senate Bill 100 in Wallowa County

In 1976, at the very beginning of the implementation of S.B. 100, Wallowa County government conducted a survey of its residents' opinions on planning and land regulations. The unscientific sample found that 70 percent favored adopting a comprehensive plan with 24 percent opposed, 74 percent favored placing prime farmland in exclusive farm use zones with 15 percent opposed, and 62 percent supported having "the Timber and Grazing lands set aside as Timber Grazing zones" with 17 percent opposing this proposal. Opinion was almost evenly divided when asked if they would "prefer Rural Residential zoning in the County": 39 percent favored that idea and 41 percent opposed it (Oregon Land Use Board of Appeals 2022).

To no one's surprise, implementing the state requirements was locally contentious. It took place during a period when two measures to repeal Senate Bill 100 were on the ballot—in 1978 and 1982. Both were defeated, but they were supported by voters in Wallowa County.

When the county took another survey of residents' opinions in 1985, the abstractions of planning and zoning had turned into complex and controversial realities. The county set the context before asking, again, about residents' attitudes toward exclusive farm use zoning: "Most of the private land in Wallowa County is used for farm, forest or grazing management. State policy calls for protection of farm use lands within areas used exclusively for farm use and to preserve forest and grazing on those lands where those activities occur. Do you favor exclusive farm use zoning to protect farmland from future conflicting uses?" Fifty-seven percent answered yes.

Delving deeper, the county asked for opinions on the appropriate land division standard for irrigated farmland. One-fifth supported 320 or 160 acres, one-third supported forty or eighty acres, and almost half (46 percent) supported allowing irrigated farmland to be divided into even smaller parcels of 5 to 20 acres. Nearly two-thirds favored allowing more residential development in rural areas (although there was no definition of what was meant by "rural") with 60 percent favoring minimum lot sizes of 5 acres or larger and 30 percent favoring rural lot sizes of 1 acre—the same density as some suburban zones in other states.

Ultimately Wallowa County adopted a 160-acre minimum parcel size to govern land divisions in the 359,054 acres (561 square miles) in its exclusive farm-use zone and an 80-acre parcel size for the 1,644,884 acres in its prime forest zone, which includes both private and public forest lands. In addition, it has 7,538 acres in a 1-acre rural residential zone, 903 acres in rural industrial zoning (mostly lumber mills), and 29 acres of rural commercial zoning. The five small cities in Wallowa County all adopted UGBs—reluctantly—as required.

How One Woman Used Oregon's Land Use Laws to Stop Sprawl in Wallowa County

During Governor McCall's career as a television journalist, he produced a documentary detailing how Oregon's water pollution control laws were being ignored. He knew that passing a law was one thing and carrying it out was another, which is why he expressed doubts about whether Senate Bill 100 would actually be implemented and enforced. He looked for support outside government to implement Senate Bill 100, and this is why one of his last public acts in office was to endorse the foundation of 1000 Friends of Oregon, which would be the watchdog for S.B. 100.

Which brings us back to Wallowa County and a woman who illustrates how Oregon's planning law, good as it is, both inspired and required local stewardship. Jean Pekarek was not trained in land use law or design—her career was in social services. But place was very important for her.

> The place, both the people and the land, shaped who my children are. So many times when they were young, I'd take them to the lake and sit on the beach watching them play with their friends in the clean water and air against the gorgeous moraine and mountain backdrop, and I would feel overwhelmed by the perfection of it all. When we would return from visiting family in Illinois, they would often thank me for moving to Wallowa County. [The opportunity] to live in a physically beautiful place shouldn't be for the wealthy alone, and that is what I observed as I passed through places around the West that have been "discovered." (Pekarek, private communication with author, September 18, 2022)

In 1991, Wallowa County approved rezoning twenty-four acres on the moraine at the foot of Wallowa Lake, from an exclusive farm-use zone to a recreational residential zone, and approved the twenty-six-lot Joseph Point residential subdivision on the property. Pekarek called 1000 Friends of Oregon for help in filing an appeal of the subdivision approval to the Oregon Land Use Board of Appeals. Yes, they told her, they would help, but she had to help as well. They asked her to get others to sign onto a LUBA appeal and to review the massive record of the proceeding to find information related to specific issues that would be the focus of the appeal: "I remember telling my husband at the time that my involvement would last three to six months max. I couldn't have imagined it would turn into decades. . . . Anyway, I called every resident who submitted testimony in opposition to the subdivision, and of those about forty individuals agreed to sign on."

Pekarek and her neighbors won their LUBA appeal in part because the county's decision violated its own land use plan, a decision affirmed in a subsequent appeal to the Oregon court of appeals. After the LUBA and court of appeals decisions, one of the three subdivision applicants cut out the silhouette of pigs from four-by-eight-foot sheets of plywood and painted them pink. They were highly visible. The frustrated applicant then alerted local and statewide media saying they were going to put a pig farm on the moraine property, since that was all they could do with it. Pekarek's daughter, who was around twelve at the time, said to her, "Mom, we should go up there and write the names Lee, Dave, and Dan on the pigs"—the first names of the three subdivision applicants.

As a result of the county's loss in its appeals, it was obliged to give serious consideration to the cultural and geological significance of the moraines. Pekarek was appointed to the advisory committee assessing the moraines, the only member who was not a government employee or who did not have some prior professional connection to the moraines. The advisory committee's decision to protect the moraines was appealed to LUBA by one of the property owners. Happily, the county decided to defend its decision—something normally left to affected property owners. Instead of representing the county in the appeal, the county counsel left it to the planning director, someone without legal training, to write most of the county's brief and to let Pekarek, another nonlawyer, handle the oral argument before the Land Use Board of Appeals. The county, with Pekarek's help, won.

Meanwhile (because land use controversies are often protracted, there is almost always a "meanwhile"), one of the property owners was granted a permit by the county to build a two-story home atop the moraine in the style of an antebellum Southern plantation mansion. Pekarek thought this might be a feint, but to be safe, she filed her own appeal of that decision. She relied on 1000 Friends of Oregon's *Citizens' Guide to Land Use Appeals*, a DIY guide for the many active citizens who couldn't afford to pay for an attorney. One of the grounds for her appeal was the adequacy of the water supply.

Her account of what happened at oral argument shows how a motivated person, without any legal training, can master the technical knowledge needed to be an effective advocate, even against a member of the bar.

> There was nothing on that page to support his statement [about proven water supply on the property] nor was there anything anywhere else in the record to support it. I viewed the inclusion of that statement as either a sign of significant ineptness or dishonesty and also found it very troubling that [the applicant's attorney] put the unsupported statement in the Summary of Material Facts rather than in his response to the assignment of errors, where such a statement should have gone. I challenged this at the very beginning of oral arguments and after the referee pinned him down, [he] finally admitted he couldn't substantiate the statement. Did he think I wouldn't notice?

With Pekarek's reputation established, when she filed another appeal with the Land Use Board of Appeals challenging a decision by the city of Joseph, the city threw in the towel and reversed its decision rather than fight. That was one of multiple development proposals for land on the moraine. That land has now been preserved (thanks largely to Pekarek's efforts) as the Iwetemlaykin State Heritage Site, adjacent to the burial site of Chief Joseph's father, Old Chief Joseph.

Jean Pekarek had many brave and determined counterparts across Oregon who used Senate Bill 100 to protect lands and resources. They included a hardscrabble rancher who never finished high school, a chain-smoking psychiatric nurse living in a mobile home park, and a high-ranking Republican party official whose high-desert farm provides much of the nation's carrot seed. These are the kind of people Tom McCall had in mind when he said, "Heroes are not statues framed against a red sky. They are people who say, 'This is my community, and it's my responsibility to make it better.'"

Just as this chapter is being written, the *New York Times* reported that the vacation rental company Vacasa ranked Wallowa Lake the number-one most profitable location to buy a winter vacation rental, and *Travel and Leisure* listed Joseph as one of America's most beautiful small towns. Not surprisingly, 40 percent of the homes in the county are now second homes. The wave of rural gentrification and displacement in the Rocky Mountains is finding its way to the shores of Wallowa Lake, which means the land use battles will, and must, continue.

Saving the Mountain West from Sprawl

Oregon's approach to land planning and regulation is unique at the state level. But other places have arrived at similar combinations of policies and regulations as a result of convergent policy evolution.

Urban growth boundaries (often with different names for the same concept) and the pairing of urban densification and redevelopment inside UGBs with rural conservation through agricultural zoning (often supplemented with conservation easement programs) can be found around the country, even where the politics vary, including Kentucky (Lexington and Fayette Counties, which started more than a decade before Oregon), Michigan (Frankenmuth Town and Township), South Carolina (Charleston City and County), and South Dakota (Sioux Falls and Minnehaha and Lincoln Counties). This pairing can also be found in several counties in California and the counties in Washington State subject to its Growth Management Act.

Examples of resident-initiated zoning in Montana, like the Springhill Zoning District outside of Bozeman in Gallatin County, show what can be done under existing laws in conservative states. Livingston, Montana, is twenty-five scant miles from Bozeman on I-90. Its planning board saw what was headed their way and in 2021 adopted a dramatically different growth policy that called for an emphasis on traditional neighborhood development, strengthening their still healthy historic downtown and designating a wide band of land outside the city limits as "pastoral/open space." In 2023, Montana's Republican-dominated legislature passed reforms of residential zoning in the state's largest cities to allow more types and higher densities of housing.

Oregon's and these other communities' experiences show that amenity-driven gentrification and sprawl in the Mountain West is not inevitable. It is not the unavoidable product of capitalism or "economic forces." It is the result of choices made by local and state elected officials and inaction or inattention by nonprofit organizations unwilling to challenge the loud voices of property rights extremists.

At this watershed moment, which way the stream of history will carry us depends on just a few people and a few organizations that believe the majesty of the West is worth saving.

12

Nihikéyah

Land Policy in the Navajo Nation

CRYSTAL CARR AND ANDREA CHRISTELLE

Crystal Carr says: *Yá'át'ééh, ádóónę́ę́ nishlinigii ei Tsé Deeshgizhnii nishlí, Biih Bitoodni báshíshchíín, Tł'ízíłání da shichei, áádóó Tá Neeszáhnii da shinálí. Shi éíyá Crystal Carr yinishyé. Tó Naneesdizídéé naashá, ákondi Tseehílíídi keehashti. Ákót'ééhgo Diné asdzaaní nishłí.* I am Rockgap, born for Deer Spring; my maternal grandfather is Manygoats and my paternal grandfather is of the Tangle People. My name is Crystal Carr. I am from Tuba City, Arizona, but I currently reside in Tsaile, Arizona.

Andrea Christelle says: Hello. My maternal grandmother is German, and my paternal grandmother is English. My maternal grandfather is Scots-Irish, and my paternal grandfather is French. My name is Andrea Christelle; I am from Ohio but currently reside in Sedona, Arizona, and Tsaile, Arizona.

The Navajo Nation—stretching across Arizona, New Mexico, and Utah—encompasses twenty-seven thousand square miles of some of the planet's most spectacular landscapes. The land attracts sightseers, tourists, and filmmakers from around the globe. Extractive industries, in cooperation with the federal government, have made billions of dollars from the coal, oil, and uranium mined out of the nation's mesas, plateaus, and canyons over the last century.

And yet, despite all the wealth outside corporations and resource colonists have pulled from the ground, many of the Navajo Nation's four hundred thousand citizens have been trapped in a housing crisis of epic proportions. Tens of thousands of homes are in various states of disrepair; nearly one-third lack electricity, indoor plumbing, or running water. It is not uncommon for three to four families to live in a substandard structure of five hundred square feet or less. In one case, a Diné man in Chilchinbeto, Arizona, dug out the side of a hill for shelter and had an old Chevy hood serving as his roof.

The causes of this dysfunction are myriad, ranging from systemic racism to intergenerational trauma to national policies that have led to wealth inequality and lack of economic mobility. Attempts at an adequate response are obstructed by paternalistic federal policies and antiquated land use laws that conspire to make the American dream of homeownership—and the development of an Indigenous entrepreneurial culture—difficult to impossible to realize.

The federal government needs to recognize these vestiges of nineteenth-century colonialism and help the Navajo Nation and its citizens move forward. The Biden administration's choice of Native Americans to head the Department of the Interior (Deb Haaland), the National Park Service (Chuck Sams), and the Bureau of Indian Affairs (Bryan Newland) suggests that greater attention will be paid to righting these wrongs. At the same time, progress on these issues means that the traditional Diné approach to land rights will need to accommodate the realities of twenty-first-century global capitalism. This essay ends with suggestions on how these goals might be advanced.

The Diné Relationship to the Land

The strong connection that Indigenous peoples have to their homeland and significant sites is the foundation of their culture and—just as importantly—their sovereignty. Today, tribal nations are reclaiming political control over their lands. Guided by Diné philosophy, our first step is to establish ties among the mind, emotions, spirit, body, and clanship: "When two strange Navajos meet, one of the first questions they ask is 'What is your clan?' In this way they establish relationships that are considered as binding as family ties" (Correll and Watson 1972).

Crystal Carr says: As a Diné woman my clanship is Rockgap, born for Deer Spring. The names of my clans are directly tied to landscapes and features, one referring to a gap in a canyon or plateau and the other signifying springs where deer often gather or rest. Tsé deeshgizhnii, or Rockgap, came from a Navajo woman who was Haashtł'ishnii and who married in the Navajo Nation's Western Agency. She and her husband set up her homestead near what my family calls Willow Springs. This area was known for peach trees and for supplying water to the nearby fields. It is located at the end of the plateau, and there is a large gap in the side of this plateau where Asdzáá Tsé deeshgizhnii lived. She had many children, and they became known as the Rockgap clan.

To this day our clan has large reunions there. Not too far from this area, my family has twenty acres of fields where we grow corn, squash, and melons. At one point there were over seventy-five clans that had similar stories on how they were tied to the land (Correll and Watson 1972). Today there are about sixty-five that are commonly used. Through our cultural protocol of clanship, we are connected to the land and to one another.

Andrea Christelle says: As a Bilagaana (non-Navajo, culturally Western person) living in the Navajo Nation, I have come to realize that land is closely tied to family, ancestry, and daily life. You would not build a starter home in Tsaile and then move to Window Rock ten years later. If you are a woman, whether you can set up a homestead and the location of that homestead depend on where you were born, which means where your mother was born.

For most of my life, I thought of myself as mainly French, but in Navajo, my French heritage is emphasized least. Each time I introduce myself in the Navajo style, which is usually in a group of mostly Diné, I am reminded of English colonialism and historical accounts of Scots-Irish brutality against Native Americans. The legacy left by my European ancestors has not been acknowledged in many histories. I am not those ancestors, and yet I am here because of them. So these introductions are an opportunity for sorting out that relationship, which for most of my life was not something I intentionally ignored, but it was invisible to me.

Recently, I have come to learn that the practice of introducing yourself is also a practice of coming to know yourself. A medicine man told me that by reminding ourselves where our ancestors came from, we are reminding ourselves of the way they understood the world and so how we understand it. Self-introduction is part of self-knowledge, and Diné revisit this inner inquiry over and over again.

Around the world, Indigenous peoples are fighting for a better life while staying true to what sets them apart from non-Indigenous peoples. An Indigenous people's relationship to their land is often compared to a mother and child relationship. For Indigenous peoples in the United States, there have been many negotiated treaties, executive orders, and court cases addressing the right to access traditional homelands. Many tribal citizens are reclaiming recognition of lands they lost.

The Land Back movement is one of the most well-known contemporary examples. Founded in 2018 by Arnell Tailfeathers, a member of the Blackfoot Confederacy, Land Back seeks to reestablish Indigenous sovereignty and political and economic control over ancestral lands. Land Back is part of a broader Indigenous struggle for decolonization. It advocates for the communal holding of land and rejects Western concepts of private land ownership. Having the largest land base of any tribal nation, the Navajo Nation struggles to manage its resources as it works to balance traditional lifeways and communities with contemporary technologies and economies.

Traditional Navajo land policies were based on community practices and collective rights associated with inheritance and customary law (Jojola 2008). Extended families and clans herded and farmed together, and land was allocated according to how it was used. Unused land was available to others in a case of use it or lose it (Rosser 2019). Land was traditionally neither bought nor sold: Western notions of private property rights, of "owning" land that one could then treat as one wishes, were foreign to Diné culture.

In 1863, the federal government deprived the Navajo people of their autonomy, their land, and the power to make decisions (under fundamental and customary law) or to govern themselves when they were forcefully displaced from their homeland. Some land and a degree of self-determination was later restored, but not all of it. Although tribal nations operate as sovereign governments, their land is also subject to U.S. Environmental Protection Agency regulations, Bureau of Indian Affairs grazing permits, and federal trust land laws. Today the Navajo Nation must negotiate all aspects of their political and legal lives, from education to housing and health care. The imposition of U.S. federal law on top of tribal governance thwarts the possibility of cultural authenticity: the Diné are not allowed to be truly who they are, rooted in a Diné epistemology and metaphysics. Colonial institutions contribute to the sociocultural suppression of traditional Diné ecological knowledge (DEK) and Diné Knowledge Systems (DKS).

History of the Diné Land

In 1863, U.S. Army field commander Kit Carson led troops across Navajo country, slaughtering sheep and goats, hacking down peach orchards and torching cornfields, and ultimately forcing some nine thousand survivors on the infamous Long Walk to Bosque Redondo in southeastern New Mexico. Brigadier Gen. James Carleton cited the motive for these crimes: "By the subjugation and colonization of the Navajo tribe, we gain for civilization their whole country, which [is] . . . by far the best pastoral region between the two oceans [and] is said to abound in the precious as well as the useful metals" (Prucha 1984, 453).

In 1868, a Navajo leader named Barboncito, who was eloquent about his people's yearning for their homeland, negotiated the Treaty of 1868 with Lt. Gen. William Tecumseh Sherman. That document laid out a reservation that was in the heart of Diné Bikéyah (the people's sacred lands) but covered only about one-eighth of the original homeland. It included very little arable or readily developable land and left out important religious sites. Still, it was home. Across the ensuing six decades, while most tribal nations were losing acreage under allotment policies, the Diné actually gained additional pieces of their original homeland back by way of executive order. The original reservation plus the additions make up what we know today as the Navajo Nation, which remains the cultural center of the Diné world.

But most of this land doesn't technically belong to the Diné. Rather, the federal government holds the title to some 90 percent of the Navajo Nation, which is held under a trust for the benefit of the nation or individual tribal members by the federal Bureau of Indian Affairs (BIA), an agency within the Interior Department. This is known as "trust land," as opposed to "fee simple" land that can be bought, sold, or used as collateral against a mortgage.

While the tribe supposedly governs the land, its self-determination has been limited by the federal government and its ultimate control of the land. In 1923, for example, the federal government established the Navajo Tribal Council, not to protect or assert sovereignty, but to have an entity that could sign off on oil leases on the Navajo Nation (Iverson 2002). It would be decades before the tribe gained the power to negotiate the terms of those leases. And even still, federal control and red tape complicate all forms of development, from an individual seeking to build a home, to a person looking to start a business, to the tribal government looking to install critical infrastructure on land that it supposedly controls.

The Navajo people have traditionally raised sheep while practicing DEK to maintain the health of the land. Many Navajo families today still practice migrating their sheep from the valley, canyon, meadow, or plains in the winter to the mountains, plateaus, or higher ground in the summer. Residing in high-elevation sheep camps in the summer remains a Navajo way of life.

The first federal regulation addressing grazing on the Navajo Nation, the Taylor Grazing Act, was passed in 1934, and after a series of policy actions, grazing regulations were adopted into the Navajo Nation Code in 1966. These policies, however, have not kept up with a changing climate, and warming temperatures, drought, erosion, and overgrazing threaten this heritage. These new conditions undermine traditional DEK. Since the 1950s, the average amount of land required to support one sheep has increased from twenty-two acres to one hundred acres.

Today grazing permits are issued by the BIA with input from the Navajo Nation. Almost 3 percent of the Navajo population has a stake in one or more of the ten thousand grazing permits. Many land use planning and development decisions are dependent on whether the grazing permittee of the grazing area where the proposed development will take place signs off for approval. Since grazing permits are only granted under the authority of the BIA, the federal government's continued control of the land is an obstacle to the enactment of Navajo sovereignty, blocking land development opportunities that would expand needed services and provide adequate housing.

Housing Challenges

The strength of the connection Diné have to their land and to significant sites is foundational to their culture. Yet a lack of resources, as well as policies that block land access and hamper homeownership, threaten the survival of that connection.

The lack of habitable housing is the most visible manifestation of the challenges facing the Navajo Nation. Most Navajo families live in multigenerational housing or are living in a housing structure with insufficient space for the number of occupants. About 30 percent of dwellings on the Navajo Nation lack electricity and running water, and the number of overcrowded households and those without adequate kitchens or plumbing continues to grow.

A 2011 Navajo Housing Authority assessment found that at least thirty-four thousand new housing units must be constructed on the Navajo Nation to meet existing needs, and another forty-seven thousand homes need to be expanded or repaired (RPI/NHA 2011). These dire numbers keep increasing. Even before the pandemic hit, the number of families who could not afford housing grew by 55 percent over just more than a decade, causing financial stress and diminishing quality of life (U.S. Commission on Civil Rights 2018).

Entrepreneurs—both Navajo and non-Navajo—also face challenges when attempting to establish businesses on the Navajo Nation, which in turn hampers the sort of economic development that could ease the housing crisis. According to the *Navajo Nation Comprehensive Economic Development Strategy* (2018), border towns such as Flagstaff, Arizona, and Farmington, New Mexico, are more supportive of small businesses, are better able to cater to the immediate needs of larger businesses, and offer more diverse employment opportunities than the Navajo Nation. While organizations like the Dineh Chamber of Commerce work to support business on the Navajo Nation and businesses run by Navajo people, they have limited resources, especially when compared with neighboring municipalities.

Navajo Nation citizens are forced to travel long distances to these border towns to buy cars or groceries or to take care of other business needs. This in turn drives up transportation costs, which eats into household budgets, diminishing quality of life while leading to car crashes. The dearth of commercial activity on the nation siphons money away from communities and into the border towns, depriving the tribe of funds that could be used to improve infrastructure and provide services.

Barriers to land access and ownership are a root cause of both the housing shortage and inadequate business development. Stringent rules govern inheritance and the transfer of land ownership. If businesses in the larger U.S. culture had to operate by the same land restrictions and bureaucratic processes associated with homesite leases and business site leases on Navajo land, there would be a national and global economic crisis. The stranglehold that the U.S. government has on Navajo land, dictating how it can be used, by whom, and under what conditions, is another (if lesser-known) legacy of colonialism that maintains the regrettable conditions of socioeconomic inequality.

For commercial uses, the Navajo Nation has a two-part process allowing land use: (1) the land withdrawal designation process where land is identified and withdrawn for a certain purpose and (2) the land lease approval process. This second step is where a legal description of what the land is going to be used for is reviewed and approved by the Navajo Nation Department of Justice as a step in the 164 Review Process.

For residential uses, Navajo citizens must complete a multistep procedure. Some steps require the applicant to pay out of pocket for required surveys—for example, a soil survey, a biological clearance survey, and an archaeological survey, each of which costs an average of $2,000. For most applications, going through this onerous process can take years. And once the lease is approved it can be almost impossible to secure a mortgage because the land isn't owned by the applicant and therefore cannot be used as collateral. Imagine what it would mean for U.S. commerce if it took years to apply to lease a commercial property or if there was almost no way to get a mortgage. People often wonder at the state of disrepair of homes on Navajo land. Imagine what the condition of most homes in the United States would be if no one were able to secure a mortgage. Most people have no idea how ensuring the lack of access to capital and ownership was the political intention when arrangements were made for the U.S. government to hold Navajo land "in trust."

Families and businesses must wait years to secure a home or storefront. The inefficiency of this administrative process contributes to many families living in dilapidated and overcrowded conditions. In what becomes a vicious cycle, the ability to address these challenges is further frustrated by high unemployment and limited economic opportunities. Many of these procedures and policies stem from the mismatch between Western notions of private property and the trust-lands relationship governing the reservation.

In 2000, Congress finally authorized the Navajo Nation to issue leases without prior approval by the secretary of the interior (Navajo Nation Trust Leasing Act 2000). By overseeing their own land leases, the Navajo Nation has gained more control over the maintenance of infrastructure and has been creating new developments to meet the needs of its people. However, there is still much work to be done in streamlining the process across multiple agencies and reforming entrenched leadership practices. Ted Jojola (2008) states that perhaps no other single aspect of community development requires as much leadership to balance the immediacy of action with a precise plan for long-term development.

The Navajo Nation Council established leasing regulations in 2013 aimed at streamlining and standardizing the land withdrawal designation process used to ensure that all necessary surveys are complete before a land use permit is issued or the leasing process begins. The applicant must provide geographic information systems (GIS) map surveys, get approval from local grazing officials, provide an approved resolution from the local chapter, and jump through numerous other bureaucratic hoops.

All enrolled members of the Navajo Nation are eligible to apply for a homesite lease. However, leasing two separate homesites is prohibited, and homesites are often challenging to transfer from one generation to the next. The process to obtain a land use permit or lease is laborious and expensive, and success in completing it is highly contingent on the applicant's financial resources and ability to negotiate the complex administrative requirements.

It is risky, for example, to invest in a land survey and lease application to determine whether a parcel is even available for lease. This risk is heightened by glitches in the often out-of-date land-tracking database. In addition, land-management-planning efforts can be politically swayed, either at the local chapter level or at the administrative level, where the director of the Navajo Nation Land Department has the sole authority to approve or reject homesite lease applications and recommend approval or disapproval to the Resources and Development Committee (RDC) of the Navajo Nation Council. This opens the door to favoritism and potentially allows people who have advantageous relationships to skip ahead in the process. Potential buyers must invest under conditions of uncertainty because the land-tracking database is difficult to access and not always up to date. The final challenge for those looking to lease land is that there is little to no enforcement of land use regulations to ensure the parcel is in fact used for the stated purpose of the lease. These outdated processes create barriers and limitations for future development and infrastructure that could help address many of the issues the Navajo Nation faces today.

In 2021, the Navajo Nation received $2.1 billion in American Rescue Plan Act (ARPA) funding. The Tribal Council, which holds the governmental purse strings, passed legislation developing a process for distributing the funds to put money into infrastructure. First, they identified the projects that were shovel ready, having gone through the necessary approval process. They also designated millions of dollars to the Navajo Tribal Utility Authority (NTUA) to expand electrical lines and broadband, with broadband projects targeted at middle-mile and last-mile projects.

In 2022, the Navajo Council passed legislation (resolution 0086-23) that designated over $600 million for housing construction, waterlines and wastewater projects, internet broadband connections, and cybersecurity upgrades. As of 2023, these efforts are barely making a dent in basic infrastructure needs. Many ARPA-approved projects have yet to spend their funding because they have been unable to acquire right of way, access to land parcels, or a homesite lease. Some of these projects are fundamental to quality of life—for instance, bringing running water to existing residences—but administrative inefficiencies are creating bottlenecks.

The Way Forward

To the extent possible, Navajo land issues need to be disentangled from federal control. This would streamline administrative processes, allowing the Navajo people to make decisions that fit their needs. Doing so would also support Navajo Nation efforts to oversee grazing permit processes, which are currently controlled by the BIA. Restructuring these long-standing administrative procedures will require careful planning in order to avoid unintended consequences so that Diné citizens and businesses can adjust their expectations. The first step in such a restructuring is to gather data on people's experiences when they apply for a homesite or grazing permit or transfer an existing permit to their name. Additional data are also needed on what policies are outdated or not enforced and on how to avoid the mismanaged housing projects of the past.

Organizations have been created to address issues of homelessness, overcrowding, electricity, and access to water. Launched in 2016, the Náátsʼíilid (Rainbow) Initiative is concerned with meeting the housing and infrastructure needs of Dinétah (Navajo land) as a way of fostering community healing. The initiative invests in cultural asset mapping and community development planning while supporting tribal governance. Its Sweat Equity Homes Project (SEHP) is building homes and other infrastructure across the Navajo Nation largely through sweat equity. Its goal is to reaffirm traditional Navajo teaching while promoting food cultivation, storytelling, and ceremonies that are adapted to contemporary lifestyles.

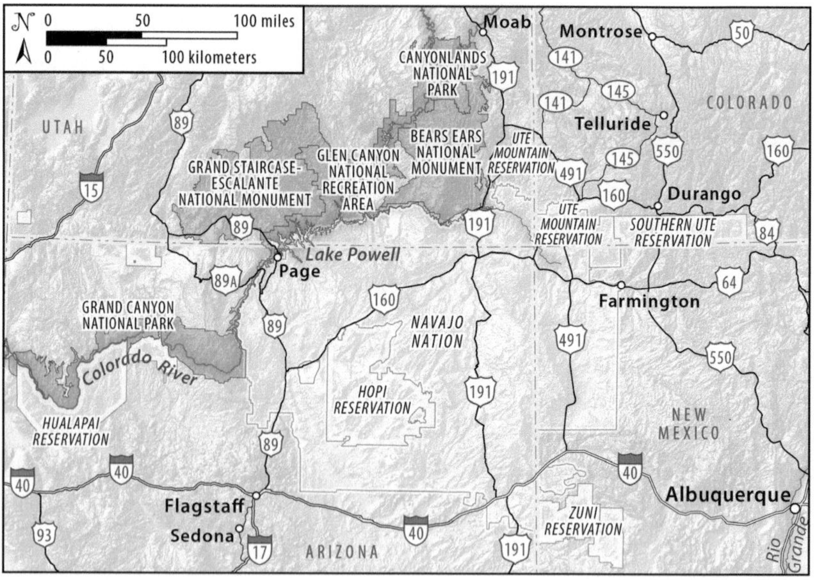

Figure 12.1 Map of the Four Corners region, showing the Navajo Nation and Bears Ears National Monument. Map credit: Chelsea Feeney.

If these processes were carried out in a timely way—with better information and less uncertainty—this would allow people to make decisions that take their needs and limitations into account. For instance, if a land transfer decision process takes more than a year, in that time, someone's financial, employment, relationship, or health status could change in a way that would lead them to make a different decision.

In the midst of these policy changes, it is also essential to draw on traditional Navajo knowledge and lifeways. Practical and legal issues intersect with traditional Diné ecological knowledge and Diné knowledge systems. In the words of George Blueeyes,

> We say Nahaszáán Shimá. Earth, My Mother.
> We are made for her.
> Even though she takes us daily, we will become part of her again.
> For we are her. The earth is our mother. (Bingham and Bingham 1984)

13

Tribal Governance of Traditional Lands
Bears Ears National Monument

REGINA LOPEZ-WHITESKUNK, INTERVIEWED BY EVELYN BRISTER

In December 2016, President Barack Obama designated 1.35 million acres of public land as the Bears Ears National Monument. Obama did so through the 1906 Antiquities Act, which empowers presidents to create national monuments from federal land to protect significant natural, cultural, or scientific features of the landscape.

Native American tribes in southeastern Utah had begun work on a proposal in 2010 in response to an effort by Senator Bob Bennett to produce a stakeholder-driven plan for Utah public lands. Over the next few years, public support for protecting the land and cultural sites of the region grew. In 2013, the Congressional delegation from Utah supported county-level committees, soliciting proposals that would inform future legislation, called the Public Lands Initiative (PLI). These consultations were presented as an open, deliberative, stakeholder-driven process to develop land policies that would strengthen conservation of valued natural areas while also allowing recreational opportunities and appropriate economic uses of public land, including energy development, mining, and grazing.

In 2015, the San Juan County, Utah, PLI committee submitted its recommendations. The recommendations left out input from the tribes, some of whom have a cultural and historical interest in the area without contemporary land ownership. In response, the tribes of southeastern Utah and the Four Corners region gathered for an unprecedented summit. Five tribal nations officially banded together in July 2015; Regina Lopez-Whiteskunk represented the Ute Mountain Ute Tribe on the Bears Ears Intertribal Coalition. In October of that year, they formally proposed Bears Ears National Monument to the Obama administration.

In 2016, as the Utah-led process for the Public Lands Initiative continued, the Utah legislature held hearings. Lopez-Whiteskunk spoke at these hearings in April, but her concerns were rudely dismissed by the lawmakers. In July, Utah's congressional delegation, including Representatives Rob Bishop and Jason Chaffetz, unveiled H.R. 5780, a statewide proposal.

Tribal and conservation interests saw the bill as undermining years of democratic process by ignoring county-level recommendations. Environmentalists further argued that the bill contradicted several key federal laws, including the Wilderness Act, the Clean Air Act, and the National Environmental Policy Act. Tribes in the region argued that the bill would violate agreements they had made with the U.S. government by placing some tribal sovereign lands under local and state management with little or no input from tribal governments.

In the months after the five tribes proposed the national monument, Regina Lopez-Whiteskunk found herself thrown into intensive work—and at the center of controversy—relating to Bears Ears. She became one of the coalition's most visible members, giving public testimony in Utah and Washington, DC, on the tribal nation's needs to protect these lands. In May 2023, I talked with her about her experience. She currently works part-time for the Montezuma Land Conservancy in Cortez, Colorado, and serves on the management advisory committee for Bears Ears National Monument. This transcription of our conversation has been edited and condensed.

Evelyn Brister: Did you grow up in the area around Bears Ears? Could you describe this landscape for people who have never seen it?

Regina Lopez-Whiteskunk: I'm a member of Ute Mountain Ute Tribe. My mother is actually of the Ute Indian Tribe of Utah, which is the Ute reservation in northeastern Utah in Fort Duchesne. I grew up going back and forth between my father's reservation and my mother's reservation. We made that drive so often, I took the landscape for granted. When we were driving back and forth, we'd stop to grab a quick bite and gas up, and that was it. As an adult, I have more appreciation for how my heritage is linked to the land between the reservations and for its striking beauty. Maybe to someone who grew up on the coasts, it looks stark, but this place is full of life. The colors of the rocks, the wide open spaces.

Brister: Could you tell me about the pivotal moment when the Intertribal Coalition came together?

Lopez-Whiteskunk: A nonprofit organization called the Utah Diné Bikéyah had been working on this since 2010. They had put effort into collecting stories, collecting and identifying significant plants, and doing a lot of engagement with the local communities in southeastern Utah. Although they had started their focus within the Navajo Nation, they began to see that San Juan County was going to be at the center of debates about how public lands in Utah would be managed and developed. They realized that as a nonprofit, they did not have the authority to speak on behalf of Indigenous people or to engage in the discussion about land management that was taking place at the county, state, and federal levels.

They worked with the Navajo Nation and Hopi leadership, who then reached out to other tribal leaders and invited us to a gathering that included representatives from the Havasupai, some Paiute tribes, the Pueblo of Zuni, and the Ute Indian Tribe of Utah. I was there to speak for the Ute Mountain Ute Tribe.

Brister: Had you been involved in tribal leadership for long? What was that meeting like, and how did it change your viewpoint?

Lopez-Whiteskunk: I had only just been elected to the Tribal Council, and—it's funny—I wasn't originally scheduled to be at that meeting and was just filling in, but it wound up being a turning point where I and others made a big commitment. The meeting was on July 15, 2015, at the casino in Towaoc. We had a very long morning with a lot of coffee, and we learned about each other. Any time you get tribal representatives together, especially with elders in the room, you have to bring along your patience as you listen to all the introductions as well as about the family ties and ties to the land. A lot of that might include lengthy stories. The morning reminded me how our history is embedded in the stories. You have to take those in and process what the connection to the land is for each individual, which ends up being what the connection is for this tribal community.

It was important to hear our elders speak of gathering willows to make the baskets and of being out on the landscape and remembering the stories of what happened between the Southern Paiute Posey and the neighboring Mormon people in 1923. The stories included everything from various kinds of controversy to descriptions of beautiful places where our families grew up and had gardens. If there was a moment that you could have embraced and recorded these stories, that morning would have been an opportune time.

Brister: How did it go after the introductions? How did a coalition that wound up having such a strong effect get formed? Was it a slow process, or did people come together pretty much spontaneously?

Lopez-Whiteskunk: Of course, people had been working behind the scenes for a while, but there comes a moment of decision. That day we were getting near our lunch break, and one of the Zuni folks, an elder named Octavius Seowtewa, who is still very active in his role as a knowledge keeper and educator, got up, and he said—and I will never forget this because I held this moment in my mind all the way through the process—that as we come together and begin to organize and strive toward one common goal, that all other business or politics from this day forward will be left outside of the room. When we came into this space for this purpose, we are all coming with mutual respect. He said that our focus would be on what we're seeking—protection and continued access to this sacred space.

It really was one of those fundamental statements and agreements that lay the groundwork for success. It helped to lay out how we would relate to one another and how we brought to the table our own unique ways of who we are, our wisdom, our knowledge, our culture, and I have to say, in that moment basically, without saying anything specific to any one group, we all acknowledged the fact that the Navajos were still having land disputes with the Hopi and had been in confrontation with the Utes over some water issues. But for this purpose, we would work together.

The meeting was being led by Eric Descheenie from the Navajo Nation and Alfred Lomahquahu from the Hopi Tribe. When we got ready to go on our lunch break, they told us, "This is an important decision that we're all coming to the table to make on behalf of our respective tribes. You may need to take this lunch break to call on other tribal leaders to run this by them, because when we come to the table after lunch, we're going to commit to this endeavor, which may end up being a heavy lift, and it may include some intense periods of planning and gathering and engaging in political process." He told us we really needed to understand what we were engaging in.

I was just a couple miles away from our main headquarters, so I quickly drove up the hill into Towaoc and sat down with Manuel Heart, who was chairman [of the Ute Mountain Ute Tribe] at that time, and he said, "You know what you have to do, and you know what is right. I've got the utmost confidence that you will make the right decision." That was huge for me because I didn't have a lot of experience in this role, and even though I didn't know exactly what would be expected of me, I felt it was important, and we couldn't afford not to be in the conversation.

I thought, *My goodness, I'm going to be representing future generations, and I'm going to have the elders and the ancestors depending on me too.* Making this decision felt like a huge weight. I went back and joined the rest of the group for lunch, and then the leaders asked the tribes who were committing to this to please come sit at the table. Those that were going to remain in a supporting role, please seat yourself away from the table. So then there were five tribes seated at the table. They were the Hopi, the Navajo Nation, the Pueblo of Zuni, the Ute Indian Tribe of Utah, and the Ute Mountain Ute Tribe.

Brister: Obviously, there were a lot of people who were really committed to the work, and it had been in the works for a long time, but I've been to a lot of community meetings where it's not clear whether good ideas are actually going to get off the ground. It seems like it's important to have a good group of people who are pulling in the same direction—and also a certain amount of luck.

Lopez-Whiteskunk: Absolutely! When the meeting continued that afternoon, with the five tribes sitting at the table, it wasn't clear what the next move should be. There was an uncomfortable stillness and quietness in the room. I asked, "Are we going to govern by Robert's Rules of Order, or what do we need to do to solidify this group as an official group?" I made the motion that the five tribes sitting at the table become a coalition group heading up the Bears Ears Initiative. I wasn't the most experienced person at the table, but putting forward this motion just seemed like it made sense, and I guess it is in line with my personality, which is that if I feel like something needs to be done, I like to get things moving. I made the motion, I had a second, and all present said aye. From that point forward, we agreed that we were going to operate on consensus. We made an agreement that we would not proceed until everybody understood and agreed on the coalition's next move. I think anyone would say that operating on consensus is one of the most difficult ways to conduct a collaboration like that, but it was necessary in this case.

Brister: Consensus decision-making is absolutely the most difficult. One problem with consensus models is that they allow someone to hijack a process by refusing to agree unless they get special dispensation for whatever their interest is. With a consensus model, you really have to trust that everyone will agree to what's good for the group as a whole.

Lopez-Whiteskunk: In our case, it was necessary because for all of us, that's how our culture and customs operate traditionally. It was certainly on our minds that we were working to preserve traditional lands, and so we should be making our decisions in a way that stemmed from the generations before us. But by the same token, we were very much operating in the present and building our current bonds. If one of us didn't understand something, everyone took time to bring them along until they did understand. We didn't move forward until everybody felt confident with what we were doing.

Brister: Although consensus decision-making is difficult, if you can get consensus, it's powerful. It provides political legitimacy. The people outside your group see how unified you are.

Lopez-Whiteskunk: That was one of the strongest reasons why the coalition was successful; it was because we did not move unless we all moved together. But like many people, I still cannot fathom how quickly we moved, and how we achieved such incredible results. We met for the first time in July 2015, and we set a deadline to have a proposal completed by that October. The day after that first meeting, we traveled as a group to the Bears Ears Buttes, which I think was the best thing we could have done. The people involved in the coalition were committing outside of our normal capacity and obligations to our tribal groups. In order for us to get this done, we committed to gather every weekend in various locations near to the five coalition tribes, so a large part of our commitment was being away from our families and communities. Thankfully, we had support from organizations like the Grand Canyon Trust, the Conservation Lands Foundation, and Southern Utah Wilderness Alliance (SUWA), who really helped us take care of the logistics of the meetings. Mind you, this was before Zoom, before real conference calling, and most of our reservations didn't have the capacity for virtual meeting anyway. It was a lot of driving, but we did it.

Brister: Could you give us a sense of why these lands were in need of preservation and a unified management plan? Why were the Navajo Nation and other tribes focusing on the landscape of southeastern Utah around Bears Ears right then?

Lopez-Whiteskunk: The Utah congressional delegation had been talking about restructuring the rules governing federal lands in Utah. There were talks ongoing with many groups, and there was a concern that their proposal would open up more vulnerabilities. There were opportunities for input, so it seemed like the process might make the management rules simpler and better able to serve what people needed and wanted. At the same time, there was a concern that a proposal might not provide adequate protection for sacred sites and the fragile ecosystem. A lot of the plants out there are unique, and the cultural artifacts are vulnerable to looting. In addition, the tribes didn't want to lose their own access rights for cultural purposes. There was also controversy over off-road motorized vehicle use and grazing in sensitive areas.

The nonprofits that had been working on these issues weren't authorized to conduct government-to-government conversations, and this is why the Navajo Nation and Hopi leadership reached out as tribal leaders to other tribal leaders to build a tribal coalition. As sovereign nations, there are legal privileges and responsibilities that tribes hold that even cities, counties, and states do not. Initially, the goal was to influence the Public Lands Initiative that had been introduced by the Utah congressional delegation.

But when the PLI proposal was presented, it became clear that it would open up more exploration for oil and gas and other minerals, and there was virtually no protection for sacred sites. In fact, there was very little written in the PLI that engaged tribes in any manner. The Navajo Nation already had some land management rights in the area, since the state of Utah does have some dealings with them. Some of the tribal money generated from oil and gas drilling gets administered through the state. That was mentioned in one sentence, and basically, that one sentence flipped the majority of control from the Navajo Nation to the state of Utah. The authors of the bill seemed unaware of the legal status that tribes have for negotiating with the federal government, and they seemed to think that tribes were subservient to state governments rather than having independent status as sovereign governments themselves. The Navajo Nation has lawyers who are trained for this, and they got involved.

Brister: Just to review the timeline here, it sounds like the story about how Bears Ears was designated as a national monument really started out years earlier, with stakeholder negotiations that had taken place since 2013 to inform a public lands bill. As that took shape, the intertribal council began meeting in 2015, and the complete text of the bill wasn't formally introduced by Utah's congressional delegation until 2016, is that right?

Lopez-Whiteskunk: Yes, that's right, and initially our coalition tried to work with Congressmen Rob Bishop and Jason Chaffetz to find other options that could meet some of our asks, but that relationship was not very equitable. We were meeting with them and proposing changes to the language that affected tribes specifically, but when we finally got a copy of the proposed PLI the day before we were supposed to meet with them, nothing had changed! I recall Congressman Bishop basically telling us, "The language is written. We're not going to amend anything." They had asked us to schedule a meeting the day after Christmas, when everybody else was enjoying their family time. Well, they called us like an hour before the meeting to tell us that their staffers were not going to make the meeting after all!

Brister: That doesn't sound like a sincere attempt to collaborate.

Lopez-Whiteskunk: It indicated how our conversations were going to be. At that point, we basically made the decision that we were going to focus our energy and time on lobbying President Obama for an Antiquities Act designation. But that also put us in the position of wanting to see the Utah Public Lands Initiative killed. We were fortunate to be able to provide testimony in a hearing with the Natural Resources Committee of the U.S. House of Representatives. So I traveled to Washington, DC, to provide testimony in opposition to the Public Lands Initiative.

Brister: So the coalition tried to cooperate, but there was just no give-and-take, and the next move involved going to Washington, DC. Had you been there before?

Lopez-Whiteskunk: Actually, yes I had. When I was eighteen I was there as part of a youth leadership experience. When I went back, the words of the late Senator Daniel Inouye of Hawaii came back to me. When I was eighteen, he had said to us, "You are the future leaders and voices of your people. You will find yourself here in this city, and this is going to be your battleground. This is where you will bring your fight for the sake of your people." When he said that, I was far from thinking I could ever be an elected leader. I'm a teenager, and I'm like, "Yeah, right. Whatever." But then some thirty years down the road, I was there playing a key role.

When I found myself walking through the halls of Congress, talking to representatives and senators, I carried his words with me. I reflected on how, when I first engaged in the conversation, my intention was to represent my tribal community specifically. But as the conversation about monument designation took shape, I realized that my voice was not only for my people or for Indigenous people. Our argument represented many land users, like the hikers, the rock climbers, the archaeological communities, as well as the country as a whole and the future generations who would like to see the ecology there intact.

Brister: Could you say something about being the only woman representing the coalition's tribes and speaking to a congressional audience that was also mostly men? Did you feel that gender mattered in that space?

Lopez-Whiteskunk: I did feel that I was treated differently by several of the elected legislators in Utah and the Utah delegation to Congress. There were pointed comments made that targeted not only the whole group as Indigenous people but also some that were directed at me specifically as a female Indigenous leader.

I will also admit that when we first started working together as a coalition, I wasn't sure how I would fit in. Specifically, although I was an elected tribal leader, in the Hopi and Pueblo of Zuni tribes, their culture does not place women in leadership or formal governance positions. I was aware of this, and I wanted to be effective, so I asked my grandmother and father for advice. I was worried that I should relinquish my spot in the coalition if being a woman was a liability. They advised me to sit down with the people I was working with and just have an honest conversation but also really listen and be prepared for the answer, which might not be what I wanted it to be.

So we did have that conversation, and I was relieved that they asked me not to leave the coalition. They went back to telling stories to explain how they felt. They see the female in the role of nurturing the community, their villages, their clans, and all the families. The female is the mother and the heart of a family. All the ceremonies and celebrations could not happen unless there was a female there. They said they were supportive of me staying in the coalition because I represented all the mothers, sisters, grandmothers, and females of our nations. I represented the heart.

Brister: That's affirming, and it probably helped them realize, too, that they needed not to overlook you.

Lopez-Whiteskunk: Yes, we had to be strong because the period of giving testimony was especially trying. I'll say, too, that Charles Wilkinson was an incredible support for us throughout. He advised us about the process and prepared us with strategies. He said, "You've got to remember one thing, Regina. When they set that little timer and you have two to five minutes to say what you want to say, you say it. That's your space. They will try to interrupt you and try to impose a question in the middle of your time. But remember, it's *your* time." One time Congressman Bishop tried to ask me some really off-the-wall questions, and I responded by saying, "Thank you for that question," and then I marched on with what I needed to say so that it could be on the record. What really matters is what goes in the federal record.

Brister: And then the Bears Ears National Monument was designated under the Antiquities Act. When did that happen?

Lopez-Whiteskunk: We presented our proposal to members of the House of Representatives and the Senate. We also presented it to the Department of Interior—to the secretary, who at that time was Sally Jewell—and to President Obama's administration, his Council on Environmental Quality. We worked very closely with the Department of Interior. One of the key things from our perspective was to maintain a unified voice and narrative, which was at times difficult when the media got involved. Congressman Bishop was adept at using the media to convey his message, and the message he put out was that the tribal communities were in need, were poor, were uneducated. But we kept our focus on speaking for the protection that the land needed.

Anyway, it happened December 28, 2016, right near the end of President Obama's term. I remember I was at a doctor's office for an appointment and got a call from the White House. It was Karen Diver, Obama's advisor on Native American Issues, and she told me that Obama was going to sign a designation for 1.35 million acres. Although this was less than the 1.9 million acres we had asked for, I told her, "Well, that's not too shabby." I had to hold my silence on that news for the rest of the afternoon until it became official. I felt so honored—proud of what we had accomplished for our tribes and the country, and also honored to be recognized for the effort I had put into it personally. The first thing I did was to call Charles Wilkinson and say, "As soon as we're done celebrating, we need to think about how to defend it."

Brister: It turned out you were right about that. A few years later, the size of the protected area in Bears Ears National Monument was reduced by the Trump administration. But under the Biden administration, that protection was restored and then some.

Lopez-Whiteskunk: It's true that we need to think about protection into the future. One thread of that is including tribes in land management decisions. President Trump reduced the size of the national monument by 85 percent. That left a lot of sacred sites with very little or no protection. It also opened up a lot of the space to more oil and gas exploration and expanded cattle grazing. President Obama had established a commission leading in the direction of collaborative comanagement between federal agencies and tribes. In addition to reducing the size of the designation and splitting it into two separate parcels, President Trump also took appointment power into his own hands. The individuals that were appointed to sit on the management advisory committees for these two smaller parcels of land were required to be residents of San Juan County, which would have excluded representation from three of the five tribes whose lands lie outside the county.

Then President Biden reestablished the national monument designation and added a little more, an additional ten thousand acres or so. That's the current designation. Biden also reinstated the commission drawn from the five tribes, and, through that, other rule changes have been initiated. I was one of the people to get one of those appointments, and so I currently sit on the Management Advisory Commission (MAC). The MAC is appointed by the secretary of the interior, who currently is Deb Haaland. It is made up of representatives of various interests, including ranchers, the outdoor recreation community, and tribes. In that role, I work with the Bureau of Land Management (BLM) and U.S. Forest Service, and we provide comments on management rules from the various perspectives, including the tribal perspective, to work toward collaborative proposals that are then open to broader public comment.

Brister: There must be a lot of considerations that go into crafting management plans.

Lopez-Whiteskunk: Indeed, there are. For one thing, you want a plan to be flexible enough to accommodate new discoveries—for instance, of cultural sites and artifacts. But you also want to be aware of the constraints that are being put on people who are trying to make their living. If someone is focused on grazing their cattle, and now they're told they have to keep the cattle out of a sacred site, how can we design this situation so it's not imposing an unfair burden, and how can we balance these values? You know, I think everything is totally possible, and managing for all these values really stems out of relationship building. We are only the best (or the worst) neighbors if we build (or fail to build) relationships. I always ask, How do I help others understand me as an Indigenous woman, and how do I also learn about you and where you come from? If I don't know that, then how can we ever meet in the middle? The hope is that we find that common ground and that we're able to shift away from a consumptive approach to the land.

And that's one of the very biggest challenges, the question of how we get to that point. We know for sure that it's going to take negotiations, and we're not always going to get what we want. It isn't an all-or-nothing world. It's about finding that common place. I think that's the biggest takeaway from my experience as a former coalition member and tribal leader—it's that continuing to highlight diversities in a form that leads to a division of people is not good for anyone. Rather, we have to create a bridge and a learning opportunity to be able to understand one another and create a better tomorrow.

14

Innovation and Collaboration on Private Lands along Wyoming's Absaroka Front

DREW E. BENNETT, TRAVIS BRAMMER, AND HILARY BYERLY FLINT

Public lands at the heart of the Greater Yellowstone Ecosystem (GYE) provide habitat for iconic wildlife species like wolves, grizzly bears, and large herds of elk. Less appreciated is the role of privately owned lands, which provide critical winter range and habitat along the migratory routes of elk, mule deer, and other large mammals. These private lands comprise nearly a third of the GYE.

Wildlife can impose significant costs on private landowners, particularly ranchers and farmers. Deep snow and harsh winter conditions drove thousands of starving elk to swarm ranches in the Jackson, Wyoming, area in 1910, tearing down fences to "devour the ranchman's stock feed," according to a vivid account from the local newspaper (Clayton 2020). Ranchers reportedly slept armed in their haystacks to keep the elk at bay. Today, agricultural landowners in Wyoming continue to face costs from elk and other wildlife that further challenge an already strapped way of life. Combined with growing pressures to sell, subdivide, or develop agricultural lands in the region, the habitat provided by private lands in the GYE is under threat.

There are tools for conserving private lands to maintain their benefits for wildlife, but these tools are generally underutilized in the GYE. The first tool, perpetual conservation easements, requires that landowners permanently give up the development rights to their property—a significant commitment as many producers face an uncertain economic future. Another tool, county zoning regulations, are rarely adopted, as local governments are unwilling to pass strict land use controls. Devising and applying new conservation tools in the region, like nonperpetual habitat leases, will be key to conserving private lands and maintaining wildlife habitat in the GYE.

Focusing on the Absaroka Front, an area in northwest Wyoming close to Cody, we highlight emerging collaborative efforts and strategies to address wildlife conflicts on private lands. In the Absaroka Front, local practitioners are developing a portfolio of options for conserving and sustaining habitat on private lands while meeting the needs of landowners. These efforts have helped build trust and a climate of collaboration among stakeholders—elements that are likely to do more to address conservation challenges in the region than any individual program or strategy. The insights being generated along the Absaroka Front are also applicable to broader challenges across the American West and beyond.

Private Lands Play a Critical Role in the GYE

On the eastern boundary of Yellowstone National Park, the rugged Absaroka Mountains rise to peaks of thirteen thousand feet before dropping dramatically to the valleys that form the flank of the GYE. Elk, mule deer, and pronghorn antelope seasonally traverse this rough landscape—leaving their summer habitats in Yellowstone to seek refuge and forage at lower elevations during the harsh winter months. These journeys take the animals across a mosaic of land ownerships, land uses, and management objectives as they move from protected lands within Yellowstone, across wilderness areas and multiple-use national forests, and into the valleys of privately owned land. These privately owned lands, including those along the South Fork of the Shoshone River southwest of Cody, Wyoming, have long been used for grazing and hay production. Increasingly, these lands are being converted into low-density residential developments.

Arthur Middleton is a prominent researcher who recognizes the importance of wildlife habitat in—and beyond—national parks. An ecologist and associate professor at the University of California, Berkeley, Middleton has spent the last decade and a half studying the seasonal movements of wildlife in the GYE. We interviewed him about his work, which has emphasized elk due to the critical role the species plays in sustaining regional food webs and its impacts on land management. He points to the South Fork of the Shoshone as an example of the conservation challenges facing the GYE. The South Fork is still relatively intact in terms of habitat and winter ranges, but it is not assured to remain that way and has already lost a significant amount of habitat.

While private lands constitute a minority of the land in the GYE (roughly 30 percent), they play a disproportionate role in supporting biodiversity. The region was historically home to as many as twenty-seven Native American tribes. The land became privatized when settlers of European ancestry claimed the first private property in the region in the 1870s under the Homestead Act of 1862. The

Homestead Act required settlers to "improve" the land by cultivating it. For that reason and the relative ease of living, claimed lands tended to be at lower elevations, tended to have more productive soils, and were more likely to be adjacent to water. The higher-elevation and less-productive lands were left to fall under public ownership. This settlement pattern contributed to the mosaic of landownership in today's GYE, where protected public lands like Yellowstone are at the core of the ecosystem and private lands form the periphery.

The importance of private land varies by species and geography across the GYE. Elk provide an example of this variability. In a study published in 2022, ecologist Laura Gigliotti worked with Middleton and others to analyze the geographic distribution of twenty-six elk herds across the GYE and compare the relative importance of public and private land to the summer, migration, and winter ranges of the herds (Gigliotti et al. 2022). Because winter ranges tend to be at lower elevations, receive less snow, and have easier access to wintertime forage and water, the scientists found that private lands were much more critical to elk in the winter. However, the importance of private lands varied among the herds, comprising 3–85 percent of each herd's winter range.

The importance of private lands in providing habitat expands beyond the species itself. Elk, along with mule deer and pronghorn antelope, play an important role in the health of the ecosystem. They are key prey species for large carnivores, and their feeding and movement patterns affect the vegetative structure and plant diversity on the landscape. These animals also provide benefits to people. Every year, millions of visitors come to Yellowstone National Park, Grand Teton National Park, and surrounding public lands to see wildlife. For some visitors, elk may be the priority, while others may come to see elusive wolves or formidable grizzly bears. Without large swaths of private lands providing seasonal habitat beyond the parks, elk and their predators are less likely to provide visitors these viewing opportunities.

As Middleton puts it, "Private lands are the hidden driver of what people identify with—even in Yellowstone and Grand Teton [National Parks]. As a thought experiment, if you barricaded all the private lands, or developed them, key wildlife populations would dramatically decline, and park visitors would no longer see the wildlife they expect to see. In fact, the National Park Service would be unable to uphold its mission to 'preserve unimpaired' the natural resources of the national parks."

There are also benefits associated with hunting elk, mule deer, and pronghorn antelope. Like park visitors, hunters come from around the globe and buy goods and services in rural communities, supporting jobs and economies around the GYE. Some hunting equipment is federally taxed to help states pay for wildlife conservation efforts. State game and fish agencies, which are responsible for ensuring the longevity of wildlife populations, are funded through those federal taxes and through hunters buying hunting tags and licenses. Because of those financial benefits and close ties to wildlife, many GYE communities hold hunting in high regard culturally.

Generally, wildlife is owned by the public, and the public gets to enjoy wildlife, whether through simply knowing that populations are healthy, seeing animals in a national park, or pursuing game species as hunters. Private landowners, however, may only realize a small share of these total benefits and may incur significant costs from the presence of wildlife on their land.

The Challenges on Private Lands in the GYE

As elk move down from the mountains in the fall, it is common to find large herds on private hay meadows during the winter months. While these herds make an impressive sight, they also create conflicts with local landowners. Elk compete with livestock for forage, eat stored hay, and damage fences. More concerning for some ranchers is the threat of brucellosis—a highly transmissible disease that moves from elk to cattle. Cows that contract the disease will lose their fetuses and may suffer other fertility issues.

Once a cow has contracted brucellosis, its owner must quarantine or slaughter the entire herd to prevent disease spread. While transmission is uncommon (there were seventeen reported cases over a ten-year period), a single brucellosis event can be devastating to a livestock operation, costing producers up to $150,000 (Middleton et al. 2022; Rhyan et al. 2013). Large predators raise additional concerns for landowners. Migrating elk herds draw grizzlies and wolves toward private lands, making them more likely to prey on livestock.

When the costs of wildlife conflict become too much of a burden on agricultural operations, eating into the already small profit margins inherent in the business, landowners may be forced to sell or change the use of their land. This may displace agriculture and accelerate residential development on the landscape. The primary threat to many Western landscapes is not typically high-density housing developments, like those found within cities, but the transition from large-acreage parcels to smaller lots—such as the subdivision of a several-hundred-acre agricultural property to five- or ten-acre "ranchettes." These new, smaller-acreage landowners build roads and fences, increasing fragmentation and reducing the ecological connectivity of the landscape. New residents may also be less knowledgeable about invasive weeds and less likely to actively manage their land, reducing habitat quality for grazing elk, mule deer, and pronghorn antelope. New residents from nonagricultural backgrounds may create social conflict with agricultural producers as they increase traffic on roads that were used to trail livestock.

In rural communities, an influx of nonagricultural landowners and residents can also reduce demand for certain goods and services and increase property values, making it more difficult for agricultural producers and support industries, like feed or tractor supply stores, to maintain profitability. Smaller lots are typically more valuable on a per-acre basis. This higher value creates incentives for larger acreage owners to subdivide or sell their land. These combined challenges reinforce a trajectory of land use change that results in habitat fragmentation and destruction.

A fundamental challenge of conservation today is confronting the forces that are driving land use conversion on private lands. This means addressing the conflicts and costs faced by landowners living with wildlife and matching the market forces that create pressure for landowners to subdivide or sell. There are no cure-all answers to this challenge. Established conservation tools, such as traditional conservation easements and zoning regulations, have an important role to play. But there are limits to what these tools can accomplish, especially in the culture of rural communities across the GYE.

Instead, this conservation challenge requires developing new tools and approaches that meet landowners' needs and foster social connections and trust. In the process, conservationists can engage stakeholders' diverse interests to work toward shared goals. This is a tall task, but we see encouraging signs in the Absaroka Front, where stakeholders are working to provide landowners new options to address the challenges of living with wildlife and maintain the important benefits their lands provide.

The Current Conservation Toolbox

Despite the threats to private lands in the GYE, there have been successful efforts to conserve habitat. Established tools for private lands conservation typically fall into one of three categories: preventing land use change from subdivision or residential development, remedying wildlife conflict on agricultural operations, and improving habitat. Each tool has its strengths and is particularly effective in certain situations.

Conservation easements and zoning/land use planning are two examples of tools intended to address land use concerns and prevent land from being converted to nonagricultural uses. Conservation easements are a long-standing and commonly used tool in private land conservation. Landowners placing conservation easements on their properties voluntarily agree to permanently restrict the use of their land. Easements significantly limit subdivision and the construction of residences or commercial facilities, while typically allowing for continued agricultural use. In return, landowners may qualify for tax incentives or, in some cases, receive a cash payment for the value of the easement. Many landowners, however, are hesitant to agree to conservation easements because of the permanent nature of the restrictions and limited awareness of the opportunity.

Alex Few is familiar with the challenges of engaging landowners in the GYE with conservation easements. After working for Western Landowners Alliance (WLA), Few became regional director of Park County Open Lands, a new community-led land trust program focused on conserving private lands along the Absaroka Front.

As Few shared with us in one of several conversations about conservation along the Absaroka Front, "If you look at the total acreage under conservation easements in the West, it's tiny. As someone who's now working with landowners to place lands under conservation easement, I recognize why. It's such a big, difficult decision for people, and it's not always the right decision. A conservation easement does not make sense for every family, and yet many of those families and businesses are incurring additional expenses by providing wildlife habitat." Many landowners also do not fully understand the financial benefits due to a lack of trusted relationships with conservation groups that can share information about conservation easement options.

Based on the analysis by Gigliotti and colleagues, less than 2 percent of the private land in elk habitat in the GYE is protected by a conservation easement. Within the Absaroka Front and other areas around Cody, there are a handful of conservation easements, but the tool has not been widely adopted in the area (Gigliotti et al. 2022).

Zoning and land use planning have also long been used to manage development on private lands. Towns and counties often create a land use plan, which outlines goals for the land in their jurisdiction. Those plans then form the basis of zoning laws, which control land development, such as where development occurs and the type of development allowed in certain areas. In the Western United States, a lack of political support for regulations and a perception of abundant open space mean that most land is not subject to zoning laws. Gigliotti and colleagues reported that 37 percent of elk range in the GYE lacked any type of zoning. Even where zoning laws are in place, land developers may receive exceptions to subdivide or develop land more intensively than the law would otherwise allow (Gigliotti et al. 2022).

Other tools help address wildlife conflicts with livestock and wildlife damage to agricultural operations. In the Absaroka Front, where large herds of elk move across private lands, landowners may receive damage compensation payments from the Wyoming Game and Fish Department (WGFD) if elk eat hay or other crops, and the WGFD will pay for fencing to help keep wildlife out of haystacks. Ranchers can also receive compensation for verified livestock losses from wolves and grizzlies. While these programs are important to help maintain tolerance for wildlife, compensation is often less than the full value of the loss.

The final category of tools currently in the conservation practitioner's toolbox are those aimed at improving habitat on private land. The U.S. Department of Agriculture's Environmental Quality Incentives Program (EQIP) provides financial incentives and technical expertise to landowners for implementing management practices that improve habitat quality. While thousands of landowners around the country have enrolled in EQIP to improve habitat, program commitments are only for a few years. The habitat improvements may be undone as soon as the agreement expires or the land passes to new owners with different management goals. And many landowners are reluctant to jump through the bureaucratic hoops required to enroll in the program.

These established tools have played important roles in habitat conservation, but their limitations demonstrate the shortcomings of current conservation strategies. Addressing these shortcomings requires innovation in the design and delivery of conservation programs to meet landowner needs. When we talked with her, Few stated the challenge:

> There are many ranchers on the Absaroka Front that have fantastic grazing plans, and because they are implementing a meaningful rest rotation program on their ranch, they're providing significant forage for big game. All that comes at an economic cost to them. [We need to] recognize that these people are doing great work. That's why the wildlife are there. That's why

> these huge migrations still exist. Because the land is intact and the owners are already stewarding their land well. So what are the tools that are necessary to protect the land from development and to help pay the costs of existing good stewardship?

While new tools are needed, so are collaborative relationships between conservationists and landowners to ensure new approaches meet landowners' needs and support the stewardship of land and wildlife.

The Need for Collaboration and Innovation

The focus on landscape connectivity for big-game species across the West (especially elk, mule deer, and pronghorn antelope) increased in 2018 when the U.S. Secretary of Interior Ryan Zinke signed Secretarial Order 3362. That order directed agencies within the Department of Interior to collaborate with Western states to conserve migratory big-game habitats. As of 2018, Wyoming had already designated one mule deer migration corridor—in Sublette County, on the southern end of the GYE. Following the secretarial order, Wyoming has designated two more corridors and appears likely to identify and designate others in the coming years.

While corridor policies were generally supported by voters, landowners in these regions saw the growing federal and state attention to corridors and connectivity and became concerned about implications for their land and agricultural operations (Gautier, Bennett, and Bonnie 2019; Paolini et al. 2023). These concerns grew after the publication of big-game movement maps, which used GPS data from collared big-game animals to show, in fine detail, migration corridors across private (and public) lands throughout large swaths of the state (see Bennett and Gautier 2019; Jones Ritten et al. 2022). Where would the designations end? Would land use restrictions on public and private lands follow? For some landowners, the focus on protecting big-game habitat seemed tone-deaf, ignoring the burdens landowners face when wildlife migrate through private land.

Conservationists in the GYE heard these landowners' concerns. In Montana's Paradise Valley, the Bozeman-based Property and Environment Research Center, or PERC, launched a multiyear process of collecting landowner feedback about concerns surrounding big game on private lands (Tilt 2020). In Wyoming, Arthur Middleton brought landowners together with conservation organizations and agencies to foster increased communication and coordination. Starting as informal conversations, these efforts led to the formation of the East Yellowstone Collaborative Working Group, whose participants include local landowners, the Western Landowners Alliance (WLA), the Nature Conservancy, the Greater Yellowstone Coalition (GYC), and Park County Open Lands. The collaborative group works "to restore, protect, and steward the lands of the Absaroka Front to support healthy wildlife populations and sustain private workings lands."

Through informal conversations and formal interviews, landowners informed conservation groups and agencies that they lacked a meaningful way to contribute to wildlife management. At public meetings, landowners felt like they were "just another seat at the table," even though the management decisions impacted their lands and livelihoods (Bennett and Gautier 2019). Other ranchers thought the science guiding policy and management on corridors was conducted in a top-down fashion and disconnected from the insights and local knowledge gained from years of observing and working on the land. These landowners desired greater recognition of the local context and the value they could provide in informing management.

Landowners identified gaps in the current conservation toolbox. They appreciated the goals of conservation easements but were often uncomfortable with permanent restrictions that would box in future generations. Many wanted to slow the loss of agricultural land, but zoning and land use regulations were nonstarters. Others lacked awareness of existing tools or were discouraged by the bureaucratic hurdles of government conservation programs, with stacks of paperwork to complete on top of running their agricultural businesses. Due to income limitations or other eligibility requirements, some landowners were not able to participate in certain government programs. There was also a political element: several landowners expressed distrust toward the federal government or had no interest in accepting government funding as a matter of principle. These landowners sought privately funded conservation. Collectively, input from landowners demonstrated the limitations of established conservation programs and highlighted the siloed nature of disparate federal, state, and private conservation efforts.

As conversations continued via the East Yellowstone Collaborative Working Group and in Paradise Valley, landowners floated new ideas. What if there were less-than-permanent conservation agreements? Could strategies be developed to mitigate financial loss from brucellosis? Landowners made suggestions and conservation groups responded by codeveloping innovative concepts. As momentum built, Middleton and PERC partnered to host a workshop that brought landowners, conservation groups, and university researchers together to develop policy recommendations for the incoming Biden administration and identify emerging strategies partners that could advance in addition to federal programs.

In 2022, PERC and GYC partnered with a Paradise Valley landowner on an "occupancy agreement." Through the occupancy agreement, elk have unfettered, livestock-free access to five hundred acres of privately owned winter range on the property. Livestock will be excluded from the winter range through the construction of a 1.25-mile fence, reducing the risk of brucellosis spread and other conflicts (Bennett and Brammer 2023). The landowners will also undertake habitat management actions—removing encroaching conifers, treating invasive weeds, and implementing controlled burns. In return, PERC and GYC reimburse the landowners for building the fence and give the landowner an additional payment for providing the winter range habitat. The agreement must be renewed on an annual basis and includes few enforcement terms to express trust between all parties.

The GYC facilitated another occupancy agreement in Wyoming, funded through private donations, that paid most of the costs of transporting cattle from a high-risk brucellosis area on a ranch to winter pasture in a low-risk area. In return, elk can freely access the property's winter range without conflict with livestock. In an effort to meaningfully address landowner concerns, these occupancy agreements have been tailored to meet the specific needs of participating landowners.

PERC also launched a Brucellosis Compensation Fund in January 2023 to mitigate the potential financial losses to livestock operators should their herd contract brucellosis. The fund will cover up to 75 percent of estimated feeding costs for a quarantined herd with a maximum payout of 50 percent of the total fund size for any single quarantine event (PERC 2022). The funding structure requires that livestock producers carry some financial risk so they are incentivized to minimize their herd's risk of exposure. While currently limited to livestock operations in Paradise Valley, the fund could also expand to other areas of the GYE, including the Absaroka Front. Success for the fund model could lay the foundation for more formal financial risk-management tools like "brucellosis insurance" or "brucellosis bonds."

The East Yellowstone Collaborative is considering how these innovations might apply to wildlife issues along the Absaroka Front, while simultaneously pursuing their own ideas. The Collaborative is exploring the concept of a "habitat lease," a less-than-permanent conservation agreement to maintain, enhance, or restore habitat in exchange for a cash or nonmonetary incentive. The goal of such a lease is to meet the needs of landowners who would not put conservation easements on their lands but still provide critical big-game habitat.

Wildlife conservation efforts along the Absaroka Front received a boost when the state of Wyoming and the U.S. Department of Agriculture (USDA) announced a formal partnership "to support the voluntary conservation of private working lands and migratory big game populations in Wyoming" in October 2022 (USDA 2022). The partnership identified the Absaroka Front as one of five initial priority areas. Projects in priority areas will be more competitive for allocated funding, which includes an initial $16 million investment for 2023. Funding is allocated to long-standing USDA programs like conservation easements and EQIP, as well as emerging tools like habitat leases. The partnership is also spurring significant investment from private state and national foundations to support resource coordinators who will be employed by nonprofit conservation organizations. These coordinator positions will conduct outreach with landowners to raise awareness of programs and help navigate the enrollment paperwork, with the aim of increasing participation.

Prior to formalizing this partnership, leadership at the USDA held several listening sessions throughout Wyoming, leveraging existing collaborative efforts such as the East Yellowstone Collaborative and the Absaroka Fence Initiative to solicit feedback. Although statutes like the Farm Bill constrain the USDA, the USDA has been able to make several adaptations to existing programs to address landowner feedback. In one example, the USDA created an exemption that allows landowners to access multiple programs simultaneously on the same land, allowing landowners to "stack" programs and meet complex resource concerns. Additionally, the USDA is exploring how other existing programs, such as its Grassland Conservation Reserve Program, might form the foundation of a more comprehensive habitat leasing effort when combined with state or private funding. The development of this concept is ongoing, as conversations continue with members of the East Yellowstone Collaborative and other stakeholders.

Alex Few told us she finds these efforts promising. She sees the discussion around this, which came to be known as the USDA-Wyoming Big Game Partnership, and the efforts to implement a habitat lease through the Grassland Conservation Reserve Program as "advancing the conversation around rewarding landowners who are already doing great things on their land."

Innovations in addressing wildlife conflict and the Wyoming-USDA partnership will not resolve the wildlife conservation challenges in the Absaroka Front. Nonetheless, they offer the chance to make headway on long-standing problems. They also represent efforts to respond to specific landowner feedback and address private costs to conserve the public's interest on private lands.

Lessons from the Absaroka Front

Looking out across the South Fork of the Shoshone River, there are only hints of the boundary lines that define landownership. A few fence lines, irrigated meadows, and signposts demark private land boundaries, agricultural operations, and the transition to public land. The landscape is still largely intact. Yet there are warning signs that the landscape is at risk. Driving along Southfork Road toward Cody, "For Sale" signs pop up in front of a handful of big open fields. Locals can point out agricultural properties that were recently subdivided into ranchettes. It is not a conservation emergency. But it is the gradual loss of conservation values and a death by a thousand cuts, where each conversion of a working farm or ranch represents a small loss, but the cumulative impact over time may be ecologically catastrophic.

The South Fork and the Absaroka Front are prime examples of the dynamics playing out across Western landscapes. So what lessons can the experiences from the Absaroka Front offer to communities across the West and beyond?

For one, focused collaboration can build social capital. The collaborative efforts in the region brought together stakeholders with different but overlapping objectives. Conservationists and landowners found common ground to better understand challenges and constraints and to identify opportunities.

The importance of conservationist and landowner dialogue is not lost on Alex Few: "We're at a time in society where we're polarized and divided. And we think we have more differences than we really do. If we actually bring people together in a meaningful way, we can see beyond whatever labels we might put on each other and find ways to work together." When he spoke with us, Arthur Middleton agreed. He feels that it is essential that efforts to conserve migrations be nonpartisan: "If you follow the science on migrations, you end up looking at states like Idaho, Montana, and Wyoming, which are all Republican-led states. So you have to come up with solutions that have broad support across parties and stakeholder interests."

Through these experiences, attention was given to developing new and innovative tools to address the shortcomings of the status quo. These new tools acted as "boundary objects," concepts that provide an opportunity to bring stakeholders together and align aims and interests. The process also created new and stronger social connections, enabling stakeholders to address complex conservation challenges over the long term.

Additionally, the Absaroka Front showed that collaborative dialogues can lead to on-the-ground conservation efforts. Pilot efforts to test new tools and the

Wyoming-USDA Big Game Partnership are direct responses to rancher feedback. The relationships that have resulted raise the hope that landowners and conservationists can continue to come to the table and address additional conservation challenges in the GYE.

Lastly, while this sort of initiative may be difficult to scale, its impact can grow by connecting with and being replicated in other regions. Already, the processes in the Absaroka Front have become part of broader efforts. The East Yellowstone Collaborative is learning from pilot projects occurring in Paradise Valley, Montana, and other regions will learn from the pilots implemented by the East Yellowstone Collaborative. The Wyoming-USDA Big Game Partnership was built from local experiences and was recently expanded to Idaho and Montana as the USDA Migratory Big Game Initiative. It may lead to similar federal-state partnerships in other Western states.

There are questions about the long-term viability of these approaches. It may prove difficult to maintain private funding for innovative strategies. Long-term political support at the state and federal levels may be challenging to sustain across different administrations. Yet there is hope that the investment in building relationships and trust can generate progress.

Partly due to his efforts along the Absaroka Front and in the GYE, Middleton was appointed as a senior advisor for Wildlife Conservation at the USDA. In Middleton's view, "What is happening reflects a real desire to do something lasting. It's something that has staying power because it represents bipartisan arrangements and is built off of genuine relationships developed through collaboration and listening to landowners."

The situation along the Absaroka Front and across the GYE is illustrative of a fundamental challenge of conservation. Collaborative and innovative conservation efforts in this region provide insight into possible strategies to balance the public's interest in wildlife and open space with the pressures faced by private landowners. New conservation tools and multistakeholder efforts to implement them can complement established tools for private lands conservation.

These tools, however, cannot be used in a vacuum. Social connections and trusted relationships are critical for collaboration. To move these efforts forward, conservationists and landowners need to be willing to work collaboratively to maintain and enhance the momentum. Will the experience in the Absaroka Front and broader GYE ultimately prove successful? That remains uncertain. But the efforts to innovate and collaborate provide hope for finding lasting solutions that work for both people and wildlife.

15

Beyond Current Boundaries

Disrupting Historical Legacies to Re-Indigenize the Crown of the Continent

MONTE MILLS AND KEKEK JASON STARK

The Rocky Mountain Front in what is now north-central Montana is a majestic landscape of unparalleled beauty, biodiversity, and wildness. From the plains, the often snowcapped peaks of the Northern Rockies rise to the clouds, sending the first droplets of some of the nation's great waterways—the Missouri, the Columbia, the Flathead, and others—on their journeys to the east and west. Through these valleys migrate elk, moose, wolverine, and black and grizzly bears, the latter often following their course out into the plains in search of late summer sustenance before fall hibernation. The area is truly the "Crown of the Continent" in both its prominent place at the top of the nation and its spectacular jewels of natural wonder.

This area is also home to the Blackfeet Nation, part of the Blackfoot Confederacy, a group of Indigenous tribes who, since time immemorial, roamed across this region. Where the plains meet the mountains remains a place of immense importance to the Blackfeet, who refer to that area as the "Backbone of the World" and continue to hunt, fish, gather, pray, and live across the landscape.

For over a century, however, this magnificent ecosystem has been divided with lines drawn on maps by those not rooted, as the Blackfeet are, in the land. From the international border between the United States and Canada, which bisected both the area and the Blackfoot Confederacy, to the more recent creations of the Blackfeet Nation's reservation, U.S. National Forests, and Glacier National Park, these boundary lines have been imbued with authority asserted under the color of U.S. law. This chapter focuses on the laws, policies, and management of resources on the United States' side of the international border, but similar efforts are also underway to redefine the historical conception and import of the international boundary imposed between the United States and Canada that split the Blackfoot Confederacy.

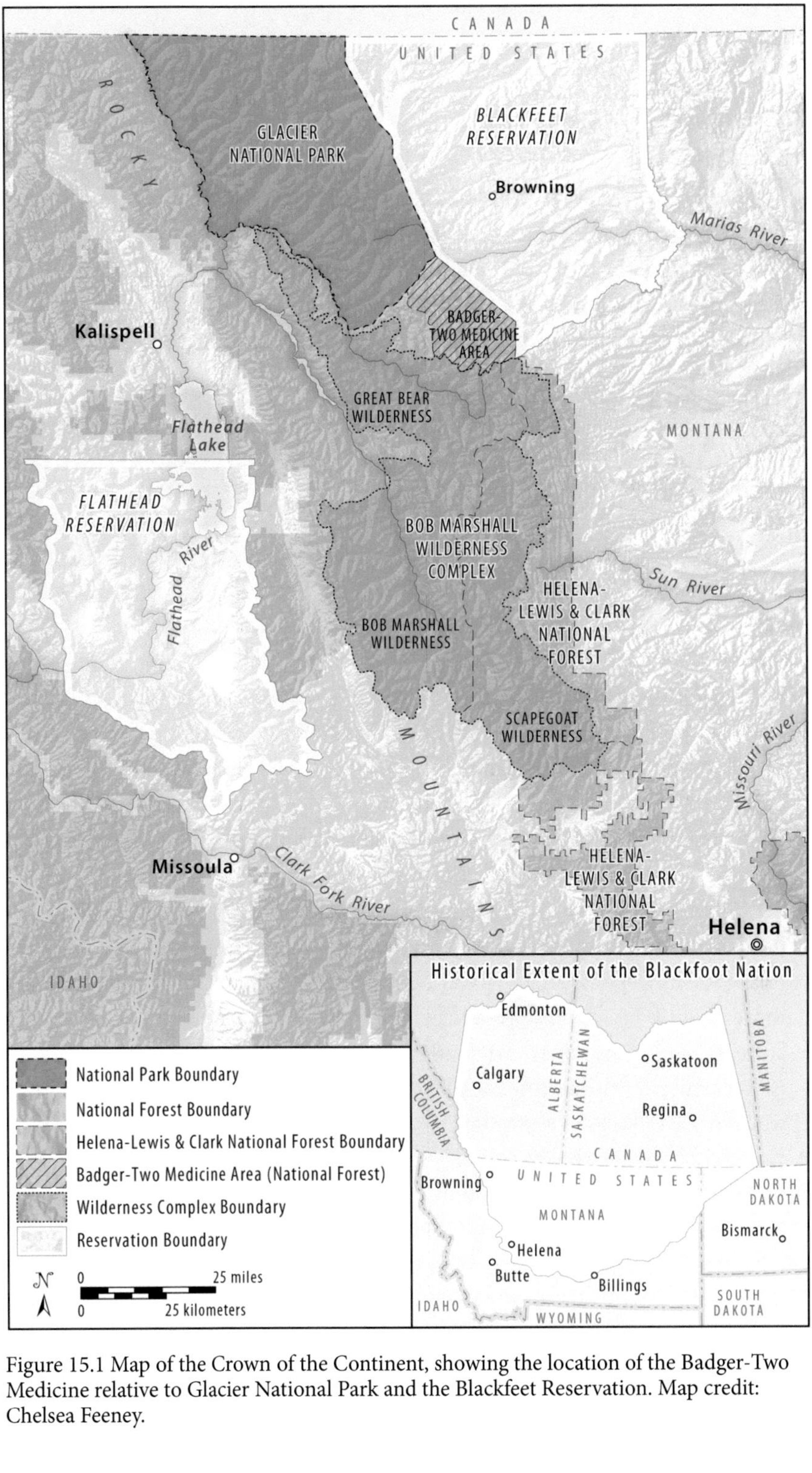

Figure 15.1 Map of the Crown of the Continent, showing the location of the Badger-Two Medicine relative to Glacier National Park and the Blackfeet Reservation. Map credit: Chelsea Feeney.

From the earliest days of that legal system, the assertion of authority and the lines that define it have relied upon conceptions of wilderness and open spaces that ignore or erase the presence of Indigenous people like the Blackfeet from the landscape. As a result, and because this mix of imposed divisions and legal power has come to define the policies, management, and decisions affecting the open spaces of the Crown of the Continent, the claiming of places in the region, like Glacier National Park or the Bob Marshall Wilderness, and the development of the area's mineral, timber, and other resources have largely excluded tribal values and viewpoints (Clow and Sutton 2001).

The historical legacies of these limits and philosophies continue to resonate across the Crown, but the Blackfeet Nation and broader Blackfoot Confederacy are now disrupting and reshaping them in meaningful ways. From long-standing efforts to protect the area known as the Badger-Two Medicine to reintroducing bison to the landscape and increasing Indigenous representation and presence at Glacier National Park, tribal voices are now overtaking the echoes of settler-colonial oppression laid down in borderlines across the landscape.

The future promises more and more impactful tribal leadership, ushering in a re-Indigenized approach to land stewardship and protection throughout the Crown of the Continent and beyond. Instead of lines and powers imposed by authorities mostly disconnected from that place, an Indigenous future for the Crown of the Continent promises a balance of connection, conservation, and authority centered in and deeply connected to the land. Bridging that future will require changes in long-held perspectives and resulting policy positions embedded into the United States' legal system. Such changes will be necessary to accommodate broader—particularly tribal—perspectives and, ultimately, to usher in a more sustainable future for the region's shared natural resources. In concert with Indigenous-led movements to protect, restore, and invigorate long-standing cultural connections at Bears Ears in the American Southwest and across the landscape, the promise of this new era will redefine the meaning of historically imposed lines and may well redraw those lines altogether.

To tell the story of these changes, this chapter begins with a brief introduction to the notion of wilderness and its connection to the legal authority animating present-day boundaries. The conception of wild spaces that has shaped the American legal landscape differs significantly from tribal notions of and connections to the land. From that framework, the chapter then examines the historical background of the Crown of the Continent, including the Blackfeet Nation's connection to the area as part of its traditional territory, as well as its treaty relationship with the United States. The third section examines the management of the area, including proposed development as well as protection efforts, before the chapter closes by setting forth the prospect of a renewed Indigenous-led future of the Crown.

Wilderness, Progress, and Power

The concept of wilderness and, in particular, the open, natural, seemingly uninhabited spaces of the American West, has become a central part of America's identity. These areas both beckon the adventurous wanderer urged on by Horace Greeley and serve as a scenic and majestic vestige of a mythic and glorious past. The potential posed by untamed expanses of lands—prime for settlement, development, and colonization—continued to shape the nation's story of itself and played an important role in defining legal rules that would invigorate the process of colonization.

In the earliest decisions of the U.S. Supreme Court, for example, the court evoked "wilderness" as a counterpoint to the more modern version of American progress, rooted in the development of the natural landscape. In fact, the court's 1823 decision in *Johnson v. McIntosh* described the as-yet-unsettled lands of what is now Illinois as "wilderness," to be acquired and utilized in the name of progress, which, in the court's view, could only happen at the hands of non-Indigenous settlers. As a result of that decision, the property rights of Native Nations to the lands they inhabited since time immemorial were made subject to an overriding interest of the United States, which could extinguish tribal ownership through purchase or conquest.

Implicit in the use and description of the wilderness theme to establish legal doctrine was the corresponding notion of the "vanishing Indian," who, at least for the Supreme Court, was inseparable from the wilderness and therefore would disappear along with it as America obtained and developed these lands. In that 1823 decision, for example, the Supreme Court justified its ruling by noting that leaving lands in the hands of its original inhabitants would be leaving it as wilderness, thereby reasoning that both the wild lands and the people intimately connected to them must be folded into America's inevitable forward march. In the effort to assimilate tribes into these Western values, the dispossession of tribal lands and removal of Indians from the landscape was a central component of the national wilderness ideal (McDonnell 1991; Wilkinson 2005).

Because it is rooted in the very foundation of the nation's identity and legal framework, the notion of unpeopled wilderness has remained a continuing foundation for the building of legal rules around tribal rights. In 2005 for example, the Supreme Court heard a case involving efforts by the Oneida Nation, in what is now New York, to restore its authority over lands that had been illegally alienated from its traditional territory but that the nation had obtained through repurchase. The court rejected the Oneida Nation's claims because, in the court's view, too much time had passed since the nation last owned and exercised its authority over those lands. According to the court, despite the history of wrongful taking of the nation's lands, recognizing tribal authority now would only serve to disrupt the settled expectations of non-Indigenous settlers. In summing up the contrast between those two possibilities, the court once again equated Indigenous authority with wilderness and modern American progress with development, saying, "It was not until lately that the Oneidas sought to regain ancient sovereignty over land converted from wilderness to become part of cities" (City of Sherrill v. Oneida Indian Nation of N.Y. 544 U.S. 197 [2005]).

Like the court, Congress has relied upon the same dichotomy between unpeopled wilderness and developed settlements, ignoring that Indigenous people inhabited these apparently (to the Western eye) "unsettled" landscapes since time immemorial. When enacting the landmark Wilderness Act of 1964, for example, Congress defined *wilderness* as follows:

> A wilderness, in contrast with those areas where man and his own works dominate the landscape, is hereby recognized as an area where the earth and its community of life are untrammeled by man, where man himself is a visitor who does not remain. An area . . . of undeveloped Federal land retaining its primeval character and influence, without permanent improvements or human habitation . . . which (1) generally appears to have been affected primarily by the forces of nature, with the imprint of man's work substantially unnoticeable; (2) has outstanding opportunities for solitude or a primitive . . . recreation; (3) has at least five thousand acres of land. (Wilderness Act 1964)

Unless one accepts the degrading assertion that an Indigenous presence in these areas is part of their "primeval character and influence," this definition leaves no room for recognition of the land's original stewards. Nonetheless, like the Supreme Court, Congress relied on this conception of wilderness when drawing this legal line that has come to define capital-*W* wilderness ever since.

The tribal understanding of *wildness* provides a clear contrast to the American theme of wilderness and the assertions of legal power that have relied on that theme. The tribal concept of wilderness is not rooted in perspectives that serve other objectives related to national interests or wealth maximization. Instead, tribal views of place derive from the traditional laws rooted in creation stories, acknowledging that tribes were placed in their respective homelands and were given responsibilities and obligations associated with these territories.

While each of these tribes, stories, and homelands provides their own unique perspectives, responsibilities, and obligations, the overarching themes of connection and continuing relations with the natural world run throughout. The tribal perspective on the concept of wilderness reflects a place where the rhythm and pulse of the territory is evident in continuous harmonious use and presence on the landscape. This view stands in stark contrast to the notion of wilderness—and the Indigenous people most deeply connected to it—as an obstacle soon to disappear beneath the wheels of progress or as an untrammeled paradise without human presence or impact.

There is no place where the clash of these two themes is more evident than in the lands encompassing the Crown of the Continent. Historically, if one ignored or removed the tribal presence and connection to the region, the Crown offered the opportunity to develop available resources in line with the dominant perspective on open spaces and progress. Those opportunities were authorized by federal agencies whose missions were rooted in similar notions of erasure and guided (ironically) by a mandate to ensure the land provided for multiple uses, even if doing so meant marginalizing the land's original and continuing users.

Drawing Lines across the Backbone of the World

Since time immemorial, the Blackfeet relied upon the yearly cycle of the seasons. Their economy centered upon the buffalo hunt and the use of resources of the mountains and eastern foothills of the Crown. Beginning in spring, various bands would disperse from their winter camps for hunting and gathering, with some headed into the mountains to gather resources while others moved east across the plains to hunt buffalo. As the summer season approached, the bands would gather in large ceremonial encampments for the annual Sun Dance and medicine lodge ceremonies. Following the ceremonies, groups would again disperse, with some hunting buffalo and others headed into the mountains to harvest lodgepoles, medicines, berries, and other foods, including hunting elk, deer, moose, bighorn sheep, mountain goats, beaver, and other small game.

Toward the fall, the bands would reconvene to engage in large communal hunts. As winter approached, they would return to the wooded river valleys along the mountains for their winter camps. To the Blackfeet, the area is home to many sacred beings including Cold Maker, Wind Maker, Thunder, Snow Shrinker, Medicine Elk, Medicine Wolf, and Medicine Grizzly Bear. As William Talks About from the Tribal Business Council of the Blackfeet Nation explains, describing this connection, "The Front is our 'backbone of the world' and a vital part of our culture since it gives us life and is utilized every day as it was by past generations of our ancestors to provide us strength, subsistence, cultural identity and to connect us with our creator" (quoted in Nie 2008, 592–93).

The geographic area encompassing the eastern portion of the Crown of the Continent was historically governed through a succession of agreements between the Blackfeet Nation and the federal government. In 1851, the United States invited all the Native Nations of the northern Great Plains to gather for a treaty council at Fort Laramie. Due to the large number of participants, the council was moved to the mouth of Horse Creek, where Nebraska and Wyoming now meet. It was the largest gathering of Plains Nations in American history, with ten to fifteen thousand people in attendance. The 1851 treaty and another treaty written in 1855 defined the aboriginal boundaries of Blackfeet Territory and other tribal territories in relation to one another and the United States.

In the Blackfeet Agreement of 1895, the Blackfeet were pressured to surrender the western portion of their lands, referred to as the "ceded strip," in the face of dire winter conditions and immense non-Indian interest in accessing the hard-rock minerals in that area. In doing so, however, the Blackfeet reserved critical rights to continue to use and access the land, including the rights to hunt, log, and travel across roughly four hundred thousand acres of ceded lands.

In 1897, President Grover Cleveland issued a proclamation creating the Lewis and Clark Forest Reserve to govern management of the region. Cleveland's proclamation acknowledged that the Blackfeet "rights and privileges . . . respecting the portion of their reservation relinquished to the United States . . . shall be in no way infringed or modified" (Cleveland 1897). The northern portion of the strip was transferred to the National Park Service for the creation of Glacier National Park, which was established by Congress in 1910 (U.S. Congress 1910).

The remaining roughly 130,000 acres of the ceded strip are in the Helena-Lewis and Clark National Forest (HLCNF). Within these acres lies the Badger-Two

Medicine region, where two drainages flow from the Rocky Mountain Front down to the plains. Like the rest of the Crown, the Blackfeet have inhabited the Badger-Two Medicine area for eons and recognize it as critical to the "oral history, creation stories, and ceremonies of the Blackfoot people, as well as an important plant gathering, hunting, fishing and timbering site which continues to be vital to the religious, cultural and subsistence survival of the Blackfoot people" (Blackfoot Confederacy 2014). The Blackfeet Nation considers this area sacred and has several reserved treaty rights on the ceded lands, but thanks to the acquisition and management of these lands by the United States, these values and rights remain threatened by oil and gas development, as well as incompatible uses and management decisions by the U.S. Forest Service (USFS) regarding the national forest that encompasses the area.

Management of the Area

The severance of the ceded strip from the Blackfeet Reservation marked a deep cut to the spirit and connectedness of the Blackfeet Nation. The subsequent creation of the national forest and inclusion of the area within what is now the Helena-Lewis and Clark National Forest further catalyzed that separation by empowering the U.S. Forest Service to manage the land and resources of the region. Through this management authority, which for much of the history of the USFS and HLCNF has been motivated by interests or concerns well removed from those of the Blackfeet, the landscape has been further shaped to encompass and reflect distant and alien concerns rather than those of the peoples most connected to it. Most damaging has been the notion, rooted in historical ideas of wilderness and progress and developed like those described above, that the best use of the region would be its development.

During the 1980s, for example, the federal government promoted the exploitation of oil and gas resources in the Badger-Two Medicine area. Led by then secretary of the interior James Watt, various agencies of the federal government sought to ramp up access to and development across the nation's public lands. As a first step toward the leasing of minerals in the Badger-Two Medicine region, the USFS conducted an Environmental Assessment (EA) in 1981, which determined that the leasing and proposed drilling on those leases would not significantly impact the quiet and solitude necessary for Blackfeet ceremonial activities or, at the very least, that such impacts could be assessed and understood for each lease. In addition, the assessment noted that a schedule of the drilling would be posted, and the Blackfeet could move farther up the mountains to get away from any disturbing sounds.

With that assessment completed, the federal government issued fifty-one oil and gas leases in the area in 1982. These parcels were not inventoried for cultural resources by the USFS, and both the "USFS and BLM [the agency responsible for monitoring subsurface development activity, the Bureau of Land Management] failed to fully consider the effects of leasing, including all phases of oil and gas activities on cultural resources, including religious values and activities, within the Badger-Two Medicine area" (Aden L. Seidlitz, quoted in Mills and Nie 2020). Despite the EA's suggestion that site- or lease-specific analysis would help identify additional impacts, no environmental analysis was conducted prior to lease issuance. Nor was there consideration of how these leases would impact the Blackfeet in their exercise of the rights reserved by the 1895 agreement with the United States. The USFS also failed to comply with the National Historic Preservation Act (NHPA) and the American Indian Religious Freedom Act (AIRFA), both of which provided additional basis on which the agency may have been required to further consider Blackfeet interests. Finally, the USFS neglected to meaningfully consult with the Blackfeet Nation, asserting that compliance would take place after lease issuance and "at the time soil disturbing activities are proposed" on each specific parcel.

Multiple objections and protests—from tribal and nontribal interests—arose in response to these controversial leases, following which the federal government soon suspended its review of the applications for permits to drill in the area. In 1993, the secretary of the interior suspended the drilling permits.

In 2013, one of the companies still holding oil and gas lease rights in the region sued the Department of the Interior to revive the stalled appeals process and to act on its 1985 drilling permits. As that litigation worked its way through protracted legal processes, the core of the conflict emerged: balancing the lessee's ability to protect a contract right to development (rooted in past ideas of exploitative use of the resource) against the federal government's ability to assess and remedy its shortcomings in recognizing the Blackfeet's connection to the region (and the harm that would result from its development) by rescinding that lease. Can a legal system long rooted in ideas of acquiring wilderness and open spaces and converting them to developable resources adequately account for the counternarrative presented by long-standing Indigenous connections to those spaces? While that litigation continues as of this writing, the existence of that conflict as a viable legal dispute is largely the result of tribal efforts to redefine the historical (mis)perception of wilderness. The work of the Blackfeet to protect the Badger-Two Medicine has been instrumental in that work.

Changing Paradigms, Shifting Boundaries

In 1992, the U.S. Congress enacted amendments to the National Historic Preservation Act. Anyone familiar with plaques on old buildings signifying their presence on the National Register of Historic Places has witnessed the impact of the NHPA; but until 1992 that law took little notice of the Indigenous history present throughout the nation. Thanks to tribal advocates, the 1992 amendments changed that. For one, the revised law broadened the type of properties possibly covered by NHPA to include traditional cultural property (TCP) and traditional cultural district (TCD) designations. These new categories of protection expanded NHPA's reach beyond just old buildings and presented the possibility of recognition for entire neighborhoods or, in the Indigenous context, landscapes of cultural import. In addition, the 1992 changes to NHPA allowed tribes to develop their own governmental capacities and offices to assume the responsibility for engaging with federal and state officials as historic preservation officers. This second change required broader federal recognition of—and consultation with—tribal officials when federal actions might impact culturally important sites.

Both of these changes have opened the door for tribal authority and perspectives to help shape federal lands management. For the Blackfeet and their region, the NHPA has been a critical tool for asserting their interests in a more proactive and synergistic fashion. For example, the Blackfeet Nation worked for years to compile the ethnographic, archaeological, and other studies of the cultural significance of the Badger-Two Medicine that resulted in its designation as a TCD in 2002.

Shortly thereafter, the Blackfeet Tribal Historic Preservation Office (THPO), the office supported by the authority of the 1992 amendments to NHPA, initiated several collaborative projects to complete the ethnographic studies of the area. In 2014, this collective work led to the Badger-Two Medicine TCD being expanded from 89,376 acres to 165,588 acres. In adding the expanded acreage to the TCD, the Keeper of the National Register's determination recognized "the remote wilderness" of the Badger-Two Medicine but provided "a more holistic and inclusive view" of the region than what was provided in 2002, recognizing it "as an interconnected traditional landscape," "a place of extreme power," and "a significant region of refuge" for many tribal members (quoted in Mills and Nie 2020, 46–47).

Designation of the Badger-Two Medicine as a traditional cultural district has proven advantageous in several ways. First, the historical and cultural studies provided the Bureau of Land Management (BLM) with an important rationale to reauthorize the suspension of oil and gas leases in the area. Second, it allowed the USFS to recommend to the Department of the Interior a federal mining withdrawal that happened administratively in 2001 and then was approved by Congress in 2006, which prevented further leasing of the area. These moves and others provided the Blackfeet and conservationists time to find more durable solutions while still working to address the leasing done in the early 1980s.

Perhaps equally important, however, these studies had an educational function as well, clearly articulating to federal agencies and political decision-makers the deep history and webs connecting the Blackfeet to the Badger-Two Medicine. By imbuing these values with an official designation under federal law, the 1992 NHPA amendments enabled federal recognition of such values within the dominant legal framework, giving federal officials a legitimate legal status to reference when considering future management decisions. Compared with the historical marginalization and denigration of those values, the TCD designation served as an important shift in federal oversight within the Badger-Two Medicine. Although this litigation continues, federal land managers are now better informed about and more attuned to the deep cultural status of those resources, which is changing their approach to planning how the region will be managed going forward.

The importance of planning in the context of federal land management activities cannot be overstated. Planning is a core principle in federal public land law and the basis for authorizing activities taking place on a piece of public land, all of which must be consistent with the governing land use plans. Plans are the vehicle for taking broad statutory mandates and more detailed regulations and applying them to particular places. Planning is particularly important on lands managed by the USFS and BLM because it is at the plan level where their broad multiple-use missions are operationalized and given meaning on the ground. In fact, the laws governing how the U.S. Forest Service carries out its duties, like the National Forest Management Act of 1976 or NFMA, require the preparation of land and resource management plans for every national forest and grassland in the National Forest System.

In 2012, new planning regulations ("2012 Planning Rule") were issued by the Obama administration. Dozens of national forests across the country are now revising plans using this rule. Consistent with the burgeoning recognition of tribal interests, these regulations include tribal provisions that are premised on the USFS's trust responsibility, its consultation duties, the unique government-to-government relationships between the federal government and tribes, and the agency's obligation to protect treaty and reserved rights.

In concert with its work to protect and help steward the Crown of the Continent, the Blackfeet Nation, through its Tribal Historic Preservation Office (THPO), engaged deeply in the revisions of the forest plan for the Helena-Lewis and Clark National Forest. That work was motivated by the Nation's recognition of the plan's ongoing implications for the Badger-Two Medicine and how the region would be managed. The revision process also provided an important opportunity to incorporate significant changes and policy developments that had happened since the original plan was prepared in 1986, like the TCD designations and the shift toward broader recognition of tribal interests, marked by other discrete federal actions such as executive orders pertaining to sacred sites and improving consultation and coordination with tribal governments. Coming as it did amid ongoing challenges to the Blackfeet's interests in, connection to, and use of the area, the Nation recognized the importance of the plan and the guidance it would provide for the region's foreseeable future.

The 2021 Land Management Plan for the Helena-Lewis and Clark National Forest provides a plan for the Badger-Two Medicine "emphasis area." Due to the efforts of the Blackfeet and their allies, many of those components are built on the explicit recognition of the TCD and Blackfeet treaty rights reserved in the area. For example, the plan sets forth a series of desired conditions that the plan is intended to achieve. One of the desired conditions developed for the 2021 Land Management Plan takes directly from the language and the vision provided by the Blackfeet THPO: "[The] Badger Two Medicine is a sacred land, a cultural touchstone, a repository of heritage, a living cultural landscape, a refuge, a hunting ground, a critical ecosystem, a habitat linkage between protected lands, a wildlife sanctuary, a place of solitude, a refuge for wild nature, and an important part of both tribal and non-tribal community values. It is important to the people who rely upon it, critical to the wild nature that depends upon it, and has an inherent value and power of its own" (U.S. Forest Service 2021). That explicit recognition of the Badger-Two Medicine as a "living cultural landscape" refutes the historical perception of the area as important only for its extractable resources. And although the Forest Service and the 2021 plan did not adhere to or adopt all the Blackfeet's recommendations, this condition marks an important starting point for the agency's management of the region.

Two of the plan's management standards suggest a similar basis for how the future management of the Badger-Two Medicine can better reflect tribal values. First, management activities will now be conducted in close consultation with the Blackfeet Nation to fulfill treaty obligations and the federal Indian trust responsibility. As such, those activities must protect and honor Blackfeet reserved rights and sacred land. The uses of this area must be compatible with desired conditions, and compatibility shall be determined through government-to-government consultation. Second, management activities shall accommodate Blackfeet tribal member access to the Badger-Two Medicine for the exercise of reserved treaty rights and for tribal members to practice spiritual, ceremonial, and cultural activities (U.S. Forest Service 2021).

The second standard is not unusual and is essentially a restatement of the Blackfeet Nation's existing treaty rights and access or accommodation policy. Nonetheless, it is an important commitment on the part of the Forest Service. The first standard, however, is far more substantive and could provide the Blackfeet greater authority to ensure that uses of the area are compatible with desired conditions. If that standard is implemented in truly "close consultation" with the nation, the resulting management decisions are far more likely to acknowledge and accommodate the nation's values, perspectives, and sovereignty.

Importantly, however, the Forest Plan did not include other of the Blackfeet's recommended provisions. Among other shortcomings, for example, the ultimate document could have done more to facilitate the Blackfeet's vision (and Tribal Business Council's proclamation) regarding the return of "original buffalo" to "original homelands." The agency could do so by taking part of the Blackfeet's proclamation and turning it into a desired condition statement or making a "suitability" of use determination regarding bison in the Badger-Two Medicine. (National Forest System Land Management Planning 2012; Scott 2023).

When viewed collectively, all these existing mechanisms, processes, and authorities—the TCD, the new desired conditions reflecting predecision tribal input and participation, the new compatibility and consultation procedures stated as enforceable standards, and existing contracting authorities—can be constructed into an approach that reflects the core principles of tribal comanagement of the forest land. If implemented in that fashion, then the firm lines of authority drawn over centuries of dispossession begin to fade and are slowly replaced by a shared perspective that better accounts for a different and more deeply connected vision of the landscape. That new, shared perspective does not (yet) restore the lands to tribal ownership or give the tribe complete control—the land remains in the hands of the federal government—and, for many tribal leaders and their constituents, it may therefore be unacceptably impotent. But notwithstanding those legitimate critiques, these changes mark important steps toward reforming the conceptual paradigm that both justified and motivated the often wrongful dispossession of those lands from Indigenous peoples. And while epitomized by the Blackfeet's work across the Crown of the Continent, this shift is happening across the nation.

Lessons for a New Era

In November 2021, the secretaries of the interior and agriculture instituted the Tribal Homelands Initiative. It called for increased efforts on the parts of both of their departments to engage in costewardship of public lands and resources. That order built on a 2016 order from former secretary of the interior Sally Jewell seeking to promote similar efforts, but stopped short of suggesting that the federal government could share management responsibilities with tribes. In September 2022, the Department of the Interior issued new guidance to federal agencies to strengthen collaboration with Native Nations in the management of public lands, water, and wildlife. This new policy supports the development of costewardship agreements to allow tribes the ability to comanage projects on public lands. In February 2023 the Forest Service released its action plan in order to advance nation-to-nation relations.

Like the forest plan governing the Badger-Two Medicine area, these policy statements are important markers toward a new era of tribal authority in the management of public lands. They present a vision of the future that integrates tribal voices across existing boundaries, reconceptualizes public lands as now and forevermore Native lands, and roots decisions about their management in a collaborative and respectful government-to-government relationship. In addition to offering hope for some measure of justice against the backdrop of a very different historical approach to wild lands and open spaces, that future also enables the promise of better, more holistic, and rooted management decisions that truly serve the entire national interest, not just those not indigenous to these lands. The bright days promised in the vision of these statements and the Blackfeet-influenced forest plan lie ahead, but only if their power is realized through the work to implement and effectuate them.

The lessons offered by history, the present, and the possible future of the Crown of the Continent can help inform the broader shift toward a new, re-Indigenized future for the American West. The starting point for considering what that shift means is critical. Critically examining the roots of the cultural values and perspectives that have resulted in lines of authority across the region can help unearth how other values and viewpoints have been excluded, diminished, or ignored. Starting with a place, its history, and the ways it has been shaped by that process creates space for those drawn out of certain stories to step back in.

In addition, the multifaceted and dedicated work of the Blackfeet to assert their interests demonstrates the numerous ways in which the historically dominant paradigms might frustrate or limit reform. The decades of work to secure TCD designation and challenge development decisions as well as extensive engagement in the Forest Service planning process have all begun to shift the tide toward meaningful recognition of the Blackfeet Nation's perspective. But none of those successes are guaranteed to result in management of the region that aligns with that perspective—all remain subject to threat by judicial decision, agency discretion, or congressional action. While some of the results of recent decisions may remain in legal limbo, they have had a meaningful impact in changing the narrative and awareness of the Blackfeet's vision of the landscape. That shift has brought together allies and alliances to support that vision, build a movement, and continue that momentum.

Durable coalitions take time, and trust, and work. Despite the progress promised by policy statements of the Biden administration, real change will continue to demand time, trust, and effort. Similarly, the power of the Blackfeet advocacy has flowed through a range of channels, pulling on a number of levers to pursue their interests. That adaptive and flexible strategy is likely key to long-term and sustainable changes.

Finally, and perhaps most importantly, the power of the progress across the Crown of the Continent is in the leadership of tribal governments and their sovereignty. As demonstrated by the story of that place, the assertion of Blackfeet authority by any means necessary, including utilizing the laws and policies of the same government that wrested these lands from tribal control, is a true call for restorative justice. Beyond its symbolic meaning, the practical result is the possibility of restoration for the public lands and resources of the West.

The boundaries and barriers to such a sustainable future have long been rooted in particular perspectives about the region's wild lands and the people who inhabited and relied on them for millennia. As demonstrated by the Blackfeet's ongoing work in the Crown of the Continent, a different, more just, and more sustainable future—one rooted in the land, guided by Indigenous connections to it, and led by Indigenous voices—is possible.

IV
COEXISTING WITH WILDLIFE AND WILDFIRE

16

Recreation as Wreckreation in the Greater Yellowstone Ecosystem

TODD WILKINSON

A few years ago, Pulitzer Prize–winning novelist Richard Ford gave a lecture at the Museum of the Rockies in Bozeman, Montana. He spoke of things people say repeatedly that just aren't true. When constantly retold without being challenged or subjected to vigorous scrutiny, these stories become part of accepted lore and are embraced as fact. Some of these include adages like "all growth is good" or the idea that living "the American dream" is equally easy to achieve for everyone.

Within the realm of the American West, the assertion that recreation is tantamount to wildlife conservation qualifies as one of those tropes. In truth, scientific studies suggest it is often just the opposite—more people, more trails, more infrastructure, and more expanded public access into wild places are not benign. Research confirms that when human visitation goes up in a habitat, negative impacts on wildlife rise too.

Despite these facts, the U.S. Congress and presidential administrations led by both political parties have worked closely with government agencies like the U.S. Forest Service, the Bureau of Land Management, the National Park Service, the U.S. Fish and Wildlife Service, and the outdoor recreation industry to dramatically increase the footprint of recreation on public lands. But at what cost to the native, indigenous biological diversity of nonhuman beings living there?

By now your dander is probably up. You might think, How could pleasure-seeking humans with good intentions and a love for nature possibly be a *problem*? Before we proceed further, let's state what is patently obvious: Like you, I live in the West because I love to recreate outside. If you presented me with a checklist of various outdoor recreation activities I have participated in during my life, I would mark the box that says, "Most of the above."

Communing with nature is what we do to re-create ourselves. Self-help books tell us what most Westerners who have lived here awhile already know: getting outside is good for us physically, mentally, and spiritually. The human-centered message has been that exercise combined with mindfulness contributes to better physical health and mental well-being. Studies indicate that people who spend more time in the natural elements, whether in a city green space or remote wilderness, tend to be happier, calmer, and more sensitive, caring, and generous (Williams 2018). We know, too, that outdoor recreation generates billions of dollars for the economy.

Much has been written about this, but reflection is mostly lacking on the consequences of large numbers of people venturing into sensitive wild areas and displacing nonhuman species that often have nowhere else to go. This is a modern phenomenon that is a growing problem for a region like the Greater Yellowstone Ecosystem, which is world-renowned for the diversity of its wildlife. Yellowstone National Park, its sister preserve Grand Teton National Park, and the other public lands surrounding them represent the cradle of American wildlife conservation, where numerous species have been brought back from the brink of extinction.

No other bioregion in the Lower 48 possesses the kind of wildness that characterizes Greater Yellowstone. On a single late summer's evening you can hear wolves howl, loons trilling, and elk bugling; watch free-ranging bison wallow and bellow; spot a grizzly bear mother with cubs; cast for wild native trout; and soak in a sense of solitude that lets you forget what year it is. Greater Yellowstone is home to all the original, free-ranging wildlife species present five hundred years ago, prior to the arrival of Europeans.

Overwhelming evidence demonstrates that when humans reduce or control the size of their individual and collective footprints, as well as the intensity of their activity, wildlife can flourish. But this requires us backing off, deliberately making space, understanding cause and effect, and following the pillar of twenty-first-century conservation—the precautionary principle. Known colloquially as "looking before one leaps," the precautionary principle requires understanding the variables to avoid actions that might be destructive and irreversible. The latter already has resulted in huge swaths of the Lower 48 where native species, once present, were eliminated and never will exist there again.

All public lands, national parks, and wilderness areas in America possess a legal designation, but they are not qualitatively equal in terms of the natural entities they contain. Some are less wild and bear the impact of human intervention and nonnative species, some are more pristine in that they still can sustain native species, and some are exceptional, like those in Greater Yellowstone, in that they have the full complement of animals from before European settlement.

So ponder this premise: If outdoor recreation supports conservation, then how does encouraging more people to use finite pieces of public and private land benefit wildlife?

Does Outdoor Recreation Lead to Stronger Public Support for Wildlife Conservation?

At the end of the twentieth century, Greater Yellowstone and other regions in the Rockies transitioned away from logging, boom-and-bust hard-rock mining, and livestock grazing, which were all industries that came at the expense of native species. After World War II, ski resorts became the first form of industrial recreation. Resort development has been bolstered by the prevailing belief, promoted by the manufacturers of gear, that outdoor recreation economies represent a better, more benevolent alternative to resource extraction. In recent years, some of the mainstream conservation organizations that cut their teeth trying to halt clearcutting of old-growth forests, energy development, and mining on public lands have forged an alliance with the outdoor recreation industry. Together they have advanced three basic arguments treated as gospel.

1. Outdoor recreation advances education and financial support for conservation.
2. Greater access for user groups to public lands translates into positive conservation outcomes and better land protection.
3. When recreation happens in landscapes vital to the survival of certain species it improves public support for conservation of those species in those places.

What is the evidence supporting these arguments? What kind of "conservation" is being achieved? For instance, how does putting more humans into spaces populated by sensitive species improve those species' survival prospects? In cases where it has become clear that recreation is causing deleterious impacts on wildlife, how often have recreationists willingly given up their access to public lands? And in an iconic, wildland bioregion like Greater Yellowstone, if wildlife conservation is not the cornerstone of generically and vaguely referenced "conservation" then what, exactly, is being sustained?

The premise that "recreation equals conservation" has been spoken so often and so rarely challenged that developers of the proposed River Bend Glamping Getaway on the banks of the Gallatin River west of Bozeman have exploited the rhetoric. The Gallatin River is a revered Western trout stream that begins in Yellowstone National Park and courses northward. It is one of three rivers that converge near Three Forks, Montana, to create the Missouri River. The Gallatin was featured as the backdrop for the 1992 movie poster of Robert Redford's film *A River Runs through It.*

In a full-page ad in the *Bozeman Daily Chronicle* on February 9, 2022, River Bend developers, heeding the advice of clever PR mavens and mimicking phrases used by conservation organizations, declared in bold letters that "Recreation Encourages Conservation." This may leave us wondering, though, how increasing river usage could accomplish that goal.

First, a crucial bit of context: In 2021, Yellowstone National Park notched nearly five million tourist visits—and since the new millennium began, tens of millions of visits in total have been recorded. During the years of the COVID-19 pandemic, parts of the Greater Yellowstone region were inundated with recreation-minded visitors and development like never before. Has this translated into a general appreciation for the conservation of nature? Are recreationists more willing to curb their use of wildlands? Have we seen a groundswell of citizens rising up to stop the sprawl that is destroying vital habitat for wildlife on private land?

Yellowstone National Park's former science chief David Hallac warned that the natural fabric of the ecosystem is not just facing death by a thousand cuts, but also death by ten thousand scratches. Small insults that seem trivial in themselves erode the ability of the land to support wildlife. Outdoor recreation, a growing number of scientists say, brings its own form of lacerating effects.

After Gallatin County commissioners approved the glampground along the Gallatin River, a number of conservation groups sued, some of whom have been avid boosters of increasing outdoor recreation on public land. One of the plaintiffs, American Rivers, and its Northern Rockies director Scott Bosse, understands the dilemma. Bosse has openly questioned the legitimacy of the "recreation encourages conservation" mantra.

Bosse has earned widespread praise among wildlife advocates around the region who believe that growing levels of industrial-strength outdoor recreation are out of control. "We used to think of, and tout, recreation as a nonconsumptive gateway to conservation, but we seriously need to revisit that," Bosse told me. "All we need to do is look around at the impacts coming to bear on public and private land. Things have changed quickly, and we need to wake up."

Bosse condemned the Gallatin River glampground in a commentary that appeared in the *Bozeman Daily Chronicle*. But he also turned heads by broaching a topic that most conservation groups in the region have largely ignored: "Let's explore the claim that 'recreation encourages conservation.' As a lifelong outdoorsman who lives to fish, hunt, paddle and ski, I'll be the first to admit that recreating in the outdoors played a huge role in turning me into a conservationist. Many of America's most celebrated conservationists—people like Teddy Roosevelt, Aldo Leopold and Mardy Murie—got their inspiration to preserve wild country from immersing themselves in the outdoors. So yes, recreation can encourage conservation" (Bosse 2022).

Bosse then addressed newspaper readers directly:

> Ask yourself this—has the explosive recreational development around Big Sky over the past few decades conserved the area's forests, wildlife and once-pristine streams? Has industrial recreation around Moab, Utah conserved the surrounding red rock canyons and created more opportunities for solitude? Of course not. While they are often linked, there's a fundamental difference between recreation and conservation. Recreation is about taking. It's a form of hedonism. Conservation is about giving. Sometimes that means giving up the opportunity to recreate in certain places or at certain times of the year to protect wildlife. Sadly, far too many recreationists take without giving anything back. That's why our conservation deficit is worsening in Greater Yellowstone and our wildlife is increasingly under siege. (Bosse 2022)

Scientific Evidence Documenting Habitat Degradation

It's ironic how American conservationists often accuse skeptics of human-caused climate change of willfully ignoring the evidence that connects the burning of carbon fuels with the greenhouse effect and rising temperatures. Aren't American conservationists doing the same thing with the mound of scientific evidence linking outdoor recreation intensity to the destruction of secure habitat for wildlife?

Shortly after she was hired to be the first director of the Montana Office of Outdoor Recreation, Rachel VandeVoort appeared at a conference on outdoor recreation organized by the Greater Yellowstone Coalition at Montana State University in Bozeman. At the time, U.S. Forest Service and Park Service officials, conservation organizations, and a coalition of advocacy groups for outdoor recreation called the Outdoor Alliance claimed there was a huge gap of understanding related to the impacts of outdoor recreation on wildlife. They said this even as the Forest

Service was rallying behind efforts to expand access to public lands in Greater Yellowstone, with the argument that there was no proof of harm.

In comments at this conference, Dr. Christopher Servheen, who for thirty-five years was the national grizzly bear recovery coordinator for the U.S. Fish and Wildlife Service, said "I've heard recreationists remark that because they never saw a grizzly bear sow and cubs flee while they were riding their bikes down a trail, it means they're not having impact. That kind of thinking is not only ignorant; it's absurd."

But VandeVoort dismissed such worries about impacts: "I have zero, zero, zero, zero, zero, zero tolerance for anybody using the term consumptive vs. non-consumptive. That is a huge bugaboo of mine and it is only creating division because every form of recreation, and recreation itself, is a renewable, sustainable use of our resources."

VandeVoort's assertion does not align with the conclusions of leading scientists like Servheen, who say industrial-strength recreation is neither renewable nor sustainable when it comes to maintaining wildlife populations. In fact, plenty of evidence existed before she made her declaration. What's more, just a year after VandeVoort spoke, a major peer-reviewed study titled "A Meta-Analysis of Recreation Effects on Vertebrate Species Richness and Abundance" was published in the journal *Conservation Science and Practice* (Larson et al. 2019).

The findings were no surprise to the lead author. Three years earlier, Dr. Courtney L. Larson had been part of another landmark study (Larson et al. 2016). Larson's research team completed the largest summary of studies gauging the effects of recreation and human activity on wildlife. Some 93 percent of the studies found at least one significant effect of recreation on wildlife, most of which were negative.

> There is growing recognition that outdoor recreation can have negative impacts on biological communities. Recreation is a leading factor in endangerment of plant and animal species on United State federal lands and is listed as a threat to 188 at-risk bird species globally. Effects of recreation on animals include behavioral responses such as increased flight and vigilance; changes in spatial or temporal habitat use; declines in abundance, occupancy, or density; physiological stress; reduced reproductive success; and altered species richness and community composition. Many species respond similarly to human disturbance and predation risk, meaning that disturbance caused by recreation can force a trade-off between risk avoidance and fitness-enhancing activities such as foraging or caring for young. (Larson et al. 2016, 2)

Often, wildlife disappear or negative impacts ensue even before land managers become aware that they have created a threat by enabling the number of human users to swell.

Problems in Greater Yellowstone are increased by the unprecedented development pressure on private lands adjacent to public land. Sprawl is transforming former farms and ranches, which used to provide vital wildlife habitat, into suburban and exurban landscapes. Dr. Servheen, when he headed U.S. grizzly recovery, had been a proponent of removing grizzlies from federal protection. But together with antipredator sentiments flaring in the states of Montana, Wyoming, and Idaho, the combination of recreation and development pressure on public and private land has caused Servheen to reverse his position. As board president of the Montana Wildlife Federation, he has noted that grizzlies are being squeezed out of important habitat, undermining the outlook for bear recovery.

How Wildlife Regard Outdoor Recreation

As I type these words, a stack of printed scientific studies, news articles, and interview notes with scientists sits before me that's half a foot deep. They speak to problems concerning wildlife across the Intermountain West near outdoor recreation towns.

Servheen has found that soaring numbers of mountain bikers threaten bear and human security in the Northern Rockies. Because bicyclists ride fast, quietly, and unpredictably, and have their eyes down on the trail, the likelihood of human-bear encounters is high. Notably, grizzlies are a kind of bellwether. One peer-reviewed study led by Dr. Charles Schwartz, former head of the prestigious Yellowstone Interagency Study Team, found that a grizzly will exhibit habitat avoidance behavior if a single house and its related infrastructure sprouts on a section of land, which is 640 acres, or equal to a square mile (Schwartz et al. 2012).

Another peer-reviewed study in Yellowstone found that grizzlies in some of the remotest corners of the park will stay away from backcountry campsites if even a few human users are present (Coleman et al. 2013). The point is not to portray an antihuman attitude; it is to accentuate the fact that wildlife have issues of tolerance when humans invade their habitat, beyond which they will abandon those areas, moving into areas that might not be as conducive to their survival.

People also often take their best friends into the wilderness with them. When people are recreating with their dogs, especially when off-leash dogs roam widely, the impacts are broadened. Dogs chase and sometimes kill wildlife; they are scourges to ground-nesting birds; they can cause dangerous run-ins with bears, wolves, and mountain lions; and they carry diseases that are shed into the environment through feces and urine.

Crowded trails became a new norm during the COVID-19 pandemic. This should serve as a wake-up call, Larson told me. "I do think there is more and more attention being paid to this topic of outdoor recreation, especially in the last few years," she said. "I think sometimes people have trouble accepting that recreation has impacts because it's an activity that 'we' [conservation advocates] typically engage in. It was easier when we could point fingers at those building developments or extracting resources, but it's harder to place blame on ourselves. The impact is also much less visible. Trails do not have a large footprint on the landscape, so it's easy to think that there are few impacts. Impacts such as wildlife avoidance, stress, and reduced reproductive success are not easily seen by the public."

Such pressures leave wildlife populations further stressed at a time when resilience is important as climate change alters habitat in myriad ways. As Servheen notes, resilience means wildlife having access to more habitat—because climate change is going to put more animals on the move. Unfortunately, habitat that is secure from human pressures is shrinking. "When we recreate, we are doing activities that are optional. It's a way to spend our leisure time. Our lives do not depend on us having to do things in a certain place or else we'll die," he said. "But that's what wildlife face by necessity."

Landscape ecologists say the dispersed nature of outdoor recreation, in every season, means that wildlife seldom get a break. Let's state this bluntly: There is no scientific data that supports the contention that soaring recreation bodes well for wildlife. There is little or no evidence to support the contention that more recreation results in better wildlife conservation overall. And there is little evidence that backs the claim that having more recreationists moving into wildlife-rich public lands, especially those with imperiled or sensitive species, results in more financial or policy support for wildlife conservation in those places. Often, recreationists will state their conditional support for putting land under conservation restrictions: only if they can use them.

The Tetons are a famous line of jagged, breathtaking mountains that rise above Jackson Hole. Their vaulting profile extends southward to Teton Pass, a beloved destination for backcountry skiers and snowboarders. It is crowned by a mecca for powder snow called Glory Bowl. Glory's mystique among locals has made it a funhog landmark. But during COVID-19 and since, its level of use by backcountry recreationists has been off the charts.

Wildlife scientists have said that these intrepid winter recreationists have disturbed and displaced sheep in their airy haunts. Wyoming Game and Fish wildlife manager Aly Courtemanche has been quoted in the local media saying it is imperative that the human presence, which stresses sheep when they are most vulnerable, be minimized. Among the options being considered by the state, National Park Service, and Forest Service are restricting access or closing portions of the range to protect sheep. At one of the public meetings when these options were discussed, a backcountry skier, incredulous that her freedom and access to public lands might be denied or limited in deference to wildlife, responded, "Well, the sheep have had these mountains for 10,000 years; now it's our turn."

Lost upon many is that the vast majority of the Lower 48 represents an area where wildlife has been forced to adapt or compromise in the face of human domination of the landscape. While intense recreation exists in other parts of the Rockies and Sierras, the likelihood of rewilding wolves, grizzlies, and wolverines there is almost nil. A region like Greater Yellowstone is a remnant: it stands as a miracle that it still possesses its biodiversity.

Negative impacts are a numbers game. They are a function of location, geography, variety of uses, frequency of users, and intensity of recreational use. Where there are a lot of people moving through secure habitat for wildlife, animals suffer negative consequences.

Outdoor Recreation Pays the Bills, but Does It Protect Biodiversity?

You can't fault anyone for wanting to make a living, provide for their family, pay their mortgage, and save for retirement—and, for many, outdoor recreation is a source of income. Politicians, gear and clothing manufacturers, outdoor retailers, state tourism offices, outfitters, guides, lobbyists in Congress, and conservation organizations cite how outdoor recreation accounts for more than 2 percent of America's gross domestic product. Generating upwards of $900 billion annually in consumer spending, outdoor recreation is the foundation for 4.3 million jobs, according to the Bureau of Economic Analysis and the Boulder, Colorado–based Outdoor Industry Association. The latter noted that their 2020 figures are probably low because they were calculated in a year of COVID-19-related restrictions. What puts outdoor recreation in a special category, promoters say, is that this economic engine is fueled by citizens spending money while engaged in enjoyable leisure activities that also make them healthier and enable them to commune with nature and use public lands that belong to them.

The Outdoor Industry Association asserts a strong link between recreation and conservation. It also notes that recreationists generally do not like getting out into deforested clear-cuts and boating on streams sullied by mining tailings. "The outdoor recreation economy depends on abundant, safe, and welcoming public lands and waters. The health of individuals, communities, and our economy is tied to opportunities for everyone to experience the benefits of parks, trails, and open spaces" (Outdoor Industry Association 2022).

Outdoor recreation has also given even conservative states a lucrative stepping-stone for pivoting away from resource extraction and the whiplash of boom-and-bust economic cycles. Recreation tourism fills motel rooms and makes cash registers ring in restaurants, helps outfitters and guides send their kids to college, enables outdoor retail gear shops to thrive, and generates tax dollars. But like all industries, business success is tied to rising profitability, which rests on the zeal to grow markets of users. This is connected in turn to unrelenting pushes to put more people into public lands, using pricey gear and recreational vehicles, without reflecting on the downsides.

This is the same kind of mindset that environmental groups have criticized extractive industries for having. In fact, it could be argued that trees will grow back in a Pacific Northwest clear-cut, but recreation pressure, represented by numbers of people and infrastructure, causes permanent damage.

Scientists are concerned that the expanding outdoor recreation complex (which involves using not just public lands but the development superstructure that supports it on public and private lands) will be a major contributing factor to the undoing of Greater Yellowstone's wildlife. The Gallatin Mountain range is a prime example. Consider this: The Gallatins today are wilder, based on the diversity of species present there now, than Yellowstone was in 1872. The only reason they are that way is because they've been protected from intense levels of traditional resource extraction and large numbers of people using them.

The Gallatins provide habitat for grizzlies, wolves, elk herds, bighorn sheep, moose, and bison wandering out of Yellowstone and, at times, rare wolverines and Canada lynx. In fact, based on the composition of species, the Gallatins would be the wildest line of mountains in nine of the twelve Western states, absent the mountains in Wyoming, Montana, and Idaho. If, based on their mammalian diversity, they were a national park, the Gallatins would be wilder than any national park outside of Yellowstone, Grand Teton, and Glacier. Notably, they would be wilder than any federally designated wilderness area in those nine other states too.

Acknowledging the Gallatin Range's stature in the upper 1 percent of true wildlands left in the Lower 48 offers a focal point for thinking about the divide between wildlife conservation advocates and outdoor recreation. Debate over the meaning of conservation is important. Similar questions arise about the commitment of conservation organizations to protecting wildlife in the public-land-rich West when, at the same time, they advocate for rising levels of recreation.

To return to Richard Ford's proposition, tropes and memes keep getting used and embraced by the public as fact when they aren't. The late conservation biologist Michael Soulé told me that much conservation thinking today seems stuck in an old paradox. Protection of wildlands, the premise goes, can't be politically justified unless wildlands are being used by people. But wildlands *are* being used, he said. They're richly inhabited wellsprings for biodiversity at a time when we are dealing with an extinction crisis. They are priceless systems that humans cannot engineer or replicate if the pieces have been stripped down or liquidated.

Moab Went Fishing for Tourism and Hooked a Great White Shark

Nearly forty years ago, Bill Hedden—along with other citizens, civic leaders, and conservationists in the desert of east-central Utah—got a sobering taste of "be careful what you wish for." With uranium mining and other natural resource extraction jobs on the wane in Grand and San Juan Counties, Hedden remembers the seductive woo of mythological sirens riding into town on two wheels. They pitched what seemed like an innocuous opportunity for community reinvention. At the time, he said, many figured, "What could Moab possibly lose by switching to a recreation economy?"

One group was composed of motorcyclists and all-terrain vehicle adherents, enthused by the emergence of more powerful off-road machines capable of transporting intrepid riders into remote terrain that was previously inaccessible. The other was made up of human-powered off-road bicyclists who had ambitions to make Moab the mountain biking capital of the world. Both imagined an extensive trail system winding through the otherworldly geology of the Colorado Plateau. They succeeded in making that vision a reality. Today that network of trails is growing; it stretches across a wide swath of slickrock mostly administered by the U.S. Bureau of Land Management.

Moab's rapid emergence as a wheeled recreation hub, combined with ramped-up advertising by the state to promote the Mighty Five—the breathtaking national parks of nearby Arches, Bryce Canyon, Canyonlands, Capitol Reef, and Zion—set the stage for a boom unlike any previous.

Looking back, Hedden, who became a commissioner on the Grand County Council, has famously said, "We went fishing for a little tourism and hooked a great white shark." Half a life later from the first flare-up between motorized and "human-powered" recreationists, Hedden admits that the optimistic prospect of consensus and collaboration, carried out by government agencies and user stakeholder groups, didn't go quite as planned—for Moab or for public lands. Valiant declarations that "balance" would be achieved between satiating the desires of recreationists to have play areas and, on the other hand, protecting sensitive wildlife and sublime scenery have failed to deliver. What's already been lost is difficult to measure.

In a recent profile that appeared after he retired from serving as executive director at the Grand Canyon Trust, Hedden offered this assessment:

> The Moab area is overridden with car traffic and people, including local residents, who "tear up and down the high desert hills and canyons in off-road vehicles, or mountain bike all over, zoom around on the river in motorboats and jet skis." Surrounding towns don't want to become another Moab, he says, yet when he asks, "Is there one activity you are willing to forbid, so that won't happen?" they look at me blankly. They don't even comprehend what I'm asking them. They're like, "Hey, this is a free country, people can do what they want." And I say, "Yes, that's what's happening in Moab." Even the animals can't find refuge. "Hunters are going into the back country with four-wheelers and shooting deer," he says. "There's no 'back of beyond' anymore because we have so many ways of getting there." (Brown 2017)

The great white shark of outdoor recreation, which wields more political influence than ever before in Washington, DC, demonstrates an insatiable appetite for seeking more terrain, enabling commercial outfitters to monetize more experiences, improving and expanding trails, and promoting the philosophy that "recreation equals conservation."

The mythical "back of beyond," a phrase Hedden applied to formerly remote and ever rarer wildlands, is shrinking every day. Today, there are tourism/recreation promoters in the Greater Yellowstone Ecosystem—in places like Big Sky, Bozeman, Jackson Hole, and Teton Valley, Idaho—who see nothing wrong with going angling for a little Moab-style outdoor recreation. Seldom acknowledged by those who tout Moab is that Greater Yellowstone still has a caliber of large mammalian wildlife diversity Moab never had and never will. Scientists warn that it doesn't take the intense levels of recreation like that occurring in Moab to have a serious impact on wildlife in Greater Yellowstone.

Front-country campsites and parking lots at trailheads are overflowing in many of Greater Yellowstone's national forests located within an hour's drive of Bozeman and Jackson Hole. Levels of river traffic recreationists have never been higher. Like the tension in Moab between motorized recreationists and fat tire riders, there's animosity between fishing outfitters and noncommercial anglers on the Upper Madison River about use levels.

On the minds of many who have watched the region change, the question is not only how much more crowded can places become, but should the objective of public land managers be to promote expanded use of areas that bureaucrats classify as "underutilized" until they become crowded? Wilderness and wilderness-caliber lands are forever being eyed for more use under the claim that they "lock people out." But viewed another way, they are among the only places left where multiple-use extraction and recreation have not invaded and where wildlife still benefit from secure habitat.

The Only Way to Safeguard Wildlife Is Limiting Human Consumption of Nature

Recent annual reports from economists working for the National Park Service have estimated that the economic value of nature tourism generated by Yellowstone and Grand Teton National Parks approaches $1.5 billion annually and is linked to fifteen thousand jobs. Next to seeing the Old Faithful geyser erupt, the top two draws to Yellowstone are grizzly bear and wolf watching. One study found that visitors would be willing to pay twice as much for an entrance fee if they were guaranteed a better chance of seeing a grizzly.

A study by the University of Montana pegged the annual value of wolf watching in Yellowstone at $82 million (RRC Associates 2022). Were the economic activities relating to the famous Jackson Hole Grizzly 399 and her cubs along with other bear-watching opportunities in Grand Teton Park to be tallied, no doubt they would also be measured in the tens of millions of dollars annually. Grizzlies are worth exponentially more to the Wyoming economy alive than dead.

As renowned Jackson Hole wildlife photographer Thomas D. Mangelsen said to me, "Grizzly 399 and the opportunity to see her year after year has given enjoyment to millions of people and inspired them to care more about wildlife. If a sport hunt of grizzlies is ever brought back, the person who gets a hunting tag will kill the bear for fun and privatize the value of that bear all for himself as he aims to turn it into a rug or stuffed animal for bragging rights."

In Forest Service lands, especially with mountain bikers, there is the problem of "user-created trails" that the agency, to date, has refused to confront. Not only do managers deny there are impacts or claim there is a paucity of evidence, but they also admit that if there are impacts, they do not possess the staffing resources to measure them or to halt the rampant creation of new trails. As scientists have told me, many user-created trails begin by riders who use game trails, and this results in wildlife being displaced.

The Forest Service is a bureaucracy driven by its "multiple-use" mission to accommodate as many kinds of human uses as possible—especially when politicians dangle enormous amounts of money in front of it. If an area becomes crowded, a local forest supervisor may say that in order to alleviate congestion, more recreation will be "dispersed" into "underutilized" areas of the front- or backcountry. What often results is that crowded areas remain crowded and traffic directed to other areas becomes more so. As if the prime objective is to fill up as much of a public land with human presence as possible!

Healthy ecosystems, which sustain biological diversity, depend on having enough terrain to support species needs and ecological function. In a time when the region's climate is trending toward being warmer and drier, there's a word often invoked when it comes to the role public lands play in maintaining healthy ecosystems: resilience. In the context of wildlife, resilience means affording wildlife the space needed to roam. Traditional and new migration paths are essential as wildlife face lower water levels, plant communities that wither, native grasslands threatened by exotic species, outbreaks of wildfires, new pathogens like West Nile and chronic wasting disease, and suburbanization of important habitat.

Protecting biodiversity means being able to empathize with other beings. To contemplate what an animal needs requires modesty and humility. What good is human prosperity when it comes at terrible cost to wildlife, diminishes the environment, and displaces working-class citizens who make huge contributions to socially holding communities together?

We need a strategy for safeguarding Greater Yellowstone. We need a national backpack tax—assessed on all outdoor gear and equipment sold, with the proceeds going back into wildlife habitat protection to offset the amount of terrain already lost. We need a new conservation ethos if we want to hold onto the miracle of wildlife in Greater Yellowstone. And it ought to have as its bedrock wildlife conservation.

Aldo Leopold anticipated the flight of masses of people from urban areas to a region like Greater Yellowstone in the 1940s: "The greater the exodus, the smaller per-capita ration of peace, solitude, wildlife, and scenery, and the longer the migration to reach them" (Leopold 1949, 280). Eventually, there could come a time in Greater Yellowstone when we recreationists set out looking for wildlife and discover they're no longer there. What kind of conservation is that?

17

Heart of the West

Wyoming's Commitment to Conserve Ungulate Migrations

EMILY REED AND MATTHEW KAUFFMAN

The small town of Superior, Wyoming, used to be a booming coal town. Pictures from the 1920s reveal sparkling new cars, a bowling alley, and other amenities supported by the wealth of the coal mines. Today, those prosperous days are nowhere to be seen. Superior doesn't have a grocery store or a gas station, and the local bar is only open occasionally. Aside from the low-slung, modest houses built into the hills around town, the most prominent structure is the county road maintenance shop.

But those hills are also dotted with mule deer—lots of them. Superior represents the southern terminus of the world's longest-recorded mule deer migration. The study of these deer has shaped how wildlife biologists think about migration, and the conservation of their corridor illustrates how science informs the management of iconic Western wildlife populations. These deer, and their story, may also represent what is possible when we recognize the habitat needs of wildlife that move across the same landscapes where we live and work.

The World's Longest Mule Deer Migration

This corner of the Red Desert outside of Superior is a great place for mule deer to spend the winter. Aside from the one paved road that runs from town to Interstate 80, seven miles to the south, most other roads are two-tracks that are largely impassible once the snow arrives and the near-constant wind hardens it into drifts. Except for the few hundred hearty humans that live here, and the occasional oil and gas truck checking on some gas wells to the west, the deer have most of the area to themselves. While this country is quite dry, the draws hold sufficient moisture to grow robust sagebrush and the forage that comes with it. Perhaps what is most important is that this country is mostly free from the ravages of the deep snow that piles up along the foothills of Wyoming's mountain ranges.

The mule deer are not full-time residents. Once the days lengthen and the snow begins to melt, they turn their noses north toward the Wind River Range, where there is the promise of abundant spring forage. Sometime in April or May, depending on the snow conditions, they cease the roundabout movement on their small winter ranges, straighten out their trajectory, and begin moving north. For the first thirty to forty miles, they move through the sagebrush habitats of the Red Desert, skirting the Killpecker Sand Dunes to climb up and over Steamboat Mountain, where some stop over briefly to forage before heading on. Then they head up to the northern end of the Red Desert, crossing State Highway 28. After crossing the highway, they take a northwesterly bearing along the western foothills of the Wind River Range.

The herd moves along the foothills, many of which are working lands used primarily for livestock grazing and mineral extraction. Such lands underpin many ungulate migrations in Wyoming, which are far too vast to be contained within the region's protected areas. Here the mule deer move across a mix of private lands, federal lands managed by the Bureau of Land Management (BLM) and U.S. Forest Service, and a few state of Wyoming parcels. This wide-open rangeland tends to support migrations of deer, elk, and pronghorn as long as they can jump or slip under the livestock fences. The ranch houses are few and far apart—even so, the migrating deer hug the mountains, giving them a wide berth. After moving about forty miles along the foothills, the herd comes to Boulder Lake, its outlet stream swollen with the snowmelt. The larger does can ford the stream, hooves stable on the rocks below, while the fawns must swim. But most make it safely across.

After Boulder Lake, the corridor starts to become busier with human activity. Another five to seven miles and the deer will no doubt see the lights and hear the vehicle noise of Pinedale, the biggest town in the Upper Green River Basin. Fueled by an oil and gas boom in the early 2000s, Pinedale and its surroundings have grown over the years. Its subdivisions are pushing up against the foothills and Fremont Lake, which juts out like a finger from town, heading northeast deep into the flanks of the Wind River Range.

As the deer approach the lake, they have limited options. The path around the lake to the right is blocked by the steep mountains, and it would be a long swim to go straight across. The best choice for the migrating deer, it seems, is to cross near a narrow outlet of the lake where it funnels into Pine Creek, which runs down into town. This choice requires the deer to navigate through an obstacle course of challenges. If they cross below the lake with a simple traverse of Pine Creek, they end up on the wrong side of an eight-foot-high woven-wire fence constructed to prevent elk from spilling onto private lands. They can stay above the fence, but that requires them to swim the tail end of the lake before it funnels into the creek. (Every year biologists recover carcasses of deer that failed to navigate the iced-over portion of the lake in spring.)

These decisions are further complicated by activity from a marina, a restaurant, and a lodge located near the bottleneck. They have come nearly a hundred miles, having left winter range a few weeks before, and the abundant forage they seek lies beyond this human-made bottleneck. Not surprisingly, many deer make a stopover just before the Fremont Lake bottleneck. This is not to forage, their typical reason for stopping over. Instead, biologists have speculated whether that particular stopover might be more of a holding spot, where the deer linger before figuring out their next move.

Mapping Migrations

The migrations of these deer weren't always known, at least not the full expanse of their movements from one end of the corridor to the other. In 2011, wildlife biologist Hall Sawyer captured and put collars on forty mule deer that were wintering down in the Red Desert near Superior. He had been funded by BLM to conduct a study to figure out the habits of deer who live "year-round" in the desert. Much to Sawyer's surprise, he couldn't find the collared deer in the Red Desert when he went to look for them during the first summer. Finally, he sent a plane in search of the radio frequencies the collars emitted. They started hearing the familiar "pings" from the collars once they got up near the Hoback Basin, the headwaters of the Hoback River. Once the collars dropped off and Sawyer could map all the locations, a picture emerged of a narrow corridor from a winter range in the Red Desert to summer ranges in the Hoback Basin—150 miles away. It was the longest migration ever recorded for the species.

Charting it across a map of southwestern Wyoming, Sawyer and his colleagues at the University of Wyoming were amazed at the migration (see figure 17.1). The length was of course impressive, but they were more impressed by the country these deer traveled. As they migrated over just one spring or fall, they moved in and out of lands managed by two federal agencies and two state agencies, crossed ranches owned by about forty different private parties, and crossed three or four

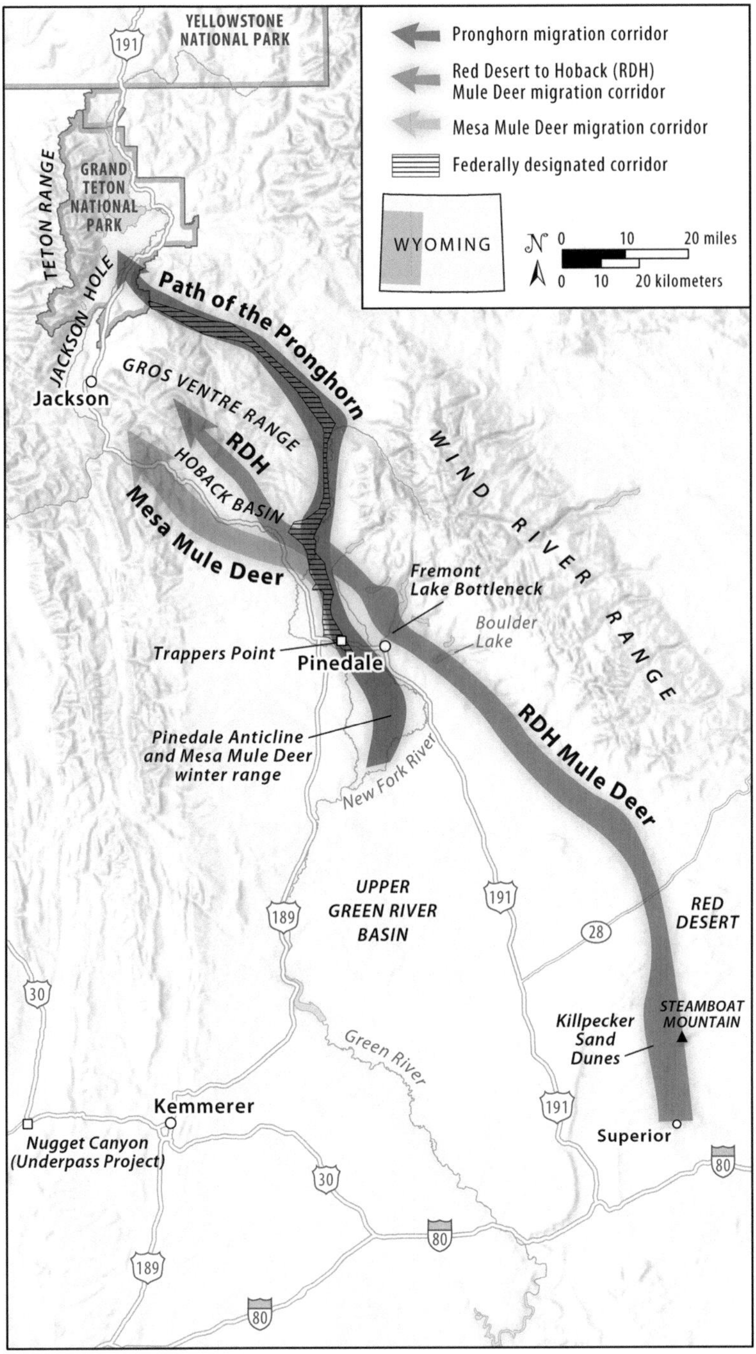

Figure 17.1 Map of select mule deer and pronghorn migrations in southwestern Wyoming. Map credit: Ian Freeman and Chelsea Feeney.

highways and about a hundred fences. The researchers decided to do something that had never been done before for ungulate migrations in the American West—they conducted a "migration assessment." First, they conducted some statistical analyses to delineate the high-use corridor (the habitats most deer moved along; Sawyer et al. 2009). Next, they intersected that high-use corridor with a map of those working lands and identified the top ten threats to deer along the corridor. The analysis revealed numerous problem spots that could potentially compromise the corridor over the long term. The number one threat the researchers identified was the Fremont Lake bottleneck.

Maps are a powerful means to convey conservation priorities, and the map of the corridor made it hard to mistake what a formidable challenge that bottleneck was. The sheer distance deer travel before and after the bottleneck spoke to how important those movements must be. Sawyer and colleagues also helped tell the story, with a glossy report, a short film, and a photo exhibit by wildlife photographer Joe Riis that toured around the state. Conservationists working in the region quickly became aware of the importance of Fremont Lake to the newly discovered migration. One of those was Luke Lynch, who worked to prevent development on private lands in the region primarily by purchasing conservation easements from willing landowners. When Luke learned that the 360-acre parcel at the outlet of the lake was up for sale and already drawn up for lakeside cottages, he saw an opportunity to conserve the parcel for the five thousand migrating deer that cross through it.

The tracked movements of the deer made it clear how important that bottleneck was to the migration, and that information combined with Luke's tenacious fundraising quickly resulted in the necessary funds ($2.1 million) being raised to purchase the property outright. That deal was completed in 2016, and the property was turned over to the Wyoming Game and Fish Department (WGFD), which created the Luke Lynch Wildlife Habitat Management Area. The deer still move through that narrow spot each spring and fall, but the fences have been removed by volunteers working with the WGFD, and the property is protected from further development in perpetuity.

Highway Crossing Structures Make Way for Migrations

Not far from the Fremont Lake Bottleneck, about five miles west of the town of Pinedale, is an open ridge dotted with sagebrush, carved out by the Green River on one side and the New Fork River on the other. The area is known as Trappers

Point, as it was a trading hub for hundreds of trappers and Native Americans in the 1830s and 1840s. Trappers Point is a natural bottleneck that acts as a one-mile-long gateway between the riparian zones of the Upper Green River Basin and the more mountainous sagebrush hills that lead into the Gros Ventre Range.

In the early days of spring, a group of about 350 pronghorn begin their ninety-mile migration from their winter range in the Upper Green River Basin to their summer range in Grand Teton National Park. This pronghorn herd makes the second-longest wildlife migration in the Lower 48 states (the first being the aforementioned deer migrating from the Red Desert to Hoback Basin). Their journey is not an easy one: they must pass through the bottleneck at Trappers Point, which has now shrunk to be a half-mile wide because of recent housing developments. As they make their way through the open space that is left, they reach their first and perhaps most dangerous barrier along the route.

Running alongside Trappers Point, bisecting their migration, is U.S. Highway 191, a busy two-lane roadway connecting Pinedale to Jackson Hole. In this exact spot, about five thousand years ago, early human hunters used the outlet of the bottleneck to ambush the pronghorn as they moved north. Archaeological evidence discovered in 1992, when a section of Highway 191 was widened, revealed one of the largest and oldest known pronghorn kill sites by early human hunters. The analysis of pronghorn teeth and fetal bones suggests that they were killed in the spring, which matches the migration timeline of pronghorn today, thereby validating the persistence of this ancient migration to the present.

Before the pronghorn even reach Highway 191, they must make it through right-of-way fencing that encompasses both sides of the blacktop. Pronghorn, in particular, struggle with crossing fences, as they prefer to duck under the bottom wire rather than jumping. In years when there are heavy spring snowstorms, snow drifts impact their ability to find sections where they can slip under the wire. Weaving between the traffic on U.S. Highway 191 became more difficult for the herd as traffic increased during the years of Pinedale's natural gas-fueled economic boom in the early 2000s. Nearby mule deer that spend their winters on the Mesa, an area just south of Trappers Point, also had to contend with the difficult crossing of U.S. Highway 191. In the 2000s, wildlife-vehicle collisions became increasingly common, with about eighty-five incidents occurring annually.

The pronghorn and mule deer who survive the crossing of U.S. Highway 191 would continue their migration. The mule deer settle into their summer ranges in the Upper Hoback Basin and the northern end of the Wyoming Range, but the pronghorn keep going. In 2008, the first forty miles of this pronghorn migration from Grand Teton National Park through the Bridger-Teton National Forest was federally designated. As of this writing, it remains one of the only herds that has part of its migration federally designated as a wildlife corridor in the United States.

Around this same time, a pilot project had been completed in another part of Wyoming that would lay the groundwork for conserving this famous pronghorn herd and many others. About one hundred miles southwest of Pinedale, near the town of Kemmerer, wildlife biologist Bill Rudd and Wyoming Department of Transportation (WYDOT) district engineer John Eddins had worked to install seven wildlife underpasses and seven miles of fencing in Nugget Canyon along U.S. 30. The project was a success: wildlife-vehicle collisions declined significantly, and trail cameras in the tunnels recorded thousands of mule deer and even a few moose using the underpasses. Transportation agencies typically give higher priority to projects that address immediate human safety concerns, such as deteriorating bridges and potholes. The Nugget Canyon Project set a new precedent for the state, addressing both human safety and deer losses. In 2010, the project was awarded the Federal Highway Administration Exemplary Ecosystem Initiative Award.

The success of Nugget Canyon propelled stakeholders back in Pinedale to think about implementing something similar. There was a looming question: Would migrating pronghorn use an overpass? With maps of migration and data on vehicle collisions in hand, a collaborative group of researchers, wildlife managers, and engineers designed a system of crossing infrastructure that included two 150-foot-wide overpasses, six underpasses, and thirty miles of fencing to help direct the animals. Pronghorn survival hinges on their speed and keen eyesight, unlike mule deer. As a result, they tend to steer clear of dark and narrow spaces such as underpasses. The overpasses would be the first of their kind in Wyoming and the first ever built specifically for pronghorn in the world. The project was completed and open for ungulate use in 2012.

Conservationists, researchers, engineers, and local community members waited anxiously for fall migration to begin to see if the newly completed project would work. As the snow began to fall in the mountains, the first pronghorn group approached the fencing, tracing back and forth along the wires until they arrived at the opening of the overpass. Then they scurried across. Over the next few days and weeks, many smaller groups followed. The project was a success, with 90 percent of pronghorn using the overpasses and 80 percent of mule deer using the underpasses, leading to an 80 percent reduction in wildlife-vehicle collisions three years postconstruction. A lesser-known yet significant outcome of the project was the expansion of winter range usage by mule deer on the Mesa. The project received numerous awards, including the Wyoming Engineering Society's 2012 President's Project of the Year and the Federal Highway Administration's 2011 Exemplary Ecosystem Initiative Award.

Although the project came with a hefty $10 million price tag, it carried an impressive return on investment. Within twelve years, the project would pay for itself by reducing property damage resulting from wildlife-vehicle collisions, which on average costs $11,600 per incident.

Reducing wildlife-road conflicts has continued to be a priority in Wyoming. In 2017, 130 people from conservation nonprofits, wildlife agencies, and universities gathered with WYDOT engineers for the Wyoming Wildlife and Roadways Summit. They identified 240 stretches of roadway that were of special concern for wildlife mortality. Each section was then evaluated by crash frequency, core wildlife habitat, and migration corridors to identify the top ten most critical projects (WGFD and WYDOT, n.d.).

Two and a half years after the Wyoming Wildlife and Roadways Summit, the state secured more than $17 million for a project along Highway 189 between La Barge and Big Piney that included eight underpasses and additional fencing. A federal grant provided the initial $14.5 million, but WYDOT and WGFD both contributed $1.25 million. Citizens of Wyoming have shown great support for these projects as well. According to a poll of four hundred registered Wyoming voters conducted by the University of Wyoming in 2019, 64 percent strongly supported constructing more crossings, while an additional 22 percent somewhat supported the initiative.

The poll also revealed that 76 percent of respondents viewed highways as a significant threat to wildlife migration. This percentage was higher than all other threats identified in the poll, including development, fencing, climate change, and oil and gas drilling. In the same year this poll was conducted, 79 percent of Teton County voters approved the allocation of $10 million in Special Project Excise Taxes (SPET) for wildlife crossing projects. Two wildlife crossing projects are funded through SPET and are expected to be completed by 2025.

In November of 2021, President Biden signed a $1 trillion infrastructure bill, with $350 million of that bill being earmarked for wildlife crossing infrastructure, the largest investment in wildlife crossings in national history. A few months later, in December of 2022, Wyoming's Republican governor, Mark Gordon, set aside $10 million of the state's $1 billion allocation of American Rescue Plan Act funding for wildlife crossing projects. The appropriation of these funds will help support an overpass for wildlife on Interstate 80 near Elk Mountain between Laramie and Rawlins, improvements to wildlife fencing and a wildlife underpass along U.S. Highway 189 near Kemmerer, and additional wildlife fences, three underpasses, and an overpass along U.S. Highway 287 near Dubois. In December of 2023, Wyoming was awarded the largest federal grant ($24.3 million) from the U.S. Department of Transportation's new Wildlife Crossings Pilot Program. The grant will build wildlife crossings for mule deer and pronghorn along a thirty-mile stretch of Highway 189 south of Kemmerer.

Despite its reputation as a fiscally conservative state, Wyoming has made significant financial investments in wildlife conservation. While we don't have any data points or sophisticated analyses that identify the social dynamics that underscore the success of wildlife crossing conservation in Wyoming, we can speculate that it really boils down to the shared human-wildlife connection. For example, the partnership between WYDOT and the WGFD can be traced back to how Eddins and Rudd shared a deep fondness for mule deer on the landscape. One could pose the question, If a WYDOT engineer did not have a personal connection to migrating mule deer, would there have been such enthusiasm for a wildlife crossing project? A deep love and attachment to these animals in people who work in transportation agencies is the catalyst for this ongoing roadway conservation success story in Wyoming.

Using Migration Maps to Plan for Energy Development

Wyoming has more mapped ungulate migrations than most other Western states, with much of that collaring work being conducted in response to ongoing oil and gas development. Many studies have been funded by the energy companies themselves, while other studies were funded by state or federal managers seeking to quantify the impacts or to collect wildlife information to guide adaptive management as gas fields were being built. Several boom periods, starting in the 2000s, illustrated the potential for wildlife habitat to be transformed rapidly by oil and gas development. It is an unfortunate coincidence that many of the best places to drill for oil and gas in Wyoming also happen to be critical habitat for ungulates to winter or migrate through on their way between their summer and winter ranges. Consequently, there are now numerous development areas that overlap with key habitats for ungulates.

One such place is the Pinedale Anticline, where world-class energy resources (natural gas) coincide with world-class wildlife habitat: namely, the sheltered winter range for the Mesa mule deer. Biologist Hall Sawyer began monitoring mule deer movements during winter in this area shortly after the development began in early 2001, and it is one of the longest-running studies to evaluate impacts from oil and gas. The results are not terribly complicated or surprising (Sawyer et al. 2017). The deer, many of which are also migratory and summer in the Hoback Basin (sharing that range with the deer that come up from the Red Desert), come down out of the mountains in early winter to the Mesa winter range.

As construction began, a clear pattern emerged wherein the deer would spend less time around the well pads, especially when they were being actively drilled. During drilling, there is nearly constant truck traffic in and out of the area as the vehicles carry supplies, equipment, and laborers. The wintering deer give these areas a wide berth, much like other wildlife avoid areas with high human activity. It is a type of indirect habitat loss, and it can mean that mule deer miss out on the forage within and around the actual footprint of the human disturbance.

Sometimes development is permitted directly within a migration corridor. Researchers have wondered if mule deer would simply stop using those migration routes. A long-term study of the Baggs mule deer herd in south-central Wyoming has provided the clearest answers. The sagebrush basin around Baggs, Wyoming, winters approximately two to three thousand mule deer, most of which migrate in a northeasterly direction across Wyoming Highway 789 up into the Sierra Madre Range for summer. The Atlantic Rim project began drilling wells for coal-bed methane in 2005, and about forty mule deer were collared on winter range at the same time. When the GPS data came back, it was immediately clear that the development area was right in the middle of a key migration corridor. A first set of studies showed a common behavioral response, where instead of avoiding human activity, the deer sped up as they moved through the well pads. The speeding up through the development came at a cost: the deer also reduced the area they used for stopovers by 60 percent (Sawyer et al. 2012).

Studies like these make clear that mule deer are capable of migrating through some level of development. They can squeak through some landscapes that are far from pristine, with the Fremont Lake bottleneck being a notable example. One way to measure the "functionality" of a migration corridor is to evaluate how well animals pace their movements with the wave of spring green-up, which allows them to access fresh, green forage when it is most digestible. This behavior—the way that deer choreograph their movements in pace with their preferred forage—is known as "surfing the green wave." In the case of the Atlantic Rim study, researchers were able to monitor the movements of mule deer throughout most of the period of gas field development. With the long-term movement data, they were able to evaluate whether the migration corridor became more difficult for mule deer to surf as well-pad densities increased over time (Aikens et al. 2022).

The results were striking. In 2005, when there were just a few wells, the mule deer kept pace with the green wave (i.e., surfed) throughout their migration. But as early as 2008, they changed their behavior: they migrated off winter range and began to congregate in a large stopover just before the development area. Some deer spent weeks held up on the edge of the development before eventually rushing through it and continuing to their summer range. But the green wave didn't stop. As the deer were held up, the green wave passed them over, moving up in elevation following the snowmelt. The deer were now behind the green wave. There was evidence that deer moved more quickly after passing through the development area to catch the wave, but the overall result was that the timing of the deer migration became increasingly mismatched with the green wave over the period of the study (2005–18). Notably, they did not habituate to the disturbance—the holding-up behavior persisted through all phases of development. Researchers estimate that their altered behavior in response to development caused mule deer to experience a 38 percent reduction in the foraging benefit of migration (Aikens et al. 2022).

These studies, and others, have established that development reduces the functionality of migration corridors—such disturbances and barriers make it more difficult for ungulates to migrate, causing them to miss out on the foraging benefits of migration (Kauffman et al. 2018). Ungulate migrations have been lost around the world, often because impermeable barriers were built that severed their movements. If such barriers are a recipe for the quick death of a migration, losing functionality is the key ingredient for a slow one. Animals like mule deer migrate because it is a profitable strategy that allows them to make a better living (food-wise) than if they stayed in one place year-round. When those foraging benefits are lost, deer are expected to put on less fat, rendering them less capable of producing healthy fawns and reducing their chances of surviving the harsh winters in Wyoming.

In essence, a population that uses a heavily developed corridor can become what ecologists call a "sink habitat"—a habitat no longer able to support positive population growth. With fewer animals produced each year than are needed to replace those that die from natural causes, animals slowly drain out of the population and off the landscape. Because migration behavior takes many generations to be learned and transmitted throughout the population, lost migrations cannot easily be restored. For example, it took bighorn sheep about forty years and moose nearly ninety years to learn new migration routes after being translocated (Jesmer et al. 2018).

Most of this science was in place in 2018 when President Trump's administration was strongly prioritizing oil and gas leasing on public lands. In its end-of-year lease sale, the BLM proposed to lease approximately a million acres in Wyoming. Dozens of those parcels overlapped the mapped corridor of the Sublette mule deer herd, which contains the herd segment that makes the migration from Red Desert to Hoback. The proposed leases were on the BLM lands that are scattered throughout the Red Desert, the last leg of the journey the mule deer make down to winter range, between the southern tip of the Wind River Range and the town of Superior.

By this time, the state of Wyoming had become focused on corridor conservation. Following the mapping of the corridor in 2014, the Wyoming Game and Fish Commission passed an Ungulate Migration Corridor Strategy in 2016 (WGFD 2016). The new policy provided a process for the WGFD to designate a migration corridor as a "vital habitat," which is meant to be managed to maintain habitat functionality so that deer can move along the corridor and derive foraging benefits. The Sublette mule deer corridor, including the Red Desert to Hoback segment, was officially designated later that same year.

Once the leases were mapped and the conflict with the corridor became clear, the letters poured in. A wide range of groups, including hunting groups like the Muley Fanatic Foundation, wrote to the WGFD and Wyoming Governor Matt Mead, requesting the leases be deferred. Some of the most powerful voices came from the county commissioners of Teton County near the summer ranges, and most importantly, Sweetwater County, where the winter range is located. For their part, the managers at the WGFD recognized the importance of the corridor, having been collaborators on most of the studies evaluating how gas development could diminish the functionality of the corridor.

Ultimately, WGFD director Scott Talbott and Governor Mead wrote a letter to Department of the Interior secretary Ryan Zinke requesting that a small number of parcels—those that were 90 percent or more within the mapped corridor—be removed from the lease sale. In July 2018, Zinke and Mead announced the deferment of nearly five thousand acres of leases that overlapped the corridor and were deemed too much of a threat to its functionality. It is presumably the first time a mapped corridor has led to oil and gas leases being removed from a lease sale to make space for migrating ungulates. Through 2019, the BLM continued to remove proposed leases from sale lists so that approximately twenty-four thousand acres within the corridor are now protected from oil and gas development.

Ongoing Challenges for Conservation

The science of ungulate migration has developed quickly—and still is (Western Migrations, n.d.). We now have a better understanding of crucial habitats and animal behavior that has led to many successful conservation projects and even agency and statewide policies. Yet there are still challenges to conserving ungulate migrations (Middleton et al. 2020). In the political landscape, policies that preserve migratory corridors across public and private lands are complex and don't offer complete protection. In 2020, Governor Gordon signed an executive order that replaced the 2016 WGFD Ungulate Migration Corridor Strategy. The executive order allows the WGFD to nominate new corridors for designation, to be reviewed by a local working group and approved or rejected by the governor.

The corridors that are approved for designation then receive some degree of protection: the state of Wyoming issues permits for a range of development types to reduce disruption to the corridor habitat. It also encourages private landowners to keep migration corridors and routes functional but does not mandate any management actions to do so. Even though Governor Gordon's 2020 executive order made Wyoming the first state to have conditions for maintaining migration functionality and to set up a state-level designation procedure protecting ungulate migration corridors, as of this writing (2024), Wyoming has not designated any new migration corridors. While conservationists appreciate that part of the new designation process includes multiple opportunities for public input, some feel that the designation process is simply too slow given the ongoing threats and expanding footprint of development of all types.

One of the candidate herds considered for designation is the Path of the Pronghorn, the corridor that received federal designation in 2008. The southern portions of the route that would be designated under the 2020 executive order are where the animals intersect with oil and gas fields. One oil and gas field on BLM is being developed and is currently under litigation from environmental groups for impacting both sage grouse habitat and the pronghorn migration. BLM has already approved the gas field development, citing that the pronghorn migration route did not have any special designations in that area. Similarly, a state of

Wyoming oil and gas lease was auctioned off and approved in an area that WGFD and conservation groups consider a bottleneck for the Path of the Pronghorn. Wildlife advocates have been vocal about the need to designate the entire Path of the Pronghorn corridor in a timely manner and ensure management of the corridor limits new oil and gas development. As of this writing, the Path of the Pronghorn is still not designated under Wyoming's executive order.

Even though dozens of migrations have been mapped in Wyoming and some have been designated, they are often not included in more localized land use decisions on private lands. One recent example is in Sublette County, where there has previously been a lot of momentum around migration conservation. This county is where the Fremont Lake bottleneck and the Trappers Point road-crossing projects are located. In 2021 and 2022, commissioners approved a 56-acre zoning change that would allow a billionaire to build an exclusive retreat. They also rezoned 299 acres of former agricultural land so it could be developed into subdivisions and approved the construction of a trauma therapy center—all within the Red Desert to Hoback migration corridor. What underscores some of these zoning decisions is the pressure on the county to expand housing, the need for rural-based mental health care, the economic interest in resort tourism, and the revenues associated with expanded commercial and residential development. The ongoing struggle of agricultural producers in the area to make ends meet or recruit the next generation to take over the operation also adds pressure to develop. Even though there is more federal funding available to support agricultural producers that are in big-game habitat areas through voluntary opportunities and incentive-based approaches such as habitat leasing and conservation easements, farms and ranches are still being developed at an alarming rate (USDA 2022).

It's clear that some of Wyoming's migratory routes are still intact today because of the open space, but we know that they are still vulnerable, especially in today's modern world. Similar to the Western boomtowns brought about by oil and gas, there are now Zoom towns, where remote workers are moving to Western gateway communities and building houses, some of which are in crucial winter range areas for wildlife. Green energy initiatives have led to solar panels and wind turbines being assembled across the prairie, sometimes within migration corridors or winter ranges of the state's abundant ungulate herds. The reality is that without adequate protections for habitat, any type of development poses a threat to migrating wildlife populations.

Conserving wildlife while providing for the needs of a growing human population is possible—it is not an either-or proposition. But it will require more cooperation. Untangling how we can make these compromises in modern society across multiple scales will require us to prioritize clear communication about what the science is telling us and integration of that information into communities for their knowledge and planning. Many Wyomingites know about the Red Desert to Hoback migration, the Fremont Lake bottleneck, and the success of the overpasses that have allowed pronghorn to more easily navigate Trappers Point. It seems clear that local knowledge of these migrations, and the connection that people have to the herds, has underpinned and prompted these conservation actions. The influence of even a single connection to an animal or a species can have a profound effect on the hearts of decision-makers, potentially paving the way for viable and lasting solutions.

18

Beyond the Science
Lessons in Human–Black Bear Coexistence

STEWART W. BRECK

From the perspective of a large carnivore ecologist working in the Western United States, we are living in remarkable and unprecedented times. Remarkable in that after a long history spent eradicating large carnivores throughout the United States, we now have growing and expanding populations of wolves, grizzly bears, black bears, mountain lions, and coyotes. Unprecedented because this restoration is occurring in a vastly changed environment—large swaths of land have been converted to crops, urban and suburban sprawl continue with no end in sight, livestock populates much of the open rangeland, and remaining wildlands are filled with people recreating.

Native carnivores are adapting to these environments. For example, we now have coyotes in every major U.S. city, black bears are common across roughly half of the United States, wolves now occupy portions of at least twelve states, and grizzly bears have recovered to the point that in Montana, there are bears that have moved out of the mountains to make their home in the grasslands known as the Eastern Front. This is not to say that recovery and conservation of these species is complete. But because of the successes, much of the focus has turned from recovering these species to figuring out how to better live with them.

Having carnivores in our modern landscapes creates new challenges, like coyotes attacking pets in cities, black bears breaking into houses, wolves and bears killing cattle and sheep on our rangelands, and grizzly bears threatening elk hunters in Montana and Wyoming. Questions about how we minimize negative interactions without resorting to killing carnivores have become a major theme. To address these questions, researchers like me have focused attention on understanding how these intelligent animals make a living in our modern landscapes, how they take advantage of our modern society's spoils (e.g., garbage, livestock, and crops), and what types of management strategies we can develop to minimize the negative interactions.

As we learn more about carnivores in our modern landscapes, the science of coexistence points convincingly toward the importance of public education and the management of anthropogenic resources as the first and most important steps in reducing conflict and creating landscapes of coexistence. But the conceptually simple solutions of securing our trash or protecting our pets and livestock have turned out to be difficult to implement. Carnivore ecologists may have insight into causes of conflict, but we lack the humility and training to be effective at understanding how to implement change when people and communities are resistant to the conclusions of scientists. In this essay, I share my experience working with black bears in the Colorado towns of Aspen and Durango, covering major findings of fourteen years of research, as well as my personal journey discovering lessons on humility and what it means to be a scientist.

Bears and Minivans

I became enamored of bears when I discovered that black bears in Yosemite National Park select minivans as their preferred vehicle to break into. Using years of data that the National Park Service had on file, we found that bears were breaking into minivans at three times the expected rate, a clear indication of them purposefully walking through a parking lot full of all types of vehicles and picking out those with the highest likelihood of a reward (Breck, Lance, and Seher 2009).

Why minivans? The answer is obvious to any parent of young children whose vehicle interiors are coated in goldfish dust and gummy bears jammed between seat cushions. Minivans are more likely to carry children, and because bears are blessed with a remarkable sense of smell, any vehicle with food is easily identified by its aroma as an optimal target for a quick meal of delicious and highly processed food, which bears love as much as we do. I was fascinated by the fact that bears could so easily figure us out and take advantage of the modern world we created. And if bears could figure out the connection between messy kids and minivans, they were undoubtedly picking up on other cues about our modern world.

My work in Yosemite occurred at the end of a decade-long effort by the park to reduce conflict with bears. During this period, bears were breaking into hundreds of cars each summer, raiding campgrounds, invading buildings, and regularly stealing campers' food off picnic tables in broad daylight. In response, park rangers and biologists were in crisis management mode: by day, they were using education and law enforcement to get people to keep food and garbage secured in bear-proof food lockers, and by night, they were playing games of cat and mouse, attempting to haze bears away from areas with people.

What wasn't happening so often was the lethal removal of bears. This was due to a mix of park philosophy that minimized lethal control and engagement by an urban public in cities like San Francisco that were expressly opposed to killing bears. Over time, the park was able to move out of crisis management and into what can be characterized as coexistence. The solution did include managing bears, but the heart of the effort focused on eliminating the availability of human foods that were the source of conflict.

The experience in Yosemite provides insight into a broader issue playing out throughout the Western United States and really anywhere black bears live in close proximity to people. Our modern environments and lifestyles create novel foraging opportunities for animals that are smart enough to figure out how to take advantage of them. Unless we find effective ways to keep bears from getting into trouble, we will remain in this mode of crisis management, which harms both people and bears. As development continues, these issues will grow until we adopt methods that will move us toward harmony. In conservation parlance, this is called coexistence and can be defined as populations of carnivores flourishing alongside thriving human endeavors with minimal human-bear conflict (Venumiere-Lefebvre, Breck, and Crooks 2022).

Achieving coexistence will be difficult. We have lost the understanding and cultural knowledge of how to live with large carnivores. For example, the elimination of wolves from Western landscapes in the early twentieth century may have been a relief for ranchers at the time. But we are suffering the consequences now, having little local knowledge of how to live with them and minimize negative interactions. Coexistence is also difficult because we are creating new environments and new relationships with carnivores that no other human culture has had before. The interactions between bears and people in national parks and the interactions between bears and people in our mountain towns are examples of these novel environments. Research will be necessary to develop insight into critical features and factors of systems that can enhance coexistence. This will involve better understanding the people and the wildlife living in the system as well as investigating those approaches that are most effective at minimizing conflict without negatively impacting either carnivores or people.

These themes were the primary motivators of my work with black bears in developed areas of Colorado. When I started in 2004, there was no research being done on bears in Colorado. This was surprising because when we plotted records of human-bear conflict, the trajectory was a steep increase from the early 1980s through 2003 (Baruch-Mordo et al. 2008). I helped form a team consisting of state biologists, graduate students, and professors, and together we set out to launch work on better understanding how bears respond to our modern environments and what we could do to minimize conflict. Like all worthwhile projects, other themes emerged that opened new and unexpected challenges. In this case, it was, What does a researcher do when the science is clear, but people are not following the science? What then is the role of scientists?

Working in Aspen

The Rocky Mountains bisect Colorado from north to south, comprising the western half of the state. The western edge of the mountains contains fertile agricultural land as the mountains trail off into the Colorado Plateau. The eastern edge of the mountains abuts the prairie and contains the majority of the human population in an area known as the Front Range. Between the western and eastern slopes are the iconic mountain ski towns of Aspen, Telluride, Steamboat, and Vail, as well as other less famous but equally beautiful towns like Durango, Glenwood Springs, Delta, and Montrose. All the mountain ranges are bear country, and since human-bear conflicts have become a main topic of concern for wildlife managers, city councils, and the governor's office, it helps to understand the history of bears in Colorado.

The 1970s were an important point in time for bears and other large carnivores in the United States. This period marks the passage of major environmental legislation and changes in societal priorities, leading to the end of outright persecution of native carnivores. For grizzly bears in Colorado, protection did not come soon enough, as the last known grizzly was killed in 1979 in a remote area of southwestern Colorado. But for black bears, the 1970s marked a new beginning, and with protection from all-out persecution, the bear population in Colorado began to grow.

Tom Beck was a bear researcher with the state at this time. His work serves as a benchmark, providing insight into the life of bears without the significant presence of people on the landscape that we have today. One key finding showed how bears dealt with times of extreme food shortage, known as natural food failures, caused by drought or late spring freezes that kill fruit or nut production from plant species like chokecherry, serviceberry, and oak. Natural food failures occur periodically, limiting the amount of food available on the landscape in late summer, when bears forage constantly to gain weight prior to hibernation. Beck's work showed that in years with poor natural food production, bears would travel widely in search of food. If they didn't find enough, they would go to their dens hungry. This didn't mean they would die of starvation, but it did mean the females would not have cubs. Survive to reproduce another day.

By 2005, when we began our research, the bear population had likely recovered to numbers more representative of the natural carrying capacity, estimated at around 20,000, and the human population had increased from around 2.5 million in the 1970s to 4.5 million. Though much of the human growth occurred in the Front Range cities of Denver and Colorado Springs, towns in the mountains also experienced increases in population, development, and wealth. Such growth impacts socioecological systems and our relationship with wildlife, including bears.

An obvious aspect of growth is the increase in anthropogenic food resources that become available to bears (e.g., garbage, bird feeders, and fruit trees) and are a major source of human-bear conflict. More wealth brings second houses and vacation homes in mountain communities that sit empty and become easy targets for bears to break into. Mountain towns also attract large numbers of visitors who may be ignorant about issues with bears, making management strategies focused on educating people and changing human behavior more difficult.

We chose the town of Aspen as our study site for a number of reasons. First, the town and surrounding development sit in the middle of prime bear habitat. Second, the town had earned a reputation for its large numbers of human-bear conflicts and the accompanying large number of bears euthanized by wildlife managers because of conflict. Finally, when we pitched the research proposal to members of the town government, our ideas were warmly received. Leaders wanted to know why bears had become such a problem in the town, not believing the prevailing hypothesis that a prevalence of trash and garbage was primarily responsible.

A major component of our research focused on understanding what factors influence bear behavior, particularly their movement relative to the developed environment. The work involved capturing bears and putting GPS collars around their necks so we could follow their movements. Using GPS collars has become largely standard practice to learn a great deal about many wildlife species. For bears, care is necessary to fit the collars correctly because bears can gain a tremendous amount of weight during hyperphagia and create situations where the collar becomes too tight, resulting in wounds on the neck. To reduce this type of impact, we would include a breakaway device on the collar that would release if the collar became too tight.

We learned a great deal from this effort: in particular, we demonstrated the importance of natural food failures in influencing bear movement (Baruch-Mordo et al. 2014). But unlike Tom Beck's work in the 1970s, where bears would wander widely during food failure years, our results showed how bears would essentially move to town. When we investigated the different types of anthropogenic food subsidies bears were finding, our results showed that the overwhelmingly preferred food type was garbage (Lewis et al. 2015). This included garbage from residential areas, large construction dumpsters placed in front of new buildings, and restaurants in the city center.

Given the clear link between garbage and bears, the next question is how to manage this problem. Some see the way to reducing conflict as managing bears through techniques like scaring them out of town, relocating them to areas away from development, or euthanizing the ones that come into town. The idea of scaring bears away from garbage sources (often referred to as "hazing") is ultimately an exercise in futility as long as the sources of anthropogenic food are readily available. Bears are smart and quickly figure out the game of chase and how to outsmart those doing the chasing. If hazing bears doesn't really work, then why not just relocate those bears involved in conflict to other areas away from town? On the surface, it seems like an easy win-win strategy, but the reality is that relocation often does not reduce conflict and can be detrimental for bears.

Part of the problem with this technique is that bears can travel incredible distances in short time periods. We may move a bear hundreds of miles only to find it has returned to its original location a few weeks later or has taken its learned conflict behavior into new environments. Furthermore, moving a bear from one area to another can put that bear into a challenging environment, where threat from other bears and a lack of understanding about the local environment can lead to lower survival rates for the relocated bears.

If scaring and moving bears doesn't work, then why not simply euthanize bears coming into town? Sometimes this does happen, but it's not a very appealing answer to the problem and often generates tremendous controversy. Indeed, the issue of killing bears to reduce conflict is the primary reason ecologists like me are hired to search for other answers. Ultimately, euthanizing bears, relocating bears, or other strategies focused on managing bears are temporary and don't solve the root issues of the conflict. It's simply a reprieve.

Given the identification of garbage as the primary problem in Aspen, our research efforts moved toward questions related to what could be done to reduce the garbage problem. We began by designing experiments to determine the influence of educational efforts on reducing the availability of garbage. Our results were discouraging, indicating that education in the form of signs encouraging people to better store their garbage and outreach through programs like "bear aware" alone would do little to solve the problems of available garbage. Our efforts may seem naive, but there is a sentiment held by many that the solution to these urban bear problems is simply a matter of educating residents to limit their garbage. This sentiment has repeatedly been shown to be false. Education is important, but alone it will do little to reduce the availability of garbage and other attractants. It needs to be linked with the development and enforcement of laws that focus on this (Baruch-Mordo et al. 2011).

Another important and unexpected discovery was the confusing pattern related to the survival and reproduction of bears in Aspen. On one hand, we saw that the extra calories bears could get in town allowed them to go into hibernation in good condition even in poor natural food years. For pregnant females, this allowed them to give birth to more bears. However, we also noticed that increases in reproduction may have been offset by increases in mortality associated with being in developed areas. We realized that our study did not address whether towns like Aspen could have impacts on the bear population and whether these impacts were positive or negative. As a result, we began planning a second phase of research with the goal of addressing the question of whether and how towns impact local bear populations (Lewis et al. 2014).

Armed with our data and results, and with a clear need to continue research, in 2010, we engaged in discussion with members of the town government in Aspen. Our research clearly highlighted the need to address the garbage issue throughout town, but the reception we received indicated that the city probably was not going to act on any of our recommendations. And further, when we brought up the idea of continuing research, the reception was tepid: the town was not going to be a supportive partner in further study. The lack of action toward better garbage management was perplexing, as it was unclear what was limiting the practical use of the knowledge we had developed. A variety of explanations seemed possible, including politics, economics, other town priorities, and apathy.

This example of how science can fail to inform policy is not unique to our work. Many books have been written on this problem across a wide range of research topics such as climate change, where it is imperative to have people alter their behavior to advance a positive outcome. In our case, a major problem is that the management of human-wildlife conflict typically falls under the purview of wildlife managers. But managing bears is not necessarily the best way of solving conflict issues. Instead, we need to manage the resources attracting the bears to actually solve the issue. Most needed is the development and enforcement of regulations related to making garbage and other food sources unavailable, the creation of incentives to encourage adoption of proven methods, improvements to infrastructure to make it easier to restrict access to garbage through bear-proof containers, and outreach to the trash hauling companies to enhance their involvement.

These are actions to be taken by cities, not wildlife managers, and to make these things happen, we need trash haulers, community planners, city governments, and social scientists working in tandem with wildlife managers. But how to get the city of Aspen to engage in this way and to take such steps was unknown to me. I became frustrated with the city and upset that our management recommendations were being ignored.

The Shift to Durango

With it clear that Aspen was no longer the best place to conduct research, in 2011, we moved our study to the city of Durango. This town was also surrounded by excellent habitat for bears and in a similar state of crisis management regarding human-bear conflicts. The research conducted in Durango would be similar to Aspen except that the team, led by Colorado Parks and Wildlife researcher Heather Johnson, would focus on understanding how the city might be impacting the bear population and continue to evaluate strategies for reducing garbage in cities.

After six additional years of work, the results were quite striking. In one bad natural food year, we documented the local bear population decreasing by over 50 percent. This demonstrated that even though females were able to attain a food subsidy that boosted reproductive output, this extra production did not make up for the increased rates of mortality that bears experienced in town. There were several causes of increased mortality: management removals due to conflict, road-related mortality, and increased mortality due to hunting (Laufenberg et al. 2018; Johnson et al. 2018).

Another important result of the work in Durango came about through a large-scale experiment to determine what would happen to levels of human-bear conflict if we gave residents bear-resistant garbage containers. We wanted to focus on understanding the benefits of reducing availability of garbage—instead of seeking to change people's behavior through education or law enforcement as we did in Aspen. If city leaders could see what results could be achieved by investing in infrastructure then perhaps this would help garner support from government entities.

We bought a thousand bear-resistant containers for residents and divided the city of Durango into experimental units where residents either did or did not receive bear-resistant containers. The results were compelling, with major decreases in conflict where there had been an investment in better equipment. The results were so persuasive that when they were presented to the city leadership, the city voted to invest an additional $600,000 in bear-resistant garbage containers for the remaining residents in Durango (Johnson et al. 2018).

I was pleased to see our research making a difference in the lives of bears and humans alike, but I remained disappointed by our failure to achieve the same success in Aspen, where the research results had pointed in the same direction. My perspective was that films were being produced about this work (*Bears of Durango* 2021) and book chapters written by famous authors (Roach 2021), so why wouldn't Aspen, or any other city for that matter, embrace our findings and double down on making the city bear-proof? With "facts" on my side and an air of superiority, I would shame the city of Aspen when reporting on the twelve years of research, thinking that would somehow help. But an experience was on my horizon, one that would knock me from my pedestal and force me to reflect on the role of science in changing policy and especially my role as scientist.

Palisade Peaches

In late summer my family goes on an annual backpacking trip in Rocky Mountain National Park as an end-of-summer celebration before school starts for my daughters. The trip requires parking at the Wild Basin parking lot on the southeast side of the park and backpacking a few miles to a high-elevation camping site. For this outing, it was questionable whether we could go because we would have to squeeze it in between my thirteen-year-old daughter's soccer game and the beginning of school. Like most families, our modern-day life can be hectic, but we were determined to get away. We hastily packed our camping and backpacking gear as well as a snack for our daughter for the one-hour car ride to the trailhead.

This snack included a Palisade peach. These luscious fruits are grown on the Western Slope of the mountains in Colorado and are arguably some of the best peaches in the world. You know it's peach season by the smell in your house—they are little orbs of aromatic gold and honey, emitting a perfume equally attractive to gods and fruit flies.

Though the trip was too short, our single night in the mountains was beautiful: we were blanketed by crisp mountain air and a sky full of stars. In the morning we packed up, had breakfast, and began heading down the trail to our car. The Greeks have a god or goddess for most events in life, and that morning, as we began hiking down the trail, I was introduced to the goddess Nemesis. I don't profess to know much about this goddess, but the little I do know is that she delivers punishment to those guilty of hubris.

About halfway to the car, we ran into a person coming up the trail. Juicy news is apparently hard to suppress, and this person informed us that a car had been broken into by a bear in the trailhead parking lot. The person had a lot to say about the incident, which I essentially ignored since I felt I knew all there was to know about the nature of bear-human conflict. The second and third groups of hikers gave more detail: the car broken into was a gray Prius, the type of car I parked there! Approaching the crowded lot full of dozens of cars, a sense of foreboding about my own vehicle held off until a nagging thought about that lovely little peach came to mind. What had we done with it? Had we disposed of it? As we continued down the trail, my last desperate hope was that there was more than one gray Prius in the parking lot. The last mile was agonizing, thinking about the ramifications of a bear breaking into my own car because I had left food in it.

Sure enough, when we got to the parking lot, there was my car with the driver's door bent back, the window blown out, bear paw prints all over the front seats, and a peach pit on the driver's seat—the remnants of the bear's meal in my car. A note from a ranger was taped to my dashboard telling me to stop by the office before leaving the park. When I went to talk to the ranger, I could hardly look him in the eye as I expressed my sincere apologies and indicated he had no idea how bad this was. He looked confused by my reaction and indicated he was not going to give me a ticket, which made me feel even more guilty. I begged him to write me up; I knew it was fair—and the least of ways I would pay.

I bent the window frame of the car door back to a position somewhat replicating normalcy, and we loaded up and started to drive off. I noticed all the signs warning people of bears in the area and not to leave food in the car—clearly informing visitors to use the provided food lockers. As we began the hour-long drive back to our home, with wind whistling through my blown-out window, I could hear my younger daughter crying. I asked if she was OK, and she asked if they were going to kill the bear because it had broken into our car. I wasn't sure but said that I doubted they would, an answer that may not have been entirely truthful. We continued driving, and about five minutes later, I could hear my daughter crying again and asked what was wrong now, and she answered with "Dad, I think this may ruin your reputation." To which I answered, "Yes, you may have a point."

Moving Forward

Our science reveals that bear populations can decline in and around our iconic mountain towns because they come looking for food, but many don't make it back out because they get run over or are euthanized for breaking into houses and cars. We've learned that this impact on bears won't jeopardize the population as a whole: black bears are not going to disappear from the landscape because of our development in mountain towns. Nonetheless, if we seek solutions that are more humane and closer to the notion of coexistence, then we need to focus on reducing the availability of our garbage and other food attractants. The science on this is clear; what isn't clear is how to do this.

Getting to the point where our mountain towns and modern landscapes are less attractive to bears will require substantial changes and investment from the citizens in communities throughout Colorado. In all the iconic mountain towns and cities, there will need to be infrastructure for better securing garbage, law enforcement willing and able to enforce ordinances regarding garbage and other attractants, and a community that supports the notion of being bear smart. Finding effective means for creating this culture offers a whole new challenge where the emphasis is less about bear ecology and more about sociology and effective policy.

Since 2022, the governor's office and Colorado Parks and Wildlife have annually made a million dollars available to towns and cities in Colorado that are struggling with human-bear conflict. The money is given to municipalities in a competitive grant process where the proposed projects must focus on reducing anthropogenic sources of food. The projects are judged by a panel, with the idea that the best ones will be funded. It's an annual million-dollar carrot meant to complement the laws and regulations passed by municipalities and counties throughout Colorado and designed to limit availability of garbage and other known attractants. How effective this type of incentive program is for reducing conflict is an important question. It undoubtedly won't solve all the problems, but hopefully it acts as an important catalyst for towns and provides opportunities for building partnerships that enhance coexistence. The question of how to coexist goes beyond black bears, extending to every large carnivore species throughout the world. The socioecological context will differ between species and systems, but the challenges of coexisting will often boil down to first figuring out how to reduce conflict by limiting access to human resources that are attractive to carnivores. Science can only help illuminate the issues; getting people to understand and make necessary changes will require cooperation among stakeholders, wildlife managers, and local governments that are not used to engaging in these types of problems. The citizens of these landscapes are critical to these efforts and need to participate in creating solutions. They will also need support to help achieve positive outcomes.

Finally, progress will require patience. Humans are fallible. Sometimes we ignore the signs and leave food in cars. And sometimes we let our egos lead us toward simplistic actions instead of understanding these are complex problems with complex solutions.

19

At Home with Forest Fires in the West

PAUL C. ROGERS

Fire screams for our attention. A forest ablaze is nature's sensational headline. The images draw a visceral reaction: do something! The response for the past century has been to suppress wildfires. National policy was to send teams of firefighters to douse ignitions before 10:00 a.m. the next day. In hindsight, suppression itself was a mistake, bringing an unprecedented menace in the form of accumulated fuels into today's forests. Yet we go on battling these flames with boundless budgets and military bravado.

A vicious cycle churns, and we seem unable to stop the crusade that exacerbates the problem. We would be better served by pressing the pause button on our reactions to fire. Let's apply what we know and learn to live with fire rather than combating it. Fire will come: the future portends mounting combustion. Bad things happen to everyone; it's how we react that determines character.

How should we respond to future fires?

Across the American West, some communities are inherently more flammable as a result of their proximity to standing forests. Such locations, when lacking resources and prone to individualistic ideologies, are particularly vulnerable to conflagrations. Island Park, Idaho, is one such community. A retreat for the middle class, Island Park is deeply rooted in conservative politics, combustible fuels, and improvised development.

The Island Park Caldera, like its younger Yellowstone neighbor, was born in cataclysm. The rhyolite soils from prior eruptions some two million years ago provide a foundation for broad expanses of fire-prone lodgepole pine. Sitting at 6,300 feet, residents of Island Park, Idaho, rest on this dormant volcano, its getaway homes spreading across landscapes also frequented by campers, fishers, and urban refugees. Unlike many of the West's iconic resort destinations, most of the dwellings in Island Park are modest. Clearly not a Santa Fe, Vail, Park City, or even nearby Jackson, Island Park's unpretentious existence still faces significant hurdles given its ripe setting for wildfire.

Chief among the challenges of Island Park are its humble trappings: wood cabins mingle with aluminum trailer homes alongside a scattering of small subdivisions. It's a middle-class model of escapism dropped into a forested Rocky Mountain setting. Dwellings in the eight-hundred- to three-thousand-square-foot range are markedly different from the likes of a Sun Valley mansion, a Park City second home, or a Telluride estate weighing in at thousands of square feet. Obviously, size isn't everything, but it does provide a measure of resources for projects like firewise landscaping (a series of actions taken to clear fuels and other materials away from homes; National Fire Protection Association, n.d.). To create a firewise landscape in Vail requires writing a check to professional arborists or landscapers. In Island Park, most homeowners will be investing in personal equipment and calloused hands for several years to clear underbrush and overhanging trees themselves. Realistically, many seasonal visitors and permanent residents will do nothing and hope for the best. This strategy of inertia ultimately results in dire outcomes, at least from the perspective of the homeowner.

A second challenge is the prevalence of individualism common to the Interior West (although many of the iconic Western resort towns are populated with extra-regional "outsiders" bringing decidedly nonindividualist philosophies). In many ways, Idaho epitomizes the libertarian bent that limits civic action and champions personal intention. In the past, however, our greatest trials have required collective action. Lessons learned from the time of Anglo-European settlement, the World Wars, the Great Depression, and myriad natural disasters have shone a bright light on Westerners uniting, sacrificing comforts, lending a hand, and compromising for the greater good. Policymakers can draw on those experiences to shape our approach to wildfires, even in communities that prize individual liberty.

How Did We Get Here?

North America didn't have a wildfire *problem* prior to Anglo-American settlement (nor water use crises!), although periodic climate fluctuations certainly presented challenges to Native people. Living within the limits of Western ecosystems means living with flames. Thomas Vale's *Fire, Native Peoples, and the Natural Landscape* shows that multiple regions across the West had similar patterns of aboriginal burning (Vale 2002). Native peoples settled in much the same areas as immigrants, showing a preference for valley bottoms with water, fertile soils, and relative ease of travel for food acquisition. While acknowledging wide variability in Native customs and forest types, a general pattern emerges of localized fires near established villages and seasonal camps, with limited human-caused fire in less-traveled mountainous terrain. No doubt, as with today's prescribed burns, Native-set blazes occasionally escaped intended areas when conditions in adjoining terrain and vegetation were susceptible.

During the nineteenth century, fire was widely applied by Anglo-Americans after intensive grazing and logging practices exhausted native vegetation. To newcomers, resources seemed boundless. Purposeful torching has sometimes been mischaracterized as negligent logging or grazing practice. Some even described Native American burning as a naive or careless custom. Native burning culture was outpaced by systemic settler torching in the 1800s. Ironically, numerous scholars have erroneously used late nineteenth-century fire patterns as a baseline to infer great successes in subsequent twentieth-century fire suppression.

As migrants learned to live in arid country, their appetite for resources led to overconsumption of wildlife, rangelands, water, soil, and forests. Burning was a common stewardship practice that was employed with abandon across widely differing woodland systems. Often such blazes—ostensibly to create forest openings and seedling fertility—were set and left until winter snows extinguished them (Hoxie 1910). As this era closed, settler impacts from intentional burning, grazing, and logging were extensive.

By the twentieth century, it was clear to settlers and government officials that unrestrained exploitation could not continue. These were not the verdant Eastern lands of their origins, where moist forests could rebound quickly. In fact, after experiencing flames, mudslides, and floods, many communities sought government intervention. Gifford Pinchot's U.S. Forest Service, established in 1905, tried to implement the methods of Old World forestry in an arid West vastly different from their place of origin. While most land was already spoken for in the East, Western highlands quickly became part of the National Forest System between 1890 and 1910.

The breaking point came with the epic 1910 inferno, where in the northern Rockies, more than three million acres of forest were scorched and eighty-six souls lost. The 1911 Weeks Act formally prohibited Native and settler light-burning traditions. As the century progressed, regulation in the form of command-and-control practices grew: forests were engineered with agrarian precision contingent on "rotations," "harvests," "stocking," "board feet," and "fire suppression" (Holling and Meffe 1996). While timber was the championed crop—even under the guise of "multiple use"—protection of this commodity included ever-mounting warfare to control wildfire's ravaging of the national woodpile. Paul Hirt's *A Conspiracy of Optimism* chronicles not only the overprojection of U.S. National Forest timber stocks but also an inflated arrogance in our ability to understand and corral nature (Hirt 1994).

Today one commonly hears the phrase "one hundred years of fire suppression" to underpin the notion of overly dense forests that are fueling wildfires often described as unprecedented. Viewed in isolation, this theory seems plausible, but the ultimate drivers of wildfire are more likely vegetation types and weather patterns. Suppressing fires, sometimes successfully, has led to more severe events in some locations and little effect elsewhere.

Late in the twentieth century, federal agencies pivoted to more holistic approaches in land management, including allowing some fires to burn. As federal agencies transitioned from managing land for optimum timber production to ecosystem stewardship with multiple goals, fire management also changed. Still, the transition to ecosystem management has not been smooth—in fact, most Western state governments remain steadfastly tied to short-term single-resource harvesting. Contrasting federal-state mandates, intermingled with private property prerogatives, undermine coordinated fire approaches. Moreover, understanding fire in the arid West requires maintaining ecosystem processes rather than the simple commodification of timber, wildlife, and water. A key tenet of modern fire management is making critical process-based linkages to climate.

According to the multicentury Palmer Drought Severity Index, the twentieth century was the wettest century of the past two millennia in much of the Interior West, even accounting for notable drought cycles of the 1930s and 1950s (Cook et al. 2004). Context matters. Relatively high moisture during the twentieth century facilitated reduced burn incidence. Generally, lower elevations tend to burn much more frequently than upper elevations (see figure 19.1). Where mixed-conifer or spruce-fir communities predominate and blazes occur every 150–450 years on average, change related to short-term climate shifts or fire suppression may have little ecological impact (Baker 2009). The brief time of effective fire suppression in these higher-elevation areas, perhaps fifty years, has likely caused little change in tree densities or related susceptibility to recent wildfires. The upshot: one need not invoke fire suppression or even climate change to explain today's big fire events. The recent transition to drought conditions, placed in the context of a wet twentieth century, is critical to understanding what is and is not unprecedented. As weather patterns shift, agility will be paramount in response to fire, perhaps taking a cue from those who preceded us.

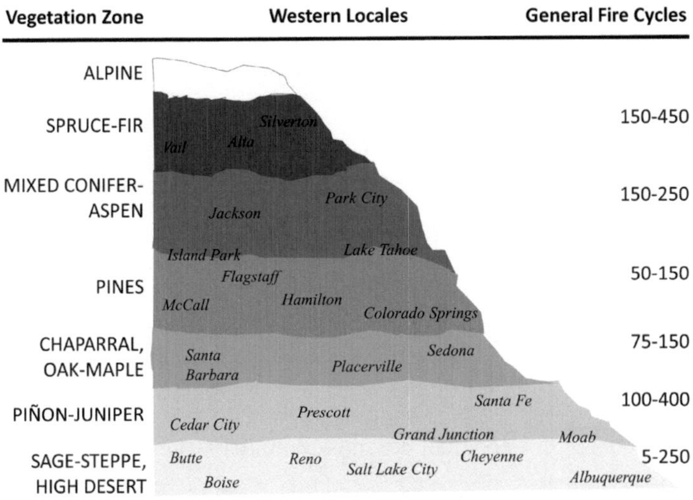

Figure 19.1 A generalized schematic of vegetation layers for Western montane forests of the United States, depicting a sampling of regional localities and average fire cycles (Baker 2009). Within elevational zones, localized variation is common and depends on topography, soil type, and moisture. In the sage-steppe zone, wide variation of fire frequency represents both grasses (short cycles) and sagebrush (medium-to-longer cycles).

Different forests burn differently. A layer cake of plant communities tracks elevation from the foothills upward: sage-steppe, piñon-juniper, chaparral and oak-maple woodlands, pines, mixed conifer-aspen, and spruce-fir. These vegetative zones generally track fire return times, with sage-steppe burning on the order of years, pines roughly decades to a century, and upper elevation forests from one to several centuries. In recent decades, more acreage of nonforested grass- and shrubland has burned than forests. This may be largely attributed to the proliferation of nonnative "flashy fire" cheatgrass that may repeat burn within only a few years. Within forest belts, subtle landscape features, such as proximity to moisture, facilitate further mixing in vegetation and burn patterns. Relatively flame-resistant forests such as quaking aspen thrive where underground water facilitates their establishment in tandem with lush plant cover (Nesbit et al. 2023). Agricultural forestry simplifies forests by selecting for species with the fastest growth, highest value, and easiest accessibility, reducing the naturally complex to the uniform.

The industrial reach of modern forest management dwarfs localized efforts by Native peoples to modify landscapes via fire and cultivation. Accessible twentieth century forests—generally lower, drier, and of mild slope angle—provided the initial inroads for wood harvest and fire protection that later encouraged recreation and home building on private lands. These woodlands have experienced the greatest transformation. Homogenous forests abutting established developments are the frontlines of contemporary fire activity. Such scenes supply flashy footage for nightly news broadcasts. The tragedies are significant, though the consequences of these practices are predictable and preventable.

A Plan for Island Park, Idaho

Many rural communities in the West aspire to fire protection. At the same time, a belief in unfettered development dominates municipal planning. Island Park, Idaho, stands out in that, unlike most amenity focused destinations, modest incomes drive much of the community's decisions about wildfire protection. This is not—or not yet—an area of imported wealth, swelling tax revenues, and glamorous entertainment. There is no nearby high-capacity airport. Instead, generations of cabin dwellers arriving by motor vehicle make up the majority of residents.

A small fraction of Island Park's eighteen thousand dwellings are occupied year-round. There are about eight hundred full-time residents. Cabins are modest, and thick forests abut most homes across this volcanic bowl bordered by Yellowstone National Park on the east, Montana's southern border to the north, and lowland sage-steppe to the west and south. With such attributes, both daunting and dazzling, residents laid claim to small allotments and built a loose assemblage of homes—collectively a municipality, of sorts—from which they now must respond to the inevitable future firestorms.

The political climate, decidedly libertarian, makes implementation of civic fire protection logistically challenging. A 2013 poll found that only 29 percent of Island Park citizens were willing to take actions such as thinning trees adjacent to homes; even fewer were onboard with replacing roofs with fireproof materials or widening access roads to dispersed cabins or concentrated developments (Resource Media 2013). Since the community survey, efforts have congealed somewhat around a working group known as Island Park Sustainable Fire Community (IPSFC).

Similar municipal groups advocating for firewise landscaping are common in fire-prone communities. Recommendations call for homeowners to establish a continuum of active forest management, with more work closer to buildings. In zone 1, immediately adjacent to buildings, this is characterized by clearing trees, brush, tall grass, dead needles, woodpiles, and other flammable materials (e.g., propane tanks, plastics) away from dwellings. In particular, overhanging trees, wooden decks, and cedar shake roofs are red flags in firewise mitigation. These are sites where an errant spark can quickly ignite a home.

In zone 2 (one to two hundred feet [thirty to sixty meters] from structures), the focus is on terrain and ladder fuels—vegetation such as shrubs and small trees that convey ground fires to crown fires. Homes on or near steep slopes are especially vulnerable to wind-propelled flames; additional measures may be required due to the speed and ferocity at which flames may advance. Firewise landscaping recommends trees be thinned in zone 2 to a spacing of at least ten feet (three meters) between tree crowns.

Zone 3, comprising lands beyond zone 2, is made up of the so-called wildlands and may require only modest tree thinning, brush and deadwood removal, and general attention to terrain, forest type, and tree ages. Oftentimes landowners do not directly control alterations farther from their homes; these decisions, particularly in Island Park, involve federal land managers. For instance, trees at a distance from houses may be younger or of deciduous types, both of which are known to be somewhat less flammable.

In the West, the most common broadleaf tree species, quaking aspen, has numerous fire-repelling properties. Some locales are actively planting or favoring aspens near housing (e.g., Breckenridge, Colorado). Recent research supports aspen's fire-resistant properties, but the authors note that further study is needed to clarify this relationship (Nesbit et al. 2023). To be clear, no vegetation type, including aspen, will deter blazes if winds are high or conditions especially dry. This leaves us with the simple firewise phrase to keep surroundings "clean and green" to staunch blazes near homes (Kuhns and Daniels 2018).

In Island Park, the consortium of individuals, homeowners' associations, civic leaders, and federal land managers (i.e., IPSFC) is making progress, though they face physical, economic, and political challenges. Fire protection merged with forest restoration is expensive.

In 2022, the state of Idaho received $1.23 from the federal government for every tax dollar paid, but it is unclear how much of that is directed toward firewise practices. (This highlights the irony of resolute individualism in places that take in more federal money than they give, particularly where citizen protection is a first principle of government.) Nonetheless, actions taken to date include setting up volunteer-run demonstration projects, gaining government grants to clear lodgepole pine along the main highway (U.S. 20), acquiring flashing highway signs to alert people to combustive conditions and evacuation plans, and improving municipal codes regarding defensible space, sprinkler requirements, and access road improvements.

The IPSFC admits, however, that enforcement of these regulations has been lacking. The group recognizes other shortcomings, pointedly phrased as "goals": to ensure multi- and single-unit rentals are included in fire prevention and safety procedures; to connect developments with loop roads rather than with one-way access; to create social media outlets for preventative actions and emergency communications; to plant fire-resistant plants and encourage aspen rejuvenation where it already exists; and to greatly increase civic education to inform people of why and where the Forest Service is removing trees (Resource Media 2013).

Even though homeowner compliance is sluggish, an unpublished draft of a 2021 IPSFC working group report centered in part on identifying regional conservation organizations to "address resistance of groups that litigate" and "fight against environmental groups who are preventing vegetation treatments." These quotes are telling: local residents see such "outside groups" as a central part of the forest management problem. However, this battle may be misplaced in terms of overall effectiveness in Island Park fire mitigation. Resistance from residents in the form of strident individualism and opposition to community action likely plays a more central role in this drama than interloping conservationists.

Acknowledging Limits

In early June 2022, I toured Island Park by foot and vehicle to gain a sense of the fire prevention setting. Newer, more prosperous neighborhoods show some broad protective elements. Though seemingly out of place is this mostly wildland setting, bluegrass lawns, exotic nursery stock trees, and sculpted shrubs lined wide asphalt access roads and driveways. These modifications will slow flames in developed spaces. However, even here, there are features that increase the likelihood a house will burn: native conifers overhanging wood decks, thick carpets of shed needles, and firewood stacked against exterior walls. I came upon one homeowner actively trimming the lower branches of a lodgepole pine near his garage. When asked whether he was taking other actions, he was circumspect about talking to a stranger but confirmed my observations: "It's every man for himself. I can barely keep up on my own property."

Passing through an older and decidedly more haphazard grouping of homes, the scene was eye-opening. Here, narrow rutted roads—some paved, some not—are encroached by tall shrubs, capped by canopies of dense conifers. Small homes, cabins, and outbuildings abut forest in every direction; propane tanks and wood caches seem tethered to each dwelling. Many of these cabins were likely built in an era very different from the dry, hot, fire-prone, and peopled forests of today. To the trained eye, it resembles a tinderbox.

When a settlement overextends itself into wildlands, the motivation is two parts profit and one part aesthetics. Our nation, in many ways, appears to be at a crossroads: one avenue says "more, more, more" toward increasing dysfunction, while the other preaches nature's limits, earnest dialogue, and adaptive action.

While the West of lore sought to reap short-term profit from nature, the region's community builders—the "stickers" in the parlance of Wallace Stegner—craft a life among these vistas through persistence and cooperation. The latter are here to make a living, while the former, the so-called boomers, strive for a killing. The essayist Bernard DeVoto described this as the perpetual fight of "the West against itself." In a 1947 essay, he summarizes, "The West has always been a society living under the threat of destruction by natural cataclysm and here it is, bright against the sky, inviting such a cataclysm" (DeVoto 1947, 13). Instead of, in his word, the "despoilers" of the early twentieth century—ranchers, timber companies, and miners—the West of today is faced with headlong development, an endless gulping from the resource trough. Without pause, we exploit the greatest dollar value from each wooded parcel until we find ourselves in the path of a raging inferno. Here, I reference the frightening infernos at Paradise, California (2018), Fort McMurray, Alberta (2016), or Waldo Canyon, Colorado (2012). To realize our limits, nature's limits, is to heed historical caution and contemporary science.

The maxim holds that if floodplains flood, we shouldn't build in them. But the forest corollary is absent. Public polling of the Island Park community found that most residents felt that wildfires could and should be prevented, though the means of doing so were not explicitly stated. Further, half of respondents felt that saving their homes was the job of firefighters and, if their homes were damaged or destroyed, their insurance would cover replacement. The sentiment that fire, a native element of Western forests, can be stopped at will is likely due to decades of command-and-control messaging, as well as tolerance of cognitive dissonance.

A flare-up in lodgepole pine, boosted by even modest winds, burns at high intensity and may transform from spark to blowup in under an hour. Still, rural Idahoans believe in individual property rights while eschewing most forms of regulation. Here and elsewhere, the challenge is to spur collective action when environmental constraints confront Western mythology. Communities, let alone individuals, cannot stop wind-driven infernos, no more than they might halt hurricanes, tornados, or floodwaters.

There is promise, however, for changing the culture to manage private land fuels. We should embrace strategic planning and slow the rate of development. Budding fire protection measures in Island Park are slowly gaining traction, but clear-eyed acknowledgment of limits to growth in the face of expanding drought, naturally combustible environs, and already overtaxed fire protection personnel will be essential. Elected officials can do more to bridge communication gaps between the public and commercial sectors, and experts can do a better job of communicating science in order to help residents better live with nature rather than battling against it.

At Home with Fire

In an earlier career, I made a living as a Forest Service nomad. We moved from north to south, traversing states, surveying with small field crews to document ecological indicators of forest conditions. Our tour landed in Glenwood Springs, Colorado, over the Independence Day weekend in 1994, where we enjoyed showers, clean motel beds, entertainment, and a brief break from the backcountry. As Tuesday morning rolled around, I was back on the interstate heading west to meet my compatriots in the small town of Meeker. Glancing up at Storm King Mountain, a waft of smoke could be seen above the oak chaparral. Federal fire response vehicles were pulled over, apparently readying themselves for an offensive. I wondered aloud, "Why are they going into that punky blaze when there's hardly a structure in sight?"

Later that day, the guilt of that quip struck. Fourteen women and men lost their lives as that fire exploded beneath them, carrying smoke and flames up a long steep gulch in an unimaginably hot whirlwind. Eight were lucky enough to escape. Billowing black-brown plumes forty-five miles away could be seen from my destination; the fatal outcome was later confirmed.

This was not the first, nor the last, of such tragedies in the name of . . . it's never quite clear what. First it was watershed protection, then it was timber, then it was structural defense. Slogging through this endless war on fire, for those in actual combat, we might toss in bravado, ego, dominion, summer income, and adventure. Following on these motives, an undertone of good versus evil prevails. The inherent sensationalism of searing flames projected across TV screens is seductive. Fire as "the villain" is an easy sell. An orphaned New Mexico bear rescued from a smoldering snag and now wearing jeans, a ranger hat, and holding a shovel strutted into the role like a marketing natural!

Among America's most iconic public relations campaigns, "Only you can prevent forest fires" overlooked how nature was the chief instigator at the time Smokey donned his dungarees. Even where humans caused fires, the brave bruin failed to communicate the futility of battling flames under extreme conditions.

But the appearance of stopping nature's fury was always more advertising ploy than grounded science. The illusion of stopping flames augmented a conspiracy of optimism that promoted public lands logging as well as the endless expansion of the forest abode. Paradoxically, the increased invasion of Western wildlands by homebuilders has altered ignitions. Smokey's words ring a bit truer now, as increasing roads, recreationists, and residents have amplified human fire starts. Aside from a tragedy here and homes lost there, the fallacy of safe scenic forest living persists. But now a climatic scene change has raised the curtain on a searing new future. The dream of a flame-free forest, bolstered by interventionist practices, should be quietly put to rest like so many smoldering embers under autumn snow.

Strategies for living with fire incorporate both ecological and social perspectives. Above all, there are layers of unpredictability in fire behavior that human engineering cannot control. Fuel breaks built to halt minor fires are easily breached with mounting winds. We should try to understand what we can but keep an open mind and practice adaptive approaches that recognize unanticipated outcomes. Such prescriptions entail a healthy dose of humility.

Approaches partnering *with* nature are more likely to succeed. This means practices will differ by forest cover. Tania Schoennagel and her colleagues provide a framework for adapting to more fire by first conceding the inadequacy of conventional practices, such as forest cutting for fuels reduction, continued suppression, and unfettered real estate development (Schoennagel et al. 2017). These authors stress that ecological resilience to fire, whether at individual homesites or spanning watersheds, starts with understanding fire types dictated by dominant vegetation. The prime goal in developed areas should be to manage landscapes such that forests can provide some ecological benefits while causing minimal home damage.

Reducing fuel continuity close to homes is paramount. The corollary, however, should also be recognized: at a distance from structures, our practice should be to minimize forest cutting and facilitate periodic fires, as well as to implement prescribed burns tactically, as Native peoples have done. If policymakers continue funding suppression and forest thinning, we will continue groping for the illusion of "command and control" where adaptive strategies underpinned by knowledge of fire-dependent systems are more appropriate.

Adopting this thinking on the regional scale, Max Moritz and his colleagues have developed a map that relies on the precepts stated above—planning, education, and community fuels buffers. They emphasize planning and curtailing development: "Deciding where and how to build our communities—arguably the key function of land use and urban planning—has ripple effects across landscapes and feedbacks to wildfire occurrence and its impacts" (Moritz et al. 2022, 2). An additional implication is that past fire responses have often been dominated by narrow interests centered on commercial forestry when more diverse perspectives are required.

Messaging is key to living with fire. The dominant narratives of popular media and government agencies are overwhelmingly negative. Cataclysmic storylines about modern "megafires" lead to the mistaken impression that human building and agricultural forestry are not culpable. Moreover, it's negligent to claim that fires have not been a historical fact of Western life. Past climatic periods spawned more widespread conflagrations, while select Native burning was common.

In our haste to lay blame for modern conflagrations, a cabal of managers, media, and some scientists have invoked increasing drought. However, what's really new is the growing number of structures, and sometimes lives, in the path of predictable flames. Rather than curtail forest sprawl directly, a woe-is-me stance emerges: something bad is being done to us! In newspeak, the resultant language is of "devastation," "destruction," "loss," "charred," "tragedy," and so on.

Rather than inflammatory language, we should kindle conversations based on ecological opportunity and social connection with wildlands. Policy strategies grounded in complexity, preparedness, and acceptance of the unpredictable will be crucial. Climate change and its evolving linkages to Western fire are daunting, but framing these challenges as frightening enemies too large to overcome discourages constructive engagement. Positioning ourselves in an adaptive stance involves learning-while-doing and nimble responses based on documented experience.

Island Park typifies a Western version of the American Dream, of living *within* nature. This locale, not unlike others in surrounding states, caters to those already residing in the region. The modest nature of such forest retreats contrasts with the region's resort towns.

The challenge of the West's various fire-exposed Island Parks is that while they are more common than the resorts, they exist outside the limelight, without the resources, planning, and infrastructure needed to protect them from the next firestorm. Facing continuous change, residents of such humble retreats invoke hindsight and independence when foresight and community are needed. As outsiders, bearing the best of intentions and armed with scientific knowledge, we are likely to be spurned. How might land stewards and municipalities codify a bigger vision that acknowledges limits to growth while living with fire?

We can start with a clear-eyed civic understanding that we cannot stop fire and that, in many instances, we need fire for healthy landscapes. And we must come to terms with unrestrained development. Real estate and tourism boosters, along with consumers' endless demands for more, are out of step with limited resources. As for wildfire, it's not unreasonable to suggest the planet is pushing back. Humility says we should listen, take note, and ask difficult questions of the relationship between our communities and natural environments. How does this Earth function? How do forests thrive with flames? How can we live compatibly?

V
RESTORING NATURE

20

Human-Driven Changes and Solutions at the Great Salt Lake

BONNIE K. BAXTER

Imagine a woman fishing along a river, the ground frozen beneath her feet. She is among the first people to live in this place we now call Utah, as the warming Earth melts the ice sheets of the Pleistocene. Before her people arrived, a large freshwater sea, Lake Bonneville, filled the watershed. But by her time (twelve thousand years ago), the bottom of this valley is home to the Great Salt Lake, and tributaries trickle from the mountains toward her village on the lakeshore.

Each day, she leaves her shelter to pass along the lush, fertile marshes (Madsen 2016). She walks upstream along the rivers that bring water and minerals to the salty lake. When she returns with her catch, she works in the small pools she has created by hand to make salt via the evaporation of the lake water. Her father will trade the salt and dried brine-fly pupae with nearby communities. When her grandfather dies, her village buries him in the marsh before they return to their cave with a lakeside view, decorated with his artwork. Her descendants, the modern Goshute and Paiute people, still live south and west of the Great Salt Lake today, as do her Ute and Shoshone cousins, whose land is northeast of the lake (Cuch 2000).

Today the shorelines of the Great Salt Lake are receding, not through the end of a glacial period but due to the actions of the humans who have flowed into Utah since the middle of the nineteenth century. Westward expansion, incentivized by the U.S. government, brought European descendants from the East in large numbers, spurred by promises of wealth, land, refuge, and opportunity. The newcomers displaced the Indigenous communities and changed the watershed in dramatic ways. They dismissed the knowledge of First Peoples who understood and respected water and its scarcity in a desert.

These human-driven changes to the watershed have led to an ecosystem in crisis, drawing the attention of national and international media. Over the last century, overuse of water has limited the flow into the Great Salt Lake, and now half of the lake bed is exposed. The lake elevation has dropped eleven feet below the healthy level. This situation raises concerns about impacts on the ecosystem as well as on the humans who live in the surrounding metropolitan areas. Dust storms from the exposed shorelines contain not only particulate pollution but also heavy metals from our history of mining in the West. This essay explores the impacts of humans on the lake, their relationship with it, and what they can do in the face of crisis. Now we who have created this disaster must try to rescue the Great Salt Lake.

A Unique and Significant Ecosystem

Rallying cries for protection of the Great Salt Lake are based on its significance as the largest lake in the Western United States and its support of ten million birds from 338 species (Sorensen, Hoven, and Neill 2020). The wetlands provide nesting habitat and a diversity of invertebrates as a food source. The birds restricted to the open water eat the brine shrimp and brine flies that flourish in the lake (Roberts 2013). The biology of the ecosystem is dependent on the spring runoff from the Wasatch Front, which keeps the salinity stabilized.

Terminal lakes such as the Great Salt Lake receive water through precipitation and inflows, and they lose water through evaporation, as no rivers run out of this low spot in the basin. Thus, the water level fluctuates as a result of inputs minus evaporation. Minerals do not leave the lake naturally, and they accumulate as they enter the system through groundwater seeps or rivers from the watershed. This makes the Great Salt Lake salty, like other terminal lakes (Saccò et al. 2021). As the lake rises and falls, the salinity of the water is affected; increased inflows can dilute the brine, and desiccating conditions can concentrate the salts. When the lake shrinks, as in recent decades, not only does it expose the shoreline, but the water also gets saltier.

In lakes like this one, high salinity limits biodiversity: only those life-forms that have evolved to balance their cells in the brine survive. The biodiversity of the ocean is immense at a salinity level of 3.4 percent, but the salinity of the Great Salt Lake is even higher, and vertebrates such as fish cannot survive. The lake's northern arm is above 30 percent salinity in the warm summer months. This part of the lake has a robust microbial community but no animals. The water is colored pink by the microbial pigments that protect the extremophiles who live there.

Not only is the salinity of the Great Salt Lake high; it also poses a challenge to organisms because it is variable. The part of the lake near Salt Lake City, the southern arm, supports the vibrant ecology that feeds many migratory and resident birds. The salinity here typically varies between 9 percent and 15 percent. Biodiversity in this area is greater than the northern arm but lower than the ocean; there are only two simple food chains, focused on either shrimp or flies.

The brine shrimp make their living in the Great Salt Lake by eating a diet of tiny algae that make their own food from the ample sunlight. Although the shrimp give birth to live young during the warm months, cold seasonal temperatures set a stress response in motion, and the shrimp create a hard cyst or shell around their embryos. These cysts are left behind in the winter when the adults die off, hatching into a healthy population of shrimp in the spring. Some birds such as northern shovelers eat the cysts, while others such as eared grebes eat the shrimp swimming in the water.

Along the margins of the lake, shorebirds feed on swarming clouds of brine flies. But most of the fly's life cycle is spent as a larva in the water of the Great Salt Lake. These tiny larvae munch on the microbial mats on the bottom. After several growth stages, the larvae attach to the mats and pupate, forming pupae that continue to develop. Adult flies emerge underwater in an air bubble formed as the pupae crack open, and the bubble delivers them to the surface. Shorebirds grab these flies as they emerge, while the phalaropes on the water will spin and create a vortex to bring the juicy pupae and larvae to the surface for their meal. Diving ducks such as goldeneye eat the larvae and pupae from the bottom of the lake. Flies, then, are important across many avian feeding zones.

This is the lake that the first people of Utah encountered. The early Great Salt Lake was highly productive, and the watershed was filled with flowing rivers and springs supplied by ample groundwater. The more recent inhabitants of the valley have wreaked havoc on this natural system, and the ecosystem is now in crisis.

An Altered Great Salt Lake

In the early twentieth century, as the young Salt Lake City grew, people began reconstructing the Great Salt Lake watershed. As the settlement prospered, the lake was used as a resource for industry. Mineral extraction, agriculture diversions, and shortcuts for the railroad would eventually impact the pristine lake that Indigenous people revered. Industrial society built dams, canals, causeways, and impoundments to sequester water. These are visible today in aerial views of the Great Salt Lake, where mineral extraction ponds have resulted in a series of colored rectangles reminiscent of Piet Mondrian paintings, and a railroad causeway splits a lake into pink- and green-colored brines.

Along the Bear, Weber, and Jordan River corridors, water was diverted as towns developed, supporting homes and agriculture. As the population grew along the Wasatch Front, uses increased, and less water made it to the Great Salt Lake at the bottom of the watershed (Null and Wurtsbaugh 2020). The overuse of water upstream from the lake continues to be the biggest threat to the lake ecosystem. It is natural for a terminal lake to fluctuate seasonally in elevation, but the rates of inputs to outputs must balance over time. If the population of the watershed uses too much water, less will trickle down, and evaporation rates may then overtake inflow rates. Studies on the watershed suggest that consumptive use (for households, industry, and agriculture) explains more than two-thirds of the diminished lake levels. The challenge is increased by Utah's population growth rate, higher than the national average and projected to increase, especially along the Wasatch Front.

The pressure of water use from home and industry pales in comparison to that from agriculture. Irrigation systems for farms take water from its sources, such as a river or reservoir. These diversions are accomplished by a series of canals, pipelines, and pumps. The efficiency of water use in agriculture varies depending on the crop and on the methods used for irrigation and water delivery. Some crops may not be sustainable as the climate changes. For example, alfalfa for livestock feed is grown by many farms in the Great Salt Lake watershed, but its water-hungry nature suggests its incompatibility with an arid desert ecosystem.

The Great Salt Lake is affected not only by these diversions but also by interventions that partition parts of the watershed (Baxter 2018). In the 1930s, Roosevelt's Civilian Conservation Corps undertook several projects to enhance waterfowl habitat. This resulted in wetlands that still exist today. Salt companies also began a large-scale extraction industry, which created dammed areas for evaporation ponds, which concentrate salt in the brine until it precipitates out in solid form. Pond construction expanded, and companies with permits for extraction grew, leading to industries on the lake that produce not only salt but also fertilizer, lithium, and magnesium.

A trestle bridge was built to encourage tourism, offering train rides across the Great Salt Lake and enabling a shortcut for the railroad. In 1960, the trestle was replaced with a rock-filled causeway, which had the unintended consequence of sequestering the northern arm from freshwater inflows, despite culverts and a small breach through which boats could pass. The causeway to the northern end of Antelope Island, which was built later in that decade, cuts off the exchange of water on the eastern side of the island.

In the latter half of the twentieth century, brine shrimp companies began harvesting the cysts of the animals for commercial aquaculture, giving the open water of the southern arm commercial value that would rival that of the salt companies. This industry depends on a functioning ecosystem that will yield healthy shrimp, and they are regulated by the Utah Division of Wildlife Resources. The harvesting of cysts has been less impactful to the Great Salt Lake than the damming required for mineral extraction.

Recently, the breach in the causeway across the lake was reconstructed by the rail company to adjust the flow between the arms. Since 2016, the water has flowed back and forth through this revised opening, but it has not mixed evenly due to the salinity (and thus density) differences between the two bodies. When the Great Salt Lake hit a historic low at the end of 2022, the state of Utah adjusted the height of the berm, piling rocks high in the opening to prevent the heavy northern arm water from bringing more salt into the southern arm, thus protecting the ecosystem by reducing the salinity.

The Additive Effect of Climate Change

The megadrought currently affecting the Southwestern United States is a cyclical natural occurrence. But human-caused climate change is exacerbating these drought conditions, as is evident in the Great Salt Lake ecosystem. Terminal lakes put cycles of drought and flooding on display, as their elevation is dependent on temperature and precipitation-evaporation cycles. In the Great Salt Lake watershed, climate science predicts hotter summers and lower levels of precipitation, with a higher proportion coming as rain instead of snow (Baxter and Butler 2020). This is a problem for the lake for several reasons, considering the dynamics of a system where snowpack stores water at the top of the watershed, and at the bottom of the basin, a terminal lake receives what's left over after human use.

Recent summer temperatures have set historic highs, and except for the heavy snowfall in the winter of 2023, recent precipitation averages (both snow and rain) have been lower. When hot spells are early or prolonged, the snow melts too quickly, running off aboveground instead of trickling through recharge zones into underground aquifers. This combination of less snow and higher rates of snowmelt leads to less flow into the Great Salt Lake. What's more, if the lake shrinks and more shore is exposed, wind events can blow lake bed dust onto the snowpack, causing it to absorb more sunlight and melt even more quickly. Once the lake enters this negative feedback loop, further shrinkage becomes difficult to stop.

The Great Salt Lake is shrinking at an alarming rate. Over almost forty years, from the historic high to the historic low, the lake dropped an astounding twenty feet (GSLST 2023). Around 70 percent of this loss is due to water diversions for consumptive uses, which have increased as the population of northern Utah has grown. In addition, global warming is adding pressure to a watershed that is already heavily taxed; the downward trend in water levels was accompanied by an average local temperature increase of three degrees. We are witnessing the additive effects of human overuse and climate change, which place more demand on the ecosystem than it can fulfill. The history of water diversions has primed the conditions for biodiversity collapse in the lake now that the ecosystem is facing the additional challenge of climate change.

The biology of the Great Salt Lake southern arm is threatened by both the loss of lake habitat and the rise in salinity (Baxter and Butler 2020). Recently, the elevation of the lake fell to a historic low that raised its salinity to unhealthy levels; the southern arm rose to 19 percent salinity in the fall of 2022, well beyond the 10–15 percent optimal range for brine shrimp, brine flies, and their food. A longer duration at this high salt concentration will eventually result in the entire lake's salinity matching that of the northern arm, meaning the loss of open water food chains.

High salinity stresses all life-forms, from microorganisms to birds to humans. When organisms have to pump salt out of their cells or build molecules up inside them in order to balance salt concentration relative to the external environment, they have less energy available for other functions. This results in slow or halted growth and metabolism. Algae and cyanobacteria slow their reproduction as the amount of salt in lake water increases, which causes food scarcity for invertebrates. The shrimp and flies can spend so much energy on managing extra salt that they shut down other systems, which is observable in their smaller size and lower reproduction rates. Elevated salinity can cause shifts in reproductive strategies, such as shrimp making cysts so early that they will leave dormancy too soon and not overwinter. High salt levels will also destabilize and even kill the microbial mats, endangering the brine-fly pupae. Fly larvae may remain suspended in the water column, too buoyant to sink. During the historic low lake elevation of 2022, we saw evidence of these disruptions.

Under such conditions, it is likely that the birds that depend on brine shrimp (e.g., eared grebes) or brine flies (Wilson's phalaropes) will lose habitat, have limited access to food, and need to devote more energy to removing excess salt from their bodies. Indeed, observations in 2022 noted different feeding habits and smaller populations of some avian species. Given that the Great Salt Lake is lauded as a site of hemispheric importance for birds, this is a concern for the entire Pacific Flyway.

A Search for Solutions

The solution sounds simple: Get more water to the Great Salt Lake. However, solving the problem is not as easy as breaking a dam and allowing water to flow. The backbone of each solution is collaboration and communication among all stakeholders, including scientists, water management agencies, state agencies, lake industries, federal agencies, elected officials, nongovernment organizations, water law firms, agriculture, and residential communities. This can be framed in terms of six points.

1. *Upgrade antiquated water law and policies.* Water rights in the West are governed by archaic federal laws from the nineteenth century that incentivized homesteading and westward expansion and did not place value on salty water with no fish. Thus, solutions for getting water to the Great Salt Lake must involve revising water law.

   The Utah state legislature recently passed bills that are good examples of how this can be accomplished at the state level to circumvent old policies such as "use it or lose it" and narrowly defined "beneficial uses." The Instream Water Flow Bill (Utah H.B. 33) of the 2022 session allows landholders to lease their water rights to the state, without forfeiture, and to donate those rights to the Great Salt Lake, which was designated as a beneficial use for water. This, along with the Secondary Water Metering Bill (Utah H.B. 242), which will measure secondary water use for irrigation, may help us address the largest water user in the system, agriculture. If we can give farmers the ability to measure their water use and optimize plantings, then they may be able to lease remaining water for the purpose of filling the lake.

   The Great Salt Lake Watershed Enhancement Bill (Utah H.B. 410) funded a $40 million trust from federal infrastructure monies. This may become a model for other states, creating an endowment that collects donations and grows funds that may be used for buying out water rights, improving water quality and quantity, and restoring healthy watershed habitats. In spring of 2023, the Church of Jesus Christ of Latter-day Saints donated water rights in perpetuity from some of their land holdings. Perhaps this is only a symbolic gesture, as water was likely flowing into the lake from these particular assets already, but this could encourage members of this prevalent church in Utah to follow suit.

The 2023 Utah state legislature was less robust in important pieces of legislation that will impact the lake, with one notable exception. A Great Salt Lake commissioner was appointed to the governor's cabinet, a role that will involve overseeing all state agencies that work on the lake and seeking solutions for cohesive management.

2. *Involve Indigenous people in making solutions.* Another outdated water policy in the Western United States invokes "first in time, first in right," which recognizes the first to claim the land as the owner of the associated water right. But the white homesteaders who claimed these rights were working in a system that ignored those who were truly first in time. All state committees should include Indigenous representation from the members of the tribes in the Great Salt Lake watershed. Learning about the watershed through the lens of those who possess the oldest oral history of Utah may teach everyone about the importance of water in the West.
3. *Address consumptive uses.* Human consumptive use for development and agriculture is largely responsible for the shrinking Great Salt Lake, and water use will be increasingly pressed by nonagriculture users as communities urbanize and grow. In a search for solutions, how to manage water use should be paramount, and human use is the only factor that can be addressed quickly; other pressures such as climate change are not easy to address on short timelines.

As the Great Salt Lake watershed communities are in a rapid growth mode, addressing household use is an important part of the conservation equation. In addition, as new companies are attracted to Utah, the state should manage the water expectations of these industries. In Utah, many cities, counties, and townships include some part of a household water bill in the resident's property taxes. This strategy hides the true cost of water use. Water bills should be transparent, and the pricing structure should reward those who conserve. During summer, when the impacts of drought are at their peak, cities along the Wasatch Front should implement water restrictions to prevent overuse. Incentivizing conservative water use is a successful strategy used in many Western states and cities, from which Utah could draw inspiration.

4. *Build bridges with other states.* The 1922 Colorado Compact has taught us many lessons about interstate solutions and shortcomings. This agreement portioned the Colorado River water across several states (and eventually included tribal nations), but the amount of water promised did not exist. How can Utah learn from this and manage water quantity needs with Idaho, which has significant water rights along its part of the Bear River corridor? Interstate agreements should be discussed in any plans to increase the amount of water delivered to the Great Salt Lake, and metering should be used to measure actual water use.
5. *Establish an elevation range and a series of actions to take when the lake elevation drops.* This solution involves the work of state agencies and their advisory committees, which includes academic scientists, state employees, and industry representatives. But the science and policies must be supported by elected officials who can create plans out of the recommendations. Current work on the state agency side is occurring on the Salinity Advisory Committee, established by the Utah Division of Forestry, Fire, and State Lands (the agency that oversees the comprehensive management plan for the lake). The new position of Great Salt Lake commissioner may elevate some of this work to the governor's office, and it may make its way to lawmakers in coming sessions. There is strong agreement and much science suggesting the optimal elevation range is 4,198 to 4,205 feet. This establishes a stable salinity as the lake fluctuates over seasons. If the lake elevation drops into the red zone, where recovery is elusive, actions such as water restrictions should be employed.
6. *Consider the pluses and minuses of interventions.* John Wesley Powell, inspired by his time with Indigenous people in the Southwest, famously warned Congress that there was not enough water for the push westward that was planned. He suggested that the people who moved West should live in the context of natural watersheds and prevent damming and diverting. Is the horse out of the barn? Can we remove structures that divert and sequester water? If not, then we must keep these ideas in mind for future alterations and consider alternative uses of existing engineering. Dams can be used to retain water, but they also can allow the immediate release of large inflows. In the case of the lake-segmenting railroad causeway discussed above, the breach berm is relatively easy to adjust temporarily. The 2023 heightening of the berm, raising it to prevent the hypersaline northern arm's water from flowing into the ecosystem of the southern arm, worked

to slow the rise in salinity. In this way, the causeway that intervened in the natural system can be used to preserve the Great Salt Lake habitat.

Reasons to Care

In this list of possible solutions, note that any one of these in isolation may have little or no impact. Multiple actions are needed if the lake will recover in a watershed that is home to more than two million people. Even if we were to bring more water to the system, this could be overshadowed by the influence of climate change and its effects, given the projected increases in temperature and evaporation. We need a quiver of arrows, not just one.

We should be buoyed by the fact that there are so many reasons to care, giving each of us motivation. While bird-watchers and duck hunters may be concerned about the loss of this enormous lake as the largest body of water on the Pacific Flyway, others might be more concerned about the reduced snow and early melt that will affect the ski resorts. Unhealthy water elevations would threaten lake-supported industries, workers' jobs, and an economic contribution to the state of nearly $2 billion.

The most acute threat of a drying Great Salt Lake to humans is air quality. Airborne dust from the exposed shorelines is a health concern for everyone along the Wasatch Front. This dust contains small particles that can compromise lung health, especially for vulnerable populations such as children and the elderly. The dust from the lake bed also contains heavy metals: for instance, mercury, which is a byproduct from historical gold smelting, selenium from copper smelting, and naturally occurring arsenic. Utah's physicians are concerned about the health impacts of airborne toxic metals. Also, a dust-filled valley may not attract new residents or relocating companies, which has broader economic consequences for Utah.

All these threats may leave one feeling overwhelmed instead of motivated. And a winter with good snowfall might breed complacency. Public engagement is crucial in keeping the issue at the forefront to engage the citizenry and to push the Utah state legislature, which can inspire others beyond the state lines. A shallow terminal lake that is shrinking rapidly is a dramatic visual reminder of the crisis of water in the Southwestern United States. Can this basin's emergency call attention to the larger problem of water in the West? The future of the Great Salt Lake reflects the future of the Western United States, and the solutions implemented here will have relevance elsewhere, spreading ripple effects over the coming decades.

21

Beaver Rewilding
Ecological Processes in the Northern Rockies

JODI BRANDT, JEN SCHNEIDER, NICK KOLARIK, EMILY ISKIN, NAWARAJ SHRESTHA, AND NANCY GLENN

In the late 1990s, after thirty years of being away, Jay Wilde returned to take over his family's cattle ranch in southeastern Idaho. He immediately noticed a major obstacle to his ranch's viability—the perennial creek of his boyhood was now intermittent: "I was sitting in my kitchen one day, and it dawned on me that there were no beavers." Thus began his mission to get beavers back to the watershed. Now there are hundreds of active beaver dams in the restored area, and the ranch has over a month of additional days with surface flow. Wilde has become a vocal beaver advocate since his view shifted from seeing beavers as pests to seeing them as assets: "The more I learned, the more it made sense that we need them in these watersheds."

In 1998, coinciding with the timing of Jay Wilde's revelation, two eminent conservation biologists, Michael Soulé and Reed Noss, published a foundational scientific article on the newly created concept of rewilding (Soulé and Noss 1998). At that time, rewilding was an extension of the concept of restoration but with a key difference: restoration aimed to return an ecosystem to a previous state, whereas the main goal of rewilding was to reestablish ecological processes to increase resilience. In its early conception, rewilding was focused on protecting biodiversity, and the main strategy was to create large protected areas and movement corridors with limited human activity and then to reintroduce large carnivores who would roam freely over these vast areas.

In practice, rewilding pairs (a) reducing human activity with (b) initial restoration actions geared toward enabling nature to play a driving role in the restoration process. The focus of rewilding on resilience, or the ability to adapt to or rebound from disturbance, is especially important in an era of climate change, changing land uses, and nonnative species. While a historically restored environment might require upkeep by humans and be less adaptable, a rewilded system that has been given the ecological tools to adapt should require less maintenance and be able to respond to change—after initial interventions that place nature and processes front and center.

Rewilding in areas that are most accustomed to human intervention and management can seem counterintuitive. It can also be difficult for some to see wildlife such as beaver not as a nuisance but as a partner in conservation and restoration efforts. This chapter explores some of the complexities involved in rewilding from scientific and cultural perspectives to give insight into how conservation efforts in the West are shifting in important ways.

Nature, Culture, and Water in the West

It's helpful to understand the concept of rewilding in its broader historical and cultural context. A variety of factors influence whether and how rewilding can be successful in different parts of the American West. The concept of rewilding might be attractive even to those who are not always particularly interested in conservation, restoration, or environmentalism. The allure of rewilding comes, in part, from a romantic conceptualization of a pure or wild nature that has held sway in the West since the late 1800s. But it also has practical, economically beneficial outcomes. Although we focus primarily on beaver rewilding, rewilding can and does involve a variety of plant and animal species.

Environmental historians of the Western United States have extensively documented the relationships among beaver, irrigation practices, and hunters and farmers. At the same time that white settlers were working to tame or dominate the lands of the West for farming and ranching under the aegis of manifest destiny, beavers were nearly eradicated by the fur trade. Farmers in particular viewed beavers as pests—they did damage to canals and laterals and, of course, damaged trees and even crops. Ranchers may have viewed them more favorably given the contributions they made to the health of those landscapes, and beaver were often moved from low-lying farmland to highland ranches (a practice that continues today). In the 1900s, there were some successful legislative efforts to bring American beaver (*Castor canadensis*) back from the brink of extinction. Beaver populations rebounded, though the construction of enormous dams along with the rapid development and channelization of many streams and rivers impacted species health throughout the twentieth century. Beaver coevolve and coexist with salmon, and the fate of the two species can be thought of as closely linked.

In the early 2000s, groups of "beaver believers" elevated the beaver to charismatic megafauna status—today, beavers have Instagram accounts, star in documentaries, and are the subject of annual conferences. Wildlife and restoration advocates, united by the potential of rewilding, have argued that beavers are nature's environmental engineers and have enlisted them in diminished riparian and other landscapes to do the work of rewilding. To put it simply, beavers are having a moment.

Thinking of beaver as engineers anthropomorphizes them—endowing them with seemingly human characteristics—and is an effort to elevate their status in a West that owes its current existence to water engineering. This may make them more palatable players in the prevailing mythos of the West. This also folds neatly into worldviews that see nature as something to be managed primarily for human benefit. On the other hand, rewilding is meant to center nature as the key actor in landscape restoration efforts. Beavers are not, in fact, engineers (though they do often design and build things). They are wild animals who engage in sometimes unpredictable and random behaviors. These competing narratives about beaver rewilding may sometimes be at odds and can result in conflicts over management practices.

Similarly, the term *rewilding* has broad appeal to those interested in reestablishing a seemingly pure natural state, free from human interference. Historians have convincingly demonstrated how the West has often been framed as Edenic, a lush garden to be wrought from the hard, dry earth of the desert through human ingenuity and effort. At the same time, the notion of Eden paradoxically implies a landscape existing in a natural, wild state unmarred by human development and the trappings of civilization. Yet virtually no part of the West has been untouched by human activity, including from Indigenous people engaged in significant landscape management efforts in the precolonial era. The idea that we can make landscapes wild again has mythic power but belies the ways humans and nature inextricably shape and act on one another. In fact, successful rewilding is often reliant on careful human engagement, policy and economic support, and long-term plans for sustainability—though to a lesser extent than other restoration practices. Such tensions must be carefully navigated and managed in rewilding projects. We explore these in greater detail below.

Why Is Rewilding Controversial?

The original intent of rewilding was as a top-down intervention: the reestablishment of apex predators like wolves, cougars, and bears that ranged freely across large landscapes, as they once did before human efforts to eradicate them. When apex predators are absent, populations of ungulates, such as deer, can become too high, leading to human-animal conflicts, overgrazing, and even population crashes. The reintroduction of large carnivores regulates grazing pressures, improving the overall balance of ecosystems. The original impetus for rewilding was that this would result in the natural regeneration of healthy prairie, sagebrush, and riparian ecosystems, together with the associated benefits of reestablishing food webs.

This large carnivore-focused vision of rewilding understandably evokes concern for those who live and work in the landscapes proposed for rewilding—humans and livestock are potential prey for these predators. In the last decade, the vision of rewilding has evolved to encompass any intervention that allows nature to play the main, active role in engineering for ecosystem sustainability. Rewilding now includes a wide variety of approaches, such as limiting wildfire suppression, reintroducing nonpredator keystone species, dam removal, and even the creation of genetically modified blight-resistant chestnut trees (Brister and Newhouse 2020; Perino et al. 2019).

Rewilding remains controversial because it will inevitably come with costs and trade-offs. For example, limiting wildfire suppression may prevent large catastrophic wildfires but will require humans to tolerate smaller, more frequent, less devastating wildfires. Likewise, reintroducing far-ranging keystone species in the Western United States, such as wolves and free-roaming bison means that people will need to accept a higher risk of wolf predation and ranchers will need to share rangeland with bison. Acceptance will require humans to have tolerance for the negative societal impacts of a rewilded system.

How Is Beaver Rewilding Different?

Recently, beaver rewilding has entered the mainstream conversation about how to create resilience in the face of climate change (Ripple et al. 2022). Beaver modify their local environment by building dams, which influence the distribution, seasonality, quantity, and quality of water both locally and downstream. On the North American continent, prior to European settlement, there were as many as 250 million beaver ponds, impounding enough water to submerge Washington, Oregon, and California (Goldfarb 2018). By the twentieth century, researchers estimate that just one hundred thousand beaver survived—less than 1 percent of the pre-fur-trapping

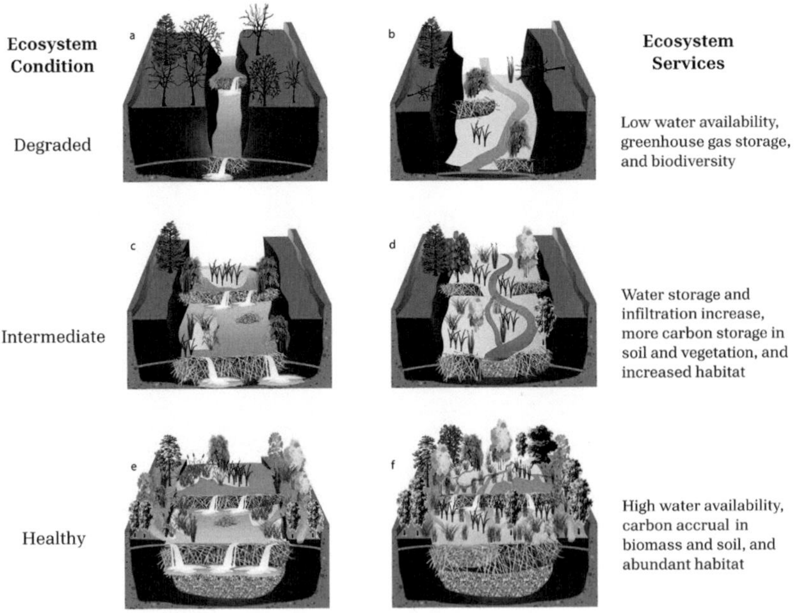

Figure 21.1 In degraded systems, beaver rewilding is a long-term process that proceeds from a degraded system (a), to initial intervention (b), to slow rehabilitation (c–e), and finally a fully restored system (f). Figure adapted from Pollock et al. (2014).

population. The absence of beaver, along with other land use changes brought about by white settlement, led to a massive deterioration of riverscapes.

In landscapes where beaver have been reestablished, people have watched the transformation of narrow, incised, dry channels into wide, wet river corridors and wetlands teeming with life (see figure 21.1). These small-scale transformations have helped people imagine an alternative to the parched and beaverless landscape that pervaded the West for the last century. Places where beaver reintroduction has transformed the landscape from dry desert sagebrush to biodiverse wetlands and ponds provide a different model of what the future could be and tap into shared desires for the reestablishment of an environmentally healthy West.

Importantly, river corridors with beaver have a greater chance of adapting to a changing climate. Beaver-restored streams are more resistant and resilient to drought and wildfire, both of which are increasing in frequency and intensity with climate change. This is a result of increased water on the landscape: on the surface in dammed ponds and in wetland vegetation and below the surface in groundwater. An estimated 90 percent of species depend on wet ecosystems at some point in their life cycle, and so beaver-rewilded systems support biodiversity, provide critical wet habitat during dry months, and are vital for the continued survival of iconic fish and bird species (Pollock 2014). Landowners also benefit from the increased water availability and resulting forage for livestock during hot, dry summers.

In what follows, we present three projects that provide insights about the promise and limitations of beaver rewilding in the Intermountain West. The first is an ideal example that demonstrates success, and the second and third demonstrate the challenges of returning beaver to the landscape.

Project 1: Beaver Rewilding Increased Water Availability for a Cattle Ranch and River Corridor. Jay Wilde's private ranch in southeastern Idaho lies along Birch Creek and has been owned by the family for generations. The creek's headwaters can be found in the forested mountains of the Caribou-Targhee National Forest, an area that is hard to access and where the few human activities are controlled hunting and fishing and Wilde's ranching. The ranch was historically dependent on the perennial water supply from Birch Creek, but the creek ran dry during the late summers in the late 1990s due to the extirpation of beaver.

Figure 21.2 An overhead view of Birch Creek flowing through U.S. Forest Service land upstream of Jay Wilde's ranch. Beaver had been extirpated, but there are now an estimated 350 beaver dams along the creek. Drone imagery credit: Boise State Visual Services.

With the primary goal of increasing water for agricultural production, Wilde began rewilding using low-tech strategies on key areas of the river corridor. The project required leveraging scarce resources and a multifaceted team with folks from the U.S. Forest Service and Utah State University. The project, implemented in the national forest, focused on modified grazing to keep cattle outside of the riparian zone and installation of beaver mimicry structures made from locally gathered woody material. Beaver were then successfully relocated to the improved sites. The project has been wildly successful: there are over 350 active beaver dams in the restored area and the ranch has forty-two additional days of streamflow each year (see figure 21.2). Beaver have also improved the riparian habitat for insects, birds, and native fish, notably Bonneville cutthroat trout (*Oncorhynchus clarkii utah*). Wilde is making ongoing improvements on his own private lands in order to extend the rewilding farther downstream. This is the most well-known beaver rewilding site in Idaho and has been featured in several online publications (for an example, see USU Restoration Consortium, n.d.).

Project 2: River Corridor Is Reset to Make Way for Natural Ecosystem Processes, Fish, and Beaver. The Big Hole River in Southwest Montana is both a premiere fly-fishing destination and the last habitat in the contiguous United States of the threatened native Arctic grayling (*Thymallus arcticus*). For much of its history since European settlement, however, mining was its heritage. Gold was first discovered in the watershed in 1864, and extensive gold placer mining left French Gulch and Moose Creek, tributaries to the Big Hole River, in a highly altered state. Cobble and boulder mine tailings covered the natural floodplain and hardened the channel banks, effectively straightening and stabilizing the channel, with no fish habitat to speak of.

Unlike Birch Creek, which was in a relatively natural state prior to rewilding, French Gulch first needed to be resurfaced from under the tailings before actions could be taken to improve habitat for beaver. The project required heavy machinery to reset the extremely degraded system and allow space for natural processes to restart. This required dealing with a series of regulatory hurdles and managing relationships with downstream neighbors concerned about how their water rights may be affected. The French Gulch project was led by the Big Hole Watershed Committee and took multiple years of planning. The project occurred along three miles of channel on public lands owned by the state of Montana, the labor was conducted by a private contractor funded by grants, and it included partnerships with agencies and landowners, eventually requiring funding from nine different entities. Ultimately, eight hundred tons of tailings and sediment were removed from the site, the historical floodplain and channel were rebuilt, and four acres of wetlands were created.

The project is considered highly successful, as historical processes have been restored and native fish have been reintroduced to the system (after elimination of nonnatives). Beaver do not occupy the site yet, but project sponsors hope that nearby beaver will migrate there naturally once habitat conditions are suitable for them. These types of highly engineered projects that use heavy machinery may, or may not, be considered beaver rewilding, depending on the goals and objectives of the restoration. On the one hand, beaver may be an eventual end goal of the project. But on the other hand, these projects require an exceptional amount of intervention, time, money, permits, and partnerships before conditions would even be suitable for beaver, and whether beaver eventually occupy the project area is highly uncertain.

Project 3: Complex Partnerships Are Formed to Save Iconic Species. Steelhead, sockeye, and Chinook salmon (*Oncorhynchus* spp.) migrate over nine hundred miles from the Pacific Ocean up the Columbia and Snake Rivers to spawn in central Idaho's headwater streams. The Pahsimeroi River, a tributary to the Snake River, historically supported a population of spawning Chinook salmon (*Oncorhynchus tshawytscha*). Currently listed as threatened under the Endangered Species Act (ESA), Chinook salmon are declining throughout their range due to a broad array of factors including ocean conditions, agricultural withdrawals, and hydroelectric dams all along their migration route. For salmon in the Pahsimeroi, at least part of the decline is related to ranching.

The Pahsimeroi River predominately runs through private land where ranchers withdraw water for agricultural production according to their legal water rights. Because of extensive water withdrawals and irrigation diversions throughout the watershed, the upper Pahsimeroi has had intermittent flow and a lack of Chinook salmon since the mid-1900s. In the 1990s, a large collaborative multistakeholder effort began that combined local-scale restoration with catchment-scale water management modifications. The main goal of the effort was to restore perennial flow to the river, reestablish native salmon spawning sites, and improve Chinook salmon populations (Copeland et al. 2021).

Like French Gulch, the Pahsimeroi River project required an exceptional amount of time, money, permits, and partnerships. Corporate mitigation funding provided by the Bonneville Power Administration (BPA) lowered financial barriers experienced by landowners with regard to modifying irrigation practices. BPA is required to spend mitigation funds to improve salmon habitat impacted by hydroelectric dams. The catchment-scale efforts, and the main strategy of the project, consisted of the ranching community switching from flood irrigation, which uses surface water diverted from the river, to sprinkler irrigation, which uses less water, and in some cases, pumped groundwater (see figure 21.3). This shift would reduce the amount of surface water diverted from the river, increasing perennial flow and removing physical barriers to fish passage.

An initial stakeholder group was formed in the early 1990s. Once BPA committed mitigation funds to the project, additional landowners and government and nonprofit partners joined too. In 1994, the first rancher switched their irrigation from flood to sprinklers, and others slowly followed suit. In 2009, the major irrigation canal diverting water from the river could be closed without negative impacts to agriculture. The closing of the diversion ditch resulted in reconnection between the middle and lower Pahsimeroi in 2009. In 2016, as a result of various other local and catchment-scale water savings activities, water flow returned to the upper Pahsimeroi. In 2020, juvenile Chinook salmon were observed in the upper Pahsimeroi for the first time in decades—a spectacular success! In 2021, however, the river ran dry due to a severe region-wide drought and the salmon disappeared.

Central to this huge collaborative effort are the ranchers who are restoring reaches of the river running through their properties to improve salmon and beaver habitat. To understand the individual perspective, we visited Big Creek Ranch on the Upper Pahsimeroi in June 2022. The owners of Big Creek Ranch would like to have beaver on their property, but the necessary water and riparian habitat are limited. The owners purchased the ranch in 2009 and immediately began shifting toward irrigation and grazing management practices to limit negative impacts on the river corridor. In 2016, in collaboration with the Idaho Department of Fish and Game and funded by grants, the ranch began low-tech restoration activities including beaver mimicry, grazing exclosures, and invasive plant management. At the time of our visit in 2022, the site was clearly better than an upstream comparison site, with more water, better instream habitat, and improved riparian quality (see figure 21.4). However, Big Creek Ranch still does not have suitable habitat for beaver due to intensive human appropriation of water and increasing drought at the regional scale.

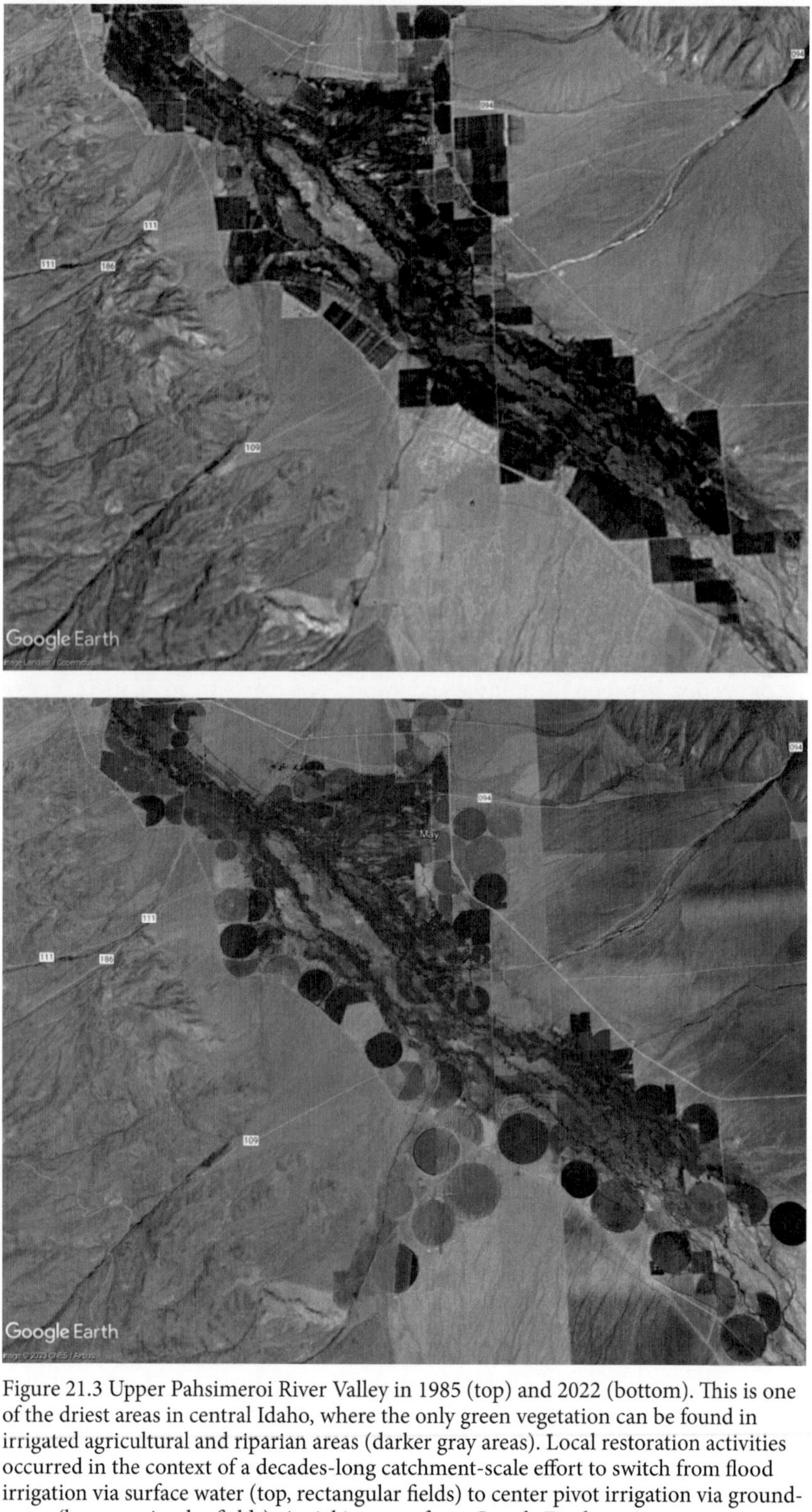

Figure 21.3 Upper Pahsimeroi River Valley in 1985 (top) and 2022 (bottom). This is one of the driest areas in central Idaho, where the only green vegetation can be found in irrigated agricultural and riparian areas (darker gray areas). Local restoration activities occurred in the context of a decades-long catchment-scale effort to switch from flood irrigation via surface water (top, rectangular fields) to center pivot irrigation via groundwater (bottom, circular fields). Aerial imagery from Google Earth.

Figure 21.4 Left: Control site directly upstream of the treatment site on the Pahsimeroi River. Right: Rewilding site on private land. Rancher-initiated interventions include grazing management, beaver mimicry structures, and invasive plant management. The restoration site has more water, better instream habitat, and a healthier riparian zone than the control site, but several years of drought have delayed rewilding progress. Photographs by Nick Kolarik.

The Promise and Limitations of Beaver Rewilding

These three examples demonstrate a range of restoration efforts and are just a small subset of the restoration projects that we have encountered. In what follows, we combine insights gained from these case studies with findings from a stakeholder workshop on riverscape restoration held at Boise State University in January 2023. The following sections highlight the main results identified in this workshop as they pertain to the promise and limitations of beaver rewilding in the American West.

Successful Beaver Rewilding Is Associated with Grazing Management and Habitat Improvement. In areas where suitable beaver habitat already exists, beaver rewilding requires only the removal of human predation pressures (such as trapping), with the hope that beaver will move in of their own volition. Through their natural activities, beaver modify the environment to make it even more habitable and sometimes expand the area suitable for beaver upstream and downstream. In some cases, translocation of beaver from areas where they come into conflict with people to areas of suitable habitat is necessary. The most famous example of this was when Idaho Fish and Game used parachutes to airdrop seventy-six beavers into what is now the Frank Church River of No Return Wilderness Area in 1948, the start of a now thriving beaver colony.

These two beaver rewilding practices (reducing human predation pressure and active beaver reintroduction) only work in areas that already have suitable habitat for beaver. However, the majority of riverscapes in the American West that were once suitable for beaver aren't any longer. The human impact has been too great (for an overview of general river degradation, see Changing U.S. Rivers, n.d.). We have observed many restoration projects occurring in these degraded riverscapes. These projects frequently have beaver rewilding as an end goal but require prebeaver interventions to create suitable habitat. The goal is for human involvement in these projects to decrease over time as the ecosystems begin to function more naturally.

Though diverse in implementation, successful examples of these types of projects typically combine two strategies. First, projects implement land management practices to reduce human disturbance. Reducing human influence in the rural West typically means restricting cattle grazing so that the woody riparian vegetation that beavers need for food, dams, and lodges can regenerate. Second, successful projects implement interventions that set the restoration process in motion. We have found that people are experimenting with different techniques, depending on the environmental context, the level of degradation, and the needs of the community.

For example, in less degraded areas, human-made structures that mimic beaver dams are popular and effective for increasing suitable beaver habitat. Just like actual beaver dams, beaver mimicry structures reduce the impact of peak flows, enable groundwater infiltration, and allow ponding and the establishment of wetlands and riparian zones. In areas with high human impact and more severe degradation, beaver mimicry may not be enough. In these cases, common practices include riparian plantings, channel reconstruction, and shifts to efficient irrigation practices to reduce surface water diversions.

We have also encountered a fair number of riparian restoration projects that do not include reestablishing beaver as an end goal, even though some of these projects have been inspired by beaver and use beaver mimicry. It is unclear whether a project counts as beaver rewilding in this case. On the one hand, the project may qualify if it is motivated by the basic tenets of rewilding. On the other hand, many projects that don't include beaver don't achieve long-term success. Beaver provide consistent maintenance of instream structures to slow down water, enabling it to both infiltrate the ground and spread out across the landscape. This maintenance is essential to resist and rebound from drought, flood, and wildfire disturbances. In the absence of beaver, humans *could* perform this role via beaver mimicry, but projects rarely have long-term resources for that type of physical maintenance.

Beaver Rewilding Is Place Based, Bottom Up, and Economically Efficient. No federal laws govern beaver management in the same way that the ESA protects wolves. While there are some beaver-specific regulations at county and state levels, those regulations are easier to change than federal law. For example, some county and state laws govern beaver trapping and hunting on public lands or prohibit beaver translocation. Because of relatively limited governmental regulation, beaver rewilding largely occurs with a bottom-up approach, and diverse stakeholders work together in the communities where they live to conduct rewilding designed for the specific environmental context and needs of their own communities and landscapes.

One key insight gained from our workshop is that economics plays a major role in beaver rewilding projects. The most obvious direct economic motivation comes when ranchers rewild in order to improve water availability for their operations. In the case of the Pahsimeroi River, many of the changes in irrigation efficiency were funded by the BPA through mitigation funds. There are also indirect economic drivers. For example, increasing habitat for species of concern is a common motivation of beaver rewilding projects, and while some stakeholders are motivated by conservation commitments, there is also an economic motivation. The listing of a species under the ESA results in restrictive land use regulations for areas harboring that species. Therefore, maintaining the landscape in a way that avoids ESA listing is a goal for those seeking to maintain productive economic use of those same resources.

Nonprofit conservation organizations also have an economic motivation—that of maintaining their own operations. These organizations are often funded by private donations and public grants, and conservation projects that balance conservation and a community's economic needs can generate a steady flow of private and public dollars. Finally, even when economic gain is not explicit, there is at least the concern of not causing economic harm, because that would likely doom a project to failure.

The Risk-to-Reward Ratio Is Low Compared to Other Species. The more well-known rewilding efforts focus on the reestablishment of broad-ranging species, such as wolf or bison. For these species, rewilding requires top-down governance because projects are implemented over large landscapes that cross jurisdictional boundaries. Furthermore, risks and trade-offs can be substantial, such as predation of large carnivores or wildfire damage. The unique aspects of beaver rewilding, on the other hand, produce a low risk-to-reward ratio.

Beavers have local, tangible benefits for diverse members of society. For ranchers like Jay Wilde, beavers increase local water availability for ranches. Beaver rewilding also creates healthy river corridors with diverse in-channel habitat, as well as wetlands and riparian zones. Wildlife is drawn to these areas, and boaters, anglers, hunters and bird-watchers all benefit.

In terms of risks, unlike wolves and other large carnivores, beavers are not a threat to livestock, pets, or humans. Beaver also do not compete with cattle for forage over vast areas, like bison do, and only require that cattle be excluded from relatively small riparian areas on the landscape. But beaver rewilding projects do come with some risks, which are predominantly local and can be categorized into two types: risk to infrastructure and risk to relationships.

Beaver dams in an area with human infrastructure can cause damage to that infrastructure, such as gradual flooding. This can be managed by removing beavers from conflict locations or implementing coexistence strategies such as tree fencing, flow devices and pond levelers.

More often, beaver rewilding poses risks to human relationships. For example, as we noted above, there is a common worry in the West about water availability, and the conflicts about perceived loss of water availability for downstream users should not be understated. Downstream water-rights holders see ponded water and wetlands upstream as water stolen from them. Although damage to infrastructure and fears over water rights can be effectively managed, beaver can still lead to conflicts with neighbors, especially given prevailing cultural biases against beavers. Historically, beaver have been seen as pests.

Thus, efforts to try to reestablish beaver are not always perceived positively. In one case we know of, project sponsors even avoid using the words *beaver* and *dams* to describe the project, instead referring to *instream restoration structures.*

Beaver Rewilding Is Not a Panacea. Not all of the West has high potential for successful beaver rewilding. From a biophysical perspective, beaver require two things: perennial water flow and dam-building materials from woody vegetation. If a riverscape system cannot provide these two essential ingredients, then beaver rewilding cannot be successful. Some channels are too steep or too narrow, or their flows are too powerful to support beaver-based rewilding. For riverscapes highly impacted by humans, years of expensive interventions are required before beaver habitation would even be possible. In terms of social considerations, many sites with suitable beaver habitat may not be eligible for rewilding because of real and perceived conflicts. Even in rural areas, flooded riverscapes may damage transportation, agriculture, and irrigation infrastructure. For all these reasons, it would be impossible for beaver to expand to their full historical range and number.

For every successful place-based beaver rewilding effort, we have observed numerous failed projects. Successful projects typically include those that combine both the reduction of human disturbance and multiple restoration interventions while having a commitment to stewardship over time. Conversely, unsuccessful projects tend to apply just one of these approaches on only a single occasion. A common project strategy is to employ beaver mimicry without reducing human disturbance and without maintenance over time. These failed projects can be highly visible and therefore present a major obstacle in terms of gaining trust from stakeholders about a project's value and potential for success. Other obstacles include a lack of funding for continued maintenance, a dearth of science-based guidance, obstructive regulatory processes, and even competition with wild ungulates in areas where cattle grazing is restricted. Some have proposed beaver and wolf are both necessary species for rewilding the West, as exemplified in the reintroduction of wolves in Yellowstone National Park.

In summary, although not a panacea, beaver rewilding is potentially an incredibly effective and inexpensive place-based strategy for building riverscape resilience in the American West. Rewilding improves degraded ecosystems by allowing nature to play a driving role in the restoration process. Diverse partnerships among ranchers, outdoors enthusiasts, hunters and anglers, big business, civil servants, conservationists, and university scientists are working together to improve ecological and economic conditions in their community. Better on-the-ground funding, science, communication, and logistical support are necessary for beaver rewilding to reach its full potential.

22

Heading Downhill

Management Challenges on the Snake River

CARLIN GIRARD

Two Ocean Plateau, just southeast of Yellowstone National Park, is one of the most remote places in the Lower 48. The water that falls there has the same chance of flowing into the Mississippi Delta as it does the Pacific Ocean. The snowfall and elevation of this region make it the headwaters for much of the West. Snowmelt that runs to the Pacific from this high plateau goes by way of the Snake River. And like every large river system, the Snake carries the flavor of the land it drains.

The Snake River in Wyoming is ringed by peaks as high as the Grand Teton, at 13,775 feet. Landscape-level conservation in Northwest Wyoming—a combination of national parks, refuges, and national forests—has left the ecosystem largely intact. The aquatic ecosystem is a clear reflection of this fact: its primary human use is ecotourism—hiking, white-water rafting, and fly-fishing for native cutthroat trout. It showcases one of the last examples of the Mountain West as it was before European settlement in the late 1800s (for images of the diverse ecosystems along the Snake River, see Anderson and Copsey 2013).

As the Snake River flows south and eventually west into Idaho at 5,600 feet, the river drops westward across Idaho's breadbasket, the lava fields of the Snake River Plain. Here, the pressure for agricultural use reigns supreme, resulting in a nearly complete loss of the ecological function that once typified central Idaho. Today, the once mighty Snake River is at times dewatered entirely for agricultural irrigation. Hydropower dams are common throughout Idaho, and the remaining 2,000 feet of elevation from Hells Canyon to the Columbia River has been turned into a hydraulic head for energy production. The impounded river slowly moves west, draining the southeastern third of Washington. It becomes the Columbia River's largest tributary in Washington State at 330 feet in elevation, still 325 miles from the Pacific Ocean.

In addition to generating energy, irrigating farmland, and carrying barge traffic to the Pacific Ocean, the river also provides for a dwindling but crucial

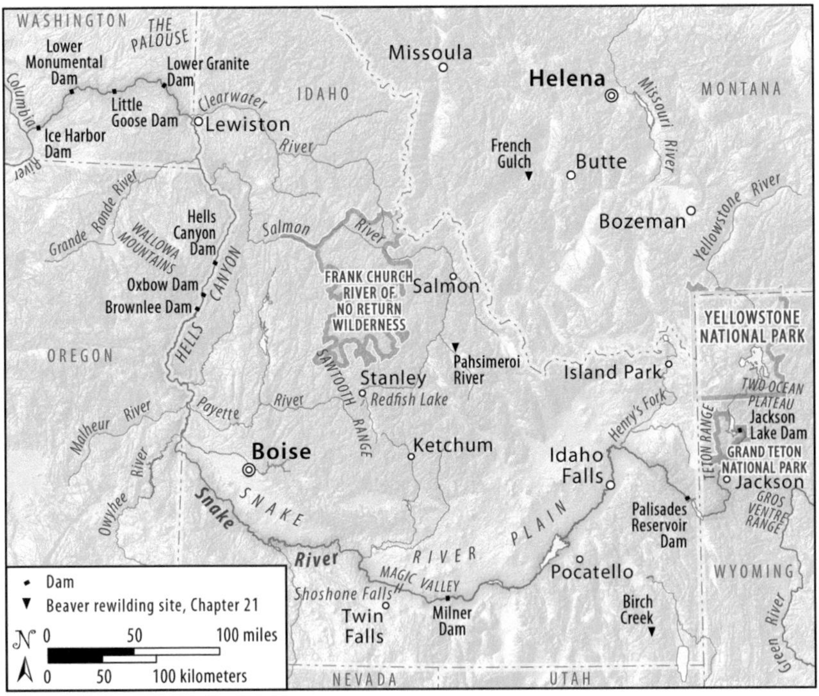

Figure 22.1 Map showing the Snake River, its main tributaries, and the locations of dams. Map credit: Chelsea Feeney.

salmon and steelhead fishery. Maintaining the compatibility of all these uses has proven extremely difficult. Despite Herculean efforts, the fishery and the Indigenous people whose culture and livelihood depend on it have suffered.

The Snake River's native fish population, once adapted to the conditions and cycles of the river, has been reshaped; many fisheries have been lost beyond recovery. While some endemic fisheries remain, disruption from dams, introduction of nonnative fish populations, and degradation of aquatic ecosystem health have made their existence precarious. On the Lower Snake, salmon and steelhead conservation are often a primary driver of river management, and since construction, retaining the fisheries has required a multibillion-dollar investment. On the midregions of the Snake, native fisheries have been lost entirely, and river management is focused on human priorities. And yet, at its headwaters, intact and connected tributaries support a native coldwater fish assemblage that is second to none in the Lower 48.

Along this one watercourse, we can find both successes and failures in fisheries and river system management. We will take a fish's-eye view on this story, running upstream from the river's Pacific Ocean outlet to its headwaters, to gain lessons in the constraints and opportunities found in the management of a large river system.

The Snake River in Washington: The Lower Snake River

As symbolic as they are imperiled, Chinook salmon in the Lower Snake River are listed as threatened under the Endangered Species Act. Being the largest of the Pacific Northwest salmon species—often weighing over thirty pounds—they are also called king salmon. The species is revered for its strength and endurance and is prized as food. Chinook salmon are central to ecological systems and are tied to the energy cycles of the forest through bugs, birds, and carnivores. But Chinook are also immensely important to people, as shown by their cultural significance and market value.

For a Snake River Chinook, running the gauntlet to spawn six hundred miles inland has gone from physically challenging to something more akin to a science-fiction adventure. Dams, overfishing, and predation by invasive and native fish have taken their toll. Even this oversimplifies matters because Chinook are diverse within their own species, and myriad impairments have degraded this fish stock.

Chinook and other anadromous fish share a common life cycle. As eggs and young, they live in streams or rivers, at times hundreds of miles from the ocean. After a year or so in freshwater, they migrate to the ocean and form schools of predators. After a few years at sea, they return to their original freshwater sites, driven by the scent of their natal spawning grounds, where they spawn and die. As recently as two hundred years ago, it is estimated that seventeen million anadromous salmon and steelhead were migrating each year up the Columbia River system. Only a tenth as many return today.

The salmon returning to the Snake River today must first swim the three-hundred-plus miles upstream from the ocean, navigating cumbersome fish passage schemes at the four hydroelectric dams on the Columbia River. Nosing into the Snake, fish encounter the first, Ice Harbor Dam, completed in 1961 and expanded in 1976, within the first ten miles. The Lower Snake River dams, operated by the Army Corps of Engineers, produce enough power to support eight hundred thousand homes (Bonneville Power Administration 2016). The Army Corps of Engineers manages these dams because of their importance in transporting goods for export, especially grain. Managing fish stocks alongside energy production and transportation on the Snake River is delicate, complex, and according to many, unrealistic.

Ice Harbor Dam, like the other dams along the Lower Snake and Columbia, employs a suite of strategies to help adult fish move upriver and smolts to move down (Army Corps of Engineers 2012). At each of the four dams on the Lower Snake, an adult Chinook needs to make its way up a roughly one-thousand-foot-long fish ladder, eventually clearing Lower Granite Dam, the last dam before reaching spawning grounds in Idaho. Even while employing every new idea and technology to pass adult and juvenile fish around and over these dams, a 2022 National Oceanographic and Atmospheric Administration (NOAA) report still identified the dams as perhaps the single largest barrier to recovery of fish in the watershed (NOAA 2022). For all these efforts, costing billions of dollars, fish passage around these dams isn't saving their populations.

The dams also shift the Snake from river habitat to lake habitat. Lake habitat now dominates in the Lower Snake in Washington, which cannot support the one thing Chinook return to do—spawn, which requires fast water and gravels. The lake habitat also inflates the predator populations that feed on outmigrating smolt.

In the dam-created lake habitat, native pikeminnow populations have multiplied enormously—so much that bounty programs are in effect in the Columbia and Snake River drainages. Run by the Washington and Oregon State Fish and Game Departments and paid for by Bonneville Power Administration, a total of 101,442 pikeminnow were removed by fishers in 2020, to the tune of $839,461, averaging $8 per fish caught and removed (Pikeminnow Sport-Reward Fishery Program, n.d.). Introduced walleye and smallmouth bass populations, which also eat smolt, have exploded in the last two decades. And it appears that where schools of smolt are especially vulnerable, such as in dam outfalls or stream mouths, predation is outpacing growth of salmon reproduction. Avian and mammalian predators also contribute to the lamentable 1 percent return rate of adult salmon. Return rates of 2–4 percent are needed to hold salmon populations stable, and so the decline of the Snake River's anadromous fish stocks continues.

Everyone wants to avoid the loss of Chinook salmon from this system, and managers are disappointed by the inability of current strategies to maintain viable fish stocks. There is a growing sentiment that creating these four dams was a miscalculation, that the predicted 48 percent reduction in adult fish returning to the Snake badly underestimated the losses, and that our ability to move fish around dams and use hatcheries where natural reproduction is lost was overestimated.

In 1855, the governor and superintendent of Indian Affairs for the Washington Territory signed a treaty with the Nez Perce tribes, vacating traditional Nez Perce homelands and ceding ownership to the U.S. government. At the same time, the tribes retained "the right of taking fish at all usual and accustomed places in common with citizens of the territory" (Indian Affairs 1855). Later court rulings in the 1970s further defined "in common with" to mean that the treaties of the mid-1800s gave these tribes a right to 50 percent of the harvestable salmon population (Dougherty 2020). These legal decisions helped to retain the historical bond of these peoples with salmon and steelhead. But it also coupled tribes to contemporary fisheries and river management in the Columbia and Snake River drainages.

Endangered Species Act funding and mitigation dollars from the Columbia, Snake, and Hells Canyon dams have fueled a complex network that supports federal, state, tribal, and private mitigation work. Millions of dollars annually, and billions of dollars since dam construction, have been invested into mitigation strategies at all levels—hatcheries, fish passage, habitat improvements, flow augmentation, and invasive fish management. Despite all these efforts, fish stocks continue to decline. As a result, dam removal is being seriously evaluated by scientists and even Congress.

Two reports completed under the Biden administration establish a path toward Lower Snake River dam removal, specifically for salmon and steelhead recovery. A champion of dam removal is U.S. senator Mike Simpson, a Republican from Idaho. He has outlined a $33.5 billion proposal to remove the dams and address the losses in energy and transportation. The Nez Perce Tribe, whose territory exists above the Snake River dams, has also come out squarely in support of dam removal. Removal would require an act of Congress, and bipartisan support is building, but as of 2023, strong opposition still exists.

Dam removal on the Lower Snake would benefit salmon but would have other costs. In the age of carbon-free energy generation, removing fully functional power-generating dams is a tough pill to swallow. In contrast to wind and solar, hydropower from twenty-two dams along the Snake River provides green energy that's available on demand. But the Elwha Dam removals on the Olympic Peninsula of Washington have shown that hydropower dam removal for fisheries restoration is possible. In 2022, authorization was granted to remove three dams on the Klamath River in California for the sake of salmon recovery (Klamath River Renewal Corporation 2020). A new era has begun, one where large dam removal proceeds when it becomes clear that fish stocks cannot otherwise survive. Momentum is building in the Lower Snake River and other locations as tribes throughout the Pacific Northwest unify around this core value.

The scale of the problems that hydroelectric dams have caused Chinook salmon and its anadromous cousins is immense. However, removing these dams for the sake of salmon is not only a net loss for green power. It also reduces flood control and drought mitigation and eliminates efficient shipping routes.

Currently, proposals for dam removal are opposed by counties in southeastern Washington, and even Democratic U.S. representatives from Washington have yet to show support. One of the largest impediments to dam removal is not being able to ensure that the plan would actually improve fish stocks, while the loss of the Lewiston, Idaho, inland port would eliminate barge transportation and thereby devastate grain producers of the Palouse. Restoring salmon needs to be a shared sacrifice, with all options on the table, even difficult ones like removing the bird and mammal predators that prey on fish and modifying the commercial salmon harvest in the ocean. Striking this balance means creating a river management system that meets human needs as well as the reproductive needs of salmon runs.

Idaho: The Middle Snake

Like many of the Snake River tributaries in Idaho, the Salmon River flows from the Sawtooth Mountains. The Sawtooths are a rugged and remote mountainous expanse with largely inaccessible rivers. The Frank Church River of No Return Wilderness Area lies in its center. The mainstem of the Salmon River flows east to west into the Snake River, south of Lewiston, Idaho. These rivers are the end of the line for anadromous fish in the Snake River because of Hells Canyon Dam.

Between Lewiston and Hells Canyon Dam are some of the most important Snake River spawning habitats currently available for salmon and steelhead. Chinook, coho, and sockeye salmon, as well as steelhead trout, persist in this reach because of intensive hatchery augmentation. Steelhead are known for being extremely strong swimmers, pushing deep into small, high-gradient tributaries to spawn. Some of the most extensive habitat suitable for steelhead spawning is found in the Clearwater River and Salmon River systems.

Steelhead are a threatened species under the Endangered Species Act, and state and federal agencies have implemented every mitigation strategy available to maintain the steelhead population. Fish screens now keep out-migrating smolt in the streams and out of irrigation ditches. Fish barriers like culverts and small dams have been systematically removed. Hundreds of floodplain and riparian projects have restored waterways after a century of logging, mining, and agricultural land use. While some of these efforts have been successful, steelhead runs are still in decline. Even in pristine sections of river, like the Middle Fork of the Salmon River, salmon and steelhead numbers are plummeting. Good habitat is not making up for losses incurred from the dam system and hostile ocean environment.

The continuation of these species in these drainages is dependent upon a robust hatchery program. Hatcheries have mitigated the damage of activities like overharvesting, logging, and dams. Unfortunately, hatcheries have also reduced the genetic diversity and adaptive capacities of fish. But there is no question that hatcheries are the only thing maintaining the beleaguered salmon and steelhead runs in the Snake River and that population scale restoration will require innovative hatchery techniques. While naturally reproducing wild fish are the recovery goal for these threatened and endangered species, the vast majority of returning adults consist of hatchery fish. "Wild" fish are those that hatch in the streambed, spawned from either wild or hatchery adults. The hatchery program is currently unable to produce a self-sustaining salmon and steelhead stock, but it does serve to help meet the obligations of the federal government to the tribes and to the Endangered Species Act. Unfortunately, it has also diluted the gene pool of fish stocks throughout Western North America.

Salmon and steelhead populations evolved to fit the conditions in each watercourse. Genetic adaptations not only produced physical differences but also hardwired behavioral traits matched to the river system and its habitats, as well as to the estuary and oceanic life stages. Hatchery practices have disregarded these adaptative traits, instead breeding salmon and steelhead smolt for the largest possible fish sizes at the greatest numbers. The result has been the disruption of the genetic life history of the species. Fish genetics and behavior no longer match their original environments, which have undergone change at the same time.

What's more, the wide range in genetics and life history strategies that once characterized the fish of the Snake River's tributaries provided the species with the built-in redundancy needed to weather storms both figurative and literal. Now, whether in terms of inland or oceanic environments, the simplified salmon and steelhead populations lack both site-specific adaptation and the ability to draw on genetic diversity to quickly adapt to change.

Nine hundred miles from the ocean, at the head of the Salmon River, near Stanley, Idaho, lies the Sawtooth Basin. The streams in these headwaters host some of the longest extant salmon and steelhead migrations in the Snake River. The sockeye salmon that migrate to this basin, spawning in the tributaries of Redfish Lake, are the farthest-known migrants of their kind and are a case study in the conservation of salmon using hatchery and dam passage techniques. Sockeye are adapted to reproduce in river systems with large on-channel lakes: they stay there eating plankton for one to two years prior to out-migration.

In 1991, Idaho sockeye were listed as an endangered species, with four adults returning to the Sawtooth Basin that year. In the span of 1991 to 1999, only 23 sockeye returned to the Sawtooth Basin, and in two of these years, sockeye were completely absent (Idaho Fish and Game 2023). Through hatchery rearing and stocking, the sockeye of the Sawtooth Basin have been kept from extinction, and while some years demonstrate that threat still exists (only 17 adults returned in 2019), progress is evident in other years (in 2014, 1,579 adults returned, and in 2022, 663 did). The tribulations that these fish endure are heroic, and the level of hands-on management that is required to keep these runs in place is astronomical.

The historical sockeye run to the Sawtooth Basin is estimated at 150,000 fish. In 2022, 2,000 sockeye made it through the Lower Snake River dams, but only 663 of those fish made it to their spawning grounds. Even after these salmon find their way past the Lower Snake River dams, their spawning run coincides with low flows and high water temperatures that are often lethal. In some low run years, such as 2021, sockeye clear the Lower Snake dams but aren't afforded the chance to swim to their spawning ground: they are instead plucked from fish ladders, where they are trucked directly to a hatchery to assure another generation of smolts are spawned through controlled hatchery techniques. A boom-and-bust cycle is natural for salmon and steelhead in the Snake River. But now a good year only holds the trend line flat, and the bad years take a toll.

The Hells Canyon Dam complex (Hells Canyon, Oxbow, Brownlee, listed from downstream to upstream) marks the end of the line for anadromous fish in the Snake River Basin, because they were not designed with fish passage infrastructure. Historically, salmon and steelhead would have spawned in the mainstem Snake River and its tributaries up to Twin Falls, Idaho, where Shoshone Falls presents a natural barrier to fish movement in central Idaho. However, since the dams were built, no sea-run fish have made it that far. This loss of available habitat between Hells Canyon and Twin Falls was particularly hard on the Snake River fall-run Chinook salmon, resulting in the loss of 80 percent of their previously utilized spawning grounds in the mainstem Snake River.

This stretch of the Snake River, Hells Canyon, remains true to its name. Among the nation's deepest gorges, Hells Canyon was nearly impassable to humans by river or land. It is now a series of lakes with small sections of flowing water between them. Hells Canyon marks the boundary between Oregon and Idaho and is a stark transition from the Lower Snake River, where large tributary after tributary adds to the river's flow. Above Hells Canyon, tributary inputs diminish, and the heavily consumed water of the Snake River becomes one of the most valuable commodities in southern Idaho (see figure 22.1).

The Snake River Plain is a distinct topography from the Washington and Wyoming stretches of the river. Whereas hydropower, barge traffic, and perhaps flood control justify the seven dams from Hells Canyon Dam downstream, irrigation begins to play an increasingly large role in the management of the dams heading east into southern Idaho. The productive volcanic soils of the Snake River Plain are missing only one ingredient essential to agriculture: water. The dams and diversions along the Snake River in Idaho are essential to the wheat, sugar beets, alfalfa, potatoes, and onions that grow in the area, and as the flows in the Snake River decrease in summer months and through periods of drought, the demand for agricultural water skyrockets.

A hot and dry wind blows across the Snake River Plain in the summer, making irrigation essential to farming. Much of the flows originate in the mountains of eastern Idaho and western Wyoming, hundreds of miles to the east. Complicating matters, the hydrologic crest of this water is in the spring and early summer, long before the highly productive agricultural lands of central Idaho need it. As a result, an additional six dams and countless irrigation diversions have been built along the Snake River in south-central Idaho to hold water until the farms need it most. This section of river is dominated by agricultural irrigation, with native fisheries virtually nonexistent. The Snake River in central Idaho goes completely dry in some summers, with all its water allocated to irrigation.

Decades-old water policy—instituted by Idaho's governing agency over water rights, the Idaho Water Resources Board—establishes what is called a Two Rivers Policy: all Snake River water above Milner Dam is allocated for use on the lands above Milner Dam. This policy encourages the full utilization of the Snake River above Milner, where water is routed from the Snake River into off-channel reservoirs for storage. Magic Valley is the end point of much of this water. It is aptly named, for it is nothing short of a miracle how the Snake River water has turned the desert of central Idaho into one of the most productive agricultural settings in America. Dam operations in this complicated reach are under the control of the Bureau of Reclamation. The bureau oversees mainstem Snake River dams and numerous smaller dams, all of which primarily serve Idaho water rights holders.

Unlike the Army Corps of Engineers, who control the dams of the Lower Snake because of their role in shipping, or the interest of Idaho Power in the Hells

Canyon Dams for energy production, the Bureau of Reclamation oversees dam operation on the Upper Snake River in Idaho and Wyoming because of the dominance of agriculture in the region. At the time of its creation in 1904, “reclamation” referred to the agency’s charge to reclaim the Western desert’s agricultural potential through water management. The management of the Upper Snake River Field Office’s ten reservoirs, culminating in full utilization of the Snake River at Milner to supply Magic Valley, exemplifies this single-minded use.

Shoshone Falls has served as a natural divide separating fish populations for millennia. On the downstream side, native redband trout, the landlocked ancestor of the Snake River steelhead runs, and bull trout are still present, but only in isolated tributary populations. Native wild trout are not present in the mainstem Snake River in eastern and central Idaho due to inadequate flow, temperature, and water quality. Hatcheries stock sterile rainbow trout in the mainstem of the Snake River for recreational fishing but little to no natural reproduction exists. These stocked rainbows live alongside nonnative fish such as smallmouth bass. Interestingly, some of the spring-fed water that arises in the volcanic bedrock cliffs of the Snake River has been developed into hatcheries and trout farms that grow trout for direct distribution to grocery stores. In this section of the Snake River, a conscious choice has been made to manage the river for agricultural production, allowing the natural flow to degrade to a point where native trout populations cannot be sustained.

To the chagrin of agricultural water users, flows in this stretch of the river are released for downstream uses. Water is spilled from dams to carry smolt through the lake system between the Lower Snake River dams. White sturgeon and the Snake River physa snail (an endangered species present only in the Snake River in central Idaho) also receive some priority in reservoir and river management but with much lesser emphasis compared to that of the anadromous fish reaches of the Snake River downstream. Moving east, however, the Snake River is once again managed for native fish, specifically for Snake River finespotted cutthroat trout (also called Yellowstone cutthroat trout).

Above Shoshone Falls, the historical fish assemblage changes. Rainbow trout were not present, and the assemblage was more typical of an inland Rocky Mountain coldwater fishery. Currently, somewhere in the vicinity of Idaho Falls, wild, native cutthroat trout and nonnative brown and rainbow trout can persist within the flow and water quality regimes of the Snake River. From this point upstream in Idaho, the river is referred to as the South Fork of the Snake River, and native trout conservation is again a priority.

The endemic Snake River finespotted cutthroat trout are now interbreeding with introduced nonnative rainbow trout (Idaho Fish and Game 2021). The resulting hybrid is called a cutbow, and the rate of mixing below Palisades Reservoir on the border of Idaho and Wyoming has prompted the Idaho Fish and Game Department to put a bounty on rainbow trout. Faced with the loss of this iconic native species, anglers have become an important tool in the management toolbox. Additionally, the Idaho Department of Fish and Game traps and removes rainbow trout in spawning tributaries. When possible, Idaho Fish and Game also collaborates with the Bureau of Reclamation to release flows from Palisades Reservoir in the early spring, before the majority of cutthroat trout spawn, with the intention of reducing spawning success for the nonnative rainbow trout. This is an example of agencies working together, managing the levers of their jurisdiction, so that the native Snake River finespotted cutthroat trout in the South Fork aren't lost to a hybrid swarm.

The Snake River and its tributaries make up the majority of the stream miles in Idaho, supporting a diversity of anadromous and inland species but also human industries vital to the state. Past decisions in the Snake and Columbia River Basins have compromised the integrity of Idaho's riverine system. Large disparity in management approaches exists, with unprecedented levels of fisheries management in place to retain anadromous fish in the Lower Basin, compared with areas in central Idaho where river conditions are so degraded that native salmon and trout fisheries have been lost and where their recovery isn't even under discussion.

Wyoming: The Upper Snake

Palisades Reservoir sits at the mouth of the Snake River Canyon and straddles the Idaho-Wyoming border at the confluence of the Salt, Greys, and Snake Rivers. The reservoir is managed by the Bureau of Reclamation, primarily for irrigation and electricity production, and despite drastic changes in water level, it often supports a productive lake fishery. The lake fishery is primarily nonnative, including kokanee salmon (introduced landlocked sockeye), introduced lake trout, and introduced brown trout but also native Snake River finespotted cutthroat trout and many native nongame fish. Emphasis on the presence of this full suite of nonnative trout is intentional. Palisades Reservoir and its nonnative fish populations have direct connectivity to the Snake River in Wyoming, but unlike almost everywhere else in the Intermountain West, nonnative trout have yet to replace the endemic Snake River finespotted cutthroat trout population.

The Snake River finespotted cutthroat trout have been able to hang on in Wyoming, with populations comparable to presettlement times. A few critical factors have led to this persistence. Perhaps the most important are the connections between rivers. Although some natural barriers exist, as do some small human-made barriers, the Snake River in Wyoming is unique for its huge amount of ecologically intact river miles that connect tributaries to the mainstem. This allows fish to move freely, migrating between seasons to utilize the best available habitats at any given time. And they do: Snake River cutthroat trout and bluehead sucker, a native sucker, have both been tracked moving extensively from tributaries to the mainstem Snake River and back. The ability to utilize different habitats is crucial at different life stages and in different seasons—in winter, when small streams freeze solid, or during spring, runoff when velocities and turbidity increase substantially. While we do not know how these fish decide to move sixty miles from one location or another, we know that they do, and it appears a crucial factor in the retention of this healthy fishery.

The largest human-made fish barrier in the Snake River in Wyoming is the last (or first) of its dams, Jackson Lake Dam. Its reservoir sits atop Jackson Lake, a natural lake along the Snake River that was over four hundred feet deep prior to dam construction. The reservoir sits at the base of the mountains in Grand Teton National Park. Jackson Lake Dam added forty feet of elevation for irrigators in Idaho, who built the dam in 1920. Aside from being a fisheries barrier, Jackson Lake Dam and the management in the reservoir it creates is the largest deviation from the priority for native fisheries management in the Snake River fishery in Wyoming. But while Jackson Lake Dam has certainly had an effect, the fisheries management history and story of the Snake River in Wyoming is one with more successes than failures.

Jackson Lake is unique from a fisheries management perspective because it is managed for trophy lake trout, a nonnative introduced species, overseen by the Wyoming Game and Fish Department. Perhaps because these lake trout reach large size, often exceeding thirty pounds, with the Jackson Lake record being fifty pounds, the fishing season for lake trout is closed during the lake trout spawning season. This is when large lake trout are most vulnerable and are found in shallow water. This management priority stands in stark contrast to the lake trout eradication program at Yellowstone Lake, a mere twenty-five miles away (National Park Service, n.d.). In Yellowstone Lake, which is not part of the Snake River drainage, millions of dollars have been spent deploying gill-netting crews to kill predacious lake trout in an exhausting attempt to bring back Yellowstone cutthroat trout populations.

The premise of inland stream and river fisheries management in the United States has nearly everywhere been the introduction of nonnative fish in order to diversify angler experience and increase fishery productivity. Humans have gone to extreme lengths to stock different fish species. Fish were moved on trains from the East Coast out West by early settlers, they were brought on horseback and in backpacks to alpine lakes by early wilderness guides, and today it isn't uncommon for helicopters to drop trout into remote lakes for recreational fishing opportunities. The efforts are almost unfathomable. But in the headwaters of the Snake River in Wyoming, the insatiable drive to stock nonnative fish was mediated by the conservation legacy surrounding Yellowstone and Grand Teton National Parks.

While nonnative fish stocking has occurred in the Snake River in Wyoming, it has not occurred for half a century. Even in the heyday of nonnative fish stocking, Snake River finespotted cutthroat trout conservation thrived in small do-it-yourself hatcheries that landowners created in spawning spring creeks on their properties. While not a recommended practice today, the ethic of Snake River cutthroat trout stewardship prevailed, thus preserving the integrity of the native fishery in the streams and rivers.

Only time will tell whether the integrity of the native fishery of the Snake River in Wyoming is strong enough to endure. The lake fisheries are far from intact, even in the headwater lakes in Yellowstone Park and the glacial lakes below the Teton Range. These include lake trout and often brown trout, both of which feed on native fish species. The population of nonnative trout exceeds that of native trout in many lakes. But the stream and river fisheries are largely intact, with only pockets of brown, rainbow, and brook trout present throughout the Snake River and its tributaries in Wyoming.

How will climate change tip the scales? It can be argued that the native Snake River finespotted cutthroat trout persist in the Snake River of Wyoming because they are uniquely adapted to the river's natural rhythms and have adaptations that overcome the bitterly cold winters, months of raging runoff, and hot dry summers. Will earlier runoff events in streams and rivers and milder winters disproportionately benefit the nonnative brown, rainbow, and brook trout? With a changing climate, are the genetics and life histories of the Snake River's native cutthroat trout plastic enough to stay ahead of the nonnative trout without significant investment and hands-on management? These questions provide a strong justification for addressing historical management errors by removing nonnative fish and protecting the river as a system. This would also be an acknowledgment that we don't know what these fish truly need to be successful, let alone how their needs might change in the future.

Terminus—and Beginning

The Snake River provides a case study in common fisheries management practices, juxtaposing catastrophically expensive failure with hands-off management of intact, self-recruiting native fish assemblages. The Snake River in Wyoming is a rare example of a successful native fisheries management regime. Over four hundred miles of congressionally designated "Wild and Scenic" rivers and streams support a successfully reproducing native fish population, and management actions in Wyoming consist of small tweaks to manage nonnative fish and address habitat loss.

The mythology of fisheries management, especially in large river systems, is defined by the misconception that such systems can be managed to meet all human needs, and that damage to native fisheries can be addressed through fisheries management techniques. The reality, as the Snake River demonstrates, is that regardless of the perceived ability for humans to artificially maintain a native fishery, native fisheries are degraded at the same rate that the river is augmented for human use.

Because fish are so highly adapted to their environment, preserving natural conditions and their genetics and life history strategies is by far the simplest and most cost-effective way to preserve and protect a fishery. Restoring fisheries once they are lost is next to impossible because the loss of the fishery is the symptom of a severely altered environment. Within the Snake River, a full spectrum of circumstances exists for native fish, from completely lost to self-sustaining. Maintaining a healthy fishery in an out-of-balance environment requires a counterbalance of equal proportions. But our understanding of fish and their aquatic habitats is so limited that the counterbalance is too commonly a list of failures.

23

A Renewed Glen Canyon Emerges

SETH ARENS

I walk upstream along the Colorado River in Utah's Cataract Canyon. It is a crisp October afternoon in 2018. Red-rock walls tower overhead as the sun dips below the canyon rim, leaving only the azure blue of a cloudless desert sky. Looking up, the scene is one of a pristine canyon wilderness.

River level offers a different scene: fifty-foot, near-vertical banks of sediment rising from the water. I lead my wife and seven-year-old twins along an indistinct riverside herd path, weaving through head-high tumbleweed and a variety of other invasive plants growing on the sediments deposited by Lake Powell.

We are on an eighty-five-mile river trip on the Colorado River through Meander and Cataract Canyons with a group of rafters. Clearwater Canyon, a once lovely and lush tributary to the river, lay under the waters of Lake Powell twenty years ago. In 2002 it partially reemerged from the reservoir, and it fully emerged in 2011 as water levels rapidly declined.

We trudge along the river toward the mouth of Clearwater Creek through challenging layers of loose sediments deposited by the reservoir. Mud comes halfway to the top of our rubber boots as we ease our way through the thick cover of sharp desert plants. The mouth of Clearwater Canyon is filled with quicksand-like mud that threatens to suck boots from feet. Traveling up the tributary canyon, it is clear the landscape is young and unstable, still trying to find its equilibrium since the waters of Lake Powell receded. A light breeze picks up the fine soil and carries it over vertical sediment cliffs like a spindrift of snow blowing off a corniced ridge. My family walks carefully around a twenty-foot-high tower of clay leaning precariously over the creek. The landscape of the tributary canyon is otherworldly, but more in a postapocalyptic than an awe-inspiring way.

Just as I begin to doubt that we will travel far enough up-canyon to see native plant regrowth, I hear a small voice from behind say, "Look, Daddy! A baby cottonwood." I look in surprise, first at my daughter for remembering the keystone riparian tree species and then at the young cottonwood seedling growing in damp soil next to the creek. Suddenly, I see the landscape not in terms of scarcity and devastation but through a lens of potential and hope. The flooding of Clearwater Canyon and a hundred similar canyons by Lake Powell irrevocably changed the landscape. But could the riparian ecosystems of these desert canyons return to some version of a natural, pre–Glen Canyon Dam state? And if so, how long would it take?

The Colorado River Basin has experienced unprecedented drought since 2000, which has caused historically low flow through the Colorado River system. By spring 2023, storage of water in the basin's two largest reservoirs, Lake Powell and Mead, dwindled to 26 percent of capacity. The crisis in water availability in the Colorado River triggered management actions in 2020–22 to increase water storage in Lakes Powell and Mead, but the actions have not stemmed the precipitous decline in reservoir levels. The most well-known management challenges pertain to water availability and hydroelectricity generation. The 180-foot drop in Lake Powell's elevation uncovered one hundred thousand acres of land, creating new ecological, recreational, and cultural resources that require management. Spontaneous ecological restoration of ecosystems is occurring throughout previously flooded portions of Glen Canyon and Cataract Canyon. Riparian ecosystems along the Colorado, Escalante, and San Juan Rivers and in over a hundred tributaries are quickly reestablishing a rich and diverse assemblage of mostly native plant species, presenting a rare positive consequence of long-term drought, climate change, and dwindling water resource availability.

The water crisis in the Colorado River Basin has been born from a combination of natural climate cycles of drought, global changes, and population growth. Rapid population growth in the arid West demands more water from the Colorado River while the region experiences long-term drought, supercharged by climate change. The spontaneous ecological restoration of Glen Canyon riparian ecosystems is a unique and unintended consequence of this water crisis. Lessons learned from a drying Lake Powell may be relevant in other large reservoir systems in the Western United States and can be applied more broadly to resource management in the West. As the population grows and the climate changes, increased pressure on natural resources will require more careful and innovative management, especially when confronted with unexpected changes such as those in the Lake Powell region.

From a River, a Lake Is Built

In 1963, the 709-foot Glen Canyon Dam was completed. On March 13, its head gates closed, and Lake Powell began to fill, first inundating Glen Canyon and later the lower half of Cataract Canyon. In 1980, when Lake Powell first filled completely, the reservoir submerged two hundred miles of the Colorado River and its tributaries. Cataract Canyon, even with half of its rapids underwater, was one of the most feared stretches of white water on the Colorado. With Lake Powell full, white-water rafters could still run the Big Drops, a series of three drop-pool rapids that fall twenty-five vertical feet in less than one mile through jagged, house-sized boulders. However, when boaters exited Satan's Gut, the most terrifying of the three, they were greeted by people lounging on houseboats or cruising on Jet Skis.

Before it became Lake Powell, the 162-mile Glen Canyon was a mild counterpart to the wild Cataract Canyon. The river's gradient mellowed to a placid two feet per mile and meandered slowly through smooth red-rock canyons topped with gently sloping domes. John Wesley Powell named the canyon for its abundance of plant life, including forests of willows, cottonwoods, and scrub oaks along the river, tributary creeks, and shady hillslopes. Glen Canyon is unique among Colorado River desert canyons because of the abundance of perennially flowing, spring-fed tributaries. Tributary canyons with flowing water were desert oases and hotspots of biodiversity, containing lush ecosystems with wetland grasses, riparian forests, and unique hanging gardens—home to plants found few other places on Earth.

For twenty years, Lake Powell was mostly full. But in 2000, Lake Powell water levels precipitously dropped due to severe regional drought. Between 2000 and 2004, the inflow of water from the Colorado, San Juan, and other tributaries dropped to half its average. In 2002, only 15 percent of the average amount of water flowed into Lake Powell, making 2002 the most severe regional drought on

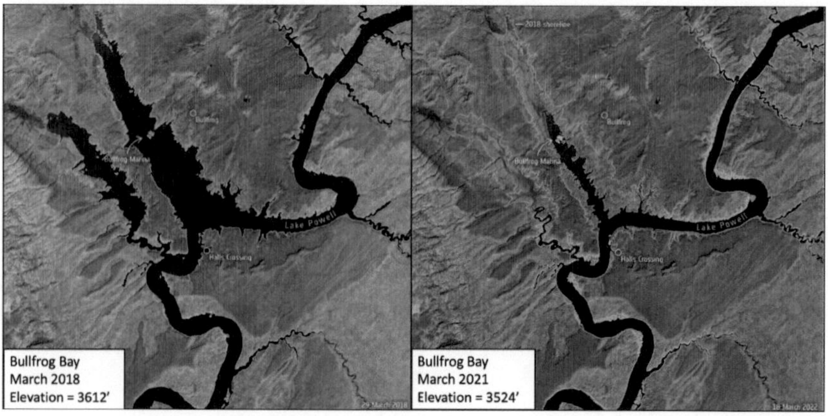

Figure 23.1 Satellite image of the Bullfrog Bay portion of Lake Powell in March 2018 (left) and March 2021 (right). Images are from modified Copernicus Sentinel data, processed by the European Space Agency.

record and one of the most significant one-year droughts in the last 1,200 years. Lake Powell's surface elevation dropped to 3,552 feet, which was, at the time, its lowest elevation since the reservoir filled and 148 feet below full pool elevation. Four extremely wet years from 2005 to 2011, including the fourth wettest on record, brought Lake Powell water levels up 100 feet but did not refill the reservoir. For the last eleven years, including four of the driest six years on record, drought conditions have prevailed, with the average inflow to Lake Powell less than 80 percent of average, causing the reservoir to drop to an all-time low elevation (see figure 23.1).

The period since 2000 is not just a drought but a megadrought, which is defined as a drought lasting more than two decades. The 2000–2021 drought was the most severe in the historical record and also the worst twenty-one-year drought in the last 1,200 years (Williams, Cook, and Smerdon 2022).

The combined effect of decreased precipitation, increased temperatures, and drier soils is evident in the record of average Colorado River streamflow. The twentieth-century Colorado River average annual streamflow was 15.3 million acre-feet (MAF), but twenty-first-century average flows dropped to a paltry 12.2 MAF (see figure 23.2). In April 2023, Lake Powell reached an all-time low elevation of 3,519 feet and was at 23 percent of full capacity. Extremely high runoff during spring 2023 raised Lake Powell water levels by 65 feet, providing temporary relief to drought.

The current crisis in Colorado River Basin water availability has been caused by a combination of drought, climate change, water use by forty million people, and the irrigation of nearly 5.5 million acres of agricultural lands in the West (U.S. Bureau of Reclamation 2012). There are several pressing management issues that arise from a near-empty Lake Powell. First, less water in Lake Powell (and Lake Mead) means that there is reduced water supply for downstream users of Colorado River water, resulting in a system less resilient to future droughts.

Second, Glen Canyon Dam supplies electricity to 3.2 million customers in the Southwest and generates reliable power to the Western electrical grid. If Lake Powell elevations drop below 3,490 feet, 30 feet lower than the April 2023 elevation, Glen Canyon Dam cannot generate electricity.

Third, Glen Canyon Dam was not designed to operate for extended periods of time at elevations below 3,490 feet. At Lake Powell elevations another 140 feet below April 2023 levels (3,370 feet), water would not be released from the dam, and the Colorado would cease to flow through the Grand Canyon.

Fourth, a low Lake Powell affects recreation. Declining Lake Powell levels have caused five of the seven marinas to permanently close since 2000. Only Wahweap

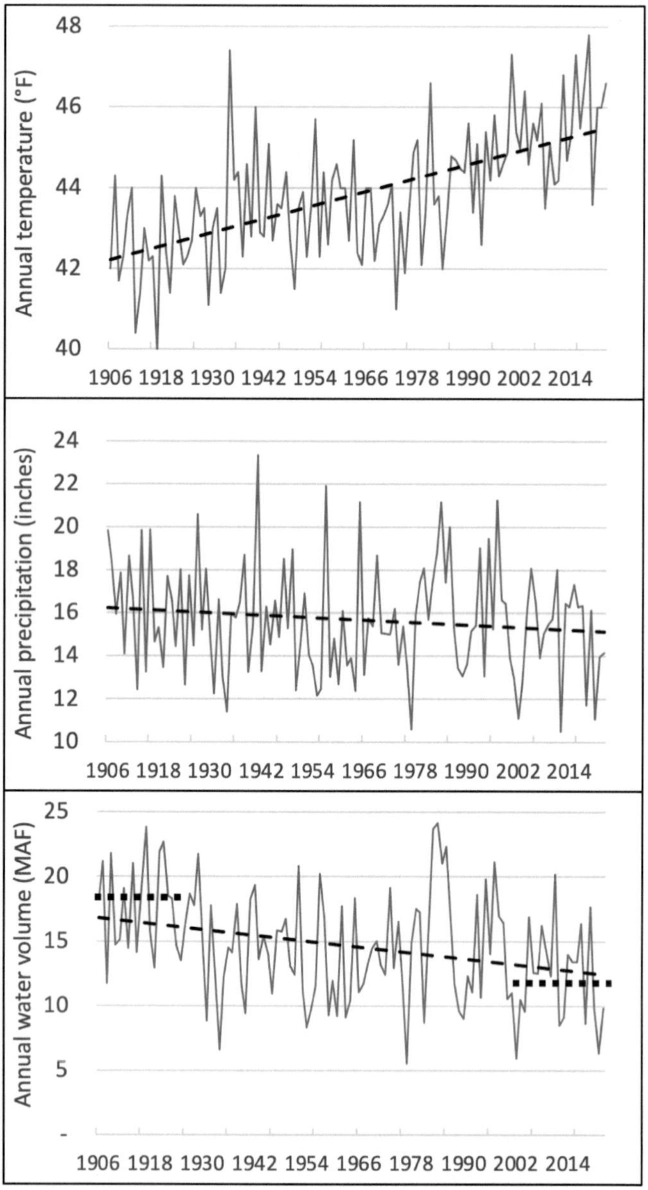

Figure 23.2 Climate and hydrology of the Upper Colorado River Basin including average annual temperature (top panel), annual precipitation (middle panel), and annual Colorado River streamflow volume in millions of acre-feet at Lees Ferry, Arizona. Dashed lines show trends in climate variables. The bold dotted line (bottom panel) shows the average annual Colorado River streamflow from 1906 to 1922 and from 2000 to 2022.

Marina, near Glen Canyon Dam, would remain open at lake elevations below 3,525 feet. River rafting on Cataract Canyon is also severely impacted by low lake levels because unstable lake sediments make it nearly impossible to maintain the North Wash boat ramp for the takeout. Further complicating logistics for rafting Cataract Canyon, a waterfall may soon form immediately below the North Wash boat ramp due to the river meandering in and out of its historical channel. If North Wash boat ramp were to close *and* a waterfall forms, then it would not be possible to raft Cataract Canyon without new infrastructure development.

Fifth, and finally, a drying Lake Powell reveals land that was once inundated by the reservoir. Lands below 3,700 feet in Glen Canyon National Recreation Area, the national park unit that contains Lake Powell, were historically managed as a reservoir. At the reservoir's April 2023 elevation, one hundred thousand acres of land that was once underwater became a terrestrial landscape. From a scientific perspective, virtually nothing is known about these landscapes. From a management perspective, few regulations exist to govern recreational use, protection of evolving and sensitive landscapes, and protection of archaeological sites with cultural significance. The park's general management plan was last updated in 1979, and its resource management plan, which covers water resources, dates to 1995. A low Lake Powell presents extreme challenges for boat-based recreation, but the emergence of new landscapes offers a new opportunity for hiking-based recreation in Glen Canyon's tributaries.

A Riparian Ecosystem Returns

The impacts of drought, climate change, and increasing water use in the West invoke images of desiccated landscapes, wilting agricultural crops, and brown lawns. From a societal perspective, these impacts are decidedly negative. The negative impacts of drought in the Lake Powell region are joined by a rare positive impact of climate change-driven drought. Many landscapes emerging from the receding waters of Lake Powell are quickly repopulating with native plant and animal species. Thriving, diverse, and rich ecosystems dominated by native plant species are establishing along the river and in many tributary canyons that flow into Lake Powell. New versions of Glen Canyon's ecosystems are reestablishing. Large areas once underwater are now open to land-based recreation. The Glen Canyon that disappeared under the waters of Lake Powell in the 1960s will never return to its pre-dam state, but a version of its former state is rapidly reestablishing as Lake Powell shrinks.

In 2019, a year after walking in Clearwater Canyon with my family, I began work to understand how ecosystems are evolving on the landscapes that emerged from Lake Powell. My research originally focused on tributaries to the Colorado River in lower Cataract Canyon and later shifted into the Glen Canyon portion of Lake Powell. I work as a research scientist for Western Water Assessment, a federally funded research program based at the University of Colorado that works regionally to understand and aid in adaptation to climate variability and change. After five years of research and exploration in Cataract and Glen Canyons, several observations about how ecosystems are reestablishing and changing have emerged: ecosystems are reestablishing very rapidly, native plants are generally outcompeting invasive, or nonnative, plants, Glen Canyon is a novel natural laboratory for studying the ecological succession of desert ecosystems, and each tributary canyon may have a unique path through succession.

Conducting ecological research in the Lake Powell region is akin to exploration. The landscapes I study are so new and so infrequently traveled since emergence that I do not know what I will see during each field visit. Native Americans inhabited the canyon for thousands of years, Spanish missionaries passed through in the eighteenth century, and John Wesley Powell led the first expedition to float the canyon in 1869. Yet many places I travel during fieldwork have not seen a human footprint since the 1960s. The emerging landscapes of Glen Canyon are simultaneously unfathomably old, achingly new, and similar to the "Great Unknown" described by Powell in his 1869 exploration of the Grand Canyon. Through survey and research, I strive to make the emergent lands of Glen Canyon known.

Very low Lake Powell elevations have created a novel system for study that has no global analogue. Rapidly declining Lake Powell elevations combine with unique geography to create a natural laboratory for studying ecological succession. As lake levels drop, tributary canyons become isolated, and each tributary canyon provides a separate natural experiment in succession. The patterns of ecological succession are more similar than different between tributary canyons, but there are also some key differences in groupings of species and abundance of nonnative plants. The drying of other large reservoirs, such as Lake Mead, is similar to that of Lake Powell in scale, but not in the conditions leading to reestablishment of native ecosystems.

Ecological succession is a process that occurs after a disturbance such as glacial retreat, fire, or flooding eliminates all flora and fauna from a landscape. A disturbed landscape of bare soil and rock goes through stages of ecosystem development where a group of plants first colonizes, then creates conditions for other

Figure 23.3 Photographs of ecological restoration in Lake Canyon taken in May of 2022: (A) Lake Canyon delta at 3,523 feet (emerged two months before), (B) Lake Canyon at 3,575 feet (emerged two years before), (C) Lake Canyon at 3,650 feet (emerged eleven years before), and (D) Lake Canyon at 3,695 feet (emerged twenty-two years before).

plants to grow in future years, ultimately replacing the early colonizers. Succession is occurring in the more than one hundred tributary canyons and valleys of Glen Canyon that were once flooded by Lake Powell. The terms *ecological succession* and *spontaneous ecological restoration* are used synonymously.

To observe succession, one would typically need to repeatedly visit a site for many years after a disturbance. In Glen Canyon, one simply needs to walk up a tributary to observe over twenty years of succession. Due to the gradual decline of Lake Powell, walking up tributary canyons of the Glen is like walking back in time. Lake Canyon provides such a tour of successional time: over four miles, the canyon climbs from reservoir level to the high-water mark of Lake Powell, depicting a twenty-two-year gradient of succession (see figure 23.3). Above 3,700 feet, riparian ecosystems were not disturbed by flooding and so represent a climax desert riparian ecosystem.

Ecosystems are reestablishing in well-watered tributaries of Glen Canyon extremely quickly. Within three years of emergence, many are dominated by native plant species. Desert ecosystems, often limited by water and nutrients, are typically slow to grow and recover from disturbances such as flooding. However, in Glen Canyon, ecosystems in many tributary canyons with flowing water have reestablished, with near-complete cover of mostly native grasses, wildflowers, and shrubs, in as little as three years. Within three to five years, willows and cottonwoods grow along riparian corridors. Ten years after emergence from Lake Powell, some creeks are lined with dense ten-foot-tall stands of willows and periodic cottonwoods up to thirty feet in height!

To the untrained eye, areas exposed since 2000 look wild and unaltered by humans. Unique hanging gardens with maidenhair ferns, monkey flowers, stream orchids and other endemic plants grow in seeps along canyon walls. Cryptobiotic soils, a symbiotic organism containing moss, lichen, and algae, begin to grow after about five years. Cryptobiotic crusts are ecologically important to desert ecosystems, serving to stabilize soil, retain water, and increase nutrient availability. The remarkable speed with which native, diverse ecosystems are reestablishing is confined to tributary canyons with flowing water. In drier locations, ecological recovery is slower but follows a similar pattern where native plants become more dominant as the landscape ages.

Nonnative plants in the Glen Canyon region grow in both previously inundated and never-flooded locations. However, the greatest abundance of nonnative plants is found in areas below 3,700 feet that recently emerged or are distant from water and very dry. From a land management perspective, nonnative plants are concerning because their dominance often leads to a less-healthy, less-resilient ecosystem that is lower in plant and animal diversity. Cheatgrass, a nonnative annual grass, increases the frequency of wildfire. Proliferation of other nonnative plants, such as tamarisk and tumbleweed (Russian thistle), decreases the recreational value of landscapes and makes travel more challenging.

Tamarisk, a nonnative shrub, is especially detrimental to restoring riparian ecosystems, but native shrubs are generally outcompeting it in Glen Canyon. Tamarisk was introduced to the United States in the late nineteenth century and is now a dominant species along much of the Colorado River and its tributaries. It dramatically alters the structure and function of riparian ecosystems, excludes native shrubs such as willow, and leads to a less diverse system. Tamarisks present in restoring Glen Canyon tributaries are found either in dying stands isolated from water on the top of sediment banks or low in abundance near water. Along the banks of tributary creeks, native coyote willow, seep willow, and willow baccharis often form dense stands, and tamarisk is infrequently present. The predominance

Figure 23.4 A tumbleweed "dam" blown into Forgotten Canyon, a tributary to Glen Canyon.

of native shrubs in Glen Canyon tributaries is unique in recently disturbed desert riparian ecosystems and sets these landscapes on a continued trajectory of healthy native ecosystem development.

Another nonnative plant of concern is tumbleweed, which begins growing early in the growing season and rapidly forms thick, head-high stands of prickly vegetation on recently exposed land surfaces or along drier terraces above the creeks. Observations in many locations in Glen Canyon show that tumbleweed does not typically persist on landscapes older than about three years. The iconic Western image of the tumbleweed rolling across the Western desert is ironically the seed dispersal strategy of a plant not native to the American West. In restoring landscapes of Glen Canyon, it is common to find a mass of dead tumbleweed completely clogging narrow canyons up to ten feet deep and a hundred feet in distance (see figure 23.4). One particularly aggressive nonnative from Southeast Asia, awned barnyard grass, colonized the first half mile of Reflection Canyon and transformed the canyon bottom from bare ground to a field of tall grass in a single growing season (see figure 23.5). The future of landscapes covered by the less-common awned barnyard grass remains unknown and future study is needed.

Figure 23.5 Invasion of the nonnative awned barnyard grass in Reflection Canyon, a tributary to Glen Canyon. Top photograph was taken in October 2021 and the bottom in August 2022.

Comparison to Post–Dam Removal Ecological Restoration

The changes occurring in Cataract and Glen Canyons due to declining water levels in Lake Powell are unique. There is no direct global analogue to the changes occurring in Glen Canyon, but research examining impacts to terrestrial ecosystems after dam removal provides a possible comparison. Although Glen Canyon Dam is not being considered for removal, human water consumption, megadrought, and climate change have reduced Lake Powell's volume so greatly and for so long that spontaneous ecological restoration (ecological succession) is occurring in a manner similar to what would happen if the dam were removed.

We can gain some relevant insights from research about spontaneous ecosystem restoration following dam removal. Plant colonization of previously flooded reservoirs typically occurs during the first year after dam removal. The speed of ecological succession and the richness and diversity of plant species in these landscapes are variable, depending on factors that include the availability of nutrients, water, soil, and seeds, as well as the climate. After dam removal, forbs and grasses are typically early colonizers, followed by riparian shrubs and eventually trees at sites in forested regions (Doyle et al. 2005).

Most studies examining ecosystem responses to dam removal occur in systems very different from Glen Canyon, where the climate is wetter and the dams much smaller than Glen Canyon Dam. In a Wisconsin study of terrestrial ecological development at thirty small-dam removal sites, the total number of trees and the number of tree species increased over time, with some tree species not appearing until thirty years after dam removal (Orr and Stanley 2006). After removal of a New Hampshire dam, wetland plant species historically growing on the margins of the small reservoir declined over time, perhaps similar to the decline in abundance of tamarisk that established during high Lake Powell elevations (Lisius, Snyder, and Collins 2018). Three years after the removal of the Glines Canyon Dam on Washington's Elwha River, spontaneous ecological restoration on land previously inundated by the reservoir caused the development of an ecosystem with similar species composition to the adjacent ecosystem that was never flooded. Nonnative plants were less abundant than expected and native ecosystem development was rapid in locations where fine sediments were present (Prach, Chenoweth, and Moral 2019). The Glen Canyon riparian ecosystem may be establishing so rapidly in part because of the abundance of fine sediments deposited by Lake Powell.

Future studies of landscapes once inundated by Lake Powell offer an opportunity to better understand how desert systems can recover from a large-scale disturbance and provide a preview of ecosystem responses and management challenges to prolonged periods of extremely low water in large reservoirs. While dam removal is not a current management option for Colorado River Basin reservoirs, study of spontaneous ecological restoration in Glen Canyon will inform any future consideration of dam removal in the arid West.

Further study of restoring ecosystems in the Lake Powell region will provide information to federal land management agencies and basin-wide water management efforts. Once-submerged landscapes must be surveyed and monitored to understand the new resources and how to manage them. Management concerns on newly exposed lands include ecological resources and cultural resources, including some of the two thousand archaeological sites identified by researchers in the 1950s. There will also be new recreation patterns. Changes have occurred so quickly and altered the region so dramatically that federal funding and management are struggling to keep pace with the change. The drop in Lake Powell coincides with the renegotiation of the 2005 Interim Guidelines of the Colorado River Compact, which determines how Lake Powell and Lake Mead are managed. The new Interim Guidelines must be in place by the start of 2026.

The Future of Glen Canyon

The trajectory of the West's warming, drying climate, together with the human demands placed on Colorado River water resources, create a future where it is unlikely that both Lake Powell and Lake Mead will ever entirely fill again. In April 2023, Lakes Powell and Mead were a combined 26 percent full—nearly thirty-nine million acre-feet (MAF) below capacity. The 2023 water year brought record amounts of snow to many locations in the Upper Colorado River Basin, and Lake Powell inflow was 166 percent of average. Lake Powell rose sixty-five feet in response to 2023's near-record snowfall, but one year of abundant water supply will not solve the basin's water crisis.

Given current Colorado River Basin consumptive use and reservoir evaporation, the Colorado River and its tributaries would need to flow at 175 percent of average for five consecutive years in order to completely fill Lake Powell and Lake Mead. This scenario is very unlikely to occur. Increasing temperatures caused by climate change dry the basin, resulting in a smaller fraction of precipitation reaching the rivers. Given the likelihood that Lake Powell will not reach full capacity again, some of the restoring ecosystems in Glen Canyon will almost certainly become permanent features of the landscape.

The ecological, cultural, and recreational resources emerging from Lake Powell are not adequately considered in how Glen Canyon National Recreation Area is managed, nor in the environmental impacts of operating Glen Canyon Dam. In the April 2023 release of a Draft Supplemental Environmental Impact Statement (DSEIS) to Near-Term Colorado River Operations, the Bureau of Reclamation gave an indication of how they would assess emerging Glen Canyon resources over the next two years and perhaps through 2045. Despite a lack of scientific study, emergent landscapes were said to be dominated by tamarisk and tumbleweed and projected to have only negative impacts on adjacent native ecosystems. Higher lake levels were expected to have a positive effect on cultural resources because inundation would prevent damage from human visitation. And most emerging recreational resources were not even mentioned. The Bureau of Reclamation has withdrawn the April 2023 DSEIS and will produce a new EIS later in 2023 following the commitment of Arizona, California, and Nevada to reduce water use.

The management decisions for Lake Powell moving forward are not binary. It is not a simplistic decision of either allowing Lake Powell to fill or draining it. Hydroclimate conditions and Colorado River Basin water management decisions will contribute to determining the future of Lake Powell and the restoring ecosystems of Glen Canyon, and many management actions are possible. Three intertwined categories of management issues are relevant to the future of Glen Canyon: water, ecological resources, and recreation.

The decision to dedicate hundreds of miles of the Colorado River to water storage was made long ago: available water should be stored in Lake Powell and Lake Mead for human consumption. However, future conditions are unlikely to produce enough runoff to fill both reservoirs. There will be wet years, such as 2023, and dry years, but the trend in declining Colorado River streamflow is very likely to continue. An iconic landscape was flooded in 1963 before its value was fully understood. Water consumption, drought, and climate change have provided a second chance to appreciate Glen Canyon's value. The renegotiation of the 2005 Interim Guidelines offers an opportunity to manage the two reservoirs differently. Previously unconsidered ecological, recreational, and cultural resources in Glen Canyon should now be considered in management decisions.

Lake Powell is no longer a barren red-rock vessel for water storage. Riparian ecosystems, especially those above 3,620 feet that emerged more than four years ago, have spontaneously reestablished and host a rich and diverse assemblage of mostly native plant species. From a perspective that values restoring ecological resources, a worst-case management scenario would preferentially fill Lake Powell over Lake Mead during a few wet years, only to have long-term drought return, such that Lake Powell drains again. In this scenario, more than twenty years of natural restoration in Glen Canyon could be undone for the purpose of temporary water storage. The value of ecological resources in the recently uncovered areas of Glen Canyon should be considered in Colorado River Basin management decisions.

While the returning ecosystems of Glen Canyon may complicate future management, they also offer opportunities. Glen Canyon, a region with geologic, ecologic, and cultural resources that might have made it worthy of National Park status at one time was lost under the waters of Lake Powell. Portions of Glen Canyon have reemerged. We should take this second chance to reconsider their value rather than again inundate an iconic canyon of the Colorado Plateau for the sake of temporary water storage. There are almost certainly management opportunities for Glen Canyon that store water and conserve ecological resources while maintaining recreation options.

The natural restoration of Glen Canyon ecosystems is one of the few bright spots in the gloomy outlook of decreasing Western water resources. Reflecting on the flooding of Glen Canyon, conservationist David Brower wrote, "Glen Canyon died . . . Neither you nor I, nor anyone else, knew it well enough to insist that at all costs it should endure. When we began to find out it was too late" (Brower 1997). But Glen Canyon is not dead. The canyon endures and life is returning to its sinuous tributaries. Ecosystems with native plants and animals are spontaneously reestablishing in rich and diverse assemblages.

References

Abbott, David R. 2003. *Centuries of Decline during the Hohokam Classic Period at Pueblo Grande*. Tucson: University of Arizona Press.

Acemoglu, Daron, and James A. Robinson. 2017. "The Economic Impact of Colonialism." In *The Long Economic and Political Shadow of History*, edited by R. F. Talley, 81–89. Vol. 1 of *A Global View*. London: Vox.

Aikens, Ellen O., Teal B. Wyckoff, Hall Sawyer, and Matthew J. Kauffman. 2022. "Industrial Energy Development Decouples Ungulate Migration from the Green Wave." *Nature Ecology and Evolution* 6:1733–41. https://doi.org/10.1038/s41559-022-01887-9.

Alexander, Ben. 2019. *Understanding Economic Transitions in Energy-Focused Communities*. Resources Legacy Fund.

All the Rooms. 2023. "Enterprise Reports: DMOs & Tourism." https://www.alltherooms.com.

Anderson, Kirk, and Doug Copsey. 2013. *Snake River Discovered: Source to Confluence*. Ketchum, ID: Kirk Anderson Photography.

Arizona State University. 2023. "Residential Survey Findings, Sedona Sustainable Tourism Plan." https://visitsedona.com/sustainable-tourism-plan/survey-results/residents/.

Army Corps of Engineers. 2012. "Columbia River Fish Mitigation." Fact Sheet. https://www.nwd.usace.army.mil/Fact-Sheets/Article/475821/columbia-river-fish-mitigation/.

August, Jack. 2007. *Dividing Western Waters*. Fort Worth, TX: TCU Press.

Baker, William Lawrence. 2009. *Fire Ecology in Rocky Mountain Landscapes*. Washington, DC: Island Press.

Baruch-Mordo, Sharon, Stewart W. Breck, Kenneth R. Wilson, and John Broderick. 2011. "The Carrot or the Stick? Evaluation of Education and Enforcement as Management Tools for Human-Wildlife Conflicts." *PLoS ONE* 6:e15681. https://doi.org/10.1371/journal.pone.0015681.

Baruch-Mordo, Sharon, Stewart W. Breck, Kenneth R. Wilson, and David M. Theobald. 2008. "Spatiotemporal Distribution of Black Bear–Human Conflicts in Colorado." *Journal of Wildlife Management* 72 (8): 1853–62.

Baruch-Mordo, Sharon, Kenneth R. Wilson, David L. Lewis, John Broderick, Julie S. Mao, and Stewart W. Breck. 2014. "Stochasticity in Natural Forage Production Affects Use of Urban Areas by Black Bears: Implications to Management of Human-Bear Conflicts." *PLoS ONE* 9 (1): e85122. https://doi.org/10.1371/journal.pone.0015681.

Baxter, Bonnie K. 2018. "Great Salt Lake Microbiology: A Historical Perspective." *International Microbiology* 21 (3): 79–95.

Baxter, Bonnie K., and Jaimi K. Butler. 2020. "Climate Change and Great Salt Lake." In *Great Salt Lake Biology: A Terminal Lake in a Time of Change*, edited by Bonnie K. Baxter and Jaimi K. Butler, 23–52. Cham, Switzerland: Springer.

Bears of Durango. 2021. Directed and produced by Dusty Hulet. Test Area North. PBS, June 28, 2021. Video, 57:11. https://www.pbs.org/show/bears-durango/.

Belote, Travis. 2019. "Diverse Interests Can Develop a Shared Vision." Letter to the editor, *Bozeman Daily Chronicle*, May 11, 2019. https://www.bozemandailychronicle.com/opinions/guest_columnists/diverse-interests-can-develop-a-shared-vision/article_7ae6f630-e0b2-5948-9df9-476435bafdbe.html.

Bennett, Drew E., and Travis Brammer. 2023. "Habitat Leasing as an Alternative to Affirmative Conservation Easements in Conserving Wildlife on Private Lands." *Wildlife Society Bulletin* 47:e1477. https://doi.org/10.1002/wsb.1477.

Bennett, Drew E., and Nicole M. Gautier. 2019. *Landowner Perspectives on Big Game Migration Corridor Conservation in Wyoming*. Laramie, WY: Ruckelshaus Institute of Environment and Natural Resources. https://www.uwyo.edu/haub/_files/_docs/ruckelshaus/private-lands-stewardship/2019-landowner-pers-report-online-accessible.pdf.

Bingham, Sam, Janet Bingham, and Rock Point School. 1984. *Between Sacred Mountains: Navajo Stories and Lessons from the Land*. Tucson: Sun Tracks, Arizona University Press.

Blackfoot Confederacy. 2014. *Proclamation of the Blackfeet Confederacy: Badger-Two Medicine*. Browning, MT: Blackfeet Tribal Business Council.

Bonneville Power Administration. 2016. *A Northwest Energy Solution: Regional Power Benefits of the Lower Snake River Dams*. Fact Sheet. https://nwriverpartners.org/wp-content/uploads/2020/02/BPA-Snake-Dams-Fact-Sheet-2016.pdf.

Bookstrom, Arthur A. 2013. "The Idaho Cobalt Belt." *Northwest Geology* 42:149–62.

Bosse, Scott. 2022. "Glamping in the Gallatin River's Floodplain Is Not Conservation." *Bozeman Daily Chronicle*, February 18, 2022. https://www.bozemandailychronicle.com/opinions/guest_columnists/guest-column-glamping-in-the-gallatin-rivers-floodplain-is-not-conservation/article_84a7030a-8284-5381-8ff8-9f1d1fb3ddbf.html.

Boyd-Fliegel, Sophia. 2022. "New Data Leads to $2.5B Estimate for Teton Housing Fix." Jackson Hole News & Guide, March 16, 2022. https://www.jhnewsandguide.com/news/town_county/new-data-leads-to-2-5b-estimate-for-teton-housing-fix/article_37ca1a7b-cf2a-5104-96f2-4cfae1826cb0.html.

Breck, Stewart W., Nathan Lance, and Victoria Seher. 2009. "Selective Foraging for Anthropogenic Resources by Black Bears: Minivans in Yosemite National Park." *Journal of Mammalogy* 90 (5): 1041–44.

Brister, Evelyn, and Andrew E. Newhouse. 2020. "Not the Same Old Chestnut: Rewilding Forests with Biotechnology." *Environmental Ethics* 42 (2): 149–67. https://doi.org/10.5840/enviroethics2020111614.

Brower, David. 1997. "Let the River Run through It." *Sierra Magazine*, July/August 1997. https://vault.sierraclub.org/sierra/199703/brower.asp.

Brown, Nell Porter. 2017. "This Land Was Made For . . . : A Utah Activist Reflects on 40 Years of Land Conservation—and What's Coming Next." *Harvard Magazine*, November–December 2017. https://www.harvardmagazine.com/2017/10/bill-hedden.

Brueckner, Martin, Angela Durey, Robyn Mayes, and Christof Pforr. 2013. "The Mining Boom and Western Australia's Changing Landscape: Towards Sustainability or Business as Usual?" *Rural Society* 22 (2): 111–24.

Brugge, David. 1971. "Problems of Electrical Power Production in the Southwest. Part V. Hearings before the Committee on Interior and Insular Affairs, U.S. Senate, 92nd Congress, 1st Session, on Environmental Problems Associated with the Production of Electrical Power by Coal-Fired Plants in the Four Corners Region of the Southwest U.S., Page, Arizona, May 28, 1971." OSTI ID: 5032850. Committee on Interior and Insular Affairs (U.S. Senate), Washington, DC.

Bullington, Joseph. 2023. "In Montana, an Avalanche of Wealth Is Displacing Workers." *In These Times*, March 30, 2023. https://inthesetimes.com/article/displaced-montana-workers-luxury-housing-2.

Cenziper, Debbie, and Will Fitzgibbon. 2021. "The 'Cowboy Cocktail': How Wyoming Became One of the World's Top Tax Havens." *Washington Post*, December 20, 2021. https://www.washingtonpost.com/business/interactive/2021/wyoming-trusts-finance-pandora-papers/.

Changing U.S. Rivers. N.d. "What Have We Wrought?" Warner College of Natural Resources, CSU. https://sites.warnercnr.colostate.edu/changing-us-rivers/.

Cheavens, Suzanne. 2022. "Commissioners Approve Rezone of Diamond Ridge Parcel." *Telluride Daily Planet*, May 18, 2022. https://www.telluridenews.com/news/article_eac5e9fa-d704-11ec-8e24-e7d9f2a0067d.html.

City of Sedona. 2023. "Chapter 5.25 Short-Term Rental Regulation." https://sedona.municipal.codes/SCC/5.25.

Clayton, John. 2020. "Stephen Leek, Father of the Elk." WyoHistory.org, November 16, 2020. https://www.wyohistory.org/encyclopedia/stephen-leek-father-elk.

Cleveland, Grover. 1897. *Proclamation 396—Withdrawal of Lands for the Lewis and Clark Forest Reserve, Montana*. February 22, 1897. https://www.presidency.ucsb.edu/documents/proclamation-396-withdrawal-lands-for-the-lewis-and-clark-forest-reserve-montana.

Clow, Richmond L., and Imre Sutton, eds. 2001. *Trusteeship in Change: Toward Tribal Autonomy in Resource Management*. Boulder: University Press of Colorado.

Coleman, Tyler H., Charles C. Schwartz, Kerry A. Gunther, and Scott Creek. 2013. "Grizzly Bear and Human Interaction in Yellowstone National Park: An Evaluation of Bear Management Areas." *Journal of Wildlife Management* 77 (7): 1311–20. https://doi.org/10.1002/jwmg.602.

Connall, D. 1982. "History of the Arizona Groundwater Management Act." *Arizona State Law Journal* 2:313–44.

Cook, E. R., U. Lall, C. Woodhouse, and D. M. Meko. 2004. *North American Summer*

PDSI Reconstructions. NOAA/NGDC, World Data Center for Paleoclimatology Data Contribution Series #2004-045. Paleoclimatology Program, Boulder, CO.

Copeland, Timothy, Demitra Blythe, Windy Schoby, Eli Felts, and Patrick Murphy. 2021. "Population Effect of a Large-Scale Stream Restoration Effort on Chinook Salmon in the Pahsimeroi River, Idaho." *River Research and Applications* 37 (1): 100–110. https://doi.org/10.1002/rra.3748.

Correll, J. L., and E. L. Watson. 1972. *Welcome to the Land of the Navajo: A Book of Information about the Navajo Indians*. Compiled and edited by Museum and Research Department, Navajo Tribe. Window Rock, AZ: Navajo Times.

Cuch, Forrest S. 2000. *A History of Utah's American Indians*. A joint project of the Utah Division of Indian Affairs and the Utah State Historical Society. Denver: University Press of Colorado.

Cypher, James M., and Raúl Delgado Wise. 2010. *Mexico's Economic Dilemma: The Developmental Failure of Neoliberalism*. Lanham, MD: Rowman and Littlefield.

Dettinger, Michael, Bradley Udall, and Aris Georgakakos. 2015. "Western Water and Climate Change." *Ecological Applications* 25 (8): 2069–93.

DeVoto, Bernard. 1947. "The West against Itself." *Harper's Magazine* 194:1–13.

Dougherty, Phil. 2020. *Boldt Decision: United States v. State of Washington*. HistoryLink.org. Essay 21084. https://www.historylink.org/File/21084.

Doyle, M. W., Emily H. Stanley, Cailin H. Orr, Andrew R. Selle, Suresh A. Sethi, and John M. Harbor. 2005. "Stream Ecosystem Response to Small Dam Removal: Lessons from the Heartland." *Geomorphology* 71:227–44.

ECONorthwest. 2022. *Effects of Proposed Grand Targhee Development on Public Services and Housing Markets in Teton County, Idaho*. July 2022. https://www.grandtargheeca.org/socioeconomics-1.

Eland, Ron. 2023. "Sedona City Council Approves Sustainable Tourism Plan." *Sedona Red Rock News*, March 28, 2019. https://www.redrocknews.com/2019/03/28/sedona-city-council-approves-sustainable-tourism-plan/.

Farrell, Justin. 2020. *Billionaire Wilderness: The Ultra-Wealthy and the Remaking of the American West*. Princeton, NJ: Princeton University Press.

Fernández-Kelly, María Patricia. 1983. *For We Are Sold, I and My People: Women and Industry in Mexico's Frontier*. Albany: State University of New York Press.

Gammage, Grady, Jr. 1999. *Phoenix in Perspective*. Phoenix: Arizona State University, Herberger Center for Design Excellence.

Gammage, Grady, Jr. 2016. *The Future of the Suburban City: Lessons from Sustaining Phoenix*. Washington, DC: Island Press.

Gammage, Grady, Jr. 2021. *Watering the Sun Corridor*. Phoenix: Morrison Institute for Public Policy, Arizona State University. Originally published 2011. https://morrisoninstitute.asu.edu.

Ganster, Paul, and Kimberly Collins. 2021. *The U.S.-Mexican Border Today: Conflict and Cooperation in Historical Perspective*. Lanham, MD: Rowman and Littlefield.

Gautier, Nicole M., Drew E. Bennett, and Robert Bonnie. 2019. *Public Opinion on Wildlife and Migration Corridors in Wyoming: Wyoming Open Spaces Initiative*. University of

Wyoming Extension Publication B1350. http://www.uwyo.edu/haub//_files/_docs/ruckelshaus/open-spaces/2019-migration-corridor-research-brief-final.pdf.

Gibson, C., and K. Jung. 2005. "Historical Census Statistics on Population Totals by Race, 1790 to 1990, and by Hispanic Origin, 1970 to 1990, for Large Cities and Other Urban Places in the United States." Working Paper no. 76. Washington, DC: U.S. Census Bureau.

Gigliotti, Laura C., Wenjing Xu, Gabriel R. Zuckerman, M. Paul Atwood, Eric K. Cole, Alyson Courtemanch, Sarah Dewey, et al. 2022. "Wildlife Migrations Highlight Importance of Both Private Lands and Protected Areas in the Greater Yellowstone Ecosystem." *Biological Conservation* 275:109752. https://doi.org/10.1016/j.biocon.2022.109752.

Goldfarb, Ben. 2018. *Eager: The Surprising, Secret Life of Beavers and Why They Matter.* Chelsea, VT: Chelsea Green.

Graham, Christopher Fox. 2023. "Sedona Chamber of Commerce to End City Partnership, Plans to Take Tourism Management in New Direction." Sedona Red Rock News, April 5. 2023. https://www.redrocknews.com/2023/04/05/sedona-chamber-to-end-city-partnership-plans-to-take-tourism-management-in-new-direction/.

Great Salt Lake Strike Team (GSLST). 2023. "Great Salt Lake Policy Assessment." https://gardner.utah.edu/wp-content/uploads/GSL-Assessment-Feb2023.pdf?x71849.

Gupta, Avijit. 2008. *Large Rivers: Geomorphology and Management.* Hoboken, NJ: John Wiley & Sons.

Hansen, Andrew J., Ray Rasker, Bruce Maxwell, Jay J. Rotella, Jerry D. Johnson, Andrea Wright Parmenter, Ute Langner, et al. 2002. "Ecological Causes and Consequences of Demographic Change in the New West: As Natural Amenities Attract People and Commerce to the Rural West, the Resulting Land-Use Changes Threaten Biodiversity, Even in Protected Areas, and Challenge Efforts to Sustain Local Communities and Ecosystems." *BioScience* 52 (2): 151–62.

Hardin, Garrett, 1968. "The Tragedy of the Commons." *Science* 162 (3859): 1243–48. https://doi.org/10.1126/science.162.3859.1243.

Hargrove, W. L., J. M. Heyman, A. Mayer, A. Mirchi, A. Granados-Olivas, G. Ganjegunte, D. Gutzler, et al. 2023. "The Future of Water in a Desert River Basin Facing Climate Change and Competing Demands: A Holistic Approach to Water Sustainability in Arid and Semi-arid Regions." *Journal of Hydrology: Regional Studies* 46:101336. https://doi.org/10.1016/j.ejrh.2023.101336.

Headwaters Economics. 2023. "The Outdoor Recreation Economy by State." *Headwaters Economics*, March 2023. https://headwaterseconomics.org/economic-development/trends-performance/outdoor-recreation-economy-by-state/.

Heyman, Josiah M. 1991. *Life and Labor on the Border: Working People of Northeastern Sonora, Mexico, 1886–1986.* Tucson: University of Arizona Press.

Heyman, Josiah M. 1998. *Finding a Moral Heart for U.S. Immigration Policy: An Anthropological Perspective.* Arlington, VA: American Anthropological Association.

Heyman, Josiah M. 2007. "Environmental Issues at the U.S.-Mexico Border and the Unequal Territorialization of Value." In *Rethinking Environmental History:*

World-System History and Global Environmental Change, edited by Alf Hornborg, J. R. McNeill, and Joan Martinez-Alier, 327–44. Walnut Creek, CA: AltaMira Press.

Heyman, Josiah M. 2012. "Constructing a 'Perfect' Wall: Race, Class, and Citizenship in US-Mexico Border Policing." In *Migration in the 21st Century: Political Economy and Ethnography*, edited by Pauline Gardiner Barber and Winnie Lem, 153–74. New York: Routledge.

Heyman, Josiah. 2017. "Border Thinking: Exclude or Relate." NACLA Border Wars Blog. https://nacla.org/blog/2017/02/27/border-thinking-exclude-or-relate.

Heyman, Josiah M., Alex Mayer, and Jessica Alger. 2022. "Predictions of Household Water Affordability under Conditions of Climate Change, Demographic Growth, and Fresh Groundwater Depletion in a Southwest US City Indicate Increasing Burdens on the Poor." *PLoS ONE* 17 (11): e0277268. https://doi.org/10.1371/journal.pone.0277268.

Hirt, Paul W. 1994. *A Conspiracy of Optimism: Management of National Forests since World War Two*. Lincoln: University of Nebraska Press.

Holling, C. S., and Gary K. Meffe. 1996. "Command and Control and the Pathology of Natural Resource Management." *Conservation Biology* 10:328–37.

Howe, Jim, Ed McMahon, and Luther Propst. 1997. *Balancing Nature and Commerce in Gateway Communities*. Washington, DC: Island Press.

Hoxie, G. L. 1910. "How Fire Helps Forestry." *Sunset* 25:145–51.

Idaho Fish and Game. 2021. "Genetic Integrity of the South Fork Snake River Yellowstone Cutthroat Trout, Part 1: Introgression/Hybridization." https://idfg.idaho.gov/blog/2021/04/genetic-integrity-south-fork-snake-river-yellowstone-cutthroat-trout-part-i.

Idaho Fish and Game. 2023. "Sockeye Salmon." https://idfg.idaho.gov/conservation/sockeye.

Imperial Irrigation District. 2023. "All American Canal." https://www.iid.com/water/water-transportation-system/colorado-river-facilities/all-american-canal.

Indian Affairs. 1855. *Treaty with the Nez Perces*. Camp Stevens. RIT_291, NAI_178309326. https://treaties.okstate.edu/treaties/treaty-with-the-nez-perces-1855-0702.

Instituto Nacional de Estadística y Geografía (INEGI). 2023. "Número de establecimientos manufactureros con Programa IMMEX y personal ocupado por condición de contratación y calificación de la mano de obra según entidades federativas y municipios seleccionadas." https://www.inegi.org.mx/temas/manufacturasexp/#Tabulados.

Iverson, P. 2002. *Diné: A History of the Navajos*. Albuquerque: University of New Mexico Press.

Ives, Joseph Christmas. 1861. *Report upon the Colorado River of the West, Explored in 1857 and 1858*. U.S. Government Printing Office.

Jesmer, Brett R., Jerod A. Merkle, Jacob R. Goheen, Ellen O. Aikens, Jeffrey L. Beck, Alyson B. Courtemanch, Mark A. Hurley, et al. 2018. "Is Ungulate Migration Culturally Transmitted? Evidence of Social Learning from Translocated Animals." *Science* 361:1023–25. https://doi.org/10.1126/science.aat0985.

Johnson, Heather E., David L. Lewis and Stewart W. Breck. 2020. "Individual and Population-Level Fitness Consequences Associated with Black Bear Use of Residential Development." *Ecosphere* 11 (5): e03098. https://doi.org/10.1002/ecs2.3098.

Johnson, Heather E., David L. Lewis, Stacy A. Lischka, and Stewart W. Breck. 2018. "An Experimental Test of Bear-Resistant Containers to Reduce Human-Black Bear Conflicts and Improve Public Perceptions." *Journal of Wildlife Management* 82 (6): 1102–14. https://doi.org/10.1002/jwmg.21472.

Johnson, Rich. 1977. *The Central Arizona Project, 1918–1968*. Tucson: University of Arizona Press.

Jojola, Ted. 2008. "Indigenous Planning—an Emerging Context." *Canadian Journal of Urban Research* 17 (1): 37–47.

Jones, Kristal, Jesse Abrams, R. Travis Belote, Bray J. Beltran, Jodi Brandt, Neil Carter, Antonio J Castro, et al. 2019. "The American West as a Social-Ecological Region: Drivers, Dynamics and Implications for Nested Social-Ecological Systems." *Environmental Research Letters* 14:115008. https://doi.org/10.1088/1748-9326/ab4562.

Jones Ritten, Chian, Amy Nagler, Kristiana M. Hansen, Drew E. Bennett, and Benjamin S. Rashford. 2022. "Incorporating Landowner Preferences into Successful Migratory Species Conservation Policy." *Western Economics Forum* 20 (1): 83–94.

Kauffman, Matthew J., James E. Meacham, Hall Sawyer, Alethea Y. Steingisser, William J. Rudd, and Emilene Ostlind. 2018. *Wild Migrations: Atlas of Wyoming's Ungulates.* Corvallis: Oregon State University Press.

Kemmis, Daniel. 2001. *This Sovereign Land: A New Vision for Governing the West.* Washington, DC: Island Press.

Klamath River Renewal Corporation. 2020. *Lower Klamath Project: Exhibit A-1 Definite Decommissioning Plan-Amended Surrender Application.* FERC no. 14803. Berkeley, CA. https://klamathrenewal.org/wp-content/uploads/2021/04/Definite-Decommissioning-Plan.pdf.

Kopinak, Kathryn, ed. 2004. *The Social Costs of Industrial Growth in Northern Mexico.* La Jolla, CA: Center for U.S.-Mexican Studies, University of California San Diego.

Kuhns, Michael and Barbara Daniels. 2018. "Firewise Landscaping for Utah." USU Cooperative Extension. First published July 2005; updated March 2018. https://extension.usu.edu/forestry/files/resources/firewise-landscaping-updated-2018.pdf.

Lara-Valencia, Francisco, Irasema Coronado, Stephen Mumme, Christopher Brown, Paul Ganster, Hilda García-Pérez, Donna Lybecker, et al. 2023. "Water Management on the US-Mexico Border: Achieving Water Sustainability and Resilience through Cross-Border Cooperation." *Journal of Borderlands Studies* 38 (4): 323–34. https://doi.org/10.1080/08865655.2023.2168294.

Larmer, Paul. 2011. "The Return of the Lords of Yesterday." *High Country News.* July 25, 2011.

Larson, Courtney L., Sarah E. Reed, Adina M. Merenlender, and Kevin R. Crooks. 2016. "Effects of Recreation on Animals Revealed as Widespread through a Global Systematic Review." *PLoS ONE* 11:e0167259. https://doi.org/10.1371/journal.pone.0167259.

Larson, Courtney L., Sarah E. Reed, Adina M. Merenlender, and Kevin R. Crooks. 2019. "A Meta-Analysis of Recreation Effects on Vertebrate Species Richness and Abundance." *Conservation Science and Practice* 1 (10): e93. https://doi.org/10.1111/csp2.93.

Laufenberg, Jared, Heather E. Johnson, Paul F. Doherty, and Stewart W. Breck. 2018. "Compounding Effects of a Natural Food Shortage and Human Development on a Large Carnivore Population along a Human Development-Wildland Interface." *Biological Conservation* 224:188–98.

Lawson, Megan. 2020. *Housing in Recreation-Dependent Counties Is Less Affordable.* Bozeman, MT: Headwaters Economics. https://headwaterseconomics.org/equity/housing-affordability-recreation-counties/.

Leopold, Aldo. 1949. *A Sand County Almanac.* New York: Oxford University Press.

Lewis, D. L., S. Baruch-Mordo, K. R. Wilson, S. W. Breck, J. S. Mao, and J. Broderick. 2015. "Foraging Ecology of Black Bears in Urban Environments: Guidance for Human-Bear Conflict Mitigation." *Ecosphere* 6 (8): 1–18. http://dx.doi.org/10.1890/ES15-00137.1.

Lewis, D. L., S. W. Breck, K. R. Wilson, and C. T. Webb. 2014. "Modeling Black Bear Population Dynamics in a Human-Dominated Stochastic Environment." *Ecological Modeling* 294:51–58.

Limerick, Patricia Nelson. 1987. *The Legacy of Conquest: The Unbroken Past of the American West.* New York: Norton.

Lisius, G. L., N. P. Snyder, and M. J. Collins. 2018. "Vegetation Community Response to Hydrologic and Geomorphic Changes following Dam Removal." *River Restoration Applications* 34:317–27.

Little, Ronald L. 1976. "Some Social Consequences of Boom Towns." *North Dakota Law Review* 53 (3): article 7. https://commons.und.edu/ndlr/vol53/iss3/7.

Locke, John. (1689) 1980. *Second Treatise of Government.* Edited by C. B. Macpherson. Indianapolis: Hackett Classics.

Madsen, D. B. 2016. "The Early Human Occupation of the Bonneville Basin." In *Lake Bonneville: A Scientific Update*, edited by Charles G. Oviatt and John F. Shroder, 504–25. Developments in Earth Surface Processes 20. Amsterdam: Elsevier.

Mammoth Lakes Tourism. 2023. "Visit Mammoth." https://www.visitmammoth.com/.

Manson, Pamela. 2023. "Park City Council Shows Support for Snow Park Redevelopment." *Park Record.* December 8, 2023. https://www.parkrecord.com/news/park-city-council-shows-support-for-snow-park-redevelopment/.

Mayer, Alex, Josiah Heyman, Alfredo Granados-Olivas, William Hargrove, Mathew Sanderson, Erica Martinez, Adrian Vazquez-Galvez, and Luis Carlos Alatorre-Cejudo. 2021. "Investigating Management of Transboundary Waters through Cooperation: A Serious Games Case Study of the Hueco Bolson Aquifer in Chihuahua, Mexico and Texas, United States." *Water* 13 (15): 2001. https://doi.org/10.3390/w13152001.

McCall, Tom. 1973. "Speech to Fifty-Seventh Oregon Legislative Assembly." January 8, 1973. In *An Oregon Story: Savings Our Beaches, Farmland and More*, produced by Jim Gilbert. Parkdale Valley Land Trust and Bergman Productions. https://www.anoregonstory.com.

McDonnell, Janet A. 1991. *The Dispossession of the American Indian: 1887–1934*. Bloomington: Indiana University Press.

Meyer, Marilyn Elliot. 1983. "Restrictions Worry Residents at Hearing." *Teton Valley News*, August 4, 1983.

Middleton, Arthur D., Hall Sawyer, Jerod A. Merkle, Matthew J. Kauffman, Eric K. Cole, Sarah R. Dewey, Justin A. Gude, et al. 2020. "Conserving Transboundary Wildlife Migrations: Recent Insights from the Greater Yellowstone Ecosystem." *Frontiers in Ecology and the Environment* 18 (2): 83–91. https://doi.org/10.1002/fee.2145.

Middleton, Arthur D., Temple Stoellinger, Drew E. Bennett, Travis Brammer, Laura Gigliotti, Hilary Byerly Flint, Sam Maher, and Bryan Leonard. 2022. "The Role of Private Lands in Conserving Yellowstone's Wildlife in the Twenty-First Century." *Wyoming Law Review* 22 (2): 237–302. https://scholarship.law.uwyo.edu/cgi/viewcontent.cgi?article=1464&context=wlr.

Mills, Monte, and Martin Nie. 2020. *Bridges to a New Era: A Report on the Past, Present, and Potential Future of Tribal Co-management on Federal Public Lands*. Missoula, MT: Margery Hunter Brown Indian Law Clinic/Bolle Center for People and Forests, University of Montana. https://www.umt.edu/bolle-center/files/mills.nie-bridges-to-a-new-era-2020.pdf.

Miroff, Nick. 2020. "Trump's Border Wall, Vulnerable to Flash Floods, Needs Large Storm Gates Left Open for Months." *Washington Post*, January 30, 2020. https://www.washingtonpost.com/immigration/trumps-border-wall-vulnerable-to-flash-floods-needs-large-storm-gates-left-open-for-months/2020/01/30/be709346-3710-11ea-bb7b-265f4554af6d_story.html.

Montana, State of. 2023. *Land Use Planning Act*, Montana Code Annotated 76-25-101 to 504.

Moritz, Max A., Rob Hazard, Kelly Johnston, Marc Mayes, Molly Mowery, Katie Oran, Anne-Marie Parkinson, David A. Schmidt, and Graham Wesolowski. 2022. "Beyond a Focus on Fuel Reduction in the WUI: The Need for Regional Wildfire Mitigation to Address Multiple Risks." *Frontiers in Forests and Global Change* 5. https://doi.org/10.3389/ffgc.2022.848254.

Mountain Luxury Real Estate. 2023. https://www.mountainluxury.com/snowbasin/.

Mumme, Stephen P. 2023. *Border Water: The Politics of US-Mexico Transboundary Water Management, 1945–2015*. Tucson: University of Arizona Press.

Murdoch, David Hamilton. 2001. *The American West: The Invention of a Myth*. Reno: University of Nevada Press.

National Fire Protection Association. N.d. "Firewise USA." https://www.nfpa.org/education-and-research/wildfire/firewise-usa.

National Forest System Land Management Planning. 2012. U.S. Code of Federal Regulation. Vol 36, sec. 219.7(e)(1)(v).

National League of Cities. 2023. "Short Term Rental Regulations: A Guide for Local Governments." https://www.nlc.org/resource/short-term-rental-regulations-a-guide-for-local-governments/.

National Oceanographic and Atmospheric Administration (NOAA). 2022. *Rebuilding Interior Columbia Basin Salmon and Steelhead*. National Marine Fisheries Service.

https://media.fisheries.noaa.gov/2022-09/rebuilding-interior-columbia-basin-salmon-steelhead.pdf.

National Park Service. N.d. *Fish Management*. https://www.nps.gov/yell/learn/management/fish.htm.

Navajo Nation Code. Title 16: Land. Chapter 1 Navajo Nation Policy on Acquisition of Lands.

Navajo Nation Comprehensive Economic Development Strategy. 2018. Navajo Nation Division of Economic Development. Prepared by Fourth World Design Group. https://navajoeconomy.org/division-administration-copy/.

Navajo Nation Trust Leasing Act. 2000. Approval of Navajo Nation Regulations, 80 Fed. Reg. 69205. November 10, 2015. https://www.federalregister.gov/documents/2015/11/10/2015-28476/navajo-nation-trust-leasing-act-of-2000-approval-of-navajo-nation-regulations.

Nesbit, Kristin A., Larissa L. Yocom, Allison M. Trudgeon, R. Justin DeRose, and Paul C. Rogers. 2023. "Tamm Review: Quaking Aspen's Influence on Fire Occurrence, Behavior, and Severity." *Forest Ecology and Management* 531:120752.

Nie, Martin. 2008. "The Use of Co-management and Protected Land-Use Designations to Protect Tribal Cultural Resources and Reserved Treaty Rights on Federal Lands." *Natural Resources Journal* 48 (3): 585–647.

Nikolewski, Rob. 2022. "Coastal Commission OKs Cap on Short-Term Rentals in San Diego—with a Key Provision." *San Diego Union Tribune*, March 9, 2022. https://www.sandiegouniontribune.com/business/story/2022-03-09/short-term-rental-vote.

Null, Sarah E., and Wayne A. Wurtsbaugh. 2020. "Water Development, Consumptive Water Uses, and Great Salt Lake." In *Great Salt Lake Biology: A Terminal Lake in a Time of Change*, edited by Bonnie K. Baxter and Jaimi K. Butler, 1–21. Cham, Switzerland: Springer.

O'Brian, Dan. 1993. "Montana's Cow Town with Charm." *New York Times*, May 9, 1993. https://www.nytimes.com/1993/05/09/travel/montanas-cow-town-with-charm.html.

O'Donnell, Kelly. 2019. *Tax and Jobs Analysis of San Juan Generating Station Closure*. O'Donnell Economics and Strategy.

Oregon Land Use Board of Appeals. 2022. Report. https://www.oregon.gov/luba/Docs/SB77%202022%20Reports.pdf.

Orr, C. H., and E. H. Stanley. 2006. "Vegetation Development and Restoration Potential of Drained Reservoirs following Dam Removal in Wisconsin." *River Restoration Applications* 22:281–95.

Ostrom, Elinor. 2015. *Governing the Commons: The Evolution of Institutions for Collective Action*. Cambridge: Cambridge University Press.

Outdoor Industry Association. 2022. "Helping the Outdoors Thrive: 2022 Policy Agenda." https://outdoorindustry.org/wp-content/uploads/2015/03/OIA-2022-Policy-Priorities.pdf.

Outdoor Recreation Satellite Account (ORSA). 2022. "Outdoor Recreation Satellite Account, U.S. and States, 2022." *U.S. Bureau of Economic Analysis*, 2022. https://www.bea.gov/sites/default/files/2023-11/orsa1123.pdf.

Paolini, Kelsey E., Abigail M. Sisneros-Kidd, Nicole Gautier, Robert Bonnie, Kenneth E. Wallen, and Drew E. Bennett. 2023. "Perpetuating Corridor Conservation: Using Public Perception to Advance Big Game Management." *Wildlife Society Bulletin* 47 (4): e1496. https://doi.org/10.1002/wsb.1496.

Perino, Andrea, Henrique M. Pereira, Laetitia M. Navarro, Nestor Fernandez, James M. Bullock, Silvia Ceausu, Ainara Cortes-Avizanda, et al. 2019. "Rewilding Complex Ecosystems." *Science* 364 (6438): eaav5570. https://doi.org/10.1126/science.aav5570.

Perry, Tim. 2023. "City of Sedona to Spend $1.67M on Tourism Program." Sedona Red Rock News, October 12, 2023. https://www.redrocknews.com/2023/10/12/city-of-sedona-to-spend-1-67m-on-tourism-program/.

Pikeminnow Sport-Reward Fishery Program. N.d. Washington Department of Fish and Wildlife. https://wdfw.wa.gov/fishing/reports/creel/pikeminnow.

Pilgeram, Ryanne. 2021. *Pushed Out: Contested Development and Rural Gentrification in the U.S. West*. Seattle: University of Washington Press.

Pollock, Michael M., Timothy J. Beechie, Joseph M. Wheaton, Chris E. Jordan, Nick Bouwes, Nicholas Weber, and Carol Volk. 2014. "Using Beaver Dams to Restore Incised Stream Ecosystems." *BioScience* 64 (4): 279–90.

Prach, K., J. Chenoweth, and R. del Moral. 2019. "Spontaneous and Assisted Restoration of Vegetation on the Bottom of a Former Water Reservoir, the Elwha River, Olympic National Park, WA, U.S.A." *Restoration Ecology* 27:592–99.

Property and Environment Research Center (PERC). 2022. *Paradise Valley Brucellosis Compensation Fund*. https://www.perc.org/wp-content/uploads/2022/12/PERC-BrucellosisCompFund-Prospectus-221207-final.pdf.

Prucha, Francis Paul. 1984. *The Great Father*. Vol. 1 of *The United States Government and the American Indians*. Lincoln: University of Nebraska Press.

Pyne, Stephen. 1998. *How the Canyon Became Grand: A Short History*. New York: Penguin Books.

Resource Media. 2013. *Message and Outreach Recommendations: Island Park Sustainable Fire Community*. Bozeman, MT.

Rhyan, Jack C., Pauline Nol, Christine Quance, Arnold Gertonson, John Belfrage, Lauren Harris, Kelly Straka, and Suelee Robbe-Austerman. 2013. "Transmission of Brucellosis from Elk to Cattle and Bison, Greater Yellowstone Area, USA, 2002–2012." *Emerging Infectious Diseases* 19 (12): 1992–95.

Ripple, William J., Christopher Wolf, Michael K. Phillips, Robert L. Beschta, John A. Vucetich, J. Boone Kauffman, Beverly E. Law, et al. 2022. "Rewilding the American West." *BioScience* 72 (10): 931–35. https://doi.org/10.1093/biosci/biac069.

Roach, Mary. 2021. *Fuzz: When Nature Breaks the Law*. New York: W. W. Norton.

Robbins, Paul, Katharine Meehan, Hannah Gosnell, and Susan J. Gilbertz. 2009. "Writing the New West: A Critical Review." *Journal of Rural Sociology* 74 (3): 356–82.

Roberts, Anthony J. 2013. "Avian Diets in a Saline Ecosystem: Great Salt Lake, Utah, USA." *Human-Wildlife Interactions* 7 (1): 158–68.

Roosevelt, Theodore. 1911. Speech. Roosevelt, AZ: Library of Congress, Manuscript Division.

Rosser, E. 2019. "Right-Sizing Use Rights: Navajo Land, Bureaucracy, and Home. Creating Private Sector Economies in Native America: Sustainable Development through Entrepreneurship." In *Creating Private Sector Economies in Native America: Sustainable Development through Entrepreneurship*, edited by Robert J. Miller, Miriam Jorgensen, and Daniel Stewart, 82–96. Cambridge: Cambridge University Press.

RPI Consulting and Navajo Housing Authority (NHA). 2011. *Phase II Housing Needs Assessment and Demographic Analysis*. https://www.navajohousingauthority.org/images/2022/Housing%20Needs%20Assessment/Navajo_Nation_Housing_Needs_Assessment_091311.pdf.

RRC Associates. 2022. *Greater Yellowstone Wildlife-Related Activity Valuation Study*. University of Montana Institute for Tourism and Recreation Research. https://www.wildlivelihoods.com/_files/ugd/94fbf7_e3af2ba3eff94781a02fc73fc8bbe38b.pdf.

Saccò, Mattia, Nicole E. White, Chris Harrod, Gonzalo Salazar, Pablo Aguilar, Carolina F. Cubillos, Karina Meredith, Bonnie K. Baxter, et al. 2021. "Salt to Conserve: A Review on the Ecology and Preservation of Hypersaline Ecosystems." *Biological Reviews* 96 (6): 2828–50.

Sadasivam, Naveena. 2018. "The US-Mexico Border Wall's Dangerous, Costly Side-Effect: Enormous Floods." *Quartz*, August 17, 2018. https://qz.com/1353798/the-us-mexico-border-walls-dangerous-costly-side-effect-enormous-floods.

Salmon Community Review. 2009. Co-Chairs: Michael Shaw and Deb Krum. Unpublished document; author's personal copy.

Sawyer, Hall, Matthew J. Kauffman, Arthur D. Middleton, Thomas A. Morrison, Ryan M. Nielson, and Teal B. Wyckoff. 2012. "A Framework for Understanding Semi-permeable Barrier Effects on Migratory Ungulates." *Journal of Applied Ecology* 50 (1): 68–78. https://doi.org/10.1111/1365-2664.12013.

Sawyer, Hall, Matthew J. Kauffman, Ryan M. Nielson, and Jon S. Horne. 2009. "Identifying and Prioritizing Ungulate Migration Routes for Landscape-Level Conservation." *Ecological Applications* 19 (8): 2016–25. https://doi.org/10.1890/08-2034.1.

Sawyer, Hall, Nicole M. Korfanta, Ryan M. Nielson, Kevin L. Monteith, and Dale Strickland. 2017. "Mule Deer and Energy Development—Long-Term Trends of Habituation and Abundance." *Global Change Biology* 23 (11): 4521–29. https://doi.org/10.1111/gcb.13711.

Schechter, K. Jonathan. 2022. "The Great Unraveling: Yes, Things Really Are Changing That Fast." Mountain and Resort Town Planners Summit, Snowmass Village, CO, October 12–14, 2022.

Schoennagel, Tania, Jennifer K. Balch, Hannah Brenkert-Smith, Philip E. Dennison, Brian J. Harvey, Meg A. Krawchuk, Nathan Mietkiewicz, Penelope Morgan, Max A. Moritz, Ray Rasker, Monica G. Turner, and Cathy Whitlock. 2017. "Adapt to More Wildfire in Western North American Forests as Climate Changes." *Proceedings of the National Academy of Sciences* 114 (18): 4582–90.

Schwartz, Charles C., Patricia H. Gude, Lisa Landenburger, Mark A. Haroldson, and Shannon Podruzny. 2012. "Impacts of Rural Development on Yellowstone Wildlife: Linking Grizzly Bear *Ursus arctos* Demographics with Projected Residential Growth." *Wildlife Biology* 18 (3): 246–57.

Scott, Tristan. 2023. "Blackfeet Bring Bison Home to Chief Mountain." *Flathead Beacon*, June 28, 2023. https://flatheadbeacon.com/2023/06/28/blackfeet-bring-bison-home-to-chief-mountain/.

Shain, Susan. 2023. "Has Montana Solved Its Housing Crisis?" *High Country News*, November 20, 2023.

Sharfstein, Daniel J. 2017. *Thunder in the Mountains: Chief Joseph, Oliver Otis Howard, and the Nez Perce War*. New York: W. W. Norton.

Shenefelt, Mark. 2022. "Morgan Ski Resort Referendum Backers Want Punitive Damages from Developer." *Standard-Examiner*, September 23, 2022. https://www.standard.net/news/local/2022/sep/23/morgan-ski-resort-referendum-backers-want-punitive-damages-from-developer/.

Smith, Darby Minow. 2023. "Montana Has a Habitat Problem." *Sierra, the Magazine of the Sierra Club*, March 14, 2023. https://www.sierraclub.org/sierra/1-spring/feature/montana-has-habitat-problem.

Smith, Henry Nash. 1947. "Clarence King, John Wesley Powell, and the Establishment of the United States Geological Survey." *Mississippi Valley Historical Review* 34 (1): 37–58.

Smith, John. 2022. "Bundy Ranch Standoff Provided a Warning of What Was to Come." *Nevada Independent*, July 17, 2022. https://thenevadaindependent.com/article/bundy-ranch-standoff-provided-a-warning-of-what-was-to-come.

Sorensen, Ella Dibble, Heidi Morrill Hoven, and John Neill. 2020. "Great Salt Lake Shorebirds, Their Habitats, and Food Base." In *Great Salt Lake Biology*, edited by Bonnie K. Baxter and Jaimi K. Butler, 263–309. Cham, Switzerland: Springer.

Soulé, Michael E. and Reed Noss. 1998. "Rewilding and Biodiversity: Complementary Goals for Continental Conservation." *Wild Earth* 8 (3): 18–28.

Spence, Mark David. 1999. *Dispossessing Wilderness: Indian Removal and the Making of National Parks*. Oxford, England: Oxford University Press.

Stegner, Wallace. 1997. *The Sound of Mountain Water: The Changing American West*. New York: Penguin Books.

Streitfeld, David, and Jack Healy. 2009. "Phoenix Leads the Way Down in Home Prices." *New York Times*. April 28, 2009. https://www.nytimes.com/2009/04/29/business/economy/29econ.html.

Taylor, Joseph E. 2004. "The Many Lives of the New West." *Western Historical Quarterly* 35 (2): 141–65.

Telluride, Town of. 2023. "A Brief History of Telluride." https://www.telluride-co.gov/566/History-of-Telluride.

Telluride Affordable Housing Guidelines. 2023. Adopted September 2007. Last modified May 9, 2023. https://smrha.org/wp-content/uploads/2023/05/2023-05-09-TAHG-.pdf.

Texas Water Development Board (TWDB). 2021. 2021 Region E Plan. https://www.twdb.texas.gov/waterplanning/rwp/plans/2021/index.asp#region-e.

Theobald, Dave. 2005. "Landscape Patterns of Exurban Growth in the USA from 1980 to 2020." *Ecology and Society* 10 (1). https://www.ecologyandsociety.org/vol10/iss1/art32/.

Thompson, Jonathan. 2015. "Lessons from Boom and Bust in New Mexico." *High Country News*, March 16, 2015.

Thompson, Jonathan. 2017. "Coal. Guns. Freedom? How the Trump Administration Has Seized Mythologies around Coal." *High Country News*, September 21, 2017.

Thompson, Jonathan. 2018. *River of Lost Souls: The Science, Politics, and Greed behind the Gold King Mine Disaster*. Salt Lake City: Torrey House Press.

Thuermer, Angus. 2023. "Elk Mountain Ranch Owner: 'We Should Have Control' of Corner-Crossing." WyoFile, April 18, 2023. https://wyofile.com/elk-mountain-ranch-owner-we-should-have-control-of-corner-crossing/.

Tilt, Whitney. 2020. *Elk in Paradise: Conserving Migratory Wildlife and Working Lands in Montana's Paradise Valley*. PERC. https://www.perc.org/wp-content/uploads/2020/07/Elk-In-Paradise.pdf.

Travis, William R. 2007. *New Geographies of the American West*. Washington, DC: Island Press.

Tsurukawa, Nicolas, Siddharth Prakash, and Andreas Manhart. 2011. "Social Impacts of Artisanal Cobalt Mining in Katanga, Democratic Republic of Congo." Freiburg, Germany: Öko-Institut.

Turner, Frederick Jackson. 1893. "The Significance of the Frontier in American History." In *Annual Report of the American Historical Association*, 197–227. https://www.historians.org/about-aha-and-membership/aha-history-and-archives/historical-archives/the-significance-of-the-frontier-in-american-history-(1893).

U.S. Bureau of Reclamation. 2012. *Colorado River Basin Water Supply and Demand Study*.

U.S. Census Bureau. 2010–21. *Current Population Survey, Annual Social and Economic Supplements* (CPS ASEC). https://data.census.gov.

U.S. Commission on Civil Rights. 2018. *Broken Promises: Continuing Federal Funding Shortfall for Native Americans*. Briefing Report before the United States Commission on Civil Rights.

U.S. Congress. 1910. Establishment; Boundaries; Trespassers; Claims and Rights under Land Laws Not Affected; Reclamation Projects; Indemnity Selection of Lands. U.S.C. Vol. 16, sec. 161.

U.S. Department of Agriculture (USDA). 1950. *Census of Agriculture*. Washington, DC: United States Department of Agriculture.

U.S. Department of Agriculture (USDA). 2022. "USDA Formalizes Big Game Conservation Partnership with State of Wyoming." October 17, 2022. https://www.usda.gov/media/press-releases/2022/10/17/usda-formalizes-big-game-conservation-partnership-state-wyoming.

U.S. Forest Service. 2021. *2021 Land Management Plan: Helena-Lewis and Clark National Forest*. R1-20-16. October 2021. https://www.fs.usda.gov/Internet/FSE_DOCUMENTS/fseprd1148266.pdf.

USU Restoration Consortium. N.d. "Low-Tech Process-Based Restoration of Riverscapes: Design Manual, Resources, Workshops." Birch Creek, Idaho. https://lowtechpbr.restoration.usu.edu/resources/casestudies/birch.html.

Vale, Thomas R., ed. 2002. *Fire, Native Peoples, and the Natural Landscape*. Washington, DC: Island Press.

Vélez-Ibáñez, Carlos G. 2017. "Continuity and Contiguity of the Southwest North

American Region." In *The U.S.-Mexico Transborder Region: Cultural Dynamics and Historical Interactions*, edited by Carlos G. Vélez-Ibáñez and Josiah Heyman, 11–43. Tucson: University of Arizona Press.

Venumiere-Lefebvre, Cassandra C., Stewart W. Breck, and Kevin R. Crooks. 2022. "A Systematic Map of Human-Carnivore Coexistence." *Biological Conservation* 268:109515. https://doi.org/10.1016/j.biocon.2022.109515.

Vila, Pablo. 2000. *Crossing Borders, Reinforcing Borders: Social Categories, Metaphors, and Narrative Identities on the U.S.-Mexico Frontier*. Austin: University of Texas Press.

Wesselhoff, Jennifer. 2023. "Park City Pulse: Bookings Look like Another Busy Season." Park Record. November 7, 2023. https://www.parkrecord.com/opinion/park-city-pulse-bookings-look-like-another-busy-season/.

Western Migrations. N.d. U.S. Geological Survey. https://www.westernmigrations.net.

Wilderness Act. 1964. Public Law 88-577 (16 U.S.C. 1131–36), 88th Congress, Second Session, September 3, 1964.

Wilkinson, Charles. 1992. *Crossing the Next Meridian: Land, Water, and the Future of the West*. Washington, DC: Island Press.

Wilkinson, Charles. 2005. *Blood Struggle: The Rise of Modern Indian Nations*. New York: W. W. Norton.

Williams, A. P., B. I. Cook, and J. E. Smerdon. 2022. "Rapid Intensification of the Emerging Southwestern North American Megadrought in 2020–2021." *Nature Climate Change* 12:232–34.

Williams, Florence. 2018. *The Nature Fix: Why Nature Makes Us Healthier, Happier and More Creative*. New York: W. W. Norton.

Wilmer, H., and M. E. Fernández-Giménez. 2015. "Rethinking Rancher Decision-Making: A Grounded Theory of Ranching Approaches to Drought and Succession Management." *Rangeland Journal* 37 (5): 517–28.

Winkler, Richelle, Donald R. Field, A. E. Luloff, Richard S. Krannich, and Tracy Williams. 2007. "Social Landscapes of the Inter-mountain West: A Comparison of 'Old West' and 'New West' Communities." *Rural Sociology* 72 (3): 478–501.

Wisevoter. 2023. "Property Taxes by State." https://wisevoter.com/state-rankings/property-taxes-by-state/#coloradohttps://smartasset.com/taxes/colorado-property-tax-calculator#colorado.

Woods, Timothy J. 2021. "'Saved': Plans for Genevieve Block Shaping Up." *Jackson Hole News and Guide*, October 6, 2021.

Wyoming Game and Fish Department (WGFD). 2016. Ungulate Migration Corridor Strategy. https://wgfd.wyo.gov/media/13364/download?inline.

Wyoming Game and Fish Department (WGFD) and Wyoming Department of Transportation (WYDOT). N.d. *Wyoming Wildlife and Roadways Initiative*. https://wgfd.maps.arcgis.com/apps/MapSeries/index.html?appid=ef666ba292b74c56a339efc10fca5332.

Yu, Ellen Pei-yi, Bac Van Luu, and Catherine Huirong Chen. 2020. "Greenwashing in Environmental, Social and Governance Disclosures." *Research in International Business and Finance* 52:101192.

Zarbin, Earl. 1997. *Two Sides of the River: Salt River Valley Canals, 1867–1902*. Phoenix: Salt River Project.

Zlolniski, Christian. 2019. *Made in Baja: The Lives of Farmworkers and Growers behind Mexico's Transnational Agricultural Boom*. Oakland: University of California Press.

Zuniga, J. 2000. *Central Arizona Project History*. Washington, DC: U.S. Bureau of Reclamation.

Contributors

Seth Arens joined the staff of Western Water Assessment in December 2015 as the Utah Research Integration Specialist. He has also worked as an environmental scientist for the Utah Division of Air Quality from 2010 to 2015.

Bonnie K. Baxter is professor of biology and director of Great Salt Lake Institute at Westminster University. Her research focuses on the lake's microbiology, leading to projects on the lake ecosystem, the limits of life in salt, and the Great Salt Lake as a model for ancient salt lakes on Mars.

Drew E. Bennett is the Whitney MacMillan Professor of Practice in the Haub School of Environment and Natural Resources at the University of Wyoming. His work focuses on strategies to balance agricultural production and the conservation of wildlife and other natural resources on private lands in the American West.

Travis Brammer is the director of conservation for the Property and Environment Research Center, where he focuses on developing and implementing innovative approaches to conservation. At the time of writing this chapter, he was the Ruckelshaus Institute Conservation Fellow at the University of Wyoming.

Jodi Brandt is a land use scientist at Boise State University with a primary focus on drought adaptation, farmland protection, and biodiversity conservation. She leads multidisciplinary teams funded by NASA, the USDA, NSF, and state agencies.

Stewart W. Breck is a research wildlife biologist in the predator project with the USDA-Wildlife Services-National Wildlife Research Center, founding member and codirector of the Center for Human-Carnivore Coexistence at Colorado State University, and a member of the Human-Bear Conflict Expert Team for the IUCN Bear Specialist Group.

Evelyn Brister is professor of philosophy at Rochester Institute of Technology. Her research focuses on evaluating land management and land use priorities and on reasoning about values in conservation science and environmental policy. She is the editor, with Robert Frodeman, of *A Guide to Field Philosophy*.

Crystal Carr (Diné) has over ten years of policy experience in tribal policy development and analysis. She is the Director of Legislative Affairs and Special Projects at Diné College, and is a doctoral candidate at Arizona State University.

Andrea Christelle is vice provost for research at Diné College. She has a PhD in philosophy from Tulane University. She is also the founder of Sedona Philosophy, which provides opportunities for reflection and conversation in the natural world.

Hilary Byerly Flint is a senior research scientist at the University of Wyoming. She has a PhD in natural resources from the University of Vermont and an MS in applied economics from Cornell University.

Robert Frodeman writes on environmental philosophy, science and technology policy, and the future of the university. He has a PhD in philosophy and an MS in geology, has held academic positions at a number of universities, and has consulted for universities and science agencies worldwide.

Grady Gammage Jr. is a practicing lawyer in Phoenix and an adjunct professor at Arizona State University. He served on the Central Arizona Project Board for twelve years, including four years as president.

Carlin Girard is the executive director of Teton Conservation District, where he works to minimize the impact from development, agriculture, and other human activities in the headwaters of the Snake River in Northwest Wyoming.

Nancy Glenn, professor in the Department of Geosciences at Boise State University, focuses on remote sensing of the environment. Many of her research projects are focused on dryland ecosystems and understanding how these ecosystems respond to changes in climate and disturbance.

Josiah Heyman is professor of anthropology and director of the Center for Inter-American and Border Studies at the University of Texas at El Paso (UTEP). He has worked in the U.S.-Mexico border region since 1982.

Shawn Hill is a city planner and conservationist. He has over twenty years of planning, conservation, and affordable housing experience. He has served as executive director for several 501(c)(3) organizations dedicated to protecting the ecosystems of the Northern Rockies through sound land use planning.

Emily Iskin is a fluvial geomorphologist, science communicator, and visual artist. Her research combines field data collection and remote sensing to answer questions focused on protecting natural rivers and restoring degraded ones.

Kristal Jones is co-owner of JG Research and Evaluation, an applied social science research firm based in southwestern Montana. Her work focuses on bringing a practical, place-based lens to work on food systems, conservation, human services, and public health.

Matthew Kauffman is a wildlife biologist with the U.S. Geological Survey's Cooperative Research Unit program, based out of the University of Wyoming. His research group investigates the long-distance migrations of Wyoming's large ungulates. Increasingly, he has sought to understand how the persistence of ungulate migration is threatened by landscape change.

Nick Kolarik is a land systems scientist with a primary focus on using freely available satellite imagery to measure the impacts of management and policy on ecosystem restoration and biodiversity conservation. He works on multidisciplinary teams funded by NASA, the USDA, and NSF.

Robert Liberty has more than forty years of experience in rural and urban land planning and regulation, acquired as a staff attorney and director of 1000 Friends of Oregon, county hearings officer, elected regional official, director of university urban sustainability programs, and attorney and planning consultant in private practice.

Regina Lopez-Whiteskunk is a former co-chair of the Bears Ears Inter-Tribal Coalition and has worked for the Montezuma Land Conservancy. She is a member of the Ute Mountain Ute Tribe.

Joan May served as director at Telluride's local community radio station KOTO from 1988 to 1997 and as executive director of the regional conservation organization Sheep Mountain Alliance from 1998 to 2007. Joan then served three terms as a San Miguel county commissioner from 2007 to 2019.

Monte Mills joined the University of Washington faculty in 2022 as the Charles I. Stone Professor of Law and the director of the Native American Law Center (NALC). He teaches American Indian law, property, and other subjects focused on Native American and natural resource–related topics.

Luther Propst is an elected county commissioner in Teton County, Wyoming. He founded the Sonoran Institute in 1991 and served as executive director until 2012. The author of three coauthored books, including *Balancing Nature and Commerce in Gateway Communities*, he has worked to balance smart growth in rural and mountain communities around the North American West for more than thirty-five years.

Betsy Gaines Quammen is a historian, conservationist, and writer in Montana. She looks at the intersection of American Western myths, land use, and extremism. She is the author of *American Zion: Cliven Bundy, God, and Public Lands in the West* and *True West: Myth and Mending on the Far Side of America*.

Emily Reed is an associate research scientist and multimedia science communicator for the Wyoming Migration Initiative at the University of Wyoming. Emily is also a freelance writer, photographer, and artist; her work has been featured in *Outdoor Life*, *Modern Huntsman*, *Western Confluence*, and more.

Wellington "Duke" Reiter, FAIA, is senior advisor to the president of Arizona State University. He is also the founder of Ten Across (10X), a nationally recognized initiative dedicated to the resiliency and adaptability of the major cities along the U.S. I-10 corridor.

Paul C. Rogers's ecosystem monitoring research has taken him around North America, Europe, Asia, Africa, and Australia. He is an adjunct professor in the Department of Environment and Society at Utah State University, a USU Ecology Center Associate, and the director of the Western Aspen Alliance.

Jen Schneider is associate dean of the College of Innovation and Design at Boise State University, where she is also professor of public policy and administration. Jen's research addresses the communication challenges presented by emerging technologies, environmental and energy controversies and change, and political polarization.

Nawaraj Shrestha is an environmental scientist with a primary focus on measurement and monitoring of water resources using remote sensing. He worked as a postdoctoral researcher at the Land Use Lab at Boise State University and is currently assistant geoscientist at the University of Nebraska–Lincoln.

Kekek Jason Stark is Turtle Mountain Ojibwe, a member of the Bizhiw (Lynx) Clan, and a practitioner of Indigenous law. Kekek is associate professor at the University of Montana's Alexander Blewett III School of Law, where he serves as codirector of the Indian Law Program, the Margery Hunter Brown Indian Law Clinic, and the American Indian Governance and Policy Institute.

Jared L. Talley is assistant professor of environmental studies in Boise State University's School of Public Service. An environmental philosopher by training and an interdisciplinary scholar in practice, he seeks to better understand how communities relate to the land and how this poses obstacles and opportunities for collaboration and governance.

Jonathan P. Thompson is a journalist, writer, and editor who mostly covers the Western United States. He publishes the *Land Desk*, is a contributing editor at *High Country News*, and is the author of *River of Lost Souls: The Science, Politics, and Greed behind the Gold King Mine Disaster* and *Sagebrush Empire: How a Remote Utah County Became the Battlefront of American Public Lands.*

Jennifer Wesselhoff is president and CEO of the Park City Chamber of Commerce & Visitors Bureau (since October 2020). Prior to arriving in Park City, Jennifer was president and CEO of the Sedona Chamber of Commerce & Tourism Bureau, which she joined in 2007.

Todd Wilkinson has been a journalist for nearly forty years and is author of several critically acclaimed books. His stories have been published in a wide variety of magazines and newspapers, ranging from *National Geographic* to the *Guardian* and *Christian Science Monitor*.

Index

Please note that italicized page numbers in this index indicate illustrations.